Song King

**MUSIC AND
PERFORMING
ARTS** OF ASIA
AND THE PACIFIC

Series Editor: Frederick Lau

Javaphilia: American Love Affairs with Javanese Music and Dance

Henry Spiller

Hearing the Future: The Music and Magic of the Sanguma Band

Denis Crowdy

Vamping the Stage: Female Voices of Asian Modernities

Edited by Andrew N. Weintraub and Bart Barendregt

Broken Voices: Postcolonial Entanglements and the Preservation of Korea's Central Folksong Traditions

Roald Maliangkay

Making Waves: Traveling Musics in Hawai'i, Asia, and the Pacific

Edited by Frederick Lau and Christine R. Yano

Song King

CONNECTING PEOPLE, PLACES, AND
PAST IN CONTEMPORARY CHINA

LEVI S. GIBBS

University of Hawai'i Press
Honolulu

Publication of this book was supported by Dartmouth College.

23 22 21 20 19 18   6 5 4 3 2 1

Library of Congress Cataloging-in-Publication Data

Names: Gibbs, Levi, author.
Title: Song king : connecting people, places, and past in contemporary China
    / Levi S. Gibbs.
Other titles: Music and performing arts of Asia and the Pacific.
Description: Honolulu : University of Hawai'i Press, [2018] | Series: Music
    and performing arts of Asia and the Pacific | Includes bibliographical
    references and index.
Identifiers: LCCN 2017047738 | ISBN 9780824869908 (cloth alk. paper)
Subjects: LCSH: Folk songs, Chinese—History and criticism. | Wang,
    Xiangrong, 1952– | Folk singers—China.
Classification: LCC ML3746.6 .G53 2018 | DDC 782.42162/951009—dc23
LC record available at https://lccn.loc.gov/2017047738

Cover photos: (*Front*) Wang Xiangrong performing at a Chinese New Year's gala in
Baoji, Shaanxi Province, on January 5, 2012. (*Back*) Wang Xiangrong and the author.
Photographs by Levi S. Gibbs.

CONTENTS

ACKNOWLEDGMENTS

Many people have contributed to the development of this book over the years. First and foremost, I want to thank Wang Xiangrong for sharing his knowledge and experience with me. Beyond what I wrote about in this book, my lengthy conversations with him taught me about what it means to be human. I also want to thank Wang's relatives and several of Wang's disciples for sharing their time with me: Feng Xiaohong, Li Chunru, Zhou Jinping, Zhang Liaojun, and Li Zhengfei.

The roots of this book began at Ohio State University, where I was fortunate to learn from Mark Bender, Kirk Denton, Ray Cashman, and Meow Hui Goh. Also during that time, I benefited from discussions with Dorothy Noyes, Heather Inwood, Ziying You, He Man, Mengjun Li, Rongbin Zheng, and Zuchao Shen. For inspiring me to pursue the social function of folk songs and folk singers in Chinese society, I am forever indebted to Su Zheng, Li Wenzhen, and Huang Bai.

More recently, my colleagues and students at Dartmouth College have provided an inspiring intellectual environment in which to finish the book. This book benefited from a Leslie Center for the Humanities Book Manuscript Review Seminar in April 2016, and I thank Graziella Parati, Dennis Washburn, James Dorsey, Gil Raz, Theodore Levin, and Victor Mair (University of Pennsylvania) for their thoughtful comments and suggestions. I also thank Barbara Will, Adrian Randolph, Hua-yuan Li Mowry, Susan Blader, Sarah Allan, Xing Wen, Sachi Schmidt-Hori, Jonathan Smolin, Lewis Glinert, Hussein Kadhim, Lucas C. Hollister, Lara Harb, Jung Ja Choi, Juwen Zhang, Joseph Lam, David Rolston, Charlotte D'Evelyn, Emily Wilcox, Sue Tuohy, Nien Lin Xie, and Hesheng Zhang.

Qiao Jianzhong was instrumental in facilitating my research in Xi'an, and I also want to thank Huang Hu, Gao Hejie, Luo Yifeng, Yang Cui, Huo Xianggui, and Li Shibin for stimulating conversations and support during my fieldwork.

Institutional support for my research over the years came from the U.S. Department of Education's Jacob K. Javits Fellowship Program; the U.S. Fulbright Program; Ohio State University's Office of International Affairs, College of Arts and Sciences, and East Asian Studies Center; the Society for Asian Music; the CHIME Foundation; Dartmouth College's Walter and Constance Burke Research Initiation Award for Junior Faculty and Junior Faculty Fellowship; Antoinet Schimmelpenninck and Frank Kouwenhoven; and Bernice Weissbourd.

Jonathan Chipman at Dartmouth College's Citrin GIS/Applied Spatial Analysis Lab produced the wonderful map.

I have presented parts of this book in its earlier stages at the University of Michigan's Confucius Institute, Shaanxi Normal University, the Xi'an Conservatory of Music, and meetings of the Association for Asian Studies, CHINOPERL, and the American Folklore Society. Chapter 4 was published in slightly altered form as "Culture Paves the Way, Economics Comes to Sing the Opera: The Rhetoric of Chinese Folk Duets and Global Joint Ventures" in *Asian Ethnology* 76, no. 1 (2017): 43–63. Part of chapter 7 will appear in "A Semiotics of Song: Fusing Lyrical and Social Narratives in Contemporary China" in Lijun Zhang and Ziying You, eds., *Chinese Folklore Studies Today: Discourse and Practice* (forthcoming from Indiana University Press).

I am extremely grateful to Frederick Lau and Masako Ikeda at the University of Hawai'i Press for all of their help and encouragement throughout this project, as well as to Cheryl Loe, Debra Tang, Katherine Fisher, Steven Hirashima, and Cindy Yen, to Lee S. Motteler for his excellent copyediting, to Kara Smith for her careful proofreading, and to the Press' anonymous readers, whose helpful suggestions and comments inspired many improvements. Any errors that remain are my own. Finally, I want to thank my parents and my brother Ian for all of their love and support over the years. I dedicate this book to my wife Aída and my daughter Rose, who inspire me in everything I do.

Song King

he was able to infuse the song with thoughts and feelings about people he had known in the past and even a TV drama he had seen in recent years.

Wang spent his childhood in a small mountain village near the intersection of the Great Wall and the Yellow River. He has journeyed on to become, first, "Folk Song King of Northern Shaanxi Province," and later, "Folk Song King of Western China." During the course of his career, Wang's life, songs, and performances have come to highlight various facets of social identity in contemporary China.[3] After winning regional contests in the late 1970s and a national contest in Beijing in 1980 where he met Deng Xiaoping, Wang was hired by a regional song-and-dance troupe, traveling on regional, national, and international tours (Zhao Le 2010). He later relocated to the provincial capital of Xi'an, assumed positions of power in several associations, and was selected as a National-Level Representative Transmitter for the Intangible Cultural Heritage of Northern Shaanxi Folk Songs in 2009 (5).[4]

When itinerant singers from the countryside become iconic artists, worlds collide. The lives and performances of representative singers such as Wang become sites for conversations between the rural and urban, local and national, folk and elite, and traditional and modern.[5] As border walkers who move from place to place, these singers straddle different groups, connecting to diverse audiences by shifting between amorphous, place-based, local, regional, and national identities, and becoming representative symbols in the process. These singers embody connections between different "heres" and "theres," offering audiences a range of viewpoints and desires to engage with—exchanges that allow audience members to resituate themselves in the larger scheme of things. This book examines the life and performances of Folk Song King of Western China Wang Xiangrong to look at how itinerant performers present audiences with traditional, modern, rural, and urban "selves" and "Others" among whom to continually redefine themselves in an evolving world. By looking at how one iconic singer has adapted and mediated between different audiences on a micro level in speech and song in specific events and connecting the insights gained to other singers in China and around the world, this book suggests that itinerant singers become iconic by modeling the socialization of self to diverse audiences.

The song Wang sang that day by the Yellow River in 2006 brought together personal and social meanings, doing so in unique ways for each audience member. The "traditional" songs Wang sings in performances act as vessels—held up for all to see—encompassing a mélange of public and private emotions. The song he performed that day also served as a marker distinguishing different groups (e.g., local, regional, national, human) against the backdrop of others. As we listened to Wang, the territory on the other side of the Yellow River (Shanxi Province) was distinct from the banks of Shaanxi Province on which we stood. Wang's song about a local migrant traveling to neighboring lands

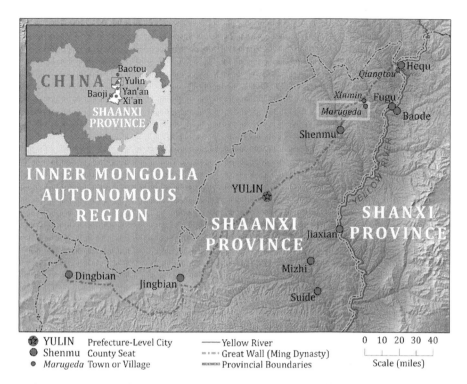

⊛ YULIN   Prefecture-Level City   ——— Yellow River   0 10 20 30 40
◉ Shenmu   County Seat   ▪ ▪ ▪ Great Wall (Ming Dynasty)   Scale (miles)
• *Marugeda*   Town or Village   ▬▬▬ Provincial Boundaries

Places mentioned in the book.

embodies local and regional identities within northern Shaanxi Province on one hand, while also bridging the two provinces and a third on the river's edge. Wang's position facing us on "this" side of the bank, in this context, was emblematic of iconic Chinese folk singers—referred to as "song kings" (*gewang* 歌王) and "song queens" (*gehou* 歌后). Facing each group from the group's edge, these singers enact exchanges between perspectives with the goal of redefining senses of self.

In many ways, singing a traditional song with a symbolic backdrop behind and a diverse audience in front is a typical setup for Wang and other iconic singers. The singers project their powerful voices toward each audience, blending together with the visual and conceptual backdrops behind the singers and their songs, presenting a fusion of the personal and social, the individual and the collective to those seated before them. Through the lives, personas, and songs of these song kings and queens, they bring together what lies behind and what sits in front—they serve as mediums between worlds. Acting as cultural mediators (cf. Filene 2000; Harker 1985), folk songs and folk singers can express the unity and diversity of a nation and/or various ethnic groups (cf. Gorfinkel 2012;

Meeker 2013). As singers such as Wang Xiangrong move from place to place and adapt material from one context to another, they take on interstitial identities, making them well suited to become representatives of larger and larger constructed regions with fuzzy borders—from locality to region to nation. In areas of the world such as China with increasing divides between countryside and city, these singers offer a sense of contact between urban centers and rural peripheries.

If the story of the song king is about mediating between what is figuratively behind the singer and who is seated in front, my place throughout this book is hovering at Wang's side, watching how it is done. During my fieldwork with Wang Xiangrong and other singers and scholars in Xi'an and various localities in northern Shaanxi Province in 2006, 2010, and especially 2011 to 2012, I documented Wang's performances in Xi'an and northern Shaanxi to see how he presented his active repertoire to a variety of audiences in different ways, interviewed Wang extensively about his life and songs, and translated those songs line by line into English. Much of my fieldwork involved looking at how Wang spoke to different audiences before, during, and after his songs. Sometimes, the performance contexts to which I accompanied Wang surprised me—they included weddings, business openings, and even Christmas concerts, in addition to more "mainstream" performances in official Chinese New Year celebrations and school anniversaries. Throughout, I combined a singer-centered approach with historical research on northern Shaanxi folk songs and singers, attempting to see connections across time and space.

That day by the Yellow River in the summer of 2006, behind Wang lay a symbolic river and an Other territory beyond, each providing a metaphorical framework for the song's performance. The song's origins lay in the past—how far back, we did not know—and the song would continue to be sung for years to come, just as the river's waters came from somewhere sight unseen, heading onward toward an unseen destination. Between the horizons of origin and end stood the singer. His song, projected at us, was rooted in past performances and tradition—the river's source—while simultaneously projecting desires for us to move toward if we so chose. Rivers suggest movement—the passage of time—but also a stillness within that movement, moments where we focus on the "now" connecting what has been and what will be, calling to mind where we come from and where we are going, offering us an opportunity to consider how our lives fit into a larger "stream" of events.[6]

Rivers, like songs, also bring to mind other places.[7] Their waters originate in some other place and flow off to yet another place. Just as the river's image encourages us to consider the past and future, it also asks us to think about our relationships with other places. Song kings and queens, as I go on to suggest, are like rivers—each singer originating in one place and meandering through ple" and elite cultural figures, song kings and queens bridge class, space, and time. They stand on the border of groups, positioning themselves as both insiders and outsiders and using that stance to authorize their construction of song worlds where different viewpoints are exchanged. In addition to performing songs representing particular groups, we see stories of iconic singers modeling how to sing as they teach people songs. During the journeys of these iconic singers, as they learn to adapt their senses of self after encountering Others, they come to share what they have discovered with audiences through representative performances and instructive models. As these singers present audiences with a range of familiar and exotic "selves" and "Others," they offer audiences the opportunity to redefine themselves through interactions with each persona, providing individual and group dialogues with difference.

At the same time, some audiences may disapprove of the models that song kings and queens provide for the meeting and merging of subjectivities. Each iconic singer stands with one foot inside and one foot outside of different groups, and that precarious, interstitial position often leads the singer's representative authority to be questioned. As groups are heterogeneous and borders often ambiguous, for everyone who might crown a singer "king" or "queen," there are others who decry the singer as a fraud. If a singer becomes too engaged in presenting a local tradition to others, people from their home region may find them too cosmopolitan and argue that they have lost their local essence and no longer merit representing the group. If, on the other hand, the singer is too local, outsiders may consider him or her parochial, and he or she will fail to mediate between groups. As identities evolve in tandem with changing relations between places, singers' designations as song kings and queens are forever contestable and always in flux.

Whether one designates a singer "song king" or "song queen" or denounces them as "interlopers" or "sellouts" is tied to individual audience members' sense of identity and whether the singer's representation aligns with that sense (Malone 2011, 2; cf. Titon 2012; Graeme Turner 2004). Objections to a singer's representativeness revolve around aspects of the singer's persona and performances that the critics feel diminish the "authenticity" of the songs, people, and places the singer is said to represent. The objection may be because, for example, the singer comes from a different place than the songs she purports to represent; because he grew up in the city, yet chooses to sing songs from the countryside; or because she uses a vocal style the critic feels unfairly represents the broader tradition. Critics who contest a singer's status as "song king" or "song queen" are in effect positioning themselves in relation to larger groups— identifying with certain groups while distancing themselves from others. By judging the representativeness of these singers, we declare who *we* are and who *we* are not, as well as who *I* am and who *I* am not. While no singer is beyond reproach, successful singers must learn to pivot between audiences, glossing over heterogeneity to construct tangible, symbolic personae that diverse audiences can relate to.

Songs as Public Conversations

The song Wang sang by the Yellow River that day presented the audience with a tapestry of meanings connected to the contexts of previous performances, situating the performed present within a historical continuum. The performances of iconic songs constitute continuous public conversations about important issues of the day—issues that change over time as society changes—forming a site for public memory (cf. Nora 1989) and the socialization of personal experience (DuBois 2006; Porter and Gower 1995). The desire for dialogue inherent to lyric song involves what Thomas DuBois calls "the communicative nature of lyric" (97). This desire seems to be rooted in a yearning for conversations with Others that in turn constitute the self. Our eagerness to travel and explore new places, peoples, and cuisines, to read novels and watch films about other places and times, to talk with people from different backgrounds, and to attend performances of dance and music—all of these lead us to notice what is familiar and different, and adjust our position accordingly. Similarly, when songs are presented from one place to another, they offer the possibility for diverse parties to meet on common ground and discuss different ways of seeing things.

The goal of such exchanges is to merge different subjectivities and find a new point of view representing a socialized self. This pattern of merging subjectivities is repeated over and over in many of Wang's songs, stories, and performances I discuss throughout this book. We see banquet attendees coming together to "strengthen their feelings," villagers communing with local gods in conversations about health and propriety, and couples exploring new terrains, sharing perspectives as a new relationship—and point of view—emerges. At the same time, we see examples of how failing to reach out to others is criticized. Songs about men and women who do not call out to others and set up mutually validating exchanges lament the failure of those individuals to secure their continued existence. If part of one's existence stems from being recognized by and forming a sense of self in conversation with others, individuals who fail to engage with others soon cease to exist.

The power of song kings and queens such as Wang is that they can create entire song worlds filled with conversing desires, ephemeral yet iterable realms populated by voiced and unvoiced personae. As those personae move through and respond to each song world, their performed desires form public conversations that audiences can join in on. At the same time, the song's personae, inflected by the singer's persona, test the audience's fluid notions of self and Other.[13] Each sung persona allows the performer to play different roles and express different types of sentiments (Fong 1990), presenting a mixture of the familiar and exotic experienced differently by each audience member. These personae provide crucial contexts that allow singers to sing what they otherwise could not and audiences to hear those lyrics in an appropriate manner. The persona of a boatman, muleteer, or revolutionary peasant singer can say things that other personae cannot. Furthermore, a persona's specificity or ambiguity can either directly address social tensions when desired or gloss over them when necessary to bridge divergent views and groups in order to bring those groups together into a larger whole.

Wang's broader repertoire of songs contains various sung personae—a muleteer, a migrant farmworker, a cowherd, a woman returning to her natal home during festival time, an audacious playboy, a pair of tender peasant lovers, a guest at a drinking party, a Mongol man and his female Han lover, a spirit medium (*shenhan* 神汉) and the spirit to whom the medium gives voice.[14] In some of Wang's more recent creations—such as his a cappella version of "The East Is Red" discussed in chapter 3 or his iconic "The Infinite Bends of the Yellow River" discussed in chapter 7—a song's persona may travel through different historical periods, offering audiences a sense of history and their place in it. By comparing the personae of Wang's childhood songs with those of the songs he performed later during his career as a representative singer, we are able to get a glimpse of how sung personae are connected to places large and small and how more specific, local personae can be developed into larger, more ambiguous, region- and nation-representing personae. During this process, the meaning embodied by the lyric "I" grows. In Wang's childhood songs that I examine in chapter 2, the "I's" of each song evoke the roles of individuals who are recognizable in the village, such as banquet hosts and guests, spirit mediums, and young people. As Wang's repertoire expanded to include the region-representing songs discussed in chapter 3, the "I's" in songs such as "Pulling Ferries throughout the Year" and "The East Is Red" become representative individuals singing on behalf of the People. By the time we reach Wang's iconic "The Infinite Bends of the Yellow River" in chapter 7, one of the many layered meanings of the song's "I" becomes that of the audience and the singer joined together through song into a collective "we."

In all of Wang's songs, the sung personae offer listeners different Others with whom to interact and gauge their senses of self. When an audience member hears a migrant farmworker sing about traveling to Inner Mongolia to find work, he or she may reflect upon what it means to stay behind and what it would be like to leave. Hearing the voice of a local spirit sung through a medium, the listener feels the spirit's presence and hears its instructions on how to cure an illness, perhaps leading the listener to consider the relationships between people and gods. When one hears a love duet sung between male and female personae, one may choose to identify with the man, the woman, both, or neither. In each case, the listener positions him- or herself in relation to the others.

In addition to these voiced sung personae, there are also other, voiceless personae—the silent, looming addressees to whom the singer calls out. In Wang's a cappella version of "The East Is Red," he calls out to the East and the sun, addressing each as "you." In another song about a tragic story from China's pre-1949 past, Wang calls out to a woman who committed suicide. The act of calling out to an Other, of singing to an addressee who is physically absent yet tangibly present in the constructed world of song, has the effect of internalizing the external—another time, place, idea, or person—summoning that intangible Other into the present "time of discourse" for the singer and listeners (Culler 2015, 225). In doing so, the singer's act of calling out pulls both singer and listeners toward a desire connected to the song's addressee. For example, calling out to a deceased female relative can express the desire to indict the tradition of arranged marriage. Calling out to the East or the sun can represent a desire for the warmth of national community.

As singers address these Others, they set up mutually defining conversations. On the one hand, the singer constructs the Other through the singer's address (Althusser 2001). A peasant singer praising the greatness of Chairman Mao constructs Chairman Mao's greatness as the singer calls out to him. A male sung persona constructs the tragedy of a deceased woman as he calls out to her. At the same time, the singer's persona is also constructed through the act of calling out to an Other (Frith 1996b, 183). By calling out to the dead woman in the example above, the male sung persona shows that persona's concern and despair. By calling out to Chairman Mao, the peasant singer persona in the earlier example constructs himself as a representative of the People. Though these exchanges are seemingly one sided—only the singer is physically present and heard—the act of address suggests a conversation that audiences can observe and join in on, identifying with the sung persona or the addressee, or choosing to stand on the sidelines (cf. Fiske 2011).

What makes these conversations unique is that they take place in front of an audience. The singer "addresses both his [or her] audience and the interlocutor of the story" via a "double directionality" (Frankel 1974, 262; Gilman 1968). Jonathan Culler (2015, 8) calls this "triangulated address," where audience members are free to position themselves at varying distances from the various personae on display (cf. Fiske 2011).[15] Just as the singer is both within and outside of the sung personae he or she embodies, the audience can also choose to identify with or objectify those personae—what John Fiske calls "implicating" and "explicating" (2011, 174–175). Allowing us to be both inside and outside of those personae with the freedom to shift between the two positions, lyric song offers us the experience of subject positions from within and without, without fully committing—"being of two minds" (Brown 2004, 133; cf. Samei 2004, 7). We as the audience have the freedom to choose, as well as the freedom not to choose—floating in between, saying while not saying, agreeing yet not agreeing.

In Wang's performances and those of other iconic itinerant singers, the singers adapt the in-betweenness of their lives, personas, and songs to each audience as they model the meeting and merging of self and Other. Mediating between the rural and urban requires singers to choose what songs to perform and how to present them—choices highlighting distinct, place-based moral aesthetics. To survive, itinerant singers must accurately assess the similarities and differences among and between groups—a skill shared by stand-up comedians and other itinerant artists (cf. Brodie 2014). Singers use this intergroup and intragroup knowledge to bridge social gaps through performance, creating level playing fields where meaningful exchanges can occur. Whether these exchanges of perspectives are sung drinking games between banquet attendees or international cultural exchanges, performance brings together different entities, allowing those entities to redefine themselves in the liminal space of the event (Gibbs 2017).

As singers present points of view in relation to which listeners can position themselves, the same song can mean different things in different contexts. When Wang Xiangrong performs a mildly suggestive local song in his home region (see chapter 5), some local audiences see it as an expression of local authenticity and perhaps nostalgic regional identity. The same song, when performed in another region, might be perceived as a reflection of risqué country bumpkinesque culture. In similarly divergent readings (or listenings, if you will), when Wang performed the song about "Going beyond the Western Pass" by the Yellow River in 2006, locals might have seen it as a symbol of local identity that had traveled and returned, maintaining authenticity while staying relevant. The outsiders, in turn, may have seen the song as an expression of local, regional, and/or national culture, while simultaneously considering how that symbolic Other related to their own senses of self. During my fieldwork, Wang's performances in his home region seemed to offer a sense of self merged with how urban, national, and foreign Others viewed that sense of self. Wang's performances in cities such as Xi'an, in turn, often displayed images of rural Others blended with urban audiences' sense of cultural history and modernity. The social Otherness of the rural identity can simultaneously constitute a form of cultural authenticity for urban audiences—an "authentic" China and Chineseness—which singers such as Wang Xiangrong and writers such as Jia Pingwa 贾平凹 (b. 1952, also from Shaanxi Province) draw on in promoting their work (cf. Yiyan Wang 2006, 213).[16]

Throughout Wang's rise from amateur folk singer to professional folk song king, we see the scope of merging subjectivities grow. Earlier songs from his home village about couples exploring new terrains as their love blossoms are later joined by love songs of the region and nation where the "couple" is transformed into Wang's solo voice and a chorus—pursuing a future together as they move forward. As itinerant singers travel, the conversations erected by their songs expand to encompass larger and more diverse groups. In the smaller village settings of Wang's childhood, songs enacted public conversations, strengthening social bonds during banquets and courtship and dealing with separation, illness, and loss in times of despair. As a singer's sphere of representation grows, larger issues regarding relations between places, time periods, and scales of identity come into play. As singers shift between and adapt to larger and ever more diverse audiences and their audience base grows, the image of each singer and the sung personae they perform become ambiguous vessels capable of meaning many things to many people (cf. Abrams 1953, 38–39), and the singers become representative icons—symbols of regions and nations.

Negotiating Place-Based Identities

China has a long history of using songs as a means to encounter other people and places. More recently, along with the rising rural-urban divide, professionally performed folk songs have played an important role in negotiating place-based identities. With the growth of provincial identities following China's market reform in the late 1970s, changing relations between places have demanded public exchanges at periodic intervals (cf. Oakes 2000). In the context of diverse viewpoints and identities, songs from other places can represent the Other, highlighting heterogeneous choices and social tensions. As China continues to move forward, folk songs can represent the past—or rather a sense of past authenticity adapted to the present (cf. Glassie 2003).

The symbolic power of stories about singer-heroes rests largely on the social and geographical meanings of songs implicit in China's long history of folk song collection. Song collection in ancient times was largely seen as a means of both political census and moral analysis. The Chinese term for "collecting folk songs" (*caifeng* 采风) is often interpreted as an abbreviation of a longer phrase meaning "to gather social customs" (*caifang fengsu* 采访风俗) (Yang Yinliu 1980, 1:47). Among ancient texts describing this practice, the *Book of Rituals* (*Li ji* 礼记), which deals with social forms, government, and ceremonial rites of the Zhou dynasty (ca. 1050–256 BCE), records that the emperor would send out officials every five years to collect songs to observe the customs of the people.[17] The *Zuo Commentary* (*Zuozhuan* 左传) tells of an official discerning the social and moral states of different kingdoms by listening to their songs (DeWoskin 1982, 29).[18] The mediation of songs between places also plays a central role in tales of "song immortals" (*gexian* 歌仙) and "song gods" (*geshen* 歌神) who are said to have appeared in localities and taught local people to sing (cf. Schimmelpenninck 1997; Loh 1984; Liang 2009; Kouwenhoven 2014). In a sense, by "founding" local song genres, song deities provided locals with a means of defining themselves in relation to others.

While David Faure and Tao Tao Liu note that "rural-urban distinctions were not a significant part of an individual's identity" during the Ming and Qing dynasties (2002, 1), scholars of China have observed a growing distance between the countryside and the city beginning in the early twentieth century (cf. Skinner 1997; Mote 1973; Faure and Liu 2002; Siu 1990). Since then, images of the country and the city are often used in contrast to one another—the "backwards" countryside serves as a foil for the "modern" city, while the city's dark side is set against romantic tropes of idyllic rurality (Creed and Ching 1997; cf. Raymond Williams 1973). Since the May Fourth period, emigration to the cities has been seen as a means of upward mobility; one "enters" the city (*jincheng*) but "goes down to" the countryside (*xiaxiang*) (Tao Tao Liu 1996). In the early twentieth century, progressive writers saw their journey from the countryside to the city as "a temporal journey from a point of traditional past to arrival at the modern present" (Leo Ou-fan Lee 1990, 122). Shanghai—the quintessential treaty-port city—became "a 'spatialization' of 'modernity'…a self-contained world cut off and set apart from the traditionalism of the surrounding countryside" (121–122). While there have also been calls to seek a sense of purity in the countryside when cities seemed lacking—a 1919 article entitled "Youth and Village" by a Beijing University literature professor named Li Dazhao (1888–1927), who would later cofound the Chinese Communist Party; Mao Zedong's 1942 "Talks at the Yan'an Conference on Literature and Art"; the "Up to the Mountains and Down to the Countryside" movement during the Cultural Revolution that sent urban youth to rural areas; and the "Root-Seeking" movement of the 1980s—these only further reinforced the sense of divide (Hung 1985; McDougall 1980).

With the growth of cities as centers of political and economic power, the symbiotic relationship between rural and urban areas has become an increasing factor in everyday life. Similar to the progressive writers of early twentieth-century China, young rural migrants in recent decades continue to see the city as "where the future lies," while "the countryside—now inhabited mainly by women, children, and the cash-strapped elderly—connotes the past, from which they wish to escape" (Wanning Sun 2014, 13). And yet, although city centers and rural peripheries are mutually defining—cities cannot consider themselves modern without pointing to other "not modern" places and a capital is only a capital when it has jurisdiction over a territory—these "centers" and "peripheries" are geographically separated.[19] How, then, are the relationships between them displayed?

Since the economic reforms beginning in the late 1970s, the number of rural migrants to cities has risen exponentially—an increase that coincided with Wang Xiangrong's move to an urban-based song-and-dance troupe in the early 1980s—and by the 1990s, the increasing divide between rural and urban was seen as a threat to "social stability" (Wanning Sun 2014, 11; Creed and Ching 1997, 2). As urban residents have increased from "twenty percent of the Chinese population" in 1990 to "almost fifty percent" by 2010, place-based identity continues to hold an important place in how people relate to each other and themselves (Rees 2016, 77; cf. Woetzel et al. 2009). In the cultural questioning following the end of the Cultural Revolution, country and city were once again brought together and compared. Some writers looked for roots in the countryside, while others extolled an "urban consciousness" (*chengshi yishi* 城市意识) as a reaction against earlier ideological depictions of the countryside (Tao Tao Liu 1996; Leo Ou-fan Lee 1990). The contrast between rural and urban is so pervasive and constitutes such a significant part of identity construction that places and identities falling in between (e.g., small county towns and rural migrants in cities) experience a "deeply felt existential angst" (Creed and Ching 1997; Sun 2014, 12). There continues to be "a vertically arranged social hierarchy" distinguishing the city from the countryside, where rural migrants belong to the lowest level of society (Sun 2014, 11).

Following China's opening up and reform in the 1980s, researchers have seen a growth of provincial identities as provinces began to promote themselves in competition with one another (Goodman 1994; Oakes 2000). In the context of promotion of place, singers and songs can make a locality, region, or nation visible and "visitable" (Dicks 2003). As singers and composers construct region-representing repertoires, the pieces they produce embody sung personae that are identifiable yet ambiguous enough to serve as unifying umbrellas for heterogeneous localities, pivoting regional identity between the local and national. The singer's persona also becomes a symbol of the region, adapting its presentation of self toward different audiences—a "fresh incarnation" of archetypal authority empowered by its resonance with parallel narratives (Connerton 1989, 63; cf. Goffman 1959; Bantly 1996). The Other territory iconic singers and their songs present offers an illusion of rootedness in the land. While tangible, this groundedness is ultimately a construction—a floating image only made "real" by listeners' perception of it as such. When singers adapt local songs into regional and national representations, they evoke fuzzy notions of "Chineseness" that are locally grounded while reinforcing the nation's identity. In addition to embodying place, iconic singers and their songs embody time as well. Behind Wang's performances lies the past as well as the future, simultaneously pointing to where audiences come from and where they are going.

Changing relations between places calls for public conversations at regular intervals. With increased rural-urban migration, the emergence of new regional identities, and the birth of new nations, negotiating new place-based identities requires exchanges between places. In an era of globalization, the local needs to be constantly redefined vis-à-vis its relationship with and appearance to the world. Rather than performing locally authentic traditions in isolation, itinerant singers embody mobile place-based authenticities through which places interact with other places. Wang's longer performances in his home region use speech and song to juxtapose local and global images, distancing the local through shifting stances and presenting the local as elevated in the eyes of others. In any performance, when an audience member hears a song originating in another context—for example, when Wang performs in the American Midwest—the audience member places the song in conversation with some aspect of him- or herself. This dialogue with difference is inherent in the work of itinerant singers like Wang who bring together different perspectives as they move between places. Presenting audiences with different ways of thinking about things and a range of traditional, modern, rural, and urban personae, these iconic singers mimic the border-crossing experiences of itinerant performers, providing audiences with miniature journeys of self-realization where each individual can position his or her sense of self in relation to others.

At the same time, there is always a degree of commonality within difference (or is it the other way around?). Both "rural" and "urban" reflect a shared notion that the places we identify ourselves with affect how we view the world. What appear to be dichotomies—"rich" versus "poor" and "modern" versus "not modern"—can be better understood as shared paradigms, spectrums along which selves define their positions among others.[20] How we designate ourselves as rural, urban, rich, poor, modern, or not depends largely on our interactions with others. In addition, what each of these terms means varies between individuals, places, and time periods, requiring one to recalibrate one's sense of self at frequent intervals. Herein lies the importance of individuals presenting "display events" where we can encounter a range of others and continually redefine who we are (Abrahams 1981).

Singers as Storytellers

As individuals in society negotiate choices between traditional and modern, rural and urban, folk and elite, local and national, personal and group identity, singers present their audiences with aesthetic, communicative experiences adapted from one context (where the songs originated) to another (the event where the audience sits before them), allowing audience members to engage in conversations with temporal and geographical Others that help define their senses of self in a changing world. As the movements of these singers between places often coincide with historic changes, the singers' geographical passages fuse with the passage of time. Within this geographical-temporal fusion, music "defines a space without boundaries," as Simon Frith notes, and "is thus the cultural form best able to cross borders" (1996a, 125). As song kings and queens travel between audiences, they bring a sense of the Other as well as the self, fusing together insider and outsider. The song kings' and queens' journeys enable them to present the audiences' roots as well as their relationships with other groups (cf. Benjamin 1969). Offering the Other of the past and the Other of other places, these singers provide audiences with the coordinates to situate themselves in time and space.

The power of Wang's lyric songs lies in the stability they provide amidst life's constant changes, made possible by the songs' combination of traditional authority and liminality.[21] Wang's performances, like those of other song kings and queens, provide a space where distinct times and places are merged together and different viewpoints are displayed and brought into conversation with one another. Ultimately, both performer and audience member take the risk to reach out and encounter something different, letting a sense of Otherness percolate briefly inside their being, and then assert their own individuality once again—giving up and then regaining subjectivity in the rhythm of the song (cf. Scott 1998; Culler 2015). Wang's audiences are "sung to" by him and "sing with" him as they listen, similar to readers of poetry, who Clive Scott suggests are "poised between…the will to control language (utter it) and the will to submit to language (assimilate it)" (1998, 89). The audiences lose themselves in each performance, before gaining a new sense of self.

Each of Wang's appearances is an event, positioned within a larger occasion. His performances of speech and song create their own time and space, separate from other constructions of the world though acknowledging the occasions in which his performances are nested—the wedding, the business opening, the Chinese New Year's performance, and so on. Wang acknowledges the audience, speaking with them if time allows and singing for them. Each of his songs creates a momentary world of its own. The songs' lyric nature brings the audience into a sense of "nowness" that unfolds with each turn of phrase (cf. Culler 2015). Rather than focusing our attention on the past as a storyteller does through the telling of narratives, Wang's lyric songs bring all of their content into the present, including those parts rooted in the past. Though the songs he performs stem from earlier versions composed, sung, and adapted by others, each of these "old" songs reaches the audience in the intimacy of the "lyric 'now'" (Culler 2015, 226). The version of "Going beyond the Western Pass" Wang sang that summer day by the Yellow River in 2006 was just as immediate as it might have been a hundred years earlier, despite the fact that the first stanza places the song around the time of a drought in 1855 (see chapter 2). Wang's performance of the song's male persona exhorting his beloved not to cry was just as immediate. The cracks in Wang's voice as he sang "don't you cry" led me to later ask him what personal tragedy he had been thinking of as he sang, to which he replied that the song's tears were part of an artistic performance.[22] What better way to express the "subjective in the collective" that "articulate[s] private but common desires, feelings and experiences" in "a shared public language" (Frith 1996a, 110; Grossberg 1992, 207).

Just as Wang's performance drew meaning from past performances, his future performances may recall performances like this one and the context that defined it. Neither first nor last, Wang's performance was a "now" entering a stream of "thens." It brought to mind the past but was not the past. It was performed in the present but was not only the present. It called out to a future beyond its scope yet seemingly within its reach. Neither past, present, nor future, Wang's performance was instead all three and at the same time none. By folding together repeatable, memorable words and music into the nowness of each performance, Wang, like other song kings and queens around the globe, brings diverse viewpoints into conversation with each other and the audience, the discursive time sustained in lyric song allowing different voices to come together and sing to one another.

Chapter Overview

What makes song kings and queens significant? As emblematic singers rise to fame, crossing boundaries and mediating between groups, their lives and performances become sites for public conversations about important issues of the day, offering audiences a means to socialize the personal. Chapter 1 looks at similarities between legendary singer-heroes of the past and contemporary Chinese folk singers, suggesting that iconic itinerant performers highlight and overcome social tensions while traveling between groups. Engaging with Others, these singers provide compelling models for audiences to negotiate their own senses of self and group in an evolving world. After outlining the archetypal singer-hero story, I look at aspects of Wang Xiangrong's life that have captured public attention as Wang moved from rural anonymity to urban fame. I suggest that Wang's image connects the mountaintop village of his youth and the provincial capital where he later came to reside, embodying tensions regarding social mobility and attitudes towards love and marriage. Life narratives such as Wang's are compelling in part because they resonate with earlier legends of song gods and goddesses, as well as contemporary Chinese folk singer biographies from the twentieth century.

As the lives of itinerant singers highlight tensions as they cross geographical, temporal, and cultural boundaries, their songs provide a means to negotiate between places. In chapter 2, I explore how the singers and songs Wang Xiangrong encountered as a youth provided models for singer authority and song as a public conversation. I suggest that songs related to village contexts—banquets, rituals, festivals, and courtship—were later adapted to represent conversations between larger entities, including regions, nations, and corporations. Providing examples of songs grounded in place—lyrical references to the topography of his home village and the surrounding area abound—I suggest that Wang went on to expand the geolyrical connection to represent larger and larger regions. Tied to this expansion is the use of different vocal masks I refer to as "sung personae"—voices constructed in songs that would later go on to embody larger collective entities. As different voices come together in the liminal "meeting ground" of song, individual desires are shared and merge, leading to the formation of new points of view.

Chapter 3 looks at how Wang used his education through song to create and perform region-representing pieces during his professional career with the Yulin Folk Arts Troupe. I explore how local traditions are adapted to make them worthy of the stage and how singers "expand" bawdy local festival tunes into somber, monumental odes to the region's history, transforming the songs' imagery, sung personae, tempo, and rhythm. After looking at a song Wang adapted for a television series in the 1980s, I suggest a similar process at work in the development of the famous revolutionary song, "The East Is Red." In addition to the reworking of song lyrics, I argue that as singers come to represent larger regions, they increasingly turn to flexible presentations of self. Citing Wang's spoken introductions in various performances between 2011 and 2012, I suggest that his role as a regional representative requires him to shift his presentation of self and the songs he sings in accordance with the place-based identities of audience members and the locations of performances (cf. Goffman 1959). I then analyze two versions Wang performs of "The East Is Red," looking at how they adapt the merging subjectivities of the songs of Wang's youth into representations of the nation and its history.

Chapter 4 looks at how the local and regional become national when performed abroad and how fuzzy notions of "Chineseness" serve as convenient symbolic sites that can pivot between audiences as various groups involved position themselves in relation to one another. I examine how Yulin Prefecture in northern Shaanxi Province used performances of song and dance, including songs and duets performed by Wang, to facilitate a joint project between the largest coal company in China and The Dow Chemical Company, a U.S.–based multinational chemical corporation. Focusing on the rhetoric surrounding the Yulin Folk Arts Troupe's 2008 performance at a "Far East Meets West" event in Dow's global headquarters, Midland, Michigan, and reciprocal, Dow-funded performances by the U.S. National Symphony Orchestra the following year in China, I explore the symbolic role of reciprocal performances amidst the forging of relationships between different localities in a global age. On the international stage, the conversations produced by song become more complicated, with multiple layers and different groups chiming in.

In addition to large-scale stage performances, song kings and queens must be able to adapt to other sorts of performance contexts. In chapter 5, I look at considerations Wang and other singers make in adapting performances to a wide range of occasions, including small, private gatherings with friends and encounters with folk song scholars. Alternative versions of songs appropriate for different audiences suggest a sensitivity to place-based views of morality that song kings and queens acquire as they travel between groups. Different interpretations of "erotic" material I encountered in conversations with Wang and two retired Shaanxi folk song collectors highlight how song performance serves as a site for discussions of public morality—a theme spanning from legends of earlier song gods to the present. Both folk singers and folk song collectors mediate between place-based rural and urban moralities in their performances and the documentation of those performances.

In chapter 6, I explore how song kings and queens allow audiences to situate themselves in a constantly changing world by creating performances that alternate between the familiar and the exotic. Examining one of Wang's appearances in his home region where I—a foreign scholar and aficionado of northern Shaanxi folk songs—became part of the emergent flow of performance, I suggest that shifts between languages, places, and melodies familiar to and more distant from audiences can act like a specialized prism—a translucent lens reflecting the audience back at themselves, projecting Others toward them, and presenting images of how they are seen by Others. I argue that these images present audiences with opportunities to resituate themselves in relation to various Others. Similar opportunities for reflection are offered when Wang challenges his audiences to listen for place-based authenticity (didao) in his songs after his return from afar, as well as the juxtaposition of Wang's performances with other acts in large, gala performances.

To maintain a sense of stability in the midst of a constant state of flux, individuals must connect their stories to other narratives that surround them, including the stories of other people, larger communities, and even entire nations. In chapter 7, I examine how Wang fuses together personal, regional, and national narratives in his performances of "The Infinite Bends of the Yellow

River," arguing that in doing so, Wang provides audiences with symbolic sites to consider what has come before and what is yet to come. I suggest that by offering performances overlaying several parallel narratives of struggle and success—Wang's personal history, recent Chinese history, and symbolic questions and answers in the song—Wang models for audience members how to connect individual lives to the larger communities and epochs in which they live.

After examining how Wang's life and songs have mediated between places, peoples, and time periods, I explore in the epilogue how the concept of "song king" and "song queen"—iconic itinerant singers highlighting and mediating between divergent points of view—can apply to singers and artists from around the world who move between rural and urban landscapes, transforming local traditions and themselves into symbols of larger regions, nations, peoples, and epochs.

CHAPTER 1

The Meanings of a Life

What is it that makes people admire them, and elect
particular singers as "kings" or "queens"?
—Antoinet Schimmelpenninck, 1997[1]

WHAT does it mean to become a song king or queen? Amidst this process of becoming, what social tensions are highlighted as a singer travels between places, mediating between perspectives? In this chapter, I suggest that the lives of itinerant singers become sites of public conversations about social issues of the day as they cross boundaries during the course of their careers. Wang's life straddles disparate places and geographical identities—the small mountain village of his youth Marugeda, the regional capital of Yulin, the provincial capital Xi'an, the national capital Beijing, and the world abroad. Wang spans social categories from poor peasant to wealthy song king, rural to urban, traditional to modern, common folk to semiofficial. He has also lived through and engaged with China's various historical periods since the founding of the People's Republic in 1949. Aspects of Wang's life—his rise in social status and his love life—have inspired multiple narratives and become sites for discussions of divergent social views.

To better understand the symbolic power of the lives of song kings and queens, I begin by looking at how the narratives of these singers build on earlier legends of Chinese singer-heroes. Noting commonalities between earlier legends and contemporary folk singer biographies, I suggest that each of these narratives focuses on an itinerant singer crossing boundaries of space and time, overcoming obstacles and coming to represent a particular region through song. The obstacles, I posit, reflect divergent views in contentious social debates. Each singer's success, then, is a result of his or her ability to engage with different Others through song in mutually defining conversations.

Many of these anecdotes—both ancient and contemporary—provide context for how we interpret the act of singing. Stories where singer-heroes encounter a range of Others provide models for what it means to sing and what it means to be a singer. These legends suggest implicit rules regarding how one should or should not engage with others and how song can be used as a powerful medium to be heard by entities from other places with divergent viewpoints. For example, when a male song god sings a flirtatious song to the female Goddess of Mercy Guanyin, he is punished for his transgression (Schimmelpenninck 1997, 104). This encounter highlights differing views of sex and morality—folk and elite, or, in this case, mundane and divine—while emphasizing the importance for singers to be able to read their audiences. When the popular female song goddess of peasant origins Liu Sanjie vanquishes male intellectuals and landlords, her victories symbolize the power of folk wisdom over elite education and capital (Loh 1984, 169). In addition, Liu's ability to bridge groups suggests that to thrive in a heterogeneous society, one must be able to mediate between divergent worldviews.

Another popular contemporary folk singer, Abao 阿宝 (b. 1969, real name: Zhang Shaochun), is described turning the hearts of bandits by singing a local song, suggesting the song's power to symbolize place, the value of local authenticity, and the ability of singing to raise one's cultural status (Wu Yue 2005). Each of these stories points to possible social functions of song—transgressing norms, gaining reprieve, and subduing and uniting groups of people. More broadly, these tales suggest the power of song to open up public conversations between divergent views, resulting in opportunities for the singer's subjectivity—and the subjectivities of those they represent—to be recognized by others.

In the following discussion of Wang's life, I offer an account of his childhood and rise to fame based on interviews, published articles, and books. Then, I focus on aspects of his life that have drawn particular attention, suggesting that these themes highlight social tensions relevant to a wider range of audiences. Life stories are inherently problematic—their components are selected from a much larger pool of material (e.g., what one ate for breakfast each day) and placed in a particular order to present a coherent image of a self at a particular point of telling (Titon 1980; Goffman 1959). Wang suggested during one of our interviews that only he could get his story right. Clearly, he desired to maintain a sense of control over the narrative, which can sometimes be reformulated when reframed by reporters, biographers, or scholars (Borland 1998; Titon 1980). And yet, such a desire to control one's own story—a desire many of us share—overlooks the fact that life stories are constructed in conversations with others (Kirshenblatt-Gimblett 1989; Linde 1993; Lawless 1991; Plummer 2001). What is seen as important is frequently what gets told. The "social demands" on how a life story is presented often connect to what has been seen as noteworthy and "storyable" in earlier narratives (Linde 1993, 7; Shuman 1986, 54; Stahl 1989).

The connections between Wang Xiangrong's life stories and those of other contemporary folk singers lie in part in what Francisca Cho Bantly (1996) calls "archetypes of selves"—"the perpetuation and embodiment of enduring biographical myths" (183). Biographies and autobiographies in general tend to model themselves on "precedent examples" (Tonkin 1992, 56). Therefore, by looking at connections between earlier legends and contemporary folk singer biographies, we can see how earlier "archetypes" might serve as "templates that a culture creates in order to shape the world into a recognizable and meaningful reality" (Bantly 1996, 179–180). Structurally, both earlier legends of singer-heroes and contemporary folk singer biographies seem to conform to general patterns found in many hero tales around the world: Their birth and childhood show hints of future greatness, they travel on long journeys, and they return (or arrive at their new home) to become king or queen (Raglan 2003, 174–175). Leaving their homes and traveling widely, the singers' period of separation during their journey is always associated with experiences that allow them to become song kings, queens, gods, or goddesses.[2] Their change in status as they transform from peasant to symbolic "king" is conceptualized in ways similar to Van Gennep's paradigm of the rites of passage (i.e., separation, transition, and incorporation), as well as Campbell's "departure," "initiation," and "return" (Van Gennep 1960, vii; Campbell 2004). The more contemporary folk singers' biographies follow in the footsteps of legends, the more the power of their stories increases. Far from being repetitious and ordinary, "the recurrent and typical in the structure of an individual life is significant," as Paul Connerton (1989) suggests, "because it traces out a pattern that is to be celebrated." Such individuals become "fresh incarnation[s] of the traditional" (63). And, the more we become aware of these "social sources of constructing lives," the more the social import of song kings' and queens' lives becomes evident—they embody public conversations between divergent viewpoints, the act of learning about one's self through the eyes of others (Plummer 2001, 399).

From Song Gods to Song Kings

Stories about itinerant singer-heroes have a long history in China. In legends of song gods and goddesses and contemporary folk singer biographies, we see stories of singers encountering difference as they travel, defining themselves in the process, and sharing conversations between viewpoints with their audiences through their lives and songs. A key element of the narrative is the singers' journey that connects them physically and aurally from one place to another, bringing together the "here" and "there." The journey is central to their rise in status. It is where they gain their experience. And upon returning home or arriving at their new destination, the singers assume the role of song god, goddess, king, or queen. During their travels, the singers run into obstacles—symbolic encounters of difference—highlighting choices about what it means to act "appropriately." These obstacles place the singers' personal actions in conversation with the expectations of different groups. By surmounting these obstacles through the power of song, these singer-heroes essentially model how to define one's sense of self in relation to others.

Legends from various parts of China tell of celebrated singer-heroes who travel from one place to another (or mysteriously appear—essentially the same thing) and teach the people to sing. We find similar journeys in biographies of contemporary folk singers, often described as the time when they learned their songs and gained experience as performers. Sometimes, the folk singer journeys alone, while other times they travel as members of a song-and-dance troupe. Regardless, the travel trope offers embodied evidence that the individual has encountered different people and places, suggesting that these singers have learned to mediate between different ways of viewing the world.

The obstacles the singers encounter during their travels highlight social tensions in contemporary issues of the day. In tales of legendary singer-heroes of the past, these obstacles often revolve around conflicting folkways and Confucian morality. In contemporary biographies, on the other hand, we see additional conflicts stemming from recent urbanization and modernization, in addition to tensions between folk and elite mores. An excellent example of the earlier legends is Third Sister Liu (Liu Sanjie), a song goddess from southwestern China who in various accounts runs up against different social forces, perhaps reflecting the concerns of different tellers at various points in history (cf. Loh 1984; Liang 2009). Many of the narratives about Liu culminate in an epic song battle where she beats all comers—scholars, landlords, and farmers. One might argue that each of the "defeated" parties represents segments of the population who fail to engage with the outside world. Limited to their own narrow views of things, they do not participate in self-defining conversations with others. Third Sister Liu, on the other hand, is able to bridge different worldviews and win the respect of all.

Many of the obstacles encountered by these singer-heroes, both past and present, deal with ideas about love, sex, and marriage. This might be due in part to a long-standing connection between singing and courtship. In some stories about Third Sister Liu, her insistence on choosing her own lover conflicts with the traditional Confucian morality of her brother and family (Loh 1984). Another legendary singer-hero, Zhang Liang, whose story is told in southern Jiangsu Province, was punished for attempting to seduce the Buddhist Goddess of Mercy by singing a licentious song (Schimmelpenninck 1997, 104). In both cases, the singers' attempts to choose a partner conflict with the desires of authority figures. Oftentimes, singers appear to mediate between elite and popular moral worldviews. Descriptions of southern Jiangsu singer-heroes range from "saints" to "incorrigible pleasure seekers," while the founders of the *hua'er* genre in Qinghai and Gansu are characterized as "behaving courageously" and "pushing back social frontiers" as they sing mountain songs described as both "popular" and "potentially illicit" (Schimmelpenninck 1997; Kouwenhoven 2014, 139). As we see with some of the stories of Wang Xiangrong's life, as contemporary folk singers achieve a level of celebrity status sufficient to elicit public interest in their private love lives, stories highlighting tensions between rural arranged marriages and free love often emerge.

Public mores—both folk and elite—act as guidelines for how one should act and what is viewed as appropriate behavior. As is noted in chapter 5, the idea of what is appropriate in what context is a particularly present aspect of performance. In adapting to a wide range of audiences as they travel, itinerant singers highlight aspects of place-based morality in the ways they adjust their performances. Conflicting views about what is appropriate extend to how one should go about improving one's position in life and the role of singing in public. Beginning with tales of legendary singer-heroes, we see conflicts highlighting divergent views about how to improve one's situation through self-expression. Social mobility in China was traditionally achieved through studying and the examination system, but stories of song gods and goddesses, similar to those of song kings and queens, suggest singing as an alternative means to raise one's status (cf. Harrison 2002).[3] When the "uneducated peasant" Third Sister Liu defeats a local scholar in a song battle, her victory "seems to challenge…elite values of education and self-cultivation," and she goes on to gain "enlightenment" and "immortality" through music (Loh 1984, 169, 167). In essence, both exam taking and singing can serve as means to redefine one's social status in relation to higher authorities. However, if singing is seen as a form of self-cultivation, disagreements arise as to how, when, and where singing should occur.

In biographies of contemporary song kings, these tensions about how to sing "appropriately" highlight broader issues emerging between rural "tradition" and urban "modernity." These tensions bubble up in struggles over the status of singers in society, appropriate linguistic and paralinguistic features for performance, and proper public behavior in urban and rural contexts. Singers in traditional society, though appreciated for the performances they contributed to rural festivals, were usually perceived as having a low social status (Tong Soon Lee 2009, 73; Lu and Xiao 2000, 240). When new regional, urban-based song-and-dance troupes were established during the reform era, membership in these new institutions offered a different type of social respectability. Singers such as Wang Xiangrong who bridged the rural/traditional and evolving urban ways of life were often caught between different views of the place of singers in society. Wang talks about his mother discouraging him from joining the song-and-dance troupe in the early 1980s, which he says was due to the perceived low status of singers in traditional society.[4] However, beginning with the increased exposure of folk singers on stage, TV, and film in the 1980s and onward, these professionals have seen an elevated rise in social status, culminating in the recent waves of song kings and star singers. When viewed in this context, Wang's mother's concerns can be understood as reflecting traditional views during a time of changing paradigms.

The tensions between rural folk and urban elite involve language and gesture (see chapter 3), as well as singing style. Though in recent years the rise in popularity of non-conservatory-trained "original ecology" (*yuanshengtai* 原生态) singing styles has led to broader acceptance of regional singing traditions, folk singers in China and elsewhere often describe clashes they experience with music conservatory-trained voice teachers over questions of style and technique.[5] Abao's biography, for example, is filled with his struggles against "experts" who don't recognize him and criticize his singing technique as "unscientific" (*bu kexue* 不科学), as well as his angst at being rejected from a music conservatory (Wu Yue 2005, 5–6).[6]

Part of the tension between folk songs and folk singers being praised with the term "original ecology" for their "untrained" quality and being criticized for their untrained quality with terms such as "unscientific" seems to stem from broader discourses of rural backwardness as a foil to urban modernity (cf. Rees 2016). What is performed onstage is implicitly advocated for—an ideal goal society is urged to move toward.[7] Music conservatory-trained voices using "scientific" techniques are often seen as elevating public culture and promoting the evolution of modernity. Rural singing styles are more problematic. Within the urban context, they often tend to call attention to the past—a rural past viewed as existing prior to urban modernity. While desires to return to cultural roots can be seen as an implicit criticism of certain negative aspects of urban modernization, they also hold the potential to threaten the positive achievements of urban modernity. The "experts" who initially rejected Abao's singing style as "unscientific" probably thought that his singing undermined the advances toward which they strove in their own work.

At the same time, broader notions of the role of singing in society have changed over time. Schimmelpenninck (1997) notes that during the 1950s in southern Jiangsu Province, it was common to hear singing during the day out in the fields and in the evening after the day's labor had ended, but by the late 1980s and early 1990s public conceptions of singing had changed. According to several of Schimmelpenninck's informants speaking during the latter period, if someone sang outdoors nowadays during the day, they would be considered psychologically suspect—such behavior was no longer socially acceptable (33–34). In recent years, appropriate contexts for singing have been limited to the stage, karaoke centers, and sometimes banquets with friends. Part of this limitation may be due to new urban notions such as noise ordinances. While singing outdoors in rural areas would have been socially acceptable in earlier periods, it was no longer so in growing urban environments. When an earlier "Folk Song King of Western China," Wang Luobin, sang operatic arias too loudly at night on the street as a child, he was jailed by the Nationalists "for disturbing the peace" (Harris 2005, 382).[8] Again, similar to the controversy regarding the social status of singers, this example suggests contradictory views of appropriate behavior in evolving urban and semiurban contexts.

Several song king biographies include the trope of being punished for singing. The instances often involve misjudging contexts, performing a song in a way that conflicts with a different performance context with which the singer is unfamiliar. This ties into the need to adapt song performances for the stage, discussed in chapter 3, as well as negotiating between different place-based moralities, discussed in chapter 4. One example, Wang Luobin, the singer who was jailed as a child for disturbing the peace, was condemned in 1960 for his "decadent" songs and sentenced by the Communist government to fifteen years in a labor camp—a case of singing songs in politically incorrect contexts (Harris 2005, 384–385). During the Cultural Revolution (1966–1976), the "King of Hua'er" Zhu Zhonglu was also jailed for singing. Around the same time, Wang Xiangrong was fired from his position as an elementary schoolteacher and accused by government officials of "not doing his job" (buwuzhengye 不务正业) when he chose to collect songs instead of studying the political rhetoric in vogue at the time (Zhang Junren 2004; Chu and Jiang 2005, 12).[9] Each instance suggests a misreading of context. At the same time, however, each singer was eventually able to excise himself from punishment and increase his social status after finding "appropriate" ways to sing connected to new contexts and audiences. Similar to Third Sister Liu's winning the song competition by finding appropriate ways to interact between groups and another legendary singer-hero Shen Qige receiving divine protection through song, singing—when adapted appropriately—can lead to salvation and a rise in status (Schimmelpenninck 1997, 104–105). Even during Zhu Zhonglu's incarceration, he was taken out of jail to perform for various international guests (Zhang Junren 2004, 58). Singing one's way out of prison was also a major theme in the legend of the American folk singer Leadbelly, who supposedly received a pardon after singing a song for the state governor recorded by the song collector John Lomax (Wolfe and Lornell 1999, 119). A similar "vindication through singing" trope is evident in Wang Xiangrong's case. After being criticized by local officials and sent back to the countryside for singing inappropriately, he later received praise from the country's leader, Deng Xiaoping, for his performance at a national contest in Beijing in 1980.

Similar to Third Sister Liu's transformation into song goddess after defeating numerous challengers in dialogue songs, singers such as Wang Xiangrong and even Peng Liyuan—the song queen turned first lady—achieved their rise through competitions and gala performances (cf. Jacobs 2012). Generations of singers from the 1950s onward share narratives mentioning how they participated in such-and-such contest or showcase and received critical acclaim and/ or won prizes.[10] In recent times, a string of televised singing competitions following the turn of the millennium have provided opportunities for younger singers to make the jump to fame (Gibbs forthcoming 2018a). A frequently cited example is Abao's rapid rise to fame after appearing on the TV singing contest *Starlight Highway* (*Xingguang dadao* 星光大道) in 2005, after which he became a highly popular media sensation, known both as the "*Xintianyou* Song King" (*xintianyou gewang* 信天游歌王) and the "Folk Song Prince," who fuses pop attraction with pseudo-northern Shaanxi folk song style (Rees 2016).

These contests and galas become symbolic turning points in the narratives of song kings and queens (Gibbs forthcoming 2018a). Moving up in the ranks from village to county to regional to provincial to national song contests parallels the song king's journey from periphery to center and often leads to meetings with national leaders. Sue Tuohy describes the process as follows:

> Village cultural centers hold competitions in which their representatives are chosen to be sent on to the next highest level and ultimately to the national stage. The selected songs and performers are labeled as typical representatives of places and genres—the best crystallizations a group has to offer for national music competitions.... Here the individual musician travels to the nation's capital as a living symbol of his or her group or region; while on the national stage, the musician is representative of and performs a particular identity and its representative music. Moreover, the musician returns to his or her locale replete with plaques and ribbons, as a national representative and is displayed as such in the village. (Tuohy 2001, 122–123)

There are many examples over the years of singers winning contests and meeting with national leaders. Ma Ziqing, a famous female northern Shaanxi folk singer of the older generation, met Zhou Enlai in the 1950s together with the other members of the northern Shaanxi a cappella troupe to which she belonged.[11] Luo Xiuying (b. 1941), a female Miao singer who worked in the Central Nationalities Song and Dance Troupe, met Mao Zedong in 1959 (Schein 2010, 147–148). Wang Xiangrong met Deng Xiaoping in 1980. Li Zhiwen 李治文 (1931–1994), an older singer who taught Wang several songs, saw Mao Zedong and Zhou Enlai while working with a national troupe and later met the national vice-chairman Wang Zhen 王震 (1908–1993) in 1990 (Yang Cui 1995, 29; Huo 2006, 2:951). The connection between meeting national leaders and achieving artistic success appears to be a nationwide (and worldwide) trend.[12] These meetings—always framed as representing recognition for the singers' talent—become symbolic sites where cultural and political capital converge, along with the periphery and center, rural and urban, folk and elite. Through competitions, galas, and meetings with leaders, singers' narratives provide compelling evidence for their rise to the level of song kings and queens, confirmed by the titles and epithets with which they are bestowed and the various positions of power they go on to hold as judges in singing contests and officials in cultural organizations. Table 1, while not comprehensive, gives a general idea of this process.

The positions of power song kings and queens attain are often seen as representing the weak and providing bridges to the disadvantaged. Members of various provincial branches of the Chinese People's Political Consultative Conference, including folk singers, writers, and artists, are seen as having an advisory role to the government on behalf of the people. Furthermore, iconic singers often provide important publicity for their home regions, serving as spokespeople for local tourism and products (figure 1.1).[13]

Song gods, goddesses, kings, and queens offer local people a means of self-expression by teaching them how to sing. In practice, "teaching" songs amounts to singing songs others have not heard before. Although those songs may appear to be "new," often that is not the case. In earlier legends when song gods and goddesses arrive from elsewhere and model songs for the people, it is as if

Figure 1.1 Advertisements for sorghum liquor and cell phone service featuring Wang Xiangrong.

Table 1 Examples of Chinese song kings and song queens

Singer	Title(s)	Select Contests/Galas	Positions of Power
Abao 阿宝 (b. 1969)	"King of Xintianyou" (信天游歌王); "Folksong Prince" (民歌王子)	Starlight Highway	Judge on TV Singing Competitions
Cui Miao 崔苗 (b. 1986)	"Song Phoenix" (歌凤凰)	Starlight Highway	N/A
He Yutang 贺玉堂 (1949–2013)	"Great King of Chinese Folksongs" (中国民歌大王); "Three Great Song Kings of Northern Shaanxi Folksongs" (陕北民歌三大歌王)	Various Competitions	Director of the Ansai 安塞 County Culture Bureau; National-Level ICH Representative Transmitter for Northern Shaanxi Folksongs
Li Youyuan 李有源 (1903–1955)	"The People's Singer" (人民歌手)	Suide Prefecture Literature and Arts Representative Meeting (1952) (绥德专区文代会)	Secretary of a Rural Government Office (wenshu 文书)
Li Zhengfei 李政飞 (b. 1980)	"Top Ten Song Kings"; "National Top Ten Red Singers"	2001 Drinking Song Contest; 2005 National Contest; 2007 Red Song Contest	Judge at Shaanxi Provincial Regionals for 2012 Red Song Contest
Li Zhiwen 李治文 (1931–1994)	"The Song King of the Loess Plateau" (黄土高原的歌王); "Real Chinese Folk-singer" (真正的中国民歌演唱家); "Peasant Folksinger" (农民歌唱家)	Various Competitions	Special Consultant for the Yulin Folk Arts Troupe
Qian Afu 钱阿福 (1909–1993)	"Great King of Shan'ge" (山歌大王); "Excellent Folk Singer" (优秀民歌手)	N/A	Honorary Member of Various Folklore Societies

Name	Title	Award/Competition	Position
Shi Zhanming 石占明 (b. 1973)	"Shepherd Song King" (羊倌歌王)	First National Folksong Competition (2002) (首届中国西北民歌擂台赛)	Artistic Committee Director for the Yulin Folk Arts Troupe; Member of the Shaanxi Provincial Chinese People's Political Consultative Conference (CPPCC)
Sun Zhikuan 孙志宽 (b. 1958)	"Xintianyou Song King" (信天游歌王); "Three Great Song Kings of Northern Shaanxi Folksongs" (陕北民歌三人歌王)	Golden Peacock (金孔雀) Cup Award (1986 National Competition)	Artistic Committee Director for the Yulin Folk Arts Troupe; Member of the Shaanxi Province Musicians' Association; Member of the Shaanxi Provincial Chinese People's Political Consultative Conference (CPPCC)
Wang Erni 王二妮 (b. 1985)	"Uncrowned King of Northern Shaanxi Folksongs" (陕北民歌的无冕之王)	Starlight Highway	Member of the Shaanxi Provincial Chinese People's Political Consultative Conference (CPPCC)
Wang Luobin 王洛宾 (1913–1996)	"Folksong King of Western China"; "Folk Song King of the Northwest" (西部歌王)	1994 Award for Outstanding Contributions to the Exchange of Western and Eastern Cultures from UNESCO	Honorary Town Head of Dabancheng in the Xinjiang Uyghur Autonomous Region
Wang Xiangrong 王向荣 (b. 1952)	"Folksong King of Western China"; "King of Northern Shaanxi Folksongs"; "Three Great Song Kings of Northern Shaanxi Folksongs" (陕北民歌三人歌王)	1980 National Rural Amateur Performance Selection in Beijing	National-Level Intangible Cultural Heritage Representative Transmitter for Northern Shaanxi Folksongs; Member of the Shaanxi Provincial Chinese People's Political Consultative Conference (CPPCC)
Zhu Zhonglu 朱仲禄 (1922–2007)	"King of Hua'er" (花儿王)	Various Gala Events	Head of the Qinghai Province Hua'er Society

Note: Select references include Wu 2005; He 2007; Yin 2007; Schimmelpenninck 1997; Xue 2005; Harris 2005; Zhao 2010; Miao 2008; Zhang 2004; Lü 1994; Huo 2006; "Cui Miao" 崔苗. http://baike.baidu.com/view/338539.htm (accessed April 8, 2013); "Sun Zhikuan" 孙志宽. http://baike.baidu.com/view/316114.htm (accessed April 8, 2013); "Wang Erni" 王二妮. http://baike.baidu.com/view/1461137.htm (accessed April 8, 2013); and "Wang Luobin, King of Songs of Western China." http://www .eventbrite.com/e/wang-luobin-king-of-songs-of-western-china-registration-7966689583 (accessed October 20, 2015). The information about Zhu Zhonglu's position as head of the Qinghai Province Hua'er Society in the 1990s is from Sue Tuohy, personal communication, October 21, 2015.

they are creating local song genres—giving a voice to the populace. This "gift" of local song genres provides the locality with a means to express a communal identity and to place that identity in relation to others that surround it (cf. Klusen 1986; Noyes 2003). By saying "this is our local song," individual and group identity are connected and positioned within a broader context that includes other groups and individuals. Furthermore, the act of presenting these "gifts" of song to a particular place (the "here") from somewhere else ("there") suggests the "here" is special, worthy of receiving gifts. By receiving and taking ownership of those songs, these mythical "gifts" become symbols of a new "here" no longer isolated from other places but instead confident in its sense of place in relation to others. By elevating the status of the giver to song "god" or "goddess," the locality's status is simultaneously raised—the "here" is worthy of a gift from the gods.

From a cursory look at several legends of song gods and goddesses, their gifts of songs seem to help delineate communities around territories and/or ethnicities. Though Third Sister Liu has become identified with the Zhuang ethnic group in Guangxi Province, earlier legends have her teaching songs to a variety of ethnic groups (Liang 2009). In stories about the origins of hua'er in Qinghai and Gansu Provinces, we also find one legend about a female deity/mysterious woman who taught a song to a local man (who then taught others) and was honored for her gift with the building of a temple to host annual gatherings where people sing (Kouwenhoven 2014, 139–140). The connection between the teaching of songs and communal solidarity is similarly evoked in another story about an argument over how to inaugurate an important regional temple. After different ethnic groups suggest ritual operas, scripture recitation, and horse races, three beautiful fairies appear singing mountain songs (hua'er), a conclusion seen as a "conciliatory" choice "shared by all ethnic groups in the region" that "may help to bridge cultural differences" (140–142).

Similar to song gods and goddesses, song kings and queens offer local people a means of self-expression and identity by teaching and performing songs. These contemporary iconic singers give guest lectures at universities and music conservatories combining local history with performance, provide theme songs for TV series and films, and model songs through recordings (CDs/Internet videos) and public performances.[14] Biographies of older singers in Shaanxi Province often portray them as talented performers who actively contributed to the public knowledge of the song tradition and the contexts in which songs were performed (cf. Lü 1994). Part of this contribution is often said to include aiding in collection efforts, teaching in universities and conservatories, and participating in officially orchestrated performances, all of which serve to model songs to others. The two-part Shaanxi volume of the *Big Anthology of Chinese Folk Songs* (*Zhongguo minjian gequ jicheng*) contains short biographies of prominent singers from earlier generations, all the way down to singers such as Wang Xiangrong, who was a young man when the collecting efforts were going full swing in the late 1970s and 1980s. Several of the biographies focus on the tireless efforts of the singers in preserving and transmitting the tradition, in addition to evidence of their vocal talents suggested by song and dance troupe membership, prizes won at song contests, and meetings with dignitaries. Some of the singers are described as collecting folk songs either during their work (e.g., at a troupe or local culture bureau) or during their free time. Special emphasis is placed on singers who shared large numbers of songs with collectors, including Yang Jinshan, Ding Xicai (who provided material for not one but two collections in the 1950s), and Wang Xiangrong, who contributed a whopping twenty-six songs included in the *Big Anthology* (*jicheng* 集成) project that began in the late 1970s (Huo 2006, 2:949–950; Lü 1994, 2:1466).

In addition to collaborating with folk song collection efforts, several singers were invited to teach at universities and/or music conservatories. Ding Xicai and Zhang Tian'en 张天恩 (1910–1969) taught at the Northwest Arts Academy (*Xibei yizhuan* 西北艺专), the predecessor of the Xi'an Conservatory of Music (Huo 2006, 2:949–950; Lü 1994, 2:1465–1466). When Zhang Tian'en lectured there in 1951, he taught students "several tens of northern Shaanxi folk songs" that later became widely sung by numerous singers (Huo 2006, 2:949). Ding Xicai went on to teach at the Shanghai Conservatory of Music (then known as the Eastern China Campus of the Central Conservatory of Music) (Lü 1994, 2:1465). During Ding's more than thirty years of teaching, he is said to have taught over one thousand students, including several who won awards. The training of younger singers by older singers continued in the 1980s. When Wang Xiangrong was hired by the Yulin Folk Arts Troupe, an older singer, Li Zhiwen, who hailed from Suide County, Shaanxi Province, was also invited as an artistic consultant for the younger generation of singers. It was from Li that Wang learned several "classic" northern Shaanxi folk songs from the Mizhi and Suide region (Yang Cui 1995). All of these examples are to some degree reminiscent of tales of legendary singer-heroes teaching the populaces of particular places to sing.

The role of song kings in teaching songs continues today with recent efforts to preserve intangible cultural heritage in China. Inspired by the various proclamations of UNESCO's Masterpieces of the Oral and Intangible Heritage of Humanity and UNESCO's 2003 "Convention for the Safeguarding of the Intangible Cultural Heritage," the China Intangible Cultural Heritage Protection Center was established within the Chinese Academy of Arts in 2006, and the first of what now total four lists of National-Level Intangible Cultural Heritage was published in that year (Rees 2012: 26, 28).[15] Connected to these lists of Chinese national-level items of intangible cultural heritage are three lists of "representative transmitters" (this is Helen Rees' translation of *daibiaoxing chuanchengren* 代表性传承人), published between 2007 and 2009 (Rees 2012). Rees has compared the idea of "representative transmitters" to the "designation of important tradition-bearers as 'living national treasures'" in Japan and South Korea (31). As of 2009, in China these "representative transmitters" totaled 1,488 individuals (32).

Building on UNESCO's push toward "education, awareness-raising and capacity-building" for traditions (2003, Article 14), the Chinese State Council's official documents use the term *chuancheng* 传承, "cultural transmission and inheritance."[16] Song kings and queens, like the seminal tradition bearers for other art forms, become "representative transmitters" (*daibiaoxing chuanchengren*) for particular song traditions. Wang Xiangrong was selected as a provincial-level representative transmitter in Shaanxi's first group of intangible cultural heritage items in June 2008 and a national-level representative transmitter in China's third group of intangible cultural heritage items in May 2009 (Yao 2015). By 2016, Shaanxi Province had five groups of provincial-level intangible cultural heritage items and China had four national-level groups.[17]

A major responsibility in assuming this role is to serve as a key figure in the generation-to-generation transmission of items of intangible cultural heritage, with the heritage seen as embodied in one's memories and skills (ZMWX 2005, 1). The representative transmitters form a bridge to previous generations, submitting a "genealogy of inheritance" (*chuancheng puxi* 传承谱系) and a history of how the aforementioned skills were inherited (*jiyi chuancheng shi* 技艺传承史) (3). After proving their place within the tradition and being officially recognized, the representative transmitters are required to actively impart their knowledge to "receivers"—in this case, younger singers—who become officially documented "disciples" (*tudi* 徒弟) of the representative transmitters, and there is even a clause warning that the representative transmitters must "hold nothing back" (SWB 2007, 1, 5, 7). The role of representative transmitter involves various means of transmission in addition to that of master-disciple (*shicheng* 师承), including social education and formal and informal instruction. Failing to maintain such relationships is grounds for having one's title removed. As Wang put it, without disciples, there are no transmitters. Without teaching songs to the populace, then, there are no song kings.

Teaching songs holds a central place in the song king narrative, tying together all elements of the story—the journey between places and peoples, the obstacles the singers encounter, and how they overcome those obstacles through song. The life stories of these singer-heroes authorize the singers to teach others songs, giving people a voice to assert themselves in conversation with others. The movement of these singers from place to place and their ascent from low to high status both embody the intersection of different social groups and ways of seeing the world in a single individual. Their humble origins and eventual rise suggest a bringing together of disparate segments of society. The singers become liminal entities valued for their ability to cross between worlds. Although they do not reach the status of emperors, they are "almost emperors" (cf. Schimmelpenninck 1997, 107). As actual kings, they would be set apart from their popular roots, while as song kings and queens they maintain their folk status and suggest the possibility of an unfettered, enduring communication between folk and elite. No longer are "the mountains high and the emperor far away." Instead, a division within society is healed and the blood of humanity flows once more.

In stories about Wang Xiangrong's life, we see elements resonating with the precedents of earlier song gods and goddesses as well as other contemporary folk singers (Gibbs 2011). Similar to the narratives discussed, Wang traveled in his youth, working with an amateur troupe, and participated in larger and larger contests, culminating in the transformational moment when he won a national contest in Beijing. Reaffirming the role of song contests in establishing new singer identities, this triumph led to his being hired by the Yulin Folk Arts Troupe and the beginning of his relocation to larger and larger cities (Yulin, Xi'an, and briefly Beijing). At the same time, the trajectory of Wang's life exposes tensions involving class, regional representation, and changing rural/urban views on love and marriage. In spite of these obstacles, or rather through the public experience of them, Wang came to serve as a representative of the people—a national-level representative transmitter of intangible cultural heritage, a delegate in the Shaanxi Provincial Chinese People's Political Consultative Conference, and a frequent lecturer on the connection between songs, geography, and history to college students and military officials. By looking at some of the different accounts of Wang's life, we see how his public image came to embody discussions of contemporary social issues.

Childhood

Wang's hometown of Marugeda 马茹疙瘩 (figure 1.2) is a small village in Fugu County, Shaanxi Province, that sits atop a mountain once covered by yellow *maru* 马茹 flowers, a type of wild rose.[18] The village's name, meaning "Maru Hill" or "cluster of *maru*," was given by two brothers—ancestors of the Wang clan—who moved there from Shanxi Province to the east.[19] Marugeda looks out upon a ravine that drops just beyond the General Guan Yu[20] Temple (*Guandi miao* 关帝庙) at its foot and another mountain ridge beyond. Walking up the village's only road, one passes several cave homes (*yaodong* 窑洞)[21] on the right and a courtyard on the left with three *yaodong* where Wang was born

Figure 1.2 Marugeda, Wang Xiangrong's home village. 2012. Photograph by author.

and grew up (figure 1.3). Soon, you reach a steeper, narrow path leading to the top of the mountain, where, surrounded by small plots of land, you can see the Dragon Mother Temple (*Longmu miao* 龙母庙) on another hill in the distance (figure 1.4). Walking over the ridge to the left, you reach the temple, from where you can view all of the surrounding area.

Wang Xiangrong was born in the year of the dragon, 1952, on the twentieth day of the sixth lunar month—the time of year when the *maru* flowers would be in full bloom.[22] Wang's mother was already old by the time he arrived—she had given birth to nine children, though only five survived. Wang was the youngest, with an elder brother and three elder sisters before him.[23] His sisters had all married by the time he was a child and lived at various distances from their natal family, with the farthest moving to Inner Mongolia in the 1950s. Wang's mother was a talented singer from whom he learned many songs. She had bound feet and planted crops all of her life. His father was a shepherd who would often sing mountain songs (*shanqu* 山曲) as he tended sheep. Wang would go up the mountain with his parents and other older relatives and neighbors—playing to one side while the adults farmed and tended sheep.

During Wang's childhood in the 1950s, there were around sixty or seventy people in the village and everyone had the surname Wang. Wang's recollec-

Figure 1.3 Courtyard with cave-homes where Wang grew up. 2012. Photograph by author.

Figure 1.4 Dragon Mother Temple. 2012. Photograph by author.

tions of his childhood evoke a sense of pastoral nostalgia, no doubt resulting from his extended residence in urban environments during recent decades. In describing Marugeda as he remembered it in his early years, Wang drew various moral and environmental contrasts with other places and times. He pointed to the village's former pristine state and abundant flora and fauna, presenting them as a foil for recent environmental effects brought on by natural resource extraction. Although he remembered the villagers of his childhood as quite poor—in contrast to the area's recent wealth—many of his descriptions of 1950s Marugeda revolve around the people's happiness and relative freedom amidst an abundance of plants, trees, and animals.

For example, Wang recalled that the stream in the ravine below the village was deep blue and purple and would often flood after heavy rainstorms. He said various people in the surrounding area had built up small embankments along the stream over the years and would sometimes divert water to irrigate their crops. Corn and potatoes were grown in the ravine, and black soybeans, mung beans, cowpeas, red beans, cabbage, and all sorts of grains, including wheat, highland barley, millet, broomcorn millet (*meizi* 糜子), and sorghum on the mountain. In addition to crops, one found numerous varieties of plants and trees, including *Artemisia scoparia* (*huanghao* 黄蒿, sometimes translated as caraway), *Caragana korshinskii* (*ningtiao* 柠条), and *Dianthera* (*xiancao* 仙草, "grass jelly"). Many types of birds inhabited the area—magpies, doves, pheasants, hawks, black ducks (*heilaoya* 黑老鸭), sparrows, and a type of red-feathered, red-beaked bird that Wang thought was particularly beautiful. When Wang visited Marugeda again a few years prior to our conversation in 2012, he noted that many of these birds had disappeared—he did not see any hawks or magpies, and even sparrows seemed to be fewer in number.[24]

On the eve of the Chinese New Year in 1966—the year the Cultural Revolution began—Wang's father died.[25] Though Wang had excelled in his studies up to that point, his school, like others during the Cultural Revolution, was soon shut down, and his dreams of going to college and becoming an official or a writer were destroyed. After Wang was forced to return to the countryside and with his father now gone, Wang's mother became anxious about finding Wang Xiangrong a wife and asked his older brother to help. At the age of sixteen, Wang's marriage was arranged, although it would be several years before the family had enough money to go through with the marriage. At seventeen, Wang became a community-supported teacher (*minban jiaoshi* 民办教师) and taught at different elementary schools for several years (Zhao Le 2010, 5).[26] During that time, he sought out local folk musicians and learned their songs. He also taught a music class to schoolchildren that was very popular. In 1972, Wang Xiangrong married.[27] Like countless couples in arranged marriages, Wang never saw his bride before the wedding day. Soon after, the couple had two daughters and a son. After Wang had taught for six years, the cadre in charge of the commune's education criticized him for spending too much time on his folk music interests and not enough time on political thought work, saying Wang was "ignoring his proper duties" (*buwuzhengye* 不务正业) (Chu and Jiang 2005, 12). Wang was warned several times, but continued to pursue his passion for folk songs, and in the summer of 1975 he went back to the fields once more as a farmer.

In 1975, after leaving his teaching position, Wang was selected to join a people's commune specialized work team (*gongshe zhuanye dui* 公社专业队) in which all the members were young people (Zhao Le 2010, 5).[28] The team worked on projects assisting various production brigades throughout the commune (Miao 2008, 73). During the day they would work, and at night when there was nothing to do, the team leader decided to put together a propaganda team (*xuanchuandui* 宣传队) and Wang became one of its mainstays (Zhao Le 2010, 5). It was at this time that Wang formally mounted the stage and soon became a well-known figure throughout the Xinmin People's Commune (*Xinmin gongshe* 新民公社, the township that included his home village, Marugeda) (Miao 2008, 73). Also during that time, Wang joined a traveling troupe that went to Inner Mongolia to perform a regionally popular folk operatic genre known as *errentai* (Lü 1994, 2:1466).

Rise to Fame

When Wang was twenty-three years old, he won a prize for singing an *errentai* piece (see chapter 3 for a description of this genre) about the "Learn from Dazhai" Campaign promoting self-reliance in agricultural production (Zhao Le 2010, 5; cf. Kwok-sing Li 1995, 297–300). Later, when the Gang of Four fell, Wang wrote a song about the event adapted from a poem published in a local newspaper and received local critical acclaim.[29] The end of the Cultural Revolution in 1976 led to an opening up of opportunities for folk songs, including Wang's position in the propaganda team mentioned earlier (Miao 2008, 73). Beginning in 1977, Wang won a string of local, then regional, then national song contests:

- In 1977, he represented Xinmin Commune in the Fugu County Arts Gala (*Fugu xian wenyi huiyan* 府谷县文艺汇演), winning first prize (Chu and Jiang 2005, 13).
- In 1978, he won first place representing Fugu County in a Yulin Prefecture artistic performance selection (*wenyi diaoyan* 文艺调演) singing "Fifth Older Brother Tends Sheep" ("Wuge fangyang" 五哥放羊) (Zhao Le 2010, 5).

- In 1979, Wang won two first-place prizes at the Shaanxi Provincial Arts Gala (*Shaanxi sheng wenyi huiyan* 陕西省文艺汇演) for the *errentai* "Earning Money" ("Da jinqian" 打金钱) and the short operatic drama "Sister-in-Law Picks Vegetables" ("Gusao tiaocai" 姑嫂挑菜) (Zhao Le 2010, 5).
- Also in 1979, Wang performed at a cultural and artistic event held in Yan'an to commemorate Mao Zedong's "Talks at the Yan'an Conference on Literature and Art." It was there that the then-head of the Yulin Cultural Bureau Shang Airen 尚爱仁 discovered Wang, paving the way for his entrance into official performances (Nan 2003, 23).

In 1980 at a National Rural Amateur Performance Selection (*Quanguo nongcun yeyu yanchu diaoyan* 全国农村业余演出调演) in Beijing,[30] Wang's performance of "Brother and Sister Go to the Market" ("Xiongmei ganji" 兄妹赶集) in cooperation with Shenmu County was chosen to be performed in Zhongnanhai, the residential compound housing top party leaders. The duet, based on an adaptation of the *errentai* folk opera melody "Liancheng Pays a New Year's Call" (see chapter 3), involves a couple buying household items in preparation for their marriage during the era of market reform.[31] Deng Xiaoping and other national leaders saw Wang's performance (Zhao Le 2010, 5).[32] The celebrated female writer Ding Ling 丁玲 (1904–1986), who had spent time in northern Shaanxi during the revolutionary period, was also present and is quoted as saying, "Having left northern Shaanxi several decades ago, today we heard real northern Shaanxi folk songs once more!" (quoted in Miao 2008, 73). Wang had stepped onto the national stage.

Several writers see 1980 as a turning point in Wang's career (Miao 2008, 73; Chu and Jiang 2005, 15). In many ways, Wang's representation of rural culture in support of new economic policies appeared in the right place at the right time. With economic decentralization following market reform, northern Shaanxi's Yulin Prefecture decided to use folk culture to advertise itself through the establishment of the Yulin Folk Arts Troupe (*Yulin minjian yishutuan* 榆林民间艺术团), which formally hired Wang in 1983 (Zhao Le 2010, 5; cf. Goodman 1994; Oakes 2000). The slogan at the time was "Culture paves the way, economics comes to sing the opera" (*wenhua pulu, jingji changxi* 文化铺路, 经济唱戏).[33] Suddenly, Wang's abilities as a singer became a professional skill.

Life as a Site for Social Discourse

Wang's move from Marugeda to Yulin City coincided with the early period of China's increased rural-urban migration fostered by economic reforms, mirroring millions of other rural residents (*nongmin*) who moved to cities to find work (Wanning Sun 2014). However, unlike more recent rural migrants who work in factories and on construction sites, Wang's transmission of a rural song tradition to the city eventually led to his being crowned song king. This blending of geographical movement and upward mobility has provided fertile grounds for a compelling story of rags-to-riches.[34] Many articles and documentaries about Wang focus on narratives describing his hard life leading up to and providing a foundation for his later development into a song king (Miao 2008; Yang Cui 1995; Zhao Le 2010). The tagline for one TV documentary, "From Shepherd Boy to the Northern Shaanxi Folk Song King of a Generation" (*Cong yige fangyangwa dao yidai Shaanbei gewang* 从一个放羊娃到一代陕北歌王), conjures up social mobility—the possibility for the rural Everyman and the "common people" (*laobaixing* 老百姓) to cross over from rural to urban, poor to rich, past to future.[35] Wang reinforces this narrative in speeches and interviews by describing how he used singing to escape from the poverty of the countryside of his youth and suggesting that young people see him as a model of how "by singing folk songs you can make it big."[36]

At the same time, the transition from rural tradition to urban modernity brings together divergent views about love and marriage. After Wang moved from the country to the city, stories about his life frequently highlighted tensions between arranged marriage and free choice. One article describes an ill-fated youthful romance with all of the trappings of a bucolic Romeo and Juliet—true love denied by the girl's parents, who decided to marry her to a rich man in far-away Inner Mongolia (Chu and Jiang 2005). Here, the writers portray Wang as a tragic figure whose heartbreak infused him with an emotional depth allowing him to move others to tears when he sang "Going beyond the Western Pass." The expression of anger toward the heartless parents parallels traditional tropes of the tragic consequences of arranged marriages we find in bridal laments from various parts of China and popular stories such as "Liang Shanbo and Zhu Yingtai" (sometimes known as "Butterfly Lovers" in English) (Cf. Mair and Bender 2011, 100–114; McLaren 2008).[37]

While the tragedy of Wang's youthful heartbreak is attributed to traditional rural society, the failure of Wang's marriage following his move to the city is often portrayed as a negative outcome caused by urban modernity and the destabilizing effects of urban life. In a book written by Wang's older brother, *Wang Xiangrong Family Chronicle* (*Wang Xiangrong jiazu jishi* 王向荣家族纪事), ostensibly a moral teaching for younger generations, there is an entire chapter devoted to Wang Xiangrong's marriage.[38] Entitled "I Arranged a Marriage for My Little Brother" ("Wo wei didi ding le qin" 我为弟弟定了亲), the chapter details the older brother's years of hard work earning money for Wang's wedding and blames Wang for the failure of his marriage (Wang Shangrong

2011, 60–70).[39] It appears that a certain level of public attention was devoted to Wang's love life after his move to Yulin, since one of his writer friends who has written several articles about Wang complained, at one point, that people focused too much on erotic stories about Wang, while failing to appreciate him as a great artist (Di 2010, 15).

The divergent views of arranged marriage and free choice we see in these examples suggest differing viewpoints along the rural-urban divide about love and marriage. In the rural context, arranged marriage is portrayed as a negative relic of the past. In the urban context, on the other hand, choosing to move away from an unhappy arranged marriage toward free love is criticized as scandalous. While by the time of my fieldwork Wang had settled into a long-term relationship, his earlier period in limbo struggling to find a new partner was sometimes presented as endemic of larger social issues as rural areas of China transitioned from arranged marriage to individual choice. Wang appeared at one point on an episode of a television program called "One Hundred Years of Love and Marriage" (*Bainian hunlian* 百年婚恋), which explored how public conceptions of love and marriage had changed over time by looking at case studies of the love lives of prominent individuals. In the episode about Wang, interview clips with him and his estranged wife were interspersed with segments shot with a sociologist and a psychologist in a TV studio. The two "experts" analyzed Wang's case and how it related to personal psychology (Wang's relationship with his mother) and broader social trends. Toward the end of the program, the psychologist concluded that Wang was in a state of limbo, caught between rural and urban social spheres, between the traditional and the progressive. She suggested that Wang still felt a sense of duty precluding him from officially divorcing his wife and had not adapted completely to more liberal urban lifestyles ("Bainian hunlian" 2003).

The interest in Wang's life as a site to discuss social mobility, the rural-urban divide, and love and marriage all stems from his rise to fame. Wang suggested that his fame began to peak in 1994, partly due to the rise of regional satellite TV stations in the early 1990s, which allowed individual artists to become more widely known.[40] Increased public interest in Wang's personal life could stem from desires to engage with ambivalent issues arising in the midst of social change. There is an intrinsically social function of celebrity "as a source of gossip, which is itself understood as an important social process through which relationships, identity, and social and cultural norms are debated, evaluated, modified and shared" (Graeme Turner 2004, 24; cf. Jeffreys and Edwards 2010; Tansman 1996; Marcus 1991; Titon 2012). Graeme Turner suggests that a public figure becomes a celebrity "at the point at which media interest in their activities is transferred from reporting on their public role (such as their specific achievement in politics or sport) to investigating the details of their personality and private lives" (2004, 8). It would follow that interest in Wang's private life resulted from his growing fame, and discussions of those aspects of his life became a site to converse about contentious social issues of the day.

Interestingly, Wang seems to have made an effort to revert his role from celebrity back to public figure after his fame crested around 2006. Following an increase in Internet use and televised singing competitions since the turn of the millennium, a younger generation of overnight superstars gradually moved him out of the spotlight (cf. Gibbs forthcoming 2018a). And along with the rise of UNESCO–inspired intangible cultural heritage preservation (cf. Howard 2012), Wang transitioned into more official roles, such as National-Level Representative Transmitter of Northern Shaanxi Folk Songs, vice-chairman of the Shaanxi Province Musicians' Association, and member of the Shaanxi Provincial Chinese People's Political Consultative Conference (Zheng-Xie 政协). During my fieldwork with Wang from 2011 to 2012, he had six younger singers officially registered as his "disciples" (tudi 徒弟) in his role as representative transmitter.[41] When I saw him again in 2016, he had twelve.[42] As vice-chairman of the Musicians' Association, he served as one of the judges at annual singing competitions, with categories including Western bel canto style (meisheng 美声), Chinese national style (minzu changfa 民族唱法), and nonconservatory-trained folk song style (yuanshengtai).[43] Wang was also frequently invited to act as a judge for other contests, such as the provincial finals for the Red Song Contest (Honggehui 红歌会) in 2012, where he was placed at the center of the judge's table—the guest of honor (figure 1.5).[44] In 2016, he was serving as a judge on the show "I Want to Be on the CCTV Gala" (Wo yao shang chunwan 我要上春晚).[45]

While Wang's transformation into a celebrity brought an increased public interest in his private life, his later transition into a public figure appears to have allowed him to reclaim some sense of separation between public and private identities. His reluctance in recent years to talk about certain aspects of his personal life, especially his romantic past, could be seen as evidence of this changed status, which is also apparent in many of his public appearances. He is more cautious about how he presents himself in public, and on many occasions he chooses to frame himself as an educator rather than just a performer. During lectures to military officials at a local political institution each year, for example, Wang mainly speaks, choosing to have his younger disciples perform the song examples. In many ways, Wang embodies Edward Said's notion of intellectuals as "individuals with a vocation for the art of representing, whether that is talking, writing, teaching, [or] appearing on television" (1996, 13).[46] His roles as vice-chairman of the provincial musicians' association and representative transmitter of northern Shaanxi folk songs carry with them responsibili-

Figure 1.5 Wang Xiangrong serving as judge in the Xi'an finals of the 2012 Red Song Contest. Photograph by author.

ties for representing and transmitting the tradition to both younger generations and outsiders. And, it is clear from his public conduct that he assumes a sense of responsibility for this representation.

As Wang is one of northern Shaanxi folk songs' "faces of tradition," the roles he has played in films, TV shows, and music videos since the early 1980s also provide interesting commentary on the portrayal of the tradition via evolving images of one individual. Wang's earliest music video following his national success in the 1980 competition was a duet called "Going to the Market" ("Ganji" 赶集; see chapter 2 for lyrics). In the video, Wang and a fellow singer represented rural residents benefiting from economic reform—visiting Yulin markets to see all of the local goods recently made available for sale following market reform.[47] Wang would later go on to perform roles highlighting northern Shaanxi's place in China's revolutionary history. He played Mao Zedong's horse groom in a film about Mao's time in northern Shaanxi and provided theme songs and soundtracks for several TV dramas set in revolutionary Yan'an, including one based on Edgar Snow's book *Red Star Over China* (*Xixing manji* 西行漫记) (Chu and Jiang 2005, 17; cf. Snow 1938).

When music videos became popular in the early 1990s with several national contests, Wang's video of "The Infinite Bends of the Yellow River" once again highlighted northern Shaanxi's importance within Chinese culture, as Wang began to approach stardom. Around the turn of the millennium, various televised documentaries depicted Wang's life with the interest reserved for celebrities, focusing once again on Wang's rise to prominence and associated social tensions. Following the emergence of Chinese intangible cultural heritage preservation in 2004, Wang's film and TV roles increasingly emphasized his preservation of tradition. In 2008, Wang was chosen as one of the Olympic torchbearers and sang a special panegyric as he ran that he composed to celebrate the Beijing Olympics (Miao 2008, 71). In 2010, he appeared as a wise old folk singer who befriends a young musicology student from Beijing in the film *I Am an Extraterrestrial* (*Wo shi waixingren* 我是外星人, English name: *A Chinese E.T. Boy*), which tells the story of a young boy from northern Shaanxi with an active imagination who dreams of becoming an astronaut and battling space aliens.

More recently, in the (2014) *Pairs of Mandarin Ducks Float on the Water* (*Yi duidui yuanyang shuishang piao* 一对对鸳鸯水上漂), Wang played a singer of the older generation who, unlike his contemporaries, refused to move to the city, instead staying on the land to preserve the tradition.[48] One article about the film calls it "China's first film about protecting and transmitting northern Shaanxi folk songs" (*Zhongguo shoubu yi chuancheng baohu Shaanbei min'ge wei zhuti de dianying* 中国首部以传承保护陕北民歌为主题的电影), coinciding well with Wang's position as national-level representative transmitter of northern Shaanxi folk songs.[49]

As Wang is a prominent face of northern Shaanxi and its folk song tradition, his appearances on film and television and the accounts of his life highlight social discourses over the years and amidst changing place relations—all part of a rural singer's journey to become a song king. As he crossed social boundaries, Wang's image as a singer highlighted social tensions between different ways of thinking, tensions reflected in anecdotes about his life in print, television, and film. Resonating with similar stories of other singers, past and present, the symbolic power of Wang's life hangs between the authority of tradition and the urgency of contemporary social issues (cf. Bauman 2004; Stahl 1989). Like other song kings and queens, Wang's life exposes tensions between peoples and places while providing a model of how to negotiate a sense of self in relation to others. When Wang's stories are seen together with the stories of other lives, the overarching song king/queen narrative is put into relief, highlighting the narrative's power to embody conversations between divergent views. While song kings and queens of all generations negotiate between conflicting social forces, the specific tensions that each individual brings to light are tied to their historical moment. Therefore, if we think of singers' life stories

CHAPTER 2

An Education through Song

Becoming a song king or queen is about learning to perform public conversations others can join in on. Over time, these conversations expand from sung dialogues between individuals—attendees at banquets paying respect to each other and villagers communicating with local gods—to cultural exchanges between regions, nations, and corporations. For singers such as Wang to come to represent regions requires finding one's voice in relation to others and learning to pivot that voice toward different audiences to build a pliable, larger-than-life whole. This chapter looks at how the songs and singers Wang was exposed to as a youth may have helped shape his vision of what it means to be a professional folk singer and, ultimately, a song king.

Though Wang's repertoire of songs from his childhood and youth spans a range of genres and contexts, each song offered ways for entities with different perspectives to gloss over differences and establish meeting grounds where they could benefit from each other's experience and find a new way forward. The sung personae and addressees of these songs have many desires—boys seeking relationships with girls, banquet attendees seeking to strengthen their relationships with other guests, fathers seeking cures for their ailing children, and spirits seeking to be honored by local villagers. Each song creates a liminal "meeting ground" where disparate desires meet on equal footing: In drinking songs, banquet attendees submit to the rules of drinking games and strengthen their social bonds within the games' liminal spaces. In spirit medium rituals, the medium's songs allow ailing children's parents to honor local spirits and the spirits to tell them how to cure the children. In songs about blossoming romances, boys and girls face new environments together—walking away from the village to pick fruit, strolling through a Chinese New Year display of lanterns, and later, exploring new markets created by economic reforms. These couples, like the banquet guests and ritual attendees, also enter liminal arenas as they merge their points of view. In each case, social constraints that might separate the participants are temporarily put aside in order to share and benefit from each other's unique perspectives and abilities. In short, the singers integrate different perspectives and identities into a public conversation.

The songs and singers from Wang Xiangrong's youth, I want to suggest, provided Wang with models of how song can serve as a conversation between entities, grounded in particular places and moments. Many of the songs contain references to the natural topography of his mountain village and the surrounding areas, which seems to have instilled in Wang an awareness of the connection between place and song (cf. Stokes 1994). In the hours and days I spent with Wang discussing the lyrics of his songs, going line by line through each stanza as I asked about the meanings of particular terms and the social contexts surrounding each song, it became evident to me that what underlies many of these songs is the ability to position oneself in relation to others and have a conversation about desires—for love, consolation, laughter, health, and comradery—for coming together to negotiate relations with others as we deal with the vagaries of life. Whether through verbal expression or silent critique, singers and listeners discuss *how things could be,* each offering their input.

In addition to the idea of song as public conversation, I want to suggest that Wang's education through song provided him with models of singer authority. The singers he admired as a child served as protomodels for what it might mean to be a song king. Several times in our discussions, Wang said that there was no such thing as a "professional folk singer" when he was young. This begs the question of how his ideas about what a singer is and does were formed. I look at two childhood models of authoritative singers—a spirit medium and a folk opera performer at temple fairs—to examine how they provided images of singers as mediums between groups. I also look at the contexts of various local genres, pointing to different ways singing functioned in social settings. Drinking songs negotiated interpersonal relations between guests and hosts at banquets; spirit-medium tunes set up conversations between villagers and local gods; love songs provided entertainment during festival time, while simultaneously opening the door for relationships between lovers.[1] Taken together, the genres of Wang's youth suggest different means through which subjectivities meet in song. Guests and hosts come together in the liminal space of an event heightened by the experience of performance. Couples going out to explore other realms offer their perspectives before coming to a new perspective together. In song, knowledge of the self and knowledge possessed by others are shared, mixed together, and form a new relational sense.

The Performancescapes of Northern Shaanxi and Marugeda

To better understand the "performancescape" of Wang's youth, we can look at how a general description of northern Shaanxi art forms intersects with the more localized traditions prevalent in the vicinity of Marugeda (Bender 2010, 120; cf. Thurston 2013, 168). Rather than forming a homogenous subsection of the larger northern Shaanxi region, Wang's home county of Fugu was in many ways isolated from other regions of northern Shaanxi to the south and southwest. Lying along the province's northern border, the area around Wang's home village formed part of a larger linguistic and folk song style region that included northwestern Shanxi Province and the Ordos region of Inner Mongolia (Miao and Qiao 1987; cf. Han 1989).

Performing genres in northern Shaanxi include folk songs, narrative singing (*Shaanbei shuoshu*), regional operatic traditions (*Qinqiang, Jinju, daoqing, errentai*), instrumental music, and dance (e.g., *yangge*, "a festive and semidramatic group dance form with singing…accompanied by percussion and often also by shawm music") (cf. Jones 2009, 12–13, 20).[2] Stephen Jones notes that these "genres, here as elsewhere in China, overlap: folk-song, narrative-singing, and opera are a continuum, and instrumental and vocal music often accompany dance" (13). There are also various types of ritual music, including ceremonies to ask for rain (*qiyu*) (22–23) and spirit-medium rituals I discuss later (cf. Ka-ming Wu 2015; Kang 2006). Among folk songs, there are several types generally referred to as "mountain songs" (e.g. *xintianyou, shanqu,* and *pashandiao*), which Wang Xiangrong (2006) notes are similar to each other.[3] These tend to have free meter and typically would be sung loudly outdoors. "Little ditties" (*xiaodiao*), on the other hand, generally have a rather solid structure, with even meter and smooth-flowing melodies (Lü 1994, 1:173).[4] While *xintianyou* mountain songs tend to have two lines of seven characters, "little ditties" often have four lines of seven characters (Wang Xiangrong 2006; Lü 1994, 1:173). Because of the frequent addition of filler words and phrases (*chenzi chenju* 衬字衬句) inserted in the middle or at the end of lines, the exact number of words can vary (Lü 1994, 1:172).[5]

Although Wang's home village is located in northern Shaanxi (near its northern edge), the culture and musical genres in Marugeda and the surrounding area were deeply influenced by the history of a migratory phenomenon known as "going beyond the Western Pass" (*zou xikou* 走西口). Many of Marugeda's villagers, including several of Wang's relatives, would travel and sometimes relocate to Inner Mongolia for economic reasons—part of a historical phenomenon where generations of men from places like northern Shaanxi and Shanxi would travel to the western sections of Inner Mongolia to find work during times of drought and hardship (YDW 1983, 2). The "Western Pass" (*xikou* 西口) referred to the gates in the western sections of the Great Wall, seen as a boundary between the area to the south ("inside the pass," *kouli* 口里) and the area to the north ("outside the pass," *kouwai* 口外). The men would head out in the spring, find jobs as shepherds, coal miners, day laborers, boatmen, and seasonal crop harvesters in Inner Mongolia, and return after the fall harvest, although some stayed "beyond the Pass" for many years and others never returned (ZYXZYY 1962, 1).

Over the years, this back-and-forth movement of Han Chinese to areas of Inner Mongolia led to cultural exchange between Han and ethnic Mongols, leading to new musical genres such as *errentai* 二人台 folk opera and Mongol-Han tunes (*Meng-Han diao* 蒙汉调).[6] *Errentai* (literally "two-person opera/stage") was a genre popular in Fugu 府谷 and Shenmu 神木 Counties in northern Shaanxi Province, Hequ 河曲 County in northwestern Shanxi Province, the Ordos region (formerly Yeke-Juu League [Yikezhaomeng 伊克昭盟], sometimes spelled Ikh-Juu or Ih-Juu), and areas near Baotou 包头 (Mongolian Bugutu) and Hohhot (Huhehaote 呼和浩特) in Inner Mongolia (YDW 1983, 1). It was often performed as a gift to the gods at temple fairs in the region on stages facing the deities. Crowds of people sat and stood in front of those stages—the songs were for them as well.[7] Two performers (traditionally both men), acting in a female role (*dan* 旦) and male clown role (*chou* 丑), would sing back and forth accompanied by a bamboo flute, four-stringed spike fiddle (*sixian* 四弦), and hammered dulcimer (*yangqin* 杨琴) (ZYXZYY 1962, 213; YDW 1983, 2). Many *errentai* songs deal with various aspects of love, while one of the genre's most representative pieces, "Going beyond the Western Pass," the aria Wang sang by the Yellow River at the beginning of this book, deals with the pain of separation.

As a child, Wang became a great fan of *errentai* and would walk great distances to see performances at temple fairs in the surrounding area.[8] Both Wang and his older brother, Wang Shangrong, tell stories about how Wang and other local children would put on their own "temple fairs" in the family courtyard or inside their family's *yaodong,* and sometimes Wang would sing while standing on top of the heated, brick platform bed (*kang* 炕), pretending it was a stage, with the other children playing the "audience" seated on the floor below (Wang Shangrong 2011).[9] In retrospect, the *errentai* genre was one of the only locally produced "professional" sorts of singing to which Wang was exposed, and for Wang and other children in the isolated villages of northern Shaanxi, *errentai* troupes were often seen as one of the only ways out of the village.[10] This may explain why Wang went on to perform *errentai* during his amateur and professional career. After working briefly in an amateur *errentai* troupe in Inner Mongolia in the 1970s, he performed an adapted *errentai*, "Brother and Sister

Go to the Market," at the national competition in Beijing in 1980, various other *errentai* pieces for the Yulin Folk Arts Troupe beginning in the early 1980s—including his first music video, "Going to the Market" (see below)—and an *errentai* duet, "The Flowers Bloom in May," at a 2008 U.S. performance involved in negotiating one of the largest joint ventures in China (see chapter 4).

One of Wang's childhood idols was a local performer of *errentai* named Sun Bin 孙宾 (1890–1983).[11] Sun was from a wealthy landlord family and had received an excellent education. Yet, instead of becoming an official or merchant, he chose to devote his time to his passion for folk songs, seeking out teachers and performing at events throughout the area (Chu and Jiang 2005). Due to the low status of singers at the time, Sun's family rejected him and neighboring villagers saw him as something of an eccentric. Later on, when Wang was older, he would often visit Sun's home to learn from him. Sadly, Sun Bin died at the age of ninety-three in 1983, the year that Wang began to work with the Yulin Folk Arts Troupe.

Another hybrid genre emerging from the region's history of migration was called "Mongol-Han tunes" (*Meng-Han diao*) in northern Shaanxi, a song genre generally considered to be most popular in Jungar Banner (Zhunge'erqi 准格尔旗) in the easternmost part of the Ordos region of Inner Mongolia, where it is now referred to as *manhandiao* 漫瀚调. Mongol-Han tunes are said to have evolved from Ordos "short song" melodies (*duandiao* 短调) with fixed Mongolian lyrics to dialogue songs with improvised Chinese lyrics or a mixture of Chinese and Mongolian, poetically referred to as "wind mixing with snow" (*feng jiao xue* 风搅雪) (E'erdunchaolu et al. 1992, 1254–1277; Yang Hong 2006, 70). Wang learned many Mongol-Han tunes from relatives returning from Inner Mongolia for visits, as well as during summer trips where he spent time with relatives in Inner Mongolia during the 1970s. During my fieldwork from 2011 to 2012, Wang's elderly aunt and other relatives were still living in Inner Mongolia, and he was frequently invited to perform in various cities in the Ordos region.

The Mongol-Han tunes Wang sings all deal with aspects of love—coming together, getting away together, and reuniting after a period of separation. The lyrics include bold declarations of love and attraction between men and women (sometimes explicitly labeled as Han and Mongol), such as "you are Older Brother's…pretty-eyed gal," "you are the round button…on Younger Sister's bosom," "you are the ache…in Older Brother's heart," and "you are Younger Sister's…dear sweetheart."[12] The songs paint images of lovers riding horses together, holding hands as they walk to find a secluded spot, and traveling over mountains and gullies to find an out-of-the-way place to kiss. The hybrid nature of this genre evokes a dialogic interaction between groups, reinforced by Wang's stories of crossing borders as he learned and performed these songs. On several occasions, I observed Wang perform a Mongolian language version of a Cultural Revolution–era revolutionary song (see chapter 6)—not a Mongol-Han tune per se, but nevertheless a testament to Wang's border-crossing experience.

Several of the songs Wang learned as a child contained references to the mountain village in which he grew up, Marugeda. One love song, "Picking *Maru* Fruits," describes a couple journeying down the mountainside and crossing the ravine (figure 2.1) to pick the fruits of the local plant after which the village was named. Even a childhood song Wang recalled about the widely told romance of Liang Shanbo and Zhu Yingtai—China's Romeo and Juliet—seemed to be mapped onto the mountainside where he grew up.[13] The village is also the setting of drinking songs and spirit-medium tunes—two genres Wang often heard in his youth. Marugeda's families lived in cave homes (*yaodong* 窑洞) carved out of the mountainside with walled courtyards in front—a traditional architectural style for many parts of rural northern Shaanxi. Some cave homes were simple, single rooms with a heated brick bed (*kang*) at one end, while others were more elaborate with one, two, or three adjoining rooms dug out on the sides and/or at the back.[14] Wang described scenes where families

Figure 2.1 Ravine below Marugeda and mountain range beyond. 2012. Photograph by author.

would invite guests to their home for a banquet, the host seating each individual on the *kang* according to relational status and communal propriety.[15] Only after everyone was properly seated would the drinking and festivities begin.

Drinking songs (*jiuqu* 酒曲) are an established folk song genre tied to local drinking culture (*jiu wenhua* 酒文化) in the northern part of northern Shaanxi (Lü 1994, 1:570).[16] The banquet or drinking party provided a space for individuals to use song and speech to strengthen their relations in mutually beneficial ways through toasting, teasing, and finger-guessing games (*huaquan* 划拳).[17] In these interactions, guests and hosts would attempt to set up "ritualized relationships" through performative gift exchange (Mayfair Mei-hui Yang 1994, 70; cf. Gibbs 2017). For example, when one banquet attendee sang a toast to another, this public singing of praise was seen as a gift, and the recipient was obligated to reciprocate by downing a glass of sorghum liquor (*baijiu* 白酒). These transactions sought to strengthen relationships via the interlocking obligations of "giv[ing]," "receiv[ing]," and "repaying" (Mauss 1966, 10–11; cf. Gibbs 2017).

While any individual at a banquet in Marugeda might have performed a song, when the host invited a singer to facilitate, that individual served a unique function in mediating between guests and host. At times, the singer would formally thank the host for the food and drink on behalf of the assembled guests. The singer might also use his mediating position to tease the host, ritualistically breaking down the social barriers that might otherwise constrict the guests' behavior (undoubtedly the guests' consumption of alcohol also helped in this regard). If one of the guests had too much to drink, the singer could also urge that individual on behalf of the host and assembled guests to slow down—thus regulating individual and collective desires. Over the course of the event, the singer would sometimes align himself with the host and at other times with the guests, acting as a representative of both and embodying the type of dual identity we have seen among song kings, queens, gods, and goddesses in chapter 1—individuals who sit on the border of two groups, participating in both and limited to neither.

We see a similar guest-host dynamic mediated by singers in another genre prevalent in Marugeda during Wang's childhood: spirit-medium tunes (*shenguandiao* 神官调). Villagers with illnesses and other maladies in the area of northern Shaanxi where Wang grew up would seek out spirit mediums to ask local gods and spirits for cures.[18] These male mediums were called "spirit officials" (*shenguan* 神官) or "spirit men" (*shenhan* 神汉), and the songs they sang during rituals were known as "spirit-medium tunes" (Lü 1994, 1:571; Huo 2006, 2:872).[19] According to Wang, the gods that the mediums communicated with served a similar function to "folk doctors" and "traveling country doctors." For all types of afflictions, including broken bones, stomach ulcers, and headaches, the spirit invited by the medium would help divine the malady's root cause, which often stemmed from the faults of one's ancestors or one's own improper actions. Occasionally, vengeful ghosts (*gui* 鬼) stirred up trouble, and the mediums held rituals to send the ghosts away. In rituals to seek cures for villagers' afflictions, the gods had to be invited, kowtowed to, presented with incense, informed in detail of the symptoms, listened to as they presented prescriptions for cures, given food for themselves and grain for their horses, and sent back on their way. In all of this, the spirit medium would serve as the representative who spoke for the spirit through song, facilitating conversations between villagers and gods.

There were several types of gods, including anthropomorphic fox spirits (i.e., foxes that became spirits) and ancestral spirits (i.e., ancestors who had become gods).[20] In the latter case, if the person had been virtuous and was worthy of respect, rather than staying in the netherworld (*diyu* 地狱) after death as a ghost, Yama, the King of Hell (*Yanwang* 阎王), could release them to ascend to the sky (*shang tian* 上天) as a god (*shen* 神).[21] In the ritual discussed later in this chapter, one of the spirits invited—the Grand Immortal of the Black Clouds—is an ancestor of the Marugeda villagers who all had the surname Wang.

Wang Xiangrong learned spirit-medium tunes from a spirit medium (*shenguan*) who lived in his village called Eldest Grandfather, who also appears to have provided Wang with one of his models for authoritative singers. For the people of Marugeda, Eldest Grandfather served as the mouthpiece for a local god and was able to command a large array of spiritual forces. Wang noted that Eldest Grandfather was very serious and had a mysterious air about him when he invited the gods to descend from their horses. He recalled that Eldest Grandfather had an incredible singing voice, often accompanying himself with the round sheepskin drum used by spirit mediums in the area. Wang also noted that Eldest Grandfather was the most knowledgeable about the village's ancient local culture. Since no one went to hospitals at that time, the villagers would ask for Eldest Grandfather's assistance whenever anyone suffered an illness. Though Wang never became a spirit medium himself, he learned many songs from Eldest Grandfather and other mediums he visited in later years.

As I translated these spirit-medium tunes into English, I found that their lyrics required the greatest degree of familiarity with local knowledge of any of the songs in Wang's repertoire. Wang mentioned that although he performed these songs occasionally for friends and scholars and was not himself a spirit medium, he felt compelled as he grew older to seek out elderly *shenguan* and learn more about the content of these songs and how they related to local culture. As I went line by line with Wang through the songs, his explanations of the subtleties of terms and the intricacies of the spirit world—couched in a deep interest in the history of local culture—reminded me of a cultural anthropologist. His efforts to interview older *shenguan* and his detailed explanations of these songs and their social contexts clearly suggest to me that Wang saw spirit medium songs as an important part of representing the local culture of his youth.

Lessons Learned

Two of the models of influential singers Wang points to from his childhood—Sun Bin and Eldest Grandfather—had dual identities authenticating their performances and aiding in their mediation between groups. Eldest Grandfather had been chosen by the gods to help communicate with the villagers of Marugeda. His ability to speak to two groups and convey messages between them is similar to the semidivine nature of song gods and goddesses and the dual identity of song kings and queens discussed in chapter 1. Sun Bin's identity also represented a unique fusion of groups, combining his elite education and social status with his passion for a popular art form usually performed by those of low status. While connecting folk and elite, as noted earlier Sun was also rejected by both groups—thrown out by his family and viewed as eccentric by local villagers—a classic border walker. We see a similar dual status in other genres from Wang's childhood. Singers of Mongol-Han tunes could bridge different ethnic groups and places. Banquet singers could float between guests and hosts. At the same time, Sun Bin's case represents a symbiotic relation of value between his divergent identities: his elite status brought attention to an otherwise "lowly" genre, while his interest in *errentai* suggested that the genre offered something of value that Sun was unable to acquire through his elite education.

Both Sun Bin and Eldest Grandfather also exhibited an ability to help groups exchange things of value. Eldest Grandfather assisted the villagers in relating requests for help to the gods and helped convey the gods' otherworldly knowledge of illnesses and cures to the villagers. He also presented gifts on behalf of the villagers to the gods through song, paying them the proper respects, and making sure they were properly provided for during their return trip. Sun's performances in temple fairs were often also done in the context of thanking gods for favors and protection.

In my conversations with Wang, it seemed that Eldest Grandfather's spirit-medium tunes helped Wang develop a sensitivity to the contexts of performance—a skill Wang would develop as he performed on stages across the nation and world. Eldest Grandfather's identity as a chosen spirit medium also showed Wang the importance of a singer's persona in authorizing the performance of a song. Spirit-medium tunes could only be properly performed by a spirit medium in the context of a ritual with an altar and other accoutrements. While Wang would sometimes sing the tunes during play as a child, it was always clear to him that his imitations did not mean the same thing as when Eldest Grandfather performed the songs in a ritual. As an ordinary child, Wang might be able to sing the words and melody, but he would not be able to communicate with the divine. Wang noted that the authority of spirit mediums was something bestowed by the gods—one could not *choose* to be a medium. Therefore, only certain individuals were authorized to perform these songs as authentic communications. The underlying idea that certain songs are only appropriate in certain contexts and certain contexts call for certain types of songs and singers was something Wang would carry with him and expand upon as he encountered a variety of audiences in the years to come.

The songs emerging in these contexts involved a variety of sung personae—images of character types suggested by the lyrics corresponding to the messages at hand. In drinking songs, the sung persona was expected to be audacious, cracking jokes and teasing the host, to achieve the "hot and noisy" (*renao* 热闹) ambience desired in banquets. Spirit-medium rituals, in turn, involved sections of song sung by the medium and other sections sung by the medium *in the voice of the spirit* in conversation with the medium. In dialogic Mongol-Han tunes, as we have seen, roles may include a Mongol man and Han woman. *Errentai* folk dramas also involved conversations between male and female personae, though both were traditionally performed by male singers. Singers could put on the mask of either persona by singing its part: a male singer in "Going beyond the Western Pass" might assume the role of the man leaving *or* the woman left behind—or sometimes both (it is not uncommon to hear one singer alternating between both roles). Each of these contexts called for sung personae capable of communicating with the participants at hand—strengthening social bonds between participants in a drinking party, conversing about an illness and its cure between humans and spirits in a ritual, and presenting a symbolic scene of parting between two individuals that connected the audience to a shared local history and geography. Later on, during the course of Wang's career, the roles he enacted through song on stage would highlight the flexible ambiguity of sung personae—vessels to be filled by different observers with a range of meanings. As I argue in the following chapter, the adaptation of sung personae formed an integral part of the development of songs representing larger and larger regions—a crucial function of the role of song kings and queens.

Both spirit-medium tunes and *errentai* catered to multiple audiences. Spirit-medium tunes represented conversations between villagers seeking help and the gods who would come to assist them. Villagers not directly involved in the ritual would also observe the exchange as secondary audiences (Brenneis 1986). Temple fairs also frequently hosted opera performances for the benefit of the spirits, with the multitudes of people comprising a parallel audience. In each case, the singers acted as authorized conduits—messengers between realms.

On separate occasions, Wang noted that both Eldest Grandfather and Sun Bin had a knowledge of local culture and history connected to their familiarity with spirit-medium tunes and *errentai* respectively. Wang suggested that Eldest Grandfather was the most knowledgeable of Marugeda's residents with regard to the village's ancient local culture. Sun Bin, in turn, was intimately familiar with the origins and variants of each *errentai* song and would present them as "living fossils" (*huo huashi* 活化石) of high cultural value that were connected to local history, sociology, folklore, geography, and other aspects of life. Wang's descriptions of Sun seem to resonate with Wang's own enthusiasm for analyzing and representing the content of songs and their social contexts to others, mentioned earlier. One article refers to Wang as a "folk music theorist" (*minjian yinyue lilunjia* 民间音乐理论家), suggesting a similar focus on analysis and representation (Chu and Jiang 2005, 15). In the context of Wang's education through song, it seems that arias such as "Going beyond the Western Pass" provided models of songs as discursive sites for audiences and singers to commune with and reflect upon the emotional landscape of life—love and separation, togetherness and loneliness.

In suggesting that Wang experienced an "education through song" in his youth, I do not mean he was a passive recipient of a tradition set in stone but rather that he acquired an expressive toolbox that would prove useful in his later work as a representative singer. David C. Rubin posits that "exposure to variants of songs is the main learning device" through which singers gain "knowledge of the genre, of individual songs, and of the constraints that function in them ... without formal teaching" (1995, 307; cf. Blader 1999). Simon J. Bronner brings up concerns about potentially hegemonic aspects of tradition, noting that "vehement argument can arise whether *following* tradition means unconsciously following a severe form of cultural authority or *choosing* from tradition that which one finds appropriate" (1998, 10, emphasis in original). But here I would suggest a happy medium between "following" and "choosing," akin to Pierre Bourdieu's notion of *habitus*—the idea of "structuring structures" inhabited by individuals, where they find a sense of agency within a set of flexible norms (1990, 53).

To be clear, Wang sees himself as an artist able to piece together bits and pieces of lyrics, melodies, and (I would suggest) sung personae from a variety of singers and places, priding himself on putting his mark on the unique style of each song he performs. The idea of "piecing together" performances from material heard elsewhere is common to many artists, such as the Suzhou *pinghua* 评话 storyteller Jin Shengbo 金声伯, who said that "parts of the story are like pieces of furniture in a room and he moves them around until the room looks good" (Blader 1983, 87). Both Wang's and Jin's conceptions of creative expression seem to be in line with Claude Lévi-Strauss' (1966) idea of the *bricoleur* who selects and assembles elements of tradition—a type of individual Ray Cashman characterizes as "a crafty recycler who constructs new possibilities out of available handed-down raw materials, meeting present needs" (Cashman, Mould, and Shukla 2011, 4; Cashman 2016, 4).[22] Before we look at how Wang put together and performed songs representing the region of northern Shaanxi, let us look at some of the pieces he was exposed to as a child.

Drinking Songs and the Negotiation of Interpersonal Relations

Several of the following drinking songs begin with metaphors for blossoming relationships, suggesting the social benefits to be gained from such events, then move on to exchanges aimed at bringing together banquet attendees in mutually beneficial ways. The songs offer a range of functions, including toasting and setting up the stage, facilitating finger-guessing games, and regulating alcohol consumption so that individual and social desires are kept in balance. The banquets begin with formal toasts where the occasion's rationale is outlined and the guests and hosts are acknowledged. Though nowadays toasting is often done through speeches (e.g., acknowledging the first time two individuals have met, praising a guest or host, and/or thanking an individual or group for a favor), traditionally in parts of northern Shaanxi, individuals could also sing toasts to each other and to the host. In recent years, banquets held at restaurants will sometimes hire professional singers to perform such musical toasts.

The lyrics in the "toasting song" (*jingjiu qu* 敬酒曲) "I Beg the Magnanimity of Our Host" (CD Track 27) stress the mutually beneficial social value of gatherings.[23] According to Wang, the song's melody is originally from Inner Mongolia and was familiar to people in the area surrounding Wang's hometown.[24] He largely credits himself for introducing such melodies to the rest of northern Shaanxi and the Xi'an area. The opening image serves as a dual metaphor for the difficulty in getting together—the meager first crop of Chinese leeks is not worth mentioning and only the second crop arrives in plentiful bunches—and the "blossoming" relationship that the gathering hopes to bring about. The imagery fuses scene and feeling in a manner similar to classical Chinese poetry, in that the scarcity of "full" bunches of leeks (*zheng baba*) matches the singer's appreciation for the scarcity of being "together" (*yi dada*) with friends (cf. Cecile Chu-chin Sun 2011). In the third and fourth lines, the singer's song and the raised cup of sorghum liquor form a gift—an offering of respect and hospitality—that the addressee reciprocates through drinking. The expectation that the listener's acceptance of the glass of liquor will bring about a closer relationship between the two is reinforced by the rhyme between "accept" (*jiexia* 接下) and "chat" (*lahua* 拉话), echoing Mauss' assertion that giving and receiving gifts establishes relationships through the obligation to "repay," bringing together the giver and receiver in a conversation (Mauss 1966, 11). While the song is itself a gift—a toast honoring the addressee—it also holds the power to transform objects into gifts.

"I BEG THE MAGNANIMITY OF OUR HOST" ("WO QING ZHURENJIA DUO DANDAI" 我请主人家多担待) (CD TRACK 27)

The second crop of Chinese leeks grows in full bunches,
It's really hard for us to get together like this,[25]
This cup of *baijiu*, please accept it,
Accept this *baijiu* and let's have a good chat.
Er chacha jiucai na zheng na baba,
Hao bu rongyi zanmen yudao na yi le dada,
Zhe beibei shao na jiu ya ni jiexia,
Jiexia zhe shao na jiu zan hao ya hao lahua.
二茬茬韭菜那整（那）把把，
好不容易咱们遇到那一（了）搭搭，
这杯杯烧（那）酒呀你接下，
接下这烧（那）酒咱好呀好拉话。

A cup of *baijiu* and several dishes,
Thanks to our host for this warm reception,
I sing poorly, my voice is no good,
I beg the magnanimity of our host.
Yi beibei na shaojiu ji diedie na cai,
Ganxie zan zhurenjia di hao zhaodai,
Wo chang de na bu na hao sangzi na lai,
Wo qing na zhurenjia nin duo na dandai.
一杯杯那烧酒几碟碟那菜，
感谢咱主人家的好招待，
我唱得（那）不（那）好嗓子（那）赖，
我请那主人家您多（那）担待。

In the second stanza, we see two more acts of exchange. The food and wine offered by the host are met with the guests' gratitude, represented by the singer. The singer then praises the host's "magnanimity" by rhetorically attacking the quality of his own voice (cf. Goffman 1967). The singer's praise of the host (lines three and four of the second stanza) acts to rhetorically "repay" the wine and food described in the stanza's beginning—the host holds the party in part to raise his social standing among peers, and the guests respond by raising his social standing (Mauss 1966, 11).

After formal toasting had taken place, pairs of guests would often play finger-guessing games, thrusting different numbers of fingers in the air and singing out guesses of the total sums in poetic phrases—"**two** people get along" (*er ren xianghao* 二人相好), "**four** happinesses bring wealth" (*si xi lai cai* 四喜来财), "**six, six,** lucky **six**" (*liu liu dashun* 六六大顺), and "the **Eight** Immortals celebrate their longevity" (*Baxian qingshou* 八仙庆寿) (emphasis added). When one player guessed correctly, the other would drink. In Wang's recording of "With a Shoulder Pole That's Soft and Flexible" (CD Track 25) below, he sang the numbers in ascending order as an example.[26]

The opening stanza of the song sets the stage for the game with another metaphor for mutually beneficial blossoming relationships—this time, the male sung persona says that when he travels south, the girls love his millet and he loves the girls. Though intentionally playful, this pairing points to the goal of many banquets: to bring together a group of individuals in a manner that shows appreciation for their unique talents without putting them into competition with each other. In a study on Shandong banquet culture, Eric Shepherd suggests, "In the banquet context, performance reduces the gaps that exist between participants by integrating them into the group at the same time that it differentiates individual performers—when they perform, individuals contribute to the group atmosphere while displaying their unique styles and abilities" (2005, 28–29). Just as the banquet participants in Shepherd's study perform songs, jokes, and poems to show devotion to the group through the vulnerability of performance while at the same time expressing their uniqueness, the mutual desires for millet and girls in the stanza below metaphorically suggest that each banquet attendee has something to offer:

"WITH A SHOULDER POLE THAT'S SOFT AND FLEXIBLE" ("YI TIAO BIANDAN RUAN LIULIU" 一条扁担软溜溜) **(CD TRACK 25)**

With a shoulder pole that's soft and smooth,
I carry yellow millet down to Suzhou, *ya me hu hei.*
Suzhou loves my soft millet,
I love Suzhou's girls, *ya me hu hei.*
Yi tiao biandan na ruanliuliu,
Dan shang huangmi wo xia Suzhou ya me hu hei.
Suzhou ai wo di ruan huangmi,
Wo ai Suzhou na daguinü ya me hu hei.
一条扁担那软溜溜，
担上黄米我下苏州呀么呼嘿。
苏州爱我的软黄米，
我爱苏州那大闺女呀么呼嘿。

Two people get along, *me hu er hai,*
Four happinesses bring wealth, *me hu er hai,*
Six, six, lucky six, *me hu er hai,*
The Eight Immortals celebrate their longevity, *me hu er hai.*

Er ren xianghao me hu er hai,
Si xi lai cai me hu er hai,
Liu liu da shun me hu er hai,
Baxian qingshou me hu er hai.
二人相好么呼儿嗨，
四喜来财么呼儿嗨，
六六大顺么呼儿嗨，
八仙庆寿么呼儿嗨。

In these finger-guessing games, both players submit to the same rules, putting the players on equal terms as they attempt to strengthen their bond. This equalizing effect is highlighted in another finger-guessing song, "A Lotus Flower Blooms on the Spot" (CD Track 24), where the two singers alternate between guesses and the refrain "strengthening our feelings together" (*jiao le yi fan qing* 交了一番情). Wang contrasted that phrase with another phrase meaning "we come to hold a grudge against each other" (*women ji le yi fan chou* 我们记了一番仇).[27] Wang suggested that the two terms reflect the ability of social events to bring people together and push them apart:

This "strengthening our feelings together" means that after drinking together, we have become friends. Perhaps tomorrow everyone will have become very good friends. Perhaps by the next day, due to some reason or other, they will no longer.... Then, it can only be said that they established friendly relations, that this thing happened.... Some [friendships] last for a long time, depending on the circumstances, depending on the development of one's character and the development of the overall state of affairs. Some, perhaps, only last for a day or just a short period of time. Before, those involved didn't know each other, but through this drinking session, it feels as though the two people have formed a friendship.[28]

The first stanza of this song once again begins with a metaphor for blossoming relationships—a blooming lotus flower. The first two lines suggest that inviting others to a banquet can result in mutually beneficial relationships—the host's invitation to drink will lead to the flowering of relationships between himself and the guests. Responding to this gracious invitation, the singer praises the host. First, the singer describes, perhaps hyperbolically, the host's immense cave home with ten rooms, and then he submits to the host's decisions about the singer's relative social rank—he will sit anywhere. There is both an awareness of a strict social hierarchy and the momentary setting aside of that hierarchy that the liminal event of the banquet allows—a chance to restructure social relationships (cf. Victor Turner 1969).

In the second stanza, Wang noted that the singer exhibits an "extremely close relationship" (*guanxi feichang miqie* 关系非常密切) with the host, poking fun at the host by criticizing the "poor quality wine [that] makes your head hurt" and the host's failure to share the good quality wine.[29] Such public ridicule in a playful manner helps define the casual nature of the event, putting at ease guests who might otherwise feel restricted by the norms of propriety. While these lines may appear to attack and thus diminish the host, in practice they are meant to elicit praise from the other guests and boost the host's status (cf. Goffman 1967).

"A LOTUS FLOWER BLOOMS ON THE SPOT" ("YI DUO LIANHUA JIU DI KAI" 一朵莲花就地开) (CD TRACK 24)

A lotus flower blooms on the spot,
Our host has invited me here to drink.
Ten rooms with large heated brick *kang, ya hai,*
Wherever the host seats me, there I shall sit, *me nai si yi ya hai, yi zier yue.*[30]
Yi duo lianhua na jiu di kai,
Zhuren qing wo shi hejiu lai.
Shi jian man jian kang ya hei,
An zai nali nali zuo me nai shi yi ya hai, yi zier yo.
一朵莲花那就地开，
主人请我是喝酒来。
十间满间炕呀嘿，
安在哪里哪里坐么，乃是咿呀咳，咿子儿哟。

In the front room the lamps are lit, the back room becomes bright,
Shedding light on our host's large wine bottles.
The good-quality wine is not for us, *ya,*
The poor-quality wine makes your head hurt, *ya me nai si yi ya hai, yi zier yue.*
Qianshi diandeng na houshi ming,
Zhaojian zhurenjia di da na jiuping.
Dahao shaojiu bu gei he ya,
Xiaoshao he di guaigu teng yame, nai shi yi ya hai, yi zier yo.[31]
前室点灯那后室明，
照见主人的大（那）酒瓶。
大号烧酒不给喝呀，
小烧喝得拐骨疼呀么，乃是咿呀咳，咿子儿哟。

The sun comes up, a little dot of red,
Shedding light on our host's wedding wine bottles.
By playing finger-guessing games we have strengthened our feelings together, *ya,*
Two people get along, strengthening our feelings together,
Four happinesses bring wealth, strengthening our feelings together,
Five of the best and brightest, strengthening our feelings together,
Six, six, lucky six, strengthening our feelings together,
The Eight Immortals celebrate their longevity, strengthening our feelings together,
A full ten have arrived, strengthening our feelings together.

Taiyang shanglai na yidianr hong,
Zhaojian zhuren di xijiu ping.
Yinwei huaquan zan jiao le yi fan qing ya,
Zan er ren xianghao me jiao le yi fan qing,
Na si xi lai cai me jiao le yi fan qing,
Na kuishou wu duo me jiao le yi fan qing,
Na liu liu da shun me jiao le yi fan qing,
Baxian qingshou me jiao le yi fan qing,
Man shi dao ya me jiao le yi fan qing.
太阳上来（那）一点儿红，
照见主人的喜酒瓶。
因为划拳咱交了一番情呀，
咱二人相好么交了一番情，
那四喜来财么交了一番情，
那魁首五朵么交了一番情，
那六六大顺么交了一番情，
八仙庆寿么交了一番情，
满十到呀么交了一番情。

As guests negotiate a complex web of relationships, the banquet singer is tasked with making sure everything goes smoothly. The singer brings liveliness to the event and also regulates the amount of drinking. Singers working as supervisors have appeared in several contexts in China. Lead singers in southern Jiangsu used work songs to regulate the pace of farm work (Schimmelpenninck 1997, 41). Spirit mediums in Wang's village would make sure the gods did not drink too much wine or tea during rituals (see below). In each case, the singers' regulation was meant to guarantee that actions were carried out at sensible paces.

In the following song, "I Urge You, Sir, to Drink Less" (CD Track 26), the banquet singer shows communal concern by asking a guest to avoid drinking too much. The singer begins by noting the good and bad qualities of *baijiu*, praising its natural ingredients and then warning of its noxious effects. He follows in the third and fourth lines with a compelling argument vilifying *baijiu* while simultaneously boosting the guest's status. *Baijiu* ruins people like rain ruins a dirt road, the singer argues, emphasizing the drink's similar effects on "gentlemen" (*junzi*) and immortals. By rhetorically grouping the guest with gentlemen and immortals, the singer preemptively returns some of guest's face that might otherwise be lost when the guest is urged to stop drinking. Furthermore, the singer places the blame for *baijiu*'s destructive effects squarely on the drink itself, avoiding any mention of the guest's complicity in becoming intoxicated.

In these five lines, the singer is able to negotiate ambivalent personal and social desires and maintain the event's conviviality. The guest may want to drink more, but doing so could be bad for his health. The other guests may want the drinking to continue, but an inebriated guest could ruin the event. In both cases, asking the guest to stop drinking is the best option for everyone involved. Through this song, the singer negotiates individual and group desires, asks the guest to stop drinking, and maintains the flow of the event with minimal hurt feelings.

"I URGE YOU, SIR, TO DRINK LESS" ("WO QUAN XIANSHENG SHAO YINJIU" 我劝先生少饮酒) (CD TRACK 26)

Baijiu is made from, *ya ha hei hei,* the water of Five Grains, *me yi ya hei,*
First it softens your arms, *ha hei hei,* and then it softens your legs, *hei ya hu hei,*
Eiiii! Wine ruins a gentleman like water ruins a road,
Even immortals can't escape from liquor's trap,
I urge you, sir, *ai hai hai hai,* to drink less. [Emphasis added]
Shaojiu na ben shi ya ha hei hei wugu shui me yi ya hei,
Xian ruan na gebo ha hei hei hou ruan tui hei ya wu hei,
Ai jiu huai junzi shui huai lu,
Shenxian chu buliao jiu di gou,
Wo quan na xiansheng ai hei hei hei shao yinjiu.
烧酒那本是呀哈嘿嘿五谷水么咿呀嘿，
先软那胳膊哈嘿嘿后软腿嘿呀呜嘿，
哎，酒坏君子水坏路，
神仙出不了酒的觳，
我劝那先生哎嘿嘿嘿少饮酒。

The use of singing in the regulation and management of relations is seen both in drinking songs and the spirit-medium tunes examined below. One spirit-medium tune contains the line "I urge the gods not to drink too much wine and tea"—a show of consideration for a ritual's divine guests similar to the lines in the drinking song above. As we see in later chapters, the idea of singer as mediator between parties extends to relations between different places and time periods as well.

Singers in these drinking songs acknowledge social hierarchies while urging all those present to meet on common grounds. Although banquet hosts must reference social status when choosing where to seat guests and which quality of *baijiu* to offer them, singers help introduce an egalitarian air by offering to sit anywhere and teasing the host for bringing out the poor-quality wine. In toasts and drinking games, individuals with different talents come together in mutually beneficial exchanges. These social interactions are similar to the spirit-medium rituals I explore below—the ritual host and spirit medium treat the gods as highly esteemed guests, meeting and exchanging favors in the ritual's intimate setting.

Spirit-Medium Tunes: Conversations between Humans and Gods

Wang's 2006 CD contains five spirit-medium tunes modeled on those he heard as a child corresponding to different sections of a ritual. The ritual's host—ostensibly a father—wants to cure an ailing family member and enlists the spirit medium to ask the gods for help.[32] In the first two songs, the spirit medium invites the gods and announces their arrival as they pass over the neighboring mountain, cross the ravine below, climb up the mountainside to Marugeda, and enter the courtyard's main gate, as the medium sets up a sacrificial altar with incense. In the third song, the medium serves as the voice of the invited god—a local deity—who sings about the illness's cause and how it might be cured. After the god finishes his instructions, the medium flies to the four directions amassing grain and fodder for the gods and their horses. In the last song, the medium sends the gods on their way.

Though not a spirit medium himself, Wang sees great value in Marugeda's spirit-medium tunes for the local knowledge they represent. David Johnson (2009) emphasizes the central place of ritual in traditional Chinese culture and the close association of performance culture with that ritual culture. Wang's interpretations and explanations concerning the spirit-medium tunes, discussed below, show a close relation between the world of the gods and the world of humans, as well as between the past and the present. "If we wish to understand how Chinese people thought and felt about the family, the community, the state, or the gods," Johnson suggests, "we must study the rituals by which those thoughts and feelings were expressed and shaped" (8). By observing social connections between the drinking songs discussed above and the spirit-medium songs discussed below, we see various underlying themes in how Marugeda's villagers related to each other and to outsiders through song.

During our conversations, Wang readily pointed out similarities between the social hierarchies of gods and humans.[33] The hierarchy of the gods is alluded to early on in the second line of the first song in the ritual below, in references to the "Sovereign" and his "soldiers." Stephan Feuchtwang (1992) has famously pointed out the "imperial metaphor" used in certain local Chinese folk beliefs, and Wang's descriptions of the gods in our conversations expanded on this metaphor to include several parallel hierarchical structures. The Sovereign (*junwang* 君王) in the lyrics that follow, sometimes also known as the General (*shuai* 帅), refers to the main god (*zhushen* 主神) invited by the medium during the ritual—usually larger, higher-ranked deities—while the soldiers (*bing* 兵) are smaller spirits lower in the hierarchy who surround the main deity on horses as he travels, ready to carry out his orders (*gei ta banshi de* 给他办事的).[34]

Wang compared this sort of hierarchy to similar structures in government and in the world of professional folk singers, two realms in which he is involved at some level.[35] When Wang talked about the Immortals of the Eight Caves (*Badong Shenxian* 八洞神仙), for example, he noted the Jade Emperor was the "head" (*zong* 总) "just like Hu Jintao (China's then president)."[36] Wang continued noting that the hierarchy of the spirits embodied the "same logic" (*yi ge daoli* 一个道理) as the way in which Hu Jintao manages all of the officials throughout China, acting as the "highest-ranking god." Wang also talked about how each of the Eight Immortals had their own set of gods beneath them and could be considered the heads (*zong*) of the gods of particular caves (immortals are believed to reside in mountain caves). Referring to the lower-ranking gods associated with a higher-ranking god, Wang called them the higher-ranking god's "disciples" (*tudi* 徒弟), using the same word he uses to refer to the younger singers with whom he has established relationships as a national bearer of intangible cultural heritage (see chapter 1).[37] Wang added, "Spirits also have generation after generation. They also take on many disciples, just like Wang Xiangrong takes on disciples."[38] When I asked if it was the same sort of relational structure, Wang replied, "Sure. Now then, below Wang Xiangrong there are Li Zhengfei, Feng Xiaohong, and them, and they also have others below them."[39] These parallel social structures offer a convenient starting point for interactions between humans and gods.

While social hierarchies influence how different entities in banquets and rituals relate to one another, the liminal performance contexts allow singers to bridge gaps in order to facilitate meaningful exchanges. Acknowledging the relative social statuses of other participants in an exchange, the singers' actions and forms of address attempt to fuse the hierarchical and the egalitarian—reflecting the different positions of the participants in relation to each other, while leveling the playing field on which to exchange perspectives (cf. Hymes 2002). We have already seen how banquet attendees use drinking games and jocular addresses of each other to promote a sense of *communitas* (cf. Victor Turner 1969). Similar attempts to "bridge the gap" between humans and gods can be seen in the offerings and inclusive terms of address used in the ritual below. By enacting successful exchanges with gods, the songs that follow and their associated ritual aim to construct a social network where the villagers are visited by and enjoy the protection of the gods, as they honor and offer sacrifices to the gods. Certain textual similarities between the lyrics of the drinking songs discussed earlier and the spirit-medium tunes discussed below belie the social nature of both contexts. When I pointed out the similar lines mentioned earlier discouraging banquet guests and gods from drinking too much wine, Wang replied, "Right! It's the same thing, the same idea."[40] I responded, "Oh, so one treats the gods the same as people," to which Wang answered, "The same, the same, the same, the same. In the past in China, people and gods were of one category (*renshen yilie* 人神一列). After all, gods are 'raised up' (*peng chulai de* 捧出来的) by people. They are molded by people. So, their system of thought still belongs to the category of the human system of thought."[41] By looking across genres in our examination of Wang's education through song, we not only see underlying commonalities in the conceptualization of social relations but also how singers are able to cull experience from one context for use in other contexts.

The manner in which spirit mediums treat the gods is similar to the guest-host interactions in the banquets discussed earlier. The lyrics and cultural contexts of these songs embody notions of social hierarchy. They portray the singer as someone who can conjure up and command various personae within the framework of a song, a power that lends itself to mediating between the positions of two or more groups. In the following ritual, entities from different realms and a range of perspectives are brought together to assist each other. Similar to the banquet singer, the spirit medium embodies a dual identity allowing him to mediate between different social realms—here, the Marugeda villagers and local gods. Spirit mediums were chosen by the gods and able to facilitate conversations between humans and spirits. The medium's liminality is reminiscent of the "semidivine" nature of song gods and goddesses discussed in chapter 1—they too were able to mediate between realms (Schimmelpenninck 1997).

In the songs below, the spirit medium performs the conversation between humans and gods using multiple sung personae and addressees, including the ritual host, the main invited spirit, a cohort of other spirits, and the medium himself. The medium's sung persona has an authoritative air. Able to command human and divine beings to carry out tasks, the medium's social status is worthy enough that when he invites the gods to the ritual they accept his invitation. He is able to fly to mystical cities in the four directions and amass a large amount of grain to feed the gods and their horses, exhibiting superhuman intelligence as he calculates the exact number of decaliters required. His voice is one that commands authority. The spirit's sung persona, in turn, exhibits intensity and intimacy as he ends each stanza by asking if the ritual host has understood what he said and acknowledging that the host has understood. The spirit has an otherworldly knowledge of the unintentional ramifications of human errors in the spirit world and the means by which the ritual host can counteract his child's resulting illness. The spirit is also pragmatic, noting that things have already reached a rather poor state, and the success or failure of the cure depends largely on the sincerity of the host's request and the gods' goodwill.

While the spirit medium and the spirit are the only two personae that "speak" in the songs, the medium populates the song world with additional addressees—silent personae made present through the singer's address. In the first song, the medium commands the ritual host to "fetch fresh chopsticks" for the visiting gods and to tell them about his problems. Calling out to the ritual host acknowledges his presence to all those within earshot, materializing him as a persona within the song world. In the fourth song, the medium, upon traveling to mystical cities in the four directions, orders the gate boy in each city to open the gate's lock and commands the storehouse keepers to go down into the granaries and retrieve what he asks. While these additional personae do not "speak" in the song, the medium's address constructs them within the song world—a world entirely controlled by the spirit medium. This aspect of spirit-medium tunes may have provided Wang with a model of performance for his later region-representing songs populated by such personae as the sun, Yellow River boatmen, and Mao Zedong. Each song creates a song world, where the singer constructs and commands a range of personae in the minds of each listener.

In the first song in the ritual, entitled "Inviting the Gods" (CD Track 28), delicacies are laid out and the spirits are invited and seated in order of seniority at a banquet of wine, tea, and incense smoke. The song models calling out to Others with an awareness of the social relations between parties—evoked through the terms of address, gifts presented, order of invitations, and hierarchical seating. In the ritual, the gods are classified socially on par with highly esteemed guests. The spirit medium formally invites the gods and shows his respect by going to the entrance to meet and greet them.[42] The best tea service, food, and wine are used for attending to their visit. Wang noted, "When lofty guests arrive, for example, when you invite the gods to your home, of course you must bring out your best table—the ivory table."[43] Though the phrases "golden lamp" and "ivory table" appear in the lyrics, Wang noted that poorer families may have used clay lamps or wooden lamps and ordinary tables instead—the fancier phrases were meant to "sound better," expressing a desire to bring out one's best in honor of esteemed guests.[44] Richard Schechner has pointed to the ability of performance to reframe how we view objects in context: "The 'other-worldliness' of play, sports, games, theater, and ritual is enhanced by the extreme disparity between the value of the objects outside the activity when compared to their value as foci of the activity" (1988, 9). This use of hyperbole not only highlights the rhetorical power of song but also suggests an awareness of and respect for the social status of the addressee(s). This awareness of social status is important when singers travel and mediate between groups. By acknowledging the status of the parties involved, the singer paints a picture of how each might see the others and themselves in the interaction, thus reinforcing a situated sense of self.

The order of the invitations is significant, with the Jade Emperor (*Yuhuang Dadi* 玉皇大帝)—usually considered to be the supreme deity—coming first.

Wang, in explaining the final line asking the gods "to be magnanimous," characterized it as a ritual saying, asking a guest to forgive the "inattentiveness" of the host.[45] In this context, he said, the line was meant to ask the gods' forgiveness if the host had been ignorant of the gods' relative rank (*guanwei daxiao* 官位大小) and unintentionally seated them in an incorrect order. This attention to the convergence of invitational order and social rank bears similarity to a discussion of funeral invitations in north-central Shaanxi, where the anthropologist Xin Liu found that "invitations to a funeral must be sent in an order that makes the hierarchy of social relations clearly visible," with those regarded as more important relative to the event at hand being invited earlier than others (2000, 47). Liu emphasizes the offense taken when parties are not invited in the order they believe they should have been.

In addition to the order of invitations, the seating arrangement outlined in the penultimate stanza has clear hierarchical implications as well. Where each god sits is an indication of their rank in relation to the other gods present in the eyes of the host. One is reminded of the line, "Wherever the host seats me, there I shall sit" in the drinking song "A Lotus Flower Blooms on the Spot" discussed earlier. Here, in the last stanza of "Inviting the Gods," the spirit medium asks the immortal guests to "be magnanimous" if, among other faux pas, he had seated them in an infelicitous order.

In the midst of all of this, we have the powerful voice of the spirit medium's sung persona. The persona's "I" has invited the gods, has the authority to tell the ritual host to fetch things, and boldly urges the gods to "be careful" and "not to drink too much wine and tea." Clearly, the spirit medium's sung persona is at the center of all—creating, populating, and directing all that occurs in the song world.

"INVITING THE GODS" ("QING SHEN" 请神) (CD TRACK 28)

Hou—hou ei hei ye hei ye hei ei!
Pay respects to the gods on the left, pay respects to the gods on the right,
In the morning, pay respects to the Sovereign, in the evening, pay respects to the Soldiers,
In the morning, pay respects to the gods with incense smoke, in the evening, pay respects to the gods with golden lamps,[46]
In the morning receiving incense smoke, in the evening receiving light,
With a golden helmet[47] on the head and body armor,[48]
The gods change their clothes, change their helmet, and get off their horses.[49]
Hou ai hei hei hei ai,
Zuo can di shen shi you can shen,
Zao can junwang shi wan can bing,
Zao can shenshen shou xiangyan, wan can shenshen shou jindeng,
Zao shou xiangyan wan shou di deng,

Ding jinkui shi chuan jinjia,
Shenshen piyi huan na jia shi lai xiama.
嗬哦哎嘿嘿嘿哎，
左参（的）神是右参神，
早参君王是晚参兵，
早参神神受香烟，晚参神神受金灯，
早受香烟晚受（的）灯，
顶金盔是穿金甲，
神神披衣换（那）甲是来下马。

Hou, hou! Hou ei hei ye hei—hei!
With a golden helmet on the head and wearing armor,
The gods change their clothes, change their helmet, and get off their horses.
An ivory table is set out,
Melons, fruits, and fresh vegetables are placed on top.
[I] tell the host to quickly fetch fresh chopsticks,[50]
Then, slowly and at ease, relate his problems to those above.
Freshly poured cold tea, full cups of clear wine,[51]
And three oil lamps serve as offerings to the Supreme Being (*Shenwang*).[52]
Hou hou hou ai hei hei hei,
Ding jinkui shi chuan jinjia,
Piyi huan jia lai xiama.
Xiangya zhuo shi fang yi zhang,
Guaguo shicai shi duanshang lai.
Jiao shizhu shi kuai huan zhu,
Xiaoyaozizai shi wang shang shu.
Qing zhen liangcha man dian di jiu,
Youhua san zhan gong Shenwang.
嗬，嗬！吼哎嘿嘿嘿，
顶金盔是穿金甲，
披衣换甲来下马。
象牙桌是放一张，
瓜果时菜是端上来。
叫事主是快换箸，
逍遥自在是往上数。[53]
清斟凉茶满奠的酒，
油花三盏供神王。

Hou—hou ei hei ye hei, hou ei, hei ei hei, hei hei hei, hei hei hei,
Hai, three cups of tea to rinse and refresh your mouth,
Four cups of wine to bring color to your cheeks.
Ai, I urge the gods not to drink too much wine and tea,
Be careful as you embark on the roads in Five Directions to save all the people.
Hai, for the gods who love tea, three cups of tea,
For the gods who love wine, four cups of wine,
And for those who are not fond of tea or wine,[54]
Please go to the Altar for the Five Immortals of the Five Directions to enjoy the
    incense smoke.[55]

Hou—hou ei hei ye hei, hou ei, hei ei hei, hei hei hei, hei hei hei,
Hai cha yin san bei shu qingliang,
Jiu yin si bei shi mianshang pi.
Ai wo quan shenshen shao yinjiu shi shao tan cha,
Xiaoxin wufang lushang jiu wanmin.
Hai haocha shenshen cha san zhong,
Haojiu shenshen shi jiu si bei,
Bu haocha bu haojiu,
Qing dao wufang tan shang shou xiangyan.
嗬哦，吼哎嘿嘿，吼哎，嘿哎嘿，嘿嘿嘿，嘿嘿嘿，
嘿哎，茶饮三杯漱清凉，
酒饮四杯是面上皮。
哎，我劝神神少饮酒是少贪茶，
小心五方路上救万民。
嘿哎，好茶神神茶三盅，
好酒神神是酒四杯，
不好茶不好酒，
请到五方坛上受香烟。

Hou—hei! Ei—
I have invited and welcomed [them],
Invited and welcomed [them].
Those of the Upper Eight Immortal Caves, those of the Lower Eight Immortal
   Caves,[56]
I am at the mouth of Eight Immortal Cave inviting the gods.
Hou hei ei,
Wo qing liao di qing shi ying liao ying,
Qing liao qing lai ying liao ying.
Shang badong shi xia ba di dong,
Wo zai badongkou shang lai qingshen.
嗬哦，嘿哎，
我请了（的）请是迎了迎，
请了请来迎了迎。
上八洞是下八（的）洞，
我在八洞口上来请神。

Hou hou hou hou ei hei ye hei,
Jade Emperor, please receive this invitation,
Taishang Laojun, please receive this invitation,
Queen Mother of the West, please receive this invitation,
Immortal Maiden of the Ninth Heaven, please receive this invitation,[57]
Four-Eyed Sky God, please receive this invitation,[58]
Pagoda-Holding Emperor, please receive this invitation,
Twenty-Eight Constellations, please receive this invitation,[59]
By the Five Directions and Five Ways, come as soon as possible.
Hou hou hou hou ei hei ye hei,
Yuhuang Dadi qing zhi ni,
Taishang Laojun qing zhi ni,

Wangmu Niangniang qing zhi ni,
Jiutian Xuannü qing zhi ni,
Siyan Tianshen qing zhi ni,
Tuota Tianwang shi qing zhi ni,
Ershiba Xiu qing zhi ni,
Wufang wudao zao daolai.

嗬嗬嗬嗬哎嘿嘿，
玉皇大帝请知你，
太上老君请知你，
王母娘娘请知你，
九天玄女请知你， 60
四眼天神请知你，
托塔天王是请知你，
二十八宿请知你，
五方五道早到来。

Ai, having invited you down, you are given seats,
I ask the gods to find their places.[61]
If you are greater, sit above at the seat of honor,
If you are smaller, sit below,
If neither big nor small, sit in the middle.
Those with horses sit on their mounts,
Those without horses sit on sedan chairs,
Those without horses or sedan chairs please lead the way to the Altar of the Five
    Directions,
Raise the flags, hang up the spirit tablet,[62]
On the wall with carved murals I seat you.[63]

Ai qing xia ni shi anxia di ni,
Wo qing shenshen sheng zuowei.
Ni kan ni shi zai da di shi zai shang zuo,
Zai xiao di shi zai xiabian zuo,
Budabuxiao shi zhongjian zuo.
You ma di shi zuozhe ma,
Shi wu ma di ni zuoshang jiao,
Wu ma wu jiao di dadao wufang tan shang,
Liqi biaogan guaxia an,
Yingbi qiang shang wo an ni.

哎，请下你是安下的你，
我请神神升座位。
你看你是在大的是在上坐，
在小的是在下边坐，
不大不小是中间坐。
有马的是坐着马，
是无马的你坐上轿，
无马无轿的达到五方坛上，
立起标杆挂下案，
影壁墙上我安你。

I ask each of the gods to be magnanimous.[64]
Wo qing gewei shenxian ni duo danqi yi.
我请各位神仙你多担起（咿）。

While the guest list outlined in "Inviting the Gods" contains the "A-listers" of the spirit world, Wang stressed that one's ability to invite higher-level deities depended largely on one's own social status. When I asked Wang why people did not automatically choose to invite the Jade Emperor over smaller, local deities—given that the Jade Emperor's power and rank was said to be the greatest—he responded as follows:

Wang: Because if you invite him directly...for example, if I invite...can I invite...can I just invite Hu Jintao whenever I feel like it?
Gibbs: Oh, you mean he wouldn't come, right?
Wang: Of course not! If you invite...if you invite Obama,[65] would *he* come?
Gibbs: Right, he wouldn't, he wouldn't.
Wang: Right. As for Obama, who can succeed in inviting him? Only congressmen. As for Hu Jintao, only the Politburo (*Zhengzhiju*), members of the Central Politburo Standing Committee (*Zhongyang zhengzhiju changwei*), and the premier—only those members of the Politburo can succeed in getting him to come. Perhaps if the Shaanxi Provincial Party Committee and Provincial Government invite Hu Jintao to visit, they still must notify the higher authorities, and after notifying those higher-ups, the higher-ups must deliberate and study (*yanjiu*) the matter and see whether Hu Jintao can go or not, whether Hu Jintao has time. They also have to make all of the arrangements. Now then, he can only go if he has time. If he is busy, they will send someone else in his place.
Gibbs: Right, right, right.
Wang: Isn't it so? The Jade Emperor is not someone you can just invite on a whim.[66]

Although the respectful rhetoric and laying out of delicacies in the above song show the host's esteem for these "lofty guests," some of the lyrics point to attempts to relate to the gods on a more personal, intimate level. In "Inviting the Gods," I asked Wang why the spirit medium would "urge the gods not to drink too much wine and tea"—after all, wouldn't that be considered a rude sort of thing for a host to do? He replied that in interactions with truly good friends or people one respects, one seeks to have them "drink just enough but not too much" and not insist that they become overly inebriated—similar to the regulating function of the singer in drinking parties mentioned earlier. Wang suggested that drinking too much tea, just like drinking too much wine, is bad for one's health, so a good friend would show care for fellow friends and not force them to carry out such destructive behavior.[67] In Robert Hymes' (2002) work on Daoist rituals and local cults, he argues that Chinese relationships with the divine are formed in two independent manners: the bureaucratic and the personal. Whereas the former implies distance and hierarchy both among the gods themselves and in their relations to mortals, the latter tends to focus on "dyadic (one-to-one)" and reciprocal connections between gods and humans, which seems to fit in with Wang's analysis of the language used above (4–5).

The first song lays out a clear hierarchy among the gods invited and attempts to treat them as honored guests, while at the same time suggesting a more intimate manner of interaction through the spirit medium's showing of concern for the gods' health. The ritual's second song, "Preparing the Sacrificial Altar" (CD Track 29), in turn, seeks to bring the gods and humans into one social group during the course of the interaction. As the gods approach, the spirit medium attempts to include them in the assembled group of people through the repeated use of the word "we" (women 我们). Speaking of the intimacy that the spirit medium creates here through his language, Wang said, "He treats this god in a very close, intimate manner. Since he has invited him in, all he thinks about is 'we'—a 'we' that includes people and gods—there is no difference among us." Wang compared this to treating guests as members of one's own family. He noted that it would be appropriate in that case to say "**we** blah blah blah, **we** blah blah blah" (women zenyang, women zenyang 我们怎样，我们怎样) instead of "**you all** blah blah blah, **we** blah blah blah" (nimen zenyang, women zenyang 你们怎样，我们怎样), continuing, "If you distinguished between 'you all' (nimen) and 'we' (women), that would place more distance between you [and them]."[68]

As the main spirit comes to join the assembled group, the path he and other accompanying spirits follow maps onto the topography of Marugeda and its surrounding area, as underlined in the lyrics below. The spirits arrive over the facing mountain, down into the ravine that lies at the foot of the village, up the mountainside to Marugeda, and in through the main gate of the courtyard where the ritual is being held. The "coal hills" the spirits climb in the third stanza relate to the villagers' practice of discarding used cooking coal by dumping it down the side of the mountain.

"PREPARING THE SACRIFICIAL ALTAR" ("SHE TAN" 设坛) (CD TRACK 29)

Look, **we**'ve all arrived, **we**'ve arrived, **we**'ve *just* arrived, *ya*, **our** Spirit.
Look, <u>down from the hill right across</u> **we** have arrived, *ya hei ei ei.*
Ni kan women lai liao lai liao cai lai liao ya, wo di xian'gen.
Ni kan women dui zheng popo xialai liao ya hei ei ei.

你看我们来了来了才来了呀，我的仙根。
你看我们对正坡坡下来了呀嘿哎哎。

Look, **we**'ve all arrived, **we**'ve arrived, **we**'ve *just* arrived, *ya,* **our** Spirit.
Look, <u>jumping over the ravine down below</u> **we** have arrived, **we** have arrived, **we** have arrived, *ei.*
Ni kan women lai liao lai liao cai lai liao ya, wo di xian'gen.
Ni kan women dui zheng gougou tiao guo lai liao lai liao lai liao ei.
你看我们来了来了才来了呀，我的仙根。
你看我们对正沟沟跳过来了来了来了哎。

Look, **we**'ve all arrived, **we**'ve arrived, **we**'ve *just* arrived, *ya,* **our** Spirit.
Look, <u>climbing up the coal hills</u>, **we** have arrived, *ya ei.*
Ni kan women lai liao lai liao cai lai liao ya, wo di xian'gen.
Ni kan women lan tan popo shanglai liao ya ei.
你看我们来了来了才来了呀，我的仙根。
你看我们蓝炭坡坡上来了呀哎。

Look, **we**'ve all arrived, **we**'ve arrived, **we**'ve *just* arrived, *ya,* **our** Spirit.
Look, <u>we have entered the main gate</u>, *ya ei hei ei.*
Ni kan women lai liao lai liao cai lai liao ya, wo di xian'gen.
Ni kan women damenkoukou jinlai liao ya ei hei ei.
你看我们来了来了才来了呀，我的仙根。
你看我们大门口口进来了呀哎嘿哎。

By including the spirit in the "we" of those assembled, the spirit medium sets up an interactive group with the Other where a conversation can happen. The spirit medium addresses multiple audiences at the same time, announcing the arrival of the spirits to the ritual host and his family, as well as their neighbors and fellow villagers. At the same time, he narrates the deities' arrival, accompanying them in song through each step and welcoming them into the group. Since the ritual host and other villagers would not have been able to see the spirits' approach and know when they were present, the spirit medium's song plays a key role in introducing the participants involved in the ritual's interaction, setting up a conversation that he facilitates in the following song.

After inviting the spirits and announcing the arrival of the main god (accompanied by others), the spirit medium enacts a conversation between the invited spirit and the ritual host in "Curing an Illness" (CD Track 30). The ritual host seeks a cure for his sick child, and the spirit dictates an herbal remedy through song for the illness in question (through the medium). The medium uses multiple sung personae to represent the different parties involved. In his own sung voice as the medium, he first points to the arrival in the sky of an ancestor who has become a local deity, the Grand Immortal of the Black Clouds (*Heiyun Daxian*) of the Wang clan. The medium then embodies the god, who announces his identity to the ritual host and those around him, asking the host why he has summoned the spirit. Wang noted that when a medium was possessed by the spirit and sang its words, there was an audible difference compared to the words sung in his own voice. Wang imitates this change in the recording of the song on his 2006 CD—there is a shift from the voice of the medium's sung persona in the first two lines to the spirit's sung persona that follows, which I put in quotation marks to indicate that the spirit is speaking. In those lines, the spirit medium reaches a state where Wang said the medium "represents the god" (*daibiao shen le* 代表神了), entering an otherworldly trance—a sort of muddleheaded, carefree (*xilihutu* 稀里糊涂) state: "Once you have arrived at this muddleheaded, carefree state, the voice that one sings out is different. It is different from the normal singing voice of that person. That is to say, people can recognize this and say, 'Oh, the god has already attached itself to his body.' He [the medium] serves as a proxy for what the god wants to say. The language he uses to say it is different."[69]

There is a fascinating progression outlined in this song, whereby the root cause of the malady is made explicit (e.g., a local spirit was disturbed when ground was broken near the home), internal and external remedies are described in detail, and possible outcomes are listed.[70] The final stanza provides a sort of "disclaimer," stating that if the cure doesn't work, it is because the gods have abandoned the cause. Elsewhere, Wang discussed the need for sincerity when asking favors from the gods and the possibility that a local god may not produce an effective result, thus necessitating the solicitation of another god from a different locality.[71] The lyrics for this section are as follows:

"CURING AN ILLNESS" ("KANBING" 看病) (CD TRACK 30)

Look, the god shouts from within the clouds,
He rides his horse atop the clouds—our ancestor turned god.[72]
"Look, if you want to know my name, my name, my name and surname,
I am the Grand Immortal of the Black Clouds of your Wang Family,[73] *ye*, are you
    clear?"
Ni kan shenshen da he shang yi sheng shi yun, shi yunli de yun,
Shenshen yuntou shang paoma ye zong wei shen.
Ni kan ni shi yao zhi wo ming, shi ming, shi ming he xing,
Wo shi ni jia Wang men de Heiyun Daxian ye ni jingming?
你看神神大喝上一声是云，是云里的云，
神神云头上跑马（耶）宗为神。
你看你是要知我名，是名，是名和姓，
我是你家王门的黑云大仙（耶）你精明？

"*Ai,* tell the host to listen carefully,
Why do you cry out to this Spirit?
State it clearly line by line,
And, line by line, the gods will show you the way."

Ai—jiao shizhu ba hua di ting,
Han dao ling shen yinwei shen?
Ni yi ju yi ju shu fenming,
Shenshen yi ju yi ju gei ni biao fenqing.
哎——叫事主把话（的）听，
喊到灵神因为甚？
你一句一句述分明，
神神一句一句给你表分清。

"*Ah,* on the west side of your house a wall was built,
On the east side of your house ground was broken (for construction),
Rolling the roller where it shouldn't be rolled,
The earth on the God of the Year's head was moved,
Disturbing your family with dog and cat calamities,
And leading your adults and children to be troubled throughout the four seasons
    of the year.
Do you understand? [You] understand."
Ai—ni jia xifang da liao qiang,
Ni jia dongbian shi dong liao tu,
An nianzi gun mo shi bushi chu,
Taisui toushang ba tu dong,
Mao yang gou yang lai dajiao,
Nao di ni jia daren wawa liao yiniansiji bu anning.
Ting kai bu yo? Ting kai liao.
啊——你家西方打了墙，
你家东边是动了土，
安碾子滚磨是不是处，
太岁头上把土动，
猫殃狗殃来打搅，
闹的你家大人娃娃（了）一年四季不安宁。
听开不哟？听开了。

"Things have already reached their present state,
Even the gods don't have a good means to fix your problem,
But since your child has come down with a severe illness,
The gods will tell you an herbal remedy prescription to use internally and externally,
Do you understand? [You] understand.
Is it clear? It is clear."
Shi dao rujin liao,
Shenshen gei ni ye meiyou hao banfa gei ni lai zhengzhi,
Zhiyou ni de hai'er xialai bing chenzhong,
Shenshen gei ni ba na yinzi fangtou shuoshang yi dao shi liwai yong,
Ting kai meiyou? Ting kai liao.
Jiekai meiyou? Jiekai liao.
事到如今了，
神神给你也没有好办法给你来整治，
只有你的孩儿下来病沉重，

神神给你把那引子方头说上一道是里外用，
听开没有？听开了。
解开没有？解开了。

"First, combine Medicine King roots,
Mountains and rivers, seven in total,
Ai, rhizome of wind-weed, fritillary bulb, winter board flower, *yin-yang* stone
    flowers,
Stone child, Chinese tamarisk, willow berries,
Then, add in atractylodes rhizome and realgar,
Mix them together and use it.
This is [the part] to be drunk internally.
There is also [the part] to be applied externally.
Line by line it is clearly explained,
Line by line, you listen carefully."
Touyi liangzi Yaowangye shi genzi wang shang di yong,
Shanshui dao dao shi qi ge zheng,
Ai, zhimu, beimu, bandong hua, yinyang shihua,
Shi shi wawa, sanchunliur, shi liushu qi,
Haiyou nage cangzhu, xionghuang,
Yi dada peishang shi wang shang yong.
Zhe shi nage nei chi de.
Haiyou nage wai tie de.
Yi ju yi ju shi shu fenming,
Ni yi ju yi ju lai tingqing.
头一量子药王爷是根子往上（的）用，
山水道道是七个整，
哎，知母、贝母、板冬花、阴阳石花、
是石娃娃、三春柳儿、是柳树杞，
还有那个苍术、雄黄，
一搭搭配上是往上用。
这是那个内吃的。
还有那个外贴的。
一句一句是述分明，
你一句一句来听清。

"*Ai,* scallion thread,
Mixed together with flour and steamed,
Mix it all together.
Ai, take it out together,
Put it in together,
After it boils, apply it to the skin.
If during seven days it sticks to the head, it has gotten the illness,
The gods will continue to descend and scare it away.
But if for seven days it doesn't stick to the head, and there is no relief,
The gods will pay no regard, mounting their horses and setting out into the sky,
    wu ou."

Ai—cong sizi,
Shi baimian yi ge dada zheng,
Ni kan ni ba ta shi he dao yi kuair liao.
Ai, yi ge dada chu,
Shi yi ge dada jin,
Gungunr xialai shi lai tuo ke.
Qi tian toushang le da liao chu, shi shou liao bing,
Shenshen gei ni jixu xialai lai nong song.
Shuo shi qi tian toushang liao bu da chu, shi bu anxin,
Shenshen yi bu guan lai er bu guan, lima dengcheng qi kongzhong wu o.
哎——葱丝子，
是白面一个搭搭蒸，
你看你把它是和到一块儿了。
哎，一个搭搭出，
是一个搭搭进，
滚滚儿下来是来拓嗑。
七天头上了打了杵，是收了病，
神神给你继续下来来弄怂。
说是七天头上了不打杵，是不安心，
神神一不管来二不管，立马登程起空中呜噢。

The power evoked by these lyrics, combined with Wang's discussion of the vocal changes and alternate sung personae when the spirit possesses the medium, suggest the authority of the singer (the spirit medium) and the sung voice to express and represent another place, person, and viewpoint—another world. At heart, the song is a conversation between mortals and immortals about how to deal with an enigmatic illness in a meaningful way. The fact that such a song was understood as emanating from a spirit only further serves to emphasize the underlying idea that something important is being conveyed from the singer to the listener through the medium of song.

Having enacted the heart of the ritual, the fourth song, "Scattering Grains and Fodder" (CD Track 31), describes the spirit medium feeding the gods and their horses with grain from mystical storehouses—it is important to feed one's guests before sending them on their way. In this song, after the ritual host has received curative advice from the gods, the *shenguan* must locate and measure out sufficient grain to feed the gods and fodder for their horses, before sending them on their way. The "three rings" in the first line refer to three iron rings (*tiehuan* 铁环) located at the bottom of the sheepskin drum (*yangpi gu* 羊皮鼓) that the *shenguan* shakes with one hand and beats with a stick in the other. There are also several smaller rings attached to the three larger rings. Other types of ritual accoutrements *shenguan* used in the past included "precious swords" (*baojian* 宝剑) and fans (*shanzi* 扇子). When I asked Wang about the significance of the number three, he at first glossed over the question by attributing it to custom but later speculated that it might have to do with notions of "heaven, earth, and people" (*tian di ren* 天地人), "people, ghosts, and gods" (*ren gui shen* 人鬼神), and/or the idea of the "three divisions of the universe" (*sanjie* 三界).

"SCATTERING GRAINS AND FODDER" ("SAN LIANGCAO" 散粮草) (CD TRACK 31)

Hou hou—hou hou hou hou hou hou hou—
(My) hand shakes three rings, clinking *ring-a-ling-a-ling*,
Turning and turning, I arrive at the East.[74]
In the East, there is a black secret city, a black secret gate,[75]
On the black secret gate hangs a black secret lock.
(I) tell the gate boy to open the lock, (I) tell the storehouse keeper to go down into the granary.
Every person gets half a pint of grain, every horse gets one and a half pints of feed.
Calculating and calculating, all together it comes to 1,850 decaliters.
Hou hou—hou hou hou hou hou hou hou,
Shou yao san huan sa lala xiang,
Wo youyouwanwan shi dao dongfang.
Dongfang you zuo qing you cheng shi qing you men,
Qing you men shang guazhe yi ba qing you di suo.
Shi jiao mentong shi lai kaisuo, jiao douzi shi lai xia cang.
Ai meiren chi di shi ban sheng liang, mei ma chi di sheng ban liao,
Suan da ji shi da suanji, gong da gong suan liao yiqian babai wushi dou.
吼吼, 吼吼, 吼吼吼吼吼,
手摇三环飒啦啦响,
我游游玩玩是到东方。
东方有座青幽城是青幽门,
青幽门上挂着一把青幽的锁。
是叫门童是来开锁, 叫斗子是来下仓。
哎, 每人吃的是半升粮, 每马吃的升半料,
算打计是打算计, 共打共算（了）一千八百五十斗。

Hou—
(My) hand shakes three rings, clinking *ring-a-ling-a-ling*,
Turning and turning, I arrive at the South.
In the South, there is a red secret city, a red secret gate,
On the red secret gate hangs a red secret lock.
(I) tell the gate boy to open the lock, (I) tell the storehouse keeper to go down into the granary.
Every person gets half a pint of grain, every horse gets one and a half pints of feed.
Calculating and calculating, all together it comes to 1,850 decaliters.
Hou—
Shou yao san huan sa lala xiang,
Youyouwanwan shi dao nanfang.

Nanfang you zuo hong you cheng, hong you men,
Hong you men shang gua di yi ba hong you suo.
Jiao mentong shi lai kaisuo, jiao douzi shi lai xia cang.
Meiren chi di ban sheng liang, mei ma chi di sheng ban liao,
Suan da ji lai da suanji, gong da gong suan yiqian babai wushi dou.
吼——
手摇三环飒啦啦响，
游游玩玩是到南方。
南方有座红幽城，红幽门，
红幽门上挂的一把红幽锁。
叫门童是来开锁，叫斗子是来下仓。
每人吃的半升粮，每马吃的升半料，
算打计来打算计，共打共算一千八百五十斗。

Hou—
(My) hand shakes three rings, clinking *ring-a-ling-a-ling*,
Turning and turning, (I) arrive at the West.
In the West, there is a white secret city, a white secret gate,
On the white secret gate hangs a white secret lock.
(I) tell the gate boy to open the lock, (I) tell the storehouse keeper to go down into the granary.
Every person gets half a pint of grain, every horse gets one and a half pints of feed.
Calculating and calculating, all together it comes to 1,850 decaliters.
Hou—
Shou yao na san huan sa lala xiang,
Shi youyouwanwan shi dao xifang.
Xifang you zuo shi bai you cheng shi bai you di men,
Bai you men shang guazhe yi ba bai you suo.
Jiao mentong shi lai kaisuo, jiao douzi shi lai xia cang.
Meiren chi di shi ban sheng liang, mei ma chi di shi sheng ban liao,
Suan da ji shi da suanji, gong da gong suan yiqian babai wushi dou.
嗬—
手摇那三环飒啦啦响，
是游游玩玩是到西方。
西方有座是白幽城是白幽的门，
白幽门上挂着一把白幽锁，
叫门童是来开锁，叫斗子是来下仓。
每人吃的是半升粮，每马吃的是升半料。
算打计是打算计，共打共算一千八百五十斗。

Hou—
(My) hand shakes three rings, clinking *ring-a-ling-a-ling*,
Turning and turning, (I) arrive at the North.
In the North, there is a black secret city, a black secret gate,
On the black secret gate hangs a black secret lock.
(I) tell the gate boy to open the lock, (I) tell the storehouse keeper to go down into the granary.

Every person gets half a pint of grain, every horse gets one and a half pints of feed.
Calculating and calculating, all together it comes to 1,850 decaliters.

Hou—
Shou yao san huan sa lala xiang,
Youyouwanwan dao beifang.
Beifang you zuo shi hei you cheng, hei you men,
Hei you men shang guazhe yi ba hei you suo.
Jiao mentong shi lai kaisuo, jiao douzi shi lai xia cang.
Meiren chi di shi ban sheng liang, mei ma chi di shi sheng ban liao,
Suan da ji lai da suanji, gong da gong suan yiqian babai wushi dou.

嗬——
手摇三环飒啦啦响，
游游玩玩到北方。
北方有座是黑幽城、黑幽门，
黑幽门上挂着一把黑幽锁。
叫门童是来开锁，叫斗子是来下仓。
每人吃的是半升粮，每马吃的是升半料。
算打计来打算计，共打共算一千八百五十斗。

Hou—
Smoke from the five sticks of incense coils upward,
Spirits of the Center, you knew it early on.
I show filial respect to the gods of the Center,
May all the gods in the sky come quickly.

Hou—
Wu zhu na xiangyan shi wang shang rao,
Zhongfang shenshen ni zao zhidao.
Wo ba zhongfang shenshen zhengzhe xiao,
Mantian shenshen zao dao lai.

嗬——
五柱那香烟是往上绕，
中方神神你早知道。
我把中方神神争着孝，
满天神神早到来。

After making sure the gods and their horses are well provided for, the spirit medium sees them off in the fifth and final song, "Sending Off the Gods" (CD Track 32), asking the gods to mount their horses and ride back into the sky:

"SENDING OFF THE GODS" ("FA SHEN" 发神) (CD TRACK 32)

Pray to the gods to disperse, pray to the gods to disperse,
I pray to the gods to disperse and get onto your horses.
Get on, get on, quickly get onto your horses,
When you get on, it will be on a multicolored horse with golden saddle and reins.

Bai shen san, bai shen san,
Wo bai shen san shi ni shangma.

Shangma shangma kuai shangma,
Yi shang shang dao jinsi liu'an shi wuyun hua.
拜神散, 拜神散,
我拜神散是你上马。
上马上马快上马,
一上上到金丝镏鞍（是）乌云花。

Pray to the gods to disperse, pray to the gods to disperse,
I pray to the gods to disperse and get onto your horses.
Red Cloud Immortal, I send you off, Black Cloud Immortal, I send you off,
Jade Emperor, you go first, Twenty-Eight Constellations will follow closely at your
    heels.
Bai shen san shi bai shen san,
Wo bai shen san shi ni shangma.
Hongyun Daxian wo song ni, Heiyun Daxian wo fa ni,
Yuhuang Dadi ni xianxing, Ershiba Xiu na jin hou gen.
拜神散是拜神散,
我拜神散是你上马。
红云大仙我送你, 黑云大仙我发你,
玉皇大帝你先行, 二十八宿（那）紧后跟嗯。

Expressing hierarchical and personal relationships (Hymes 2002), spirit-medium tunes embody interpersonal relations within a social hierarchy. We have seen interesting parallels between how spirits invited to a ritual and guests invited to a banquet are treated with wine, food, and song with the goal of cultivating alliances. Both attempt to blend the hierarchical and the personal, bringing everyone together while realigning social stratifications. The guest-host relationship exhibited is also present in folk opera performances in temple fairs, discussed below, and extends to discussions in later chapters of visits Wang and the Yulin Folk Arts Troupe made to other localities over the length of his career. While banquets, spirit-medium rituals, and international cultural exchanges all form liminal spaces where relations are negotiated, many of the songs Wang learned as a child projected that liminality into an "other" space—one that looked beyond the scope of the village and sometimes beyond the scope of the present. In the love songs I discuss next, we see how individuals from different backgrounds meet and redefine their subjectivities in new, liminal territories.

Couples Going Out

Some of the earliest songs Wang remembers are songs about love—songs that often contain allusions to Marugeda's landscape and the surrounding area, fusing together images of the purity of nature with the honesty and wholesome love of its people. In interviews with journalists and scholars, Wang sometimes introduces a song he learned from his mother, "Picking *Maru* Fruits" ("Da maruru" 打马茹茹), that describes the blossoming love between a boy and a girl as they travel along the topography of Wang's youth.[76] In this song of variable length, the courting couple goes down the mountainside and crosses the gulley below to "pick *maru* fruits"—ostensibly to get away from prying eyes.[77] The gulley is a ravine next to the mountain on which Marugeda is located.[78] There is a small stream below, which the female protagonist is playfully carried across in the song, and the fact that she is surnamed Wang coincides with the fact that everyone in Marugeda was surnamed Wang (even some of the gods, as we have seen).

This ravine seems to represent the boundary between the "here" of the village and the "elsewhere" beyond in several of the songs from Wang's youth. Lovers descend the mountain and cross it to get away, while spirits invited by the local medium arriving over the facing mountain cross the ravine on their way to enter the village (see "Preparing the Sacrificial Altar" below). In many ways, "Picking *Maru* Fruits" is an exemplary model of numerous songs about couples heading out into unknown territories that Wang has performed during his career. In many of these songs, the couple begins at home and travels together, engaging with the scenery they find along the way. As they travel, they exchange gifts, including physical objects, favors, praise, and new perspectives. Their alternating subjectivities as they react to their new surroundings become merged into a new combined subjectivity—that of the couple. The first stanza's second line offers a metaphor for the "blooming" relationship situated precisely in the gulley that separates the "here" and "there"—blossoming *maru* flowers:

"PICKING *MARU* FRUITS" ("DA MARURU" 打马茹茹)

Now you are exactly twenty-one,
In the sixth month, at the bottom of the gulley, the *maru* flowers are red, Older
    Brother's dear Little Sister.[79]
Xianzai ni rujin ershiyi nian zheng ya,
Liuyue li goudi li maru hong ya, gege na xiao meizi.
现在（你）如今二十一年正呀，
六月里沟底里马茹红呀，哥哥那小妹子。

Next door, there is an Aunt Wang,
(When I) head out to pick *maru,* she follows along, Older Brother's dear Little
    Sister.[80]
Gebi na you ge Wang le da di niang ya,
Da maruru zou qishen xianggen shang ya, gege na xiao meizi.
隔壁那有个王勒大的娘呀，
打马茹茹走起身相跟上呀，哥哥那小妹子。

When other people pick *maru*, they go in large groups,
When we go to pick *maru*, it's just the two of us, Older Brother's dear Little Sister.
Renjia na da maruru yi le da di qun ya,
Zan er ren da maruru liang ge ren ya, gege na xiao meizi.
人家那打马茹茹一勒大的群呀，
咱二人打马茹茹两个人呀，哥哥那小妹子。

(Say) when others pick it, they get two or three decaliters,
When we pick it, we don't get that many, Older Brother's dear Little Sister.
Shuo ren le jia ni da le er le san di dou ya,
Zan er ren da buxia gai gong zen ya, gege na xiao meizi.
说人（勒）家你打了二（勒）三的斗呀，
咱二人打不下该公怎呀，哥哥那小妹子。

I ask my Older Brother to carry me on his back,
After he carries me over the river, I'll be sure to repay his kindness, Older
　　Brother's dear Little Sister.
Jiao le yi sheng gege bei le gei xia wo ya,
Bei le guohe nabian bu enqing ya, gege na xiao meizi.
叫了一声哥哥背了给下我呀，
背了过河那边那补恩情呀，哥哥那小妹子。

Place the sack on the lower millstone,
And the bamboo pole on the top one, Older Brother's dear Little Sister.[81]
Kou le dai na fang zai mo le pan di shang ya,
Zhu le gan gan fang zai na modingshang ya, gege na xiao meizi.
口勒袋那放在磨勒盘的上呀，
竹勒竿竿放在那磨顶上呀，哥哥那小妹子。

During the course of these stanzas, the couple offers each other mutual aid amidst suggestions of the two lovers coming together as one. He carries her across the river and she "repay[s] his kindness." They pick the fruit in a group of two and do not get as much as other groups—clearly, the couple has greater concerns at hand. The fact that their coming together occurs elsewhere, across the ravine that serves as the village's boundary, lines up with other songs about couples going out as they form new subjectivities. From an interactive viewpoint, the two individuals are responding together to another place, forming a bond as they react together to what they see. At the same time, their journey into this other place serves as a metaphor for the new, merged subjectivity that they are moving toward. As they negotiate back and forth through song between their individual subjectivities, they seek a common ground that combines each of their viewpoints and desires into a new point of view situated in a new place. That place is neither where he or she comes from but where they are traveling together.

Other songs from Wang's youth are also clearly situated on Marugeda's mountainside and hint at this trope of "couples going out." Another love song that Wang learned from his mother, a short folk song version of the classic romance "Liang Shanbo and Zhu Yingtai" (sometimes glossed as the Chinese version of Romeo and Juliet) has a line about the lovers "going down the mountain"—in Marugeda, they too must descend the mountain in pursuit of courtship:[82]

"LIANG SHANBO AND ZHU YINGTAI" ("LIANG SHANBO YU ZHU YINGTAI" 梁山伯与祝英台)

Older Brother Liang Shanbo and Zhu Yingtai,
Brother and Sister, down the mountain we come.
Liang Shanbo gege, Zhu Yingtai,
Zan xiongmei er ren xiashan lai.
梁山伯哥哥、祝英台，
咱兄妹二人下山来。[83]

Though this story is told and sung in many versions throughout China, the reference here to "down the mountain we come" clearly maps it onto the topography of Marugeda. The merging of subjectivities also takes on an interethnic dimension in some of the Mongol-Han tunes Wang learned when he was young. "Happy in My Heart, A Smile on My Face" (CD Track 33) is sung by a Mongol male to his female Han lover. After each of them praises the positive qualities that the other brings to the relationship—her beauty and his height— the Han female suggests they "go for a walk...to an out-of-the-way place." Again, the implication is to get away from prying eyes, and yet here again we see the developing of a relationship and the merging of subjectivities in a place characterized as a liminal other. By the third stanza, the Mongol male is declaring oaths of eternal love, suggesting a newly formed combined subjectivity with "interconnected roots" more durable than either of their individual selves:

"HAPPY IN MY HEART, A SMILE ON MY FACE" ("XIN LITOU LE LAI LIANLIAN SHANG XIAO" 心里头乐来脸脸上笑) (CD TRACK 33)

With happiness in my heart and a smile on my face,
I can't help but want to sing a Mongol-Han tune.
Han little sister is pretty,
And Mongol older brother strikes a tall figure.
Xin litou le lai lianlian shang xiao,
Zhi bu zhu xiang chang ge Meng le Han diao.
Han na jia meimei zen zhangde qiao,
Mengren gege na ge le tou gao.
心里头乐来脸脸上笑，
止不住想唱个蒙（了）汉调。

汉（那）家妹妹（怎）长得俏，
蒙人哥哥（那）个（勒）头高。

You see your dear[84] with fondness, I see Older Brother as a good person,
Who does everything he can to be together with his Little Sister.
Don't be shy, I'm not ashamed,
Let's go for a walk hand-in-hand to an out-of-the-way place.
Ni kan qinqin qin na lai wo kan gege hao,
Yixinyiyi he na meimei jiao.
Ni bu paxiu lai wo ye bu haisao,
Zan shoulashou zai beigelaolao zou yizao.
你看亲亲亲（那）来我看哥哥好，
一心一意和那妹妹交。
你不怕羞来我也不害臊，
咱手拉手在背圪佬佬走一遭。

The pine and cypress trees on Daqing Mountain have interconnected roots,
Little Sister and I have interconnected hearts.
Flesh sticks on bones and bones connect to tendons,
In life and in death, we will never be separated.
Flesh sticks on bones and bones connect to tendons,
In life and in death, we will never be separated.
Daqing Shan songbai gen lian gen,
Wo he meimei na xinlianxin.
Rou tie gutou gu lian jin,
Yaosiyaohuo zan yong na bufen.
Rou tie gutou gu lian jin,
Yaosiyaohuo zan yong bufen.
大青山松柏根连根，
我和妹妹那心连心。
肉贴骨头骨连筋，
要死要活咱永（那）不分。
肉贴骨头骨连筋，
要死要活咱永不分。

In the third and final stanza, the Mongol male paints a natural scene on a well-known mountain in Inner Mongolia—a key landmark for migrants who "walked beyond the Western Pass"—to suggest that in such liminal territory the couple would together find a new, intertwined point of view. This interethnic romance in places that are both liminal (e.g., "out-of-the-way") and grounded (e.g., Daqing Mountain) again points to the potential for individuals from different backgrounds to come together in a new place, while at the same time celebrating the border region whose history gave birth to these songs. Like the references to the area surrounding Marugeda in "Picking *Maru* Fruits," the images in this Mongol-Han tune situate the love it expresses within the regional topography of the land and the history of its people.

Several of the *errentai* pieces Wang learned follow this "couple going out" pattern. Similar to the songs examined above, they involve walking out into new territory, although we often notice a lack of specific place markers. Here, the contexts are frequently widely celebrated festivals, such as the Lantern Festival accompanying Chinese New Year, so the couple's journey into another space suggests a journey into another time as well—a potential future together in the coming year and the years to come. Wang would develop these songs into his award-winning performance in 1980 at the national competition in Beijing and his representative performance in the United States in 2008, discussed in chapter 4.

In one traditional *errentai* duet, "Ten *Li* Markers" (CD Track 18), the couple first exchanges courtesies at the woman's home. She invites him in and he presents her with a leg of mutton, a common gift during the Chinese New Year in northern Shaanxi.[85] The remainder of the song uses the pretext of her walking him home as an opportunity for playful flirtation. As they walk, they look at lanterns (presumably during the Lantern Festival) and stars and talk about their mutual desires for each other. The "ten *li* markers" refer to ten road markers, designating distances of one *li* 里 each (approximately a third of a mile), by which the couple passes as they walk together. As they mark the distance covered in the journey towards the man's home (a distant realm from the perspective of the starting point at the woman's home), this journey also serves as a metaphor for the merging subjectivities of the couple as they head toward a new point of view.

This merging of subjectivities is reinforced by an alternation between individual voices and the two singers in unison in the following version Wang arranged in collaboration with others. Wang said earlier versions of this song would have the male and female persona alternating entire stanzas, but this proved rather monotonous. Instead, he worked out a version with a playful back and forth between the performers *within* each stanza. The long strings of rapid-fire nonsense syllables add to the excitement of the performance and showcase the performers' vocal techniques. In addition, the alternation between each individual voice and the couple in unison highlights the effect of two subjectivities merging into one—each adding something to the mix and then singing together in the common ground they have created as they walk out into another land:

"TEN *LI* MARKERS" ("SHILI DUN" 十里墩) (CD TRACK 18)

Sister, open the door, Sister, open the door,
Use both hands for your Older Brother, come and pull the door open,
Aiyo, your Older Brother has brought you a leg of mutton.

Meizir kaimen lai, meizir, ni kaimen lai,
Shuang shoushou nage gei gege ba men lakai,
Aiyo, gege gei ni ti hui na yang le tui tui lai.
妹子儿开门来，妹子儿，你开门来，
双手手那个给哥哥把门拉开，
哎哟，哥哥给你提回那羊（了）腿腿来。

Gu ge na la der gai,[86]
One *li* marker, *ya ha si lu lu lu yi ya ha hei,*
One *li* marker, *ya ha ge ba ba ba yi ba yi ba beng,*
The one *li* marker is close, close, close,
Ai yi yo yo, ai yo yo yo, yo yi yo yo,
Looking at the lanterns, *ya,* looking at the stars, *ya,*
Xi liu liu liu, pa la la la, si lu lu lu, gei guar gei guar, gu lu lu lu, everything is green.
Gu ge na la der gai,
Yi li dun lai ya ha shu lu lu lu yi ya ha hei,
Yi li dun lai ya ha ge ba ba ba yi ba yi ba beng,
Yi li ge dun jin jin jin,
Yo yi yo yo, ai yo yo yo, yo yi yo yo,
Guan mingdeng ya, guan mingxing ya,
Na xi liu liu liu, pu la la la, shu lu lu lu, gei gur gei gur, gu lu lu lu, yang ya a yang
    qing.
咕个那啦嗒儿该，
一里墩来呀哈倏噜噜噜一呀哈嘿，
一里墩来呀哈格吧吧吧一吧一吧蹦，
一里圪墩近近近，
哟咿哟哟，哎哟哟哟，哟咿哟哟，
观明灯呀，观明星呀，
那唏溜溜溜，扑啦啦啦，倏噜噜噜，该咕儿该咕儿，咕噜噜噜，样呀啊样青。

I think of my dear Little Sis, but I can't see your face,
Whether dreaming or not, Older Brother, come over tonight.
Ai yo, happy in the heart, a smile on Little Sister's face.
Wo na xiang nage meimei jian bu shang ni di mian,
Meng na ye nage bu meng gege ni jintian wanshang lai.
Aiyo, xi zai xinshang xiao zai na meimei de lian.
我（那）想那个妹妹见不上你的面，
梦（那）也（那个）不梦哥哥你今天晚上来。
哎哟，喜在心上笑在那妹妹的脸。

Gu ge na la der gai,
One *li* marker, *ya ha si lu lu lu yi ya ha hei,*
One *li* marker, *ya ha ge ba ba ba yi ba yi ba beng,*
The one *li* marker is close, close, close,
Ai yi yo yo, ai yo yo yo, yo yi yo yo,
Looking at the lanterns, *ya,* looking at the stars, *ya,*
Xi liu liu liu, pa la la la, si lu lu lu, gei guar gei guar, gu lu lu lu, everything is
    green.[87]

Gu ge na la der gai,
Yi li ge dun lai ya ha shu lu lu lu yi ya ha hei,
Yi li dun lai ya ha ge ba ba ba yi ba yi ba beng,
Yi li ge dun jin jin jin,
Yo yi yo yo, ai yo yo yo, yo yi yo yo,
Guan mingdeng ya, guan mingxing ya,
Xi liu liu liu, pu la la la, shu lu lu lu, gei gur gei gur, gu lu lu lu, yang ya a yang qing.
咕个那啦嗒儿该，
一里圪墩来呀哈倏噜噜噜一呀嘿，
一里墩来呀哈格吧吧吧一吧一吧蹦，
一里圪墩近近近，
哟咿哟哟，哎哟哟哟，哟咿哟哟，
观明灯呀，观明星呀，
唏溜溜溜，扑啦啦啦，倏噜噜噜，该咕儿该咕儿，咕噜噜噜，样呀啊样青。

We see a similar alternation between individual and united voices in the songs that follow, including the one Wang sang at the national contest in 1980 and the duet he sang in the United States in 2008 to facilitate a joint venture (see chapter 4).

Another festival-themed *errentai*, "Liancheng Pays a New Year's Call" (CD Track 21), tells the story of a couple paying their respects to each other for the coming year (*bainian* 拜年) and then going out to look at the impressive variety of lanterns on display during the Lantern Festival held on the fifteenth day of the first lunar month. The good wishes that they offer each other establish their relationship for the audience, and that relationship is then developed as the singers list the colorful variety of lantern shapes found at the festival in alternating lines with an ever-increasing tempo—watermelon, cabbage, Chinese chives, coriander, eggplant, cucumber, dragon, phoenix, and tiger, finally ending in unison on a climactic, onomatopoeic rendition of the sound of two firecrackers. Again, we see alternating male and female voices juxtaposed with singing in unison. In the lyrics below, there is a clear progression from relatively simple alternation in the first stanza to more complicated shifting back and forth in the second, and even more in the third. In the third stanza, the two singers take turns pointing out and commenting on what they see, culminating in the final line in unison. As they each offer observations from their respective points of view, they are sharing their perspectives and ultimately contributing to a new shared perspective. As Barbara Herrnstein Smith notes,

When we exclaim to a companion, "Look at this interesting photo," or urge someone to taste what we are tasting or listen to what we are hearing...we are, no doubt, partly engaged in verbal gift giving, and thus in seeking to please those whose pleasure and goodwill are of general value to us. When all this is granted, however, there does seem to remain another aspect to our motives when we attempt, sometimes straining language to its furthest reaches, to make known to our companions the most subtle features of our experiences. It might seem, in fact, that there is an irreducible satisfaction to be gained from the sense that there are people around us who not only occupy the same gross physical environment as we do, but who also to some extent share the same experiential environment, seeing what we see, tasting what we taste, feeling what we feel. (1978, 91)

In light of the "couple going out" paradigm, the alternation and fusion of voices symbolizes each subjectivity offering input on their new surroundings as they merge into a new subjectivity in that new space. Since the Lantern Festival represents a liminal period looking forward to the coming year, the couple's "walking out" in this context metaphorically engages with the future—modeling how they might respond together to events to come.

"LIANCHENG PAYS A NEW YEAR'S CALL" ("LIANCHENG BAINIAN" 连成拜年) (CD TRACK 21)[88]

(M) Passing the New Year, on the very first day,
(F) I invite Older Brother Liancheng to my home to pay his New Year's respects.
Guo le ba da le nian touyi ha ha ha tian,
Wo qing nage Liancheng gege lai wojia baishang yi hui nian.
过（了）罢大（勒）年头一哈哈哈天，
我请那个连成哥哥来我家拜上一回年。

(M) Entering the door, (F) he bends at the waist,
(M) Left hand dragging him, (F) my right hand helps him up,
(MF) *Nai shi yi ya hai,*
(MF) What year is this for which we pay our respects, *nai si yi ya hai!*[89]
Yi jin na menr ba yao wan,
Zuoshou na la lai na youshou chan,
Nai shi yi ya hai,
Zan xiongmei er ren bai di yi ge shenme nian nai shi yi ya hei!
一进那门儿把腰弯，
左手那拉来那右手搀，
乃是咿呀咳，
咱兄妹二人拜的一个什么年，乃是咿呀咳！

(M) The first lunar month on the fifteenth day, we celebrate the Lantern Festival,
(F) I go to watch the lanterns with my Older Brother Liancheng.
(M) The watermelon lantern, *ei,* (F) is a brilliant red,
(M) The cabbage lantern, *ei,* (F) is a glistening green,
(M) The Chinese chives lantern, *hei hei hei,* (F) is broad and upright,
(M) The coriander lantern, (F) has numerous little pieces,

(M) The eggplant lantern (F) is sparkling purple,
(M) Twists and turns (F) has the cucumber lantern,
(M) The dragon lantern (F) has a body covered in scales,
(M) The phoenix lantern (MF) is covered in myriad colors,
(MF) The tiger lantern has impressive power and dignity,
(MF) Playfully shaking its head and wagging its tail is the lion lantern,
(MF) The lamp with multiple exploding shells, *nai si yi ya hai*—
(MF) And two *drrrrrrrr-ping-pang-ping-pang* firecracker lanterns, *nai si yi ya hai!*[90]

Zheng na yue shi na wu nao huadeng,
Wo he wo nage Liancheng gege qu guandeng.
Xigua deng ai hong tengteng,
Baicai deng ai lü ge yingying,
Jiucai deng hei hei hei kuan ge zhengzheng,
Na yansui deng sui ge fenfen,
Qiezi deng zi yinyin,
Na qiniubawan na huanggua deng,
Long'er deng manshen lin,
Feng'er deng hua shengsheng,
Laohu deng a shi weifeng a,
Yaotoubaiwei shizi deng a,
San da jin paodan da deng, nai shi yi ya hai,
Haiyou na shu lululu qihuo dai pao pingpang pingpang liang zhan deng ya, nai shi yi ya hai!

正（那）月十（那）五闹花灯，
我和我那个连成哥哥去观灯。
西瓜灯哎红腾腾，
白菜灯哎绿（个）莹莹，
韭菜灯嘿嘿嘿宽（个）铮铮，
那芫荽灯碎（个）纷纷，
茄子灯紫阴阴，
那七扭八弯那黄瓜灯，
龙儿灯满身鳞，
凤儿灯花生生，
老虎灯啊实威风啊，
摇头摆尾狮子灯啊，
三打金炮弹打灯，乃是咿呀咳，
还有那傄噜噜起火带炮乒乒乒两盏灯呀，乃是咿呀咳！

The couple's journey through the Lantern Festival as a metaphor for facing the future together aligns with how Wang adapted this song, together with the composer and scholar Li Shibin, for his performance at the 1980 National Rural Amateur Performance Selection in Beijing.[91] While the Lantern Festival through which the couple walks in "Liancheng Pays a New Year's Call" conjures up a festive mood each year with thoughts of things to come, the "other" place in Wang and Li's adaptation, "Brother and Sister Go to the Market," was the new public market made possible after economic reform instituted in the late 1970s. Wang developed this idea of a forward-looking rural couple walking into post-reform modernity in his first music video, "Going to the Market," produced in 1982 or 1983.[92] As the couple in that song marvels at the wide range of goods available from various parts of northern Shaanxi, they are in a sense stepping into a post-economic reform "modern" version of themselves. As they enter and respond to this new other, the couple expresses their transformed point of view, interpreting and appreciating the benefits of the commodity economy. Once again, their arrival at this new understanding and identity follows the pattern of alternating viewpoints leading to a fusion of viewpoints. Note how they encourage each other as they approach the market, pointing out and describing the attributes of products they see, and end by declaring in unison the mantra of this new ideology: "The market is open to the people."

"GOING TO THE MARKET" ("GANJI" 赶集)[93]

(M) The sun comes up, shining on the western mountain,
(F) I'm going with my Third Elder Brother to the market,
(M) Third Younger Sister, *ai*, hurry up, (F) Older Brother, *ai*, let's hold hands,
(MF) *Ai hai yo*, the two of us are walking together, *ai*—
Yangpo shanglai zhao yame zhao Xishan,
Wo he wo de san gege ba ji gan,
San meimei ai kuai dian zou, jiao gege ai zan shou la shang shou,
Ai hai yo, zanmen er ren xianggen shang zou ai—
阳婆上来照呀么照西山，
我和我的三哥哥把集赶，
三妹妹哎快点走，叫哥哥哎咱手拉上手，
哎嗨哟，咱们二人相跟上走哎—

(M) Look at all the people going to the market, strung together in a bunch,
(F) Big carts, *ya*, small carts, *yo ho*, bustling about,
(M) Over mountains (F) and crossing rivers, (M) dashing about (F) to enter the market,
(MF) Today there are tons of people, a noisy bustling village scene.
Ai hai yo, bustling people, horses neighing, it's truly lively and exciting.
Ni kan na ganji de ren'er liancheng na yi chuan chuan,
Dache ya xiaoche yo he pao de huan,
Fan guo shan tiao guo he, jin gan ji bu jin shichang,
Jintian zhe ren'er shizai duo, renhuanmajiao naorangrang.
Ai hai yo, jichang shang na renhuanmajiao zhen yame zhen honghuo.
你看那赶集的人儿连成那一串串，
大车呀小车哟嗬跑得欢，
翻过山跳过河，紧赶几步进市场，

今天这人儿实在多，人欢马叫闹嚷嚷。
哎嗨哟，集场上那人欢马叫真呀么真红火。

(M) Mountain products, local specialties, all kinds are available,
(F) Oil cakes, *ya,* are fragrant, rice wine is sweet,
(M) Melons from Jingbian, (F) dates from Jiaxian, (M) Yulin's tofu (F) has a great flavor,
(F) Quick, Older Brother, look over there, (M) there are so many cows, donkeys, mules, and horses,
(F) Donkeys from Jiaxian and Mizhi are nice and tall, (M) horned cattle jump along *ge beng beng,*
(F) Buying and selling at reasonable prices, everyone laughing ha ha ha, (M) the open market has opened to the people,
(MF) *Ai hai yo,* the open market has opened to the people.

Shanhuo techan yang ya yangyang quan,
Yougao ya xiang lai mijiu tian,
Jingbian de gua, Jiaxian de zao, Yulin de doufu weidao hao,
Gege ni kuai wang nabian qiao, niu lü luo ma zhen bu shao,
Jia-Mi de maolü zhang de gao, qiao jiao huangniu ge beng beng tiao,
Gongmaigongmai haha xiao, jishi maoyi kaifang liao,
Ai hai yo, jishi maoyi kaifang liao.

山货特产样呀样样全，
油糕呀香来米酒甜，
靖边的瓜，佳县的枣，榆林的豆腐味道好，
哥哥你快往那边瞧，牛驴骡马真不少，
佳米的毛驴长得高，翘角黄牛格崩崩跳，
公买公卖哈哈笑，集市贸易开放了，
哎嗨哟，集市贸易开放了。

As I suggest in the following chapters, the "couple going out" pattern can be seen in many of the songs Wang developed and performed throughout his career representing the region and the nation at home and abroad. While in some cases, the couple continues to be a male and a female persona similar to "Picking *Maru* Fruits" and various *errentai,* in other cases the pairings take on a metaphorical nature—a boatman and his passengers, Mao and the People, Wang and his audience. The advantage of this pattern is that it brings together different viewpoints in a sense of shared desire, a rhetorical move applicable to a range of contexts. The viewpoints of various localities in northern Shaanxi can merge into a desire for the region. The desires of different entities in China and the United States can be brought together in the facilitation of a joint venture (see chapter 4). The desires of the individual can meet and merge with the desires of the collective. In each case, the "couple going out" allows for a discussion of different points of view, while suggesting that they can exist together in a harmonious "new" way.

Two-Person Opera as a Site of Public Discourse

"Going beyond the Western Pass" (CD Track 17), one of the most popular *errentai*, tells the story of a Han man who must leave his wife Yulian 玉莲 and travel to Inner Mongolia to find work, highlighting the emotional torment of separation through song (ZYXZYY 1962, 201). There are many genres of songs on this same theme, but the *errentai* versions offer the most complete narrative, and given *errentai*'s embedded development within the history of "going beyond the Western Pass," this aria seems to hold a special place within the genre. This piece is often listed as one of Wang's most representative and was the song Wang performed in the scene by the Yellow River at the beginning of the book.

In the following excerpt, there is an interesting shift between who the sung persona addresses through the course of the lyrics. In the first two stanzas, the male persona appears to narrate the story to an assembled crowd (remember that *errentai* were often sung to crowds at temple fairs). Then, in the third stanza he switches to address his beloved Yulian directly.[94] The fourth stanza, in turn, could be read as addressing both Yulian and the audience, merging together personal and collective experience.

"GOING BEYOND THE WESTERN PASS" ("ZOU XIKOU" 走西口) (CD TRACK 17)

In the fifth year of Xianfeng's reign,[95]
Shaanxi Province met with a year of famine.[96]
Those with money had granaries filled to the brim,
While each and every suffering farmer was truly pitiful.
Xianfeng zheng ya wu nian ai,
Shaanxi sheng ya na zao xia na nian de jin.
You na qian di na youqian di liang na man de cang,
Shouku di ren'er yi ge yi ge shishi kelian.
咸丰正呀五年哎,
陕西省呀那遭下那年（的）馑。
有那钱的，那有钱的粮（那）满（的）仓，
受苦的人儿一个一个实实可怜。

Second cousin has sent a letter,
He says that beyond the Western Pass there's a good harvest.
I have it in mind to go beyond the Pass,
But I'm afraid Yulian won't agree.
Er gujiu shaolai na yi feng xin,
Ta shuo shi na xikou ai hao shou de cheng.
Wo na youxin na wo youxin zou le kou de wai,
You pa na Yulian bu ya na bu yicong.

二姑舅捎来那一封信，
他说是那西口哎好收（的）成。
我（那）有心，那我有心走了口（的）外，
又怕那玉莲不呀那不依从。

Dear sis—*ai hei*—sister, *ai*,
Don't you cry for me.
If you cry, I can't endure the ache in my heart,
At sixes and sevens, all in a bustle, my heart's in deep trouble.
Mei ai hei meimei ai,
Ni buyao gei gege wo ku.
Ni ku di nage ge na ge wo xinyang nannai,
Qishangbaxia, pumangluanzao, xinshang bu haoguo.
妹哎嘿妹妹哎，
你不要给哥哥我哭。
你哭得那个哥（那）哥我心痒难耐，
七上八下，扑忙乱燥，心上不好过。

Heaven has met with disaster,
The five grains are withered and even grass doesn't grow.
If one doesn't go beyond the Western Pass,
The days of the poor are truly numbered.
Tian zao nage huang na han,
Zhe wugu hemiao baicao na ye na bu zhang.
Bu zou xi na kou,
Qiongren di rizi zhe shishizaizai mei banfa guo.
天遭那个荒（那）旱，
这五谷禾苗百草（那）也（那）不长。
不走西（那）口，
穷人的日子这实实在在没办法过。

There are additional stanzas in other versions of this piece where the woman responds, expressing her sadness at seeing the man go and offering suggestions for how he should keep himself safe during the journey, such as taking big roads to avoid bandits, staying in big inns to avoid thieves, sitting in the back of boats to avoid falling in the water, and eating hot food to avoid getting sick (YDW 1983, 73; Lü 1994, 1:191–192, 199, 197). The dilemma framing their exchange is that they will not have food if he does not leave, but they are individually weaker and may not be able to reunite if they separate. While each option offers a potential benefit—staying, leaving, urging him to stay, letting him leave—none of them comes without a cost.

Each party is able to express their ambivalent desires through the sung dialogue. Both of them reaffirm their connection to each other by expressing a desire to be together and offering assurances of continued fidelity. At the same time, each offers a unique benefit for the other during their time of separation. He wants to earn money and return, gaining wealth during his journey to another place and then returning to share that transformation with Yulian. She, in turn, wants him to be safe and not abandon her. Her advice for him on how to stay safe—a listing of potential dangers and how to avoid them—in a sense reflects her desire to accompany him as he journeys into an unknown territory so that he (and by extension she) can benefit from the experience without being diminished by it. While she does not physically travel with him, she desires to do so through song. Thus, the sung dialogue represents a shared effort to deal with an unknown using the unique perspectives of each party. It is about how a couple responds to external constraints, searching for a shared point of view in the process. While "going beyond the Western Pass" was a historical reality, as a performed metaphor the couple's journey (though he travels alone, she accompanies him in her song) represents two subjectivities coming together as they face the world—a merging of viewpoints and desires through song.

At the same time, we must remember that this dialogue is observed by an audience, who may interact with what they see and hear in various ways. When this duet was performed in earlier times, there were men in the audience who might have gone beyond the Western Pass and returned or perhaps were debating whether or not to go. There might be women in the audience whose husbands were going to leave or had already left. These women might not have known if their husbands would ever return or if they were still alive. One of the earlier contexts for performances of this piece was during the Ghost Festival on a temple stage next to the banks of the Yellow River in northwestern Shanxi Province, a place where many men died attempting to cross over to Inner Mongolia on their way to find work (Yang Hong 2006, 41, 200–201). Since the *errentai* in this temple fair were meant to be consumed by wandering ghosts, those departed men also served as a potential audience for the performed dialogue of separation.

In recent times, audiences might relate to these performances in different ways. Couples in long-distance relationships might resonate with the performed pains of living apart from one's beloved. Nowadays, performances of "going beyond the Western Pass" also become nostalgic symbols of the region— markers of place-based identity connected to the region's history. There are karaoke versions of songs about going beyond the Western Pass, as well as TV dramas. While watching the parting couple in an *errentai* performance, each audience member is free to identify with any, all, or none of the performed personae: the man who must leave, the woman who is being left behind, both, or neither (cf. Frith 1996b, 184). Rather than assuming that listeners identify with the same persona throughout the duration of the performance, we might view each person in the audience as a free agent. When the emotions, demeanor, and situation of any persona resonate with an audience member, he or she can "implicate" with the persona, and when the audience member is no longer inclined to identify with the persona, he/she may "explicate" him/herself from such alignment (Fiske 2011, 174–175). The act of implicating and explicating with particular persona, lyrics, and situations during the course of the performance offers the audience members a chance to pass judgment, to determine what aligns with their point of view and what does not.

Part of the emotive power of the song stems from its convenient ambiguity—though the song expresses emotions in a public manner, the form of that expression essentially provides a vessel within which to place a range of real life experiences. In singing to "Yulian," the singer and those identifying with his sung persona may imagine themselves addressing a person from their past or even a fictional character from a story. As the surrounding audience is none the wiser, the song provides an opportunity for individuals to experience private emotions in a public, sympathetic environment. Several singers with whom I spoke told me that during certain periods of their lives, they infused emotions related to specific individuals into songs they sang about going beyond the Western Pass. When I asked Wang in one of my first interviews with him in 2006 what he thinks about while singing, he mentioned particular individuals from his past whom he thought about when he sang this song. When I asked him again towards the end of my fieldwork in 2012, Wang expanded on his previous answer to include not only his own experience but the experiences of people he had known in his village who had traveled to Inner Mongolia, each with a unique story, as well as stories from TV dramas and novels about people going beyond the Western Pass. While the latter may be the stories of fictional characters, the emotive content of their stories is palpable and can contribute to a singer's accumulated understanding of and emotional interaction with the song. What is "true" is the emotional reaction to it, regardless of whether the individuals are real or fictional.

A good number of the songs Wang sings deal with "going beyond the Western Pass," often in the context of the sorrow of parting from one's beloved. One of these pieces for which he has become well known is "The One Who Walked beyond the Western Pass Has Returned" (CD Track 6). This song, of the "mountain tune" (shanqu 山曲) genre, describes the anticipation with which a migrant farmworker prepares to return from "beyond the Western Pass" to his home village and his beloved. Steeped in the memories of countless individuals who have left Wang's home area for Inner Mongolia, Wang's performances of this song in recent years appear to have added a new layer of meaning. At a New Year's performance sponsored by the local government in his hometown area in December 2011 (see chapter 6), Wang preceded his performance of this song with a speech about Fugu's rapid economic rise in recent years, which he said allowed those residents who had left out of poverty to return home. During that event, Wang chose to sing this song as his finale. Just like the nameless migrant peasant embodied by the song's persona, Wang too had returned after many years.

"THE ONE WHO WALKED BEYOND THE WESTERN PASS HAS RETURNED" ("ZOU XIKOU DE REN'ER ZHUAN HUILAI" 走西口的人儿转回来) (CD TRACK 6)

Not at all big, *ai hei*, that *little* black horse, I feed it an extra two pints,
A three-day, *ai hei*, journey—darling, I'll make it in two.
Bu da da ai hei nage xiao qing ma ma na duo wei shang er sheng liao,
San tian di ai hei nage lucheng qinqin wo liang ya me liang tian dao.
不大大哎嘿那个小青马马那多喂上二升料，
三天的哎嘿那个路程，亲亲，我两呀么两天到。

The water flows, *ai hei*, a thousand *li*, returning to the vast ocean,
The one, *ai hei*, who has walked beyond the Western Pass, darling, I've turned around and come back.
Shui liuliu ai hei nage qian li a na gui ya na gui dahai,
Zou xikou ai hei nage ren'er qinqin wo zhuan ya me zhuan huilai.
水流流哎嘿那个千里啊那归呀那归大海，
走西口哎嘿那个人儿，亲亲，我转呀么转回来。

Daqing Mountain, *ai hei*, is tall, darling, Wula Mountain, *ai*, is short,
With a snap, *ai hei*, of the horse whip, darling, I return inside the Pass.
With a snap, *ai hei*, of the horse whip, darling, I return inside the Pass.
Daqing Shan ai hei nage gao lai qinqin na Wula Shan ei di,
Mabianzi ai hei nage yi shuai qinqin wo hui ya na hui kouli.
Mabianzi ai hei nage yi shuai qinqin wo hui ya me hui kouli.
大青山哎嘿那个高来，亲亲，那乌拉山哎低，
马鞭子哎嘿那个一甩，亲亲，我回呀那回口里。
马鞭子哎嘿那个一甩，亲亲，我回呀么回口里。

If we view "Going beyond the Western Pass" as Yulian accompanying her departing lover through song on his journey into the unknown, "The One Who Walked beyond the Western Pass Has Returned," in turn, symbolizes the benefits gained through that journey. The man returns not only with material wealth but with a transformed subjectivity to share. Rather than the couple physically exploring the Other together, one of them explores, visiting the Other, and returns, reuniting the couple. The underlying lesson, however, is the same: to survive and thrive in a fluid world, one must engage with others and embrace new senses of self.

When Desires Fail to Merge

We can add further depth to the pattern of "Couples Going Out" when we look at different versions of particular songs where one version has the couple going out and coming together and another relates how things go wrong and the couple fails to unite, often leaving one of them weaker for it. One such song, "Drinking Opium" (CD Track 3), is sung both by Ma Ziqing (the famous female northern Shaanxi folk singer mentioned in chapter 1) and Wang Xiangrong in different versions. Ma's version, often referred to as "If Your Mother Beats You, You Can Tell Your Older Brother" ("Ni mama da ni, ni gei gege shuo" 你妈妈打你你给哥哥说), is a playful, somewhat flirtatious dialogue between a young woman and a traveling muleteer (*jiaofu* 脚夫) (Lü 1994, 1:99). In contrast, Wang's version is a male sung persona's exhortation of an absent female. While Ma's version suggests that the woman might join the muleteer (by extension enacting the "couple going out" paradigm), Wang's version laments the female addressee's choice to remain in isolation and the downfall caused by that decision.

Ma Ziqing sings verses alternating between the male and female persona, suggesting that they are meant to form a dialogue. In the first stanza, the muleteer tells the woman that if her mother beats her, she should tell him rather than trying to kill herself by drinking opium paste.[97] She responds in the second stanza by saying that she had no one to talk to, and only then did she drink the opium. He then playfully pokes fun at her by suggesting that it was her own fault that her mother beat her—she wore her fancy red shoes on the muddy road.[98] She flippantly defends herself, saying that if she chooses to wear red shoes, it's only because she wants to look good—what does that have to do with a lowly donkey driver like him? The muleteer ends the exchange by complaining in the final stanza that she drives his heart wild when she wears the red shoes while standing above him on the edge of a hill.

The mood of Wang's version of the song is completely different—subdued, forlorn, and evoking a sense of pain. The three stanzas he recorded in 1994 appear to be sung by a male persona who refers to himself as Older Brother. His sorrowful wailing receives no answer—the female addressee remains silent. When I asked Wang where the absent woman was, he replied, "She is dead." As he talked about this song, he said that it expressed the man's anger at the woman for taking her own life—for succumbing to her bitter fate instead of rebelling against it.

"DRINKING OPIUM" ("HE YANGYAN" 喝洋烟) (CD TRACK 3)

If your mother beat you, you should have told your Older Brother about it,
Why did you drink opium and kill yourself?

Ni ge mama da ni ya ni gei gege shuo ya ei,
Ni weishenme na yao ba nage yang na yanr he ya ei.
你（格）妈妈打你呀你给哥哥说呀哎，
你为什么那要把那个洋（那）烟儿喝呀哎。

If your father scolded you, you shouldn't have cried so,
You should have known that your dad had a surly temper.
Ni ge dada na ma ni nage ni buyao ku ya ei,
Ni gai zhidao ni da nage pi na qi jue ya ei.
你（格）大大那骂你那个你不要哭呀哎，
你该知道你大那个脾（那）气倔呀哎。

If your older brother gave you a lesson, you shouldn't have gotten so mad,
You should have known that your brother had a bad temper.
Ni na gege na xun ni nage ni na buyao qi ya ei,
Ni gai zhidao ni gege na hui na piqi yo ei.
你那哥哥那训你那个你（那）不要气呀哎，
你该知道你哥哥那灰（那）脾气哟哎。

When I asked Wang whether he had heard of people committing suicide through drinking opium when he was a child, he told me that his mother used to tell him stories about one of his older female cousins who had killed herself in the 1940s, before Wang was born, after suffering in an unhappy arranged marriage. Wang said that he sensed his mother's disapproval of and resentment towards the old "feudal" system of arranged marriage from her tone of voice and other paralinguistic features as she would tell the story. Though he did not go into further detail, Wang said that a lot of his own views were embodied in his performance of the song.[99]

Wang's description of "Drinking Opium" made me realize that personal views, which are very much connected with one's personal life, can also be gleaned from one's descriptions of seemingly objective things like "traditional" song lyrics. Even if Wang didn't connect a song to his own life, his description of the song could be quite telling. Reflecting on the personal through discussions of the traditional is perhaps another lesson learned in Wang's education through song. John McDowell (2011) notes how individuals tell stories assumed to be communally standardized and "objective"—he is looking at mythic narrative traditions of Andean peoples in Colombia and Ecuador—but the stories those individuals tell often belie their own views and lives in the perspectives and characterization used in the telling. Similar to Wang's descriptions of "Going beyond the Western Pass" and "Drinking Opium," the personal cannot help but leak into performances and discussions of the traditional. Another example of this phenomenon is found in Ray Cashman's (2011) analysis of an Irish storyteller from County Donegal, Packy Jim McGrath, who juxtaposed traditional, biblical stories with more personal narratives during his ongoing dialogue with Cashman. According to Cashman, by combining biblical stories with a personal narrative about dealing with a rude individual in a tavern, Packy Jim allowed for additional meanings and rhetorical moves to be attached to a seemingly traditional story.[100]

In each of these cases, traditional forms of expression can help individuals make sense of their lived experience (DuBois 2006). In a study of the Scottish Traveller singer Jeannie Robertson, James Porter and Herschel Gower write, "The songs do not simply recount emotional high points in this experience, but crystallize and transform the lived reality into formal, coherent expressive structures" (1995, 269). Likewise, Cashman suggests, "Tradition provides Packy Jim both an explanation for evil in the world and a charter for his own moral behavior, helping him comprehend injustice and have faith that in the end the deserving will triumph" (2011, 378). Similar to Jeannie Robertson and Packy Jim, Wang's songs and his discussions of them provide Wang with a platform through which to reflect on, crystallize, and express his views on a range of personal and social issues.

Both Wang's version of "Drinking Opium" and a festival tune he discusses about an old bawdy boatman who fails to consummate a relationship with a girl he takes down south (see chapter 3) constitute critiques of isolated individuals who fail to reach out to others when they still have the chance. In "Drinking Opium," the singer implores the now deceased woman to "tell Older Brother," suggesting that she turn to help outside of the family when continued isolation would ultimately lead to her demise. In the bawdy boatman's case, he is rejected due to his age, and his tale is a humorous reminder to young people to find partners while young to avoid the social stigma of permanent bachelors (*guanggun* 光棍).[101] While the cruel fate of the woman in "Drinking Opium" involves the isolation brought on by the arranged marriage system (in Wang's version), in the festival tune, it is the isolation brought on by poverty and low social status, ultimately culminating in rejection. Without calling out to an Other while they still had the chance, both individuals essentially fade away without social support. In both cases, the underlying idea is that calling out to an Other secures one's continued existence, and failure to do so leads one to become a ghost drifting in the wind. The contrast between songs about individuals with different viewpoints coming together to help each other and form a new point of view and songs critiquing isolated individuals who fail to call out to others and suffer for it reinforces the idea that song is a public conversation that we benefit from joining in on. It positions us in relation to others and allows us to reap the benefits of others' unique abilities while asserting our own senses of self.

In sum, the songs and singers that Wang heard as a child had a profound influence on him. They instilled in him the understanding of song as a means of communicative mediation between people. They showed him the power of song in building and strengthening relationships amidst life's twists and turns and finding points of commonality through which to relate to one another. They also impressed upon him the ability of the singer to serve as a representative—standing in for the host in a banquet or ritual, the guests at a drinking party, a spirit in a curative act, or two lovers on their way into uncharted territory. In this chapter, I have suggested that the power and authority of the singers from Wang's childhood provided models for how to facilitate conversations between divergent voices through song, influencing Wang's image of what it meant to be a professional folk singer and a song king in the years to come. Following Wang's move to the city and his exposure to different audiences, he used this experience with different contexts, songs, and sung personae to construct regional and later national personae that could be adapted to different events—a process that is explored in greater depth in the following chapter.

CHAPTER 3

Representing the Region

Dᴜʀɪɴɢ Wang's career at the Yulin Folk Arts Troupe (figure 3.1), he helped construct a regional identity amidst evolving relations between places. Wang found that the troupe's stage represented a context different from any he had encountered before, and he felt a lack of large-scale pieces that could symbolize all of northern Shaanxi, representing the history, land, and people of the Loess Plateau onstage.[1] While Marugeda's banquet singers and spirit mediums performed conversations between local people and gods and *errentai* actors performed in temple fairs throughout the triprovincial area of "going beyond the Western Pass," for Wang to represent the region of Yulin and northern Shaanxi as a whole to disparate localities within the region and outsiders as well, he needed to shift the songs he sang and how he presented himself.

Following China's economic reform, one of the Yulin Folk Arts Troupe's goals was to advertise the region through song and dance and help it establish economic relationships in China and abroad. Yulin's regional identity would need to link various local identities within the region to a broader sense of Chineseness—similar to the bridge between local and national provided by provincial identities (Goodman 2002). This endeavor called for a shift in the geographical representations of songs. Regional song-and-dance troupes required songs with expanded imagery and sung personae that outsiders and audiences throughout the heterogeneous region would recognize, sung by singers deemed worthy of representing the region as a whole. Mentions of local scenes would fail to represent the region as a whole, and expressive genres popular only in particular localities, such as *errentai* and spirit-medium tunes, could potentially fracture the "imagined community" of northern Shaanxi (Anderson 1991).

Instead of lyrics referring to local topographies—Marugeda's ravine, for example—the region required identifiable images that would unite the region, such as the Loess Plateau and the Yellow River. The sung personae of these new

Figure 3.1 Exterior of the Yulin Folk Arts Troupe. Yulin, Shaanxi. 2012. Photograph by author.

songs had to be general enough to be recognizable to a range of audiences, yet clearly tied to the region. Following Bella Dicks' notion of the "visitability" of places, in order for localities to become legible sites accessible to outsiders, representations of places must present them as distinct others in a relatable way, satisfying "the touristic... desire to experience something different, something which is part of the lives of others but which can be related back to the self" (2003, 8). Therefore, local sung personae such as the boisterous banquet singers and mystical spirit mediums of Wang's childhood were replaced with opaque yet relatable personae whose ambiguity could tie together a range of meanings and places in a wider variety of contexts. The singers of these region-representing songs would also set aside local identities when audiences needed a singer evoking a regional identity to unite them, glossing over subregional differences. Singers such as Wang had to be flexible in how they presented themselves—shifting their claims to place-based identity in order to find common ground with each audience.

To better understand the contours of this process, I begin with a general discussion of how local song traditions around China have adapted to the aesthetics of the stage in recent years. After briefly looking at issues of musical accompaniment, gestures, and language, I turn to some examples of how Wang constructed his regional repertoire by borrowing songs from various localities and adapting local tunes into region-representing masterpieces. Adaptations of local songs into regional songs often involve altering metaphors to expand their symbolic potential. I point to similar developments of the "couple going out" paradigm and related imagery in Wang's "expanding" of a local song from his youth into a regional symbol and stories about the composition of the emblematic folk song-cum-regional-cum-national anthem "The East Is Red" ("Dongfang hong" 东方红). Citing Wang's onstage banter as he presents his active repertoire to audiences in different localities, I look at how he as a regional singer must shift his presentation of place-based identity and particular songs, bringing each audience together in relation to his persona as "Folk Song King of Northern Shaanxi" and glossing over subregional differences. Finally, I explore Wang's performances of two versions of "The East Is Red," suggesting how they adapt the "couple going out" paradigm into representations of the region and nation.

Constructing Stageworthy Performances

Wang often noted during our interviews whether a certain song could be performed onstage, an idea I refer to as "Stageworthiness."[2] Certain songs were not appropriate for the stage, although Wang would perform them in other contexts that I explore in chapter 5. Part of the idea of Stageworthiness involves adapting song performances to the aesthetics of the stage—what Qiao Jianzhong (2011) calls "stageification" (*wutaihua* 舞台化). To meet audiences' expectations for stage performances in large venues, singers must be attentive to melody, pace, vocal technique, length, and associated gestures (Qiao 2011).[3] Another aspect of Stageworthiness is that singers must be able to recognize and adapt to different performance contexts—noting the occasion, people in the audience, and mood—and respond with prepared (though variable) repertoires, presented in ways that connect those repertoires to the audience at hand. Such variability is highlighted in versions of "The East Is Red" Wang performs that I discuss below.

Many scholars have noted how Chinese regional song traditions adapt as they move from "village traditions" to the stage and television (Davis 2005; Ingram 2012; Qiao 2011; Gorfinkel 2012).[4] In Catherine Ingram's (2012) work on Kam big song in southeastern Guizhou Province, she discusses two major performance contexts—"the Kam 'village tradition' and the stage"— where the former refers to traditional singing events held in the local drum tower (*dare low*) during New Year celebrations and the latter includes TV performances and tourist concerts. The Kam people with whom Ingram spoke would "distinguish these two different performance formats by location and context—as, respectively, *nyao dare low song lao ga* (exchanging song in the *dare low*) and *cha tai dor ga* (going onstage to sing)" (56). Similarly, Sara Davis notes a "split between song and dance staged for tourists and song performed for locals" in her research on contemporary performances of Tai Lüe music in Yunnan, referring to these two contexts as "front stage" and "backstage" respectively (2001, 38; 2005, 22).

Both Ingram and Davis suggest that the performance styles and content of traditions are transformed when traditions pivot from targeting in-group to out-group audiences. Noticeable changes have been seen in the performance of "folk" song and dance traditions at large-scale events directed at cultural outsiders. In Jing Li's (2013) examination of ethnic minority folk song and dance performances from Yunnan Province at the 2007 Smithsonian Folklife Festival in Washington, D.C., she notes that although the Yunnan officials accompanying the delegation agreed to performances by "peasant artists from fields and villages" (77) onstage, one high-ranking cultural official suggested it was necessary to mix them with professionally trained performers:

> We felt that this was such an influential event, we needed the participation of professional troupe members. We selected the programs in the same way, systematically integrating the two [i.e., folk and professional], because folk (*minjian*) artists often performed individually or in a pair. It was somewhat monotonous and dull (*dandiao*). [The National Mall was] such a significant site, so many people, our performances needed to produce a certain atmosphere (*qifen*). If a dance was performed by ten or twenty people, the atmosphere would be better. (77)

The officials' considerations of the performance context (e.g., "such a significant site") and their desired effect (e.g., "our performances needed to produce a certain atmosphere") clearly led to alterations in repertoire and style.

We see a similar sense of aesthetic adaptation in Anthony Shay's discussion of folk dance companies from various countries. Shay cites the founder and director of a national state-sponsored folk dance company based in Mexico City, Amalia Hernandez (1917–2000), who said, "There is no way to move village dancers directly onto a professional stage. Everything must be adapted for modern eyes—costumes, lighting, steps, *espectaculo*. . . . What we make are theater pieces based on folklore" (Hernandez, cited in Carriaga 1969, F1, cited in Shay 2002, 36, cited in Wilcox 2013).[5] A similar sentiment was expressed by a well-known Korean dancer, Ch'oe Sŭng-hŭi, who performed in the United States between 1938 and 1940. In a newspaper article at the time, she is quoted as saying that certain traditional dances were "too long to perform on stage or too short and simple to perform on stage. So I wanted to create something original and new which fits this contemporary era" (cited in Van Zile 2001, 201). Each of these examples points to a concern with the aesthetics of the stage.

The need to adapt pieces to the expectations of stage performances is evident in Wang's adaptation of a bawdy festival tune into "Pulling Ferries throughout the Year" (CD Track 23), which I discuss below. Wang's desire in composing this song was to create a dramatic piece fitting for the stage that could represent the entire region. Patia Isaku (1981) notes a similar phenomenon of adapting "local" pieces for presentation to audiences from other regions in Japan, where "local songs often become well known throughout the country, but usually in an altered form" (10). In Wang's case, he slowed down the melody and adapted a humorous, bawdy boatman persona from the earlier festival context into a dramatic boatman figure, embattled by the elements as he ferries a boatload of people to the other shore. The boatman in Wang's composition is still a recognizable sung persona, and yet its resemblance to a heroic helmsman borders on the epic, offering a figure that a wide variety of audiences could relate to that would symbolize larger fuzzy identities, such as the region and the nation. The earlier sung persona from the festival tune, on the other hand, the bawdy boatman—while humorous in local contexts—would not be relatable to urban audiences and would have run counter to the goal of evoking a larger "imagined community" by reinforcing negative stereotypes of "backwards" rural populaces (Anderson 1991). Similarly, stories of the composition of "The East Is Red" describe a now-famous peasant singer coming up with the first stanza in a flash of inspiration, and that peasant composer—nicknamed "The People's Singer"—provides a relatable sung persona for national Chinese audiences.

Stage performances also carry expectations regarding accompaniment—at the very least, instrumental accompaniment, and sometimes including a chorus as well—and background dancers in the case of large-scale performances. Until relatively recently, it was uncommon to find songs performed a cappella onstage in China, and recordings of folk songs almost always included MIDI accompaniment or a full orchestra (cf. Gorfinkel 2012). Wang's (2006) CD, *Northern Shaanxi Song King, Wang Xiangrong,* is a telling example: recorded in 1994 at the Music Research Institute in Beijing, the album's a cappella renditions of regional folk songs made it unpublishable for over a decade. It took twelve years for musical trends to shift enough for China Record Corporation to finally publish it as the first in a series of "original ecosystem" (*yuanshengtai* 原生态) folk songs. Though trends have changed enough for singers to perform a cappella *yuanshengtai* folk songs onstage, many audiences still expect stage performances to have musical accompaniment.

In addition to musical accompaniment, a performance's Stageworthiness also involves issues of language and gesture. When rural singers come to the city, unspoken rules about how to sing, speak, and move onstage come into play. If the singers continue to perform using local dialect, they can be criticized by audiences who expect to hear a performance in nationally understood Mandarin Chinese. The "Shepherd Song King," Shi Zhanming, was rejected from a local county opera troupe for not speaking Mandarin and for lacking a "stage presence" (Xue 2005, 12). Even Wang Xiangrong was criticized for his subregional dialect, which certain scholars felt was not representative of northern Shaanxi as a whole—an issue I discuss below. On the other hand, if folk singers choose to sing in Mandarin, local audiences from their home region may feel that they have lost the local "flavor" of the song, thus diminishing their perceived authenticity as a folk singer (cf. Tuohy 2003).

At the same time, stage performances have implicit expectations about how a singer should carry him/herself onstage, and the gestures that appear natural in performances need to be carefully learned and practiced. When I spoke with a senior scholar who worked with Wang Xiangrong in the early stages of Wang's career, the scholar poked fun at Wang's "rustic" stage presence at that time and explained how Wang had to be taught how to walk and move his arms while onstage. Shi Zhanming also struggled to get used to the stage during the early stages of his career, when he reportedly had to adapt from singing to his sheep to singing to large audiences from atop a stage (Xue 2005). In large-scale performances, a singer is often accompanied by an array of background dancers, and the ability to play one's part in a massive choreography is key. These examples reflect influences of Western-inspired ideals of performance and national language policy that have generally dominated stage practices of singers in China during recent times.

As Wang Xiangrong transitioned to the expectations of these newly created stages, he found a need for an expanded repertoire of songs worthy of representing the region. One means he used was to borrow songs from various parts of northern Shaanxi that presented general impressions of the region. Another method Wang used was to borrow songs from neighboring regions, which in some cases resulted in the songs becoming popularized as northern Shaanxi folk songs as Wang performed them during the course of his career. A third method was to adapt local songs into region-representing masterpieces, the process of which I examine further later in this chapter.

Borrowing Songs

One means to expand a repertoire worthy of the stage was borrowing and adapting songs from other areas within and outside of northern Shaanxi. Wang learned several songs from central-northern Shaanxi's Suide-Mizhi region during Li Zhiwen's tenure as a consultant for the Yulin Folk Arts Troupe. Certain scholars have suggested that Suide and Mizhi's relative isolation from the stylistic influences of other provinces and areas makes them more representative of the unique character of northern Shaanxi (cf. Liu Yulin et al. 2010; Huo Xianggui interview, March 22, 2012). Li Zhiwen, a native of Suide, taught Wang several songs from the region, including "Herding Livestock" ("Gan shengling" 赶牲灵) and "Song of the Muleteer" ("Jiaofu diao" 脚夫调)—both love songs featuring muleteer figures who have become synonymous with northern Shaanxi (Yang Cui 1995, 29). Both of these muleteer personae are vague enough to represent the region and characteristic enough to distinguish the region from others (cf. Dicks 2003). "Herding Livestock" describes a mule train driving draft animals from one place to another, while a village woman calls out to the muleteer from a distance asking him to wave his hand if he is her sweetheart. The animals and dialect words in the song's lyrics place the song in northern Shaanxi, but no specific place names are mentioned. "Song of the Muleteer" describes a muleteer stopping in the middle of a journey to "visit a friend." While it does mention specific place names, they are general-sounding enough to evoke images of the region as a whole: "Zhang Family Field," "Liu Family Hill," "Lamb Mountain." Wang mentioned that although he had never heard certain melodies from Suide and Mizhi as a child, he felt that learning to sing and appreciate those songs was part and parcel of becoming an inheritor of the broader northern Shaanxi folk song tradition.

With Wang's identity as a northern Shaanxi folk singer established, he was also able to adapt songs from outside the region that became part of the northern Shaanxi canon through his performances. During the late 1970s, Wang had the opportunity to learn songs from across the Yellow River in neighboring Shanxi Province while attending gala performances (*huiyan*). While attending one such gala performance in 1977 held in Qiangtou 墙头—a village along the Yellow River in northern Shaanxi across from Hequ, Shanxi Province—he heard the following song sung by a singer, Yang Zhongqing 杨仲青 from Baode 保德 County, Shanxi Province, which lies directly across the Yellow River from Fugu County Town. Wang soon began performing the song, which has since become considered a northern Shaanxi folk song (despite its Shanxi origins), and many singers in northern Shaanxi have done variations of it. Once again, we see generalized male and female personae and natural imagery that evoke northern Shaanxi without being tied to any particular locality—a mountain ridge, a grass-covered hillside, a gully. The melody is also relatively slow and powerful, evoking the great distances the male lover's song had to travel to reach its target, while simultaneously conjuring up the vast expanses of the region of northern Shaanxi.

"WHO IS THAT?" ("NA SHI YI GE SHUI" 那是一个谁**) (CD TRACK 7)**

Across the way on the other ridge, *ya*, who is that?
That's my Second Younger Sister, who'll be the death of me.
On the hillside grow ten kinds of grasses,
Seeing ten kinds, Little Sister is better than nine.
I stand on this ridge, Little Sister, you are in that gully,
If you choose me, Little Sis, wave your hand,
If you choose me, Little Sis, wave your hand.

Dui panpan nage geliangliang shang na shi yi ge ya shui?
Na jiu shi wo na yaoming di ge er meimei.
Shanpopo shang zhang zhe nage shi ya na shi yangyang cao,
Shi yangyang de nage kanjian meizi ni jiu jiu yangyang hao.
Wo zhan zai zhe geliangliang shang na meimei ya ni zai na gou,
Kanzhong liao nage gege meizi ni jiu zhao yi zhao shou,
Kanzhong liao nage gege meizi ni jiu zhao yi zhao shou.
对畔畔那个圪梁梁上那是一个呀谁?
那就是我那要命的个二妹妹。
山坡坡上长着那个十呀那十样样草,
十样样的那个看见妹子你就九样样好。
我站在这圪梁梁上那妹妹呀你在那沟,
看中了那个哥哥妹子你就招一招手,
看中了那个哥哥妹子你就招一招手。

While "Who Is That?" went on to join the canon of commonly identifiable northern Shaanxi folk songs, another song Wang learned from Yang Zhongqing at the same gala event did not. Although Wang added a few verses and went on to produce a music video of "Lighting a Lamp on East Mountain, West Mountain Becomes Bright" ("Dongshan shang diandeng xishan shang ming" 东山上点灯西山上明), that song remains identifiable as a Shanxi song and is not widely popular in northern Shaanxi. In comparing the two songs, one notes a faster pace and more intricate melody in "Lighting a Lamp on East Mountain, West Mountain Becomes Bright"—both of which place it stylistically as coming from Shanxi—whereas "Who Is That?" has the slower tempo, wider jumps from low to high, and falling glissando typical of other northern Shaanxi songs.

Melody and tempo were key factors in producing what Wang described as "solemn and dignified" (*cangliang houzhong* 苍凉厚重) works that could represent the region on large-scale stages. Quick, humorous melodies from local festivals often would not do. In addition, certain genres Wang grew up with such as *errentai,* while popular in the area around Marugeda and neighboring sections of Shanxi and Inner Mongolia, were foreign to other parts of northern Shaanxi and could not represent the region. This subregional heterogeneity was highlighted years later when Wang tried to teach his repertoire of *errentai* to his first two official disciples after he was chosen as a national-level representative transmitter in 2009. The two disciples—Feng Xiaohong and Li Chunru— came from other parts of northern Shaanxi to the south and west and were unfamiliar with the *errentai* melodies.[6] When I interviewed Feng Xiaohong about the pieces he had learned from Wang, Feng noted, "There are many of them that I can't sing. For many of them, it's because they are from Inner Mongolia, Shanxi, Ordos...*ai,* for a lot of them, when he sang them, I had never even heard the melody before."[7] When a song has a distinctive melody or dialect pronunciation placing it as "other," it is difficult to adapt into a region-representing piece. Instead, audiences tend to favor songs they have heard before and know how to sing—Feng Xiaohong called these "familiar songs" (*shuge* 熟歌).[8] At the same time, Feng's partner Li Chunru noted that songs can shift in popularity over time—she discussed how songs that were not popular earlier on gained popularity through public exposure in musicals, TV song contests, TV dramas, and other contexts.[9]

However, the appropriation of songs from various places was not enough. Wang needed a means to transform what he considered to be local songs into large-scale, region-representing pieces and felt that stage performances required dramatic works worthy of the region's history. The complex issues involved in adapting "small" songs into "big" songs can be seen in Wang's composition of "Pulling Ferries throughout the Year" and stories about the composition of another region-representing song, "The East Is Red," which I discuss below.[10]

Expanding the Local

After struggling with finding a suitable repertoire for the Yulin Folk Arts Troupe stage, in the late 1980s Wang was asked to compose a theme song evoking the history of the region for a TV drama. After becoming familiar with the plot of the series, Wang searched for a suitable melody and decided to adapt a tune he had heard during rural Lantern Festival gatherings when he was young. The piece was sung in the voice of an old boatman bragging about taking a young woman on a river excursion down south, only to have her to run off with a younger man after they reached their destination. Wang sang two stanzas from the festival song with varying first and second lines and the same third and fourth lines—showing the flexibility of emergent oral performance. The boatman refers to the young woman as a "white peony":

In my boat, there sat this white peony,
I took that peony down to Jiangnan.
In Jiangnan, there was her sweetheart,
And she left me, this old boatman, out in the cold.
Wo chuanli zuo zhege bai mudan,
Ban shang na mudan xia Jiangnan.
Jiangnan you ta de nanzihan,
Ba wo zhe lao shaogong gechaozhuan.
我船里坐这个白牡丹，
扳上那牡丹下江南。
江南有她的男子汉，
把我这老艄公圪超转。

If you say I have it hard, I really have it hard,
I steered my boat down to Jiangnan.
In Jiangnan, there was her sweetheart,
And she left me, this old boatman, out in the cold.
Shuo wo nan, wo zhen ye nan,
Ban shang na shuichuan xia Jiangnan.
Jiangnan you ta de nanzihan,
Ba wo zhe lao shaogong jiu gechaozhuan.
说我难，我真也难，
搬上那水船下江南。
江南有她的男子汉，
把我这老艄公就圪超转。[11]

The TV director liked Wang's melody and asked him to come up with whatever
lyrics he felt would be appropriate, assuming Wang's experience as a folk singer
would guarantee something with an authentic feel. Wang chose to transform
the image of the boatman from a bawdy, humorous figure to a tragic hero with
a hard life—someone whose personality Wang described as strong, valiant, and
tenacious, someone who puts his heart and soul into everything he does no
matter how much he suffers. This transformation of the song's sung persona to
convey a new message to a new audience coincided with what Wang learned
from the genres of songs he had gathered over the years. The newly crafted
boatman had an emblematic quality embodying various levels of meanings—a
purposeful ambiguity stemming from Wang's experience dealing with multiple
audiences.

"PULLING FERRIES THROUGHOUT THE YEAR" ("YI NIAN SIJI BAN SHUICHUAN" 一年四季扳水船) (CD TRACK 23)

When you mention my hometown, *ai,* it's known throughout the land,
On the banks of the Yellow River—Qileng Village.
For generations, [we] have endured poverty,
I steer my boat, passing the time.
Tiqi wojia ai jia youming,
Huanghe na pan shang zhe Qilengcun.
Zuzu na beibei shou pinqiong,
Wo ban chuan na baidu guo shang na guangjing.
提起我家哎家有名，
黄河那畔上这碛楞村。
祖祖那辈辈受贫穷，
我扳船那摆渡过上那光景。

If you say I have it hard, I truly have it hard,
Ai, throughout the year, in every season, steering my boat.

The scorching sun on the top of my head, my foot pressed on the plank,
Ai, in the wind and in the rain, I bore through the waves.
Ai hai hai hai hai hai hai ya,
In the wind and in the rain, I bore through the waves.
Shuo wo nan, wo zhen ye nan,
Ai, yi nian na siji ya ban shuichuan.
Touding shang lieri wo jiao ta shang ban,
Ai, feng li na yu li zai lang litou zuan.
Ai hai hai hai hai hai hai ya,
Feng li na yu li zai lang litou zuan.
说我难，我真也难，
哎，一年那四季呀扳水船。
头顶上烈日我脚踏上板，
哎，风里那雨里在浪里头钻。
哎嘿嘿嘿嘿嘿嘿呀，
风里那雨里在浪里头钻。

Rowing is hard, ferrying is difficult,
My feet are planted on two worlds—*yin* and *yang.*
The wind blows, rain pours, the waves billow to the sky,
Ai, a boatload of people floats on the crest of a big wave.
Ai hai hai hai hai hai hai ya,
A boatload of people floats on the crest of a big wave.
Huachuan na ku, baidu nan,
Jiao ta na yinyang zhe liang shijie.
Guafeng na xiayu zhe lang taotian,
Ai, yi chuan ren fu zai zhe da lang jian.
Ai hai hai hai hai hai hai ya,
Yi chuan ren fu zai zhe da lang jian.
划船那苦，摆渡难，
脚踏那阴阳这两世界。
刮风那下雨这浪滔天，
哎，一船人浮在这大浪尖。
哎嘿嘿嘿嘿嘿嘿呀，
一船人浮在这大浪尖。

Several changes in the lyrics' imagery appear to reflect common trends in the construction of region-representing songs. Unlike the bawdy boatman of the festival tune, whose purpose was to entertain local people at a particular time of year, Wang's composition needed imagery that would connect several broader concepts: history, the region, the common people, and the nation.

Wang's discussion of slowing down the festival melody and his desire to compose a dramatic song for the stage point to choices in music and accompaniment involved in producing region-representing songs. Following Dicks' notion of "visitability," such songs had to be "distinct" while at the same time "relatable" (Dicks 2003, 8). One way to create new pieces with the gravitas to represent the region was to adapt local melodies and change the lyrics. Wang cited a key example of this with his composition of "Pulling Ferries throughout the Year," the lyrics of which I analyze further below. Starting with a melody he had heard in festival performances as a child, Wang slowed down the tempo and changed the voice with which he sang it. The original tune's tempo had been quick and playful, matching the story it told of a bawdy old boatman who unsuccessfully tried to court a young woman. The song was meant to provoke a great deal of laughter and amusement at rural festivities. In retrospect, Wang saw the festival performances as too focused on local entertainment and lacking a sense of "deep feeling." This was not a song that could represent all of northern Shaanxi. Wang decided to slow down the melody and use a "solemn and dignified male voice" to "call out" (*han chulai* 喊出来)—a gesture coinciding with Wang's desire for the new song to reach a larger audience. He said, "I enlarged upon (*fangda le* 放大了) [the festival tune], because when you look at it in a small way, it's a little tune used for a [festival] skit, but when you magnify and amplify it, it becomes a great music that captures this entire region of land. A very big…momentous music [*sings his new version*]."[12]

Scholars have also described the composition of "The East Is Red" as a transformation from an "unrefined folk song" to what is variously termed a "solemn, dignified, stately ode" and "a powerful, dignified, revolutionary ode," and we see a similar process of changes in tempo and rhythm in that and other region-representing songs (Wei 2004, 65; Zhao 1994, 79; Wang Changfa 1998, 84–85). Changes in tempo are highlighted in Wang's multistanza a cappella version of "The East Is Red," discussed below, where he slows down certain stanzas to make them more dramatic, then picks up the pace in other stanzas to encourage the audience to clap along.

Wang's composition of "Pulling Ferries throughout the Year" parallels similar stories of region-representing tunes evolving from "smaller" festival tunes. Songs such as "The East Is Red" and "The Infinite Bends of the Yellow River" are often described by scholars along the lines of "small songs from small places that evolved into big songs representing big places," and often part of this transformation is tied to transformed symbols and expanded metaphors—similar to Wang's transformation of a bawdy, old boatman into a heroic, pensive helmsman. "The Infinite Bends of the Yellow River" also expands the boatman trope into a national symbol, as I discuss later in chapter 7. Based on melodic comparisons, the scholar Yang Cui (2007) speculates that "The Infinite Bends of the Yellow River" (also known as "The Song of the Yellow River Boatman") may have been based on an earlier bawdy festival tune called "The Two Wives." The process in which Yang describes the development of the later song from this earlier bawdy tune bears a certain similarity to Wang's rhetoric of "little festival tunes" and his desire to "enlarge upon" their meaning. Yang writes, "This piece, 'Two Wives,' was a *small* piece performed in *small* gatherings of *yang'ge*" (12, italics added). The repetition of the word "small" (*xiao* 小) indicates a dismissive attitude toward the song, as the word has often been used to describe non-elite art forms, frequently with implications of immorality and bawdiness (e.g., novels [*xiaoshuo* 小说, lit. "small speech"], folk plays [*xiaoxi* 小戏, lit. "small plays," as contrasted against large-scale, mainstream productions, like Beijing opera, etc.], pornographic films [*xiao dianying* 小电影, lit. "little movies"], etc.). At the same time, the "small" can also be understood as referring to a geographically limited scope, similar to Wang's discussion of "small" pieces in need of being expanded geographically. The connection implied between the geographical and the moral is significant to the transmission of folk songs, and I discuss place-based morality further in chapter 5.

Whereas the earlier festival tune was meant to entertain during rural festivities, in Wang's composition the boatman's struggle with wind and waves merges different senses of time—it is both timeless and deeply rooted in Chinese history. His crossing from one bank to the other as he battles crashing waves is an experience of suffering and uncertainty, combined with a sense of determination. The statement "For generations, [we] have endured poverty" suggests that the boatman persona represents generations who have come before him. The song is potentially situated in any time—no mention of a specific year is given—and that ambiguity adds to the sense that the boatman is connected to a long string of history. Furthermore, the boatman is ever-present—unlike the bawdy festival boatman who was tied to a particular time of year, this persona exists "throughout the year, in every season." The cyclical flowering and decline of the seasons and the ebb and flow of the waves evoke the cycles of history. Speaking of this ebb and flow, Wang cited the flourishing of the Tang dynasty and the weakness of the late Qing with invasions from foreign powers as examples. In talking about these difficult periods of Chinese history, Wang spoke of the thin line between life and death: "When things went well, they went well, and when they went badly, [people] died." Wang highlighted this liminal state in the boatman's stance between two worlds and the boat's position on the crest of the wave—it may quickly and safely deliver its occupants to the other shore, or it may suddenly capsize and drown them.

Seen in the context of the earlier festival tune, I suggest that Wang's composition is an expansion of the "couple going out" paradigm. The boatman is transformed from a lecherous man into a fearless leader, while the woman he carries becomes the boatload of people. In both cases, the "couples" are heading toward particular destinations and the boatmen are defined by their partners. In the festival tune, the couple is headed to the Jiangnan region to the southeast—the boatman hoping to develop a relationship with the woman and the woman using the ride to reach her young lover. The disconnect between the couple's goals forms the narrative defining the old boatman as a tragicomic character. Rather than merging their subjectivities, as suggested in the examples given in chapter 2, the boatman ends up alone and worse off for it. He has been seen by an Other and rejected. By narrating the story to festivalgoers, he pokes fun at himself and provokes laughter, while reiterating the idea that couples can only come together when they have characteristics that mutually benefit each other.

In "Pulling Ferries throughout the Year," the boatman and the boatload of people are headed toward the other shore of a river—a destination they move toward but do not reach during the course of the song. The boatman guides the boatload of people, attempting to take them to their destination as he protects them from potential disaster, while they support him with their trust, imbuing him with the qualities of a leader. One cannot be a leader without a territory and a populace to lead, and the boat and boatload of people provide convenient metaphors for these notions. That the people depend on the boatman's leadership to avoid disaster and reach their destination suggests the mutual support of a leader and a populace as they head toward an uncertain future together.

Creating a Mythic Boatman

The boatman's transformation in Wang's composition is an example of how sung personae are adapted to represent larger regions and time periods. As the sentiments to be conveyed change, so do the personae (Fong 1990). The bawdy boatman persona from Wang's youth fit the humorous mood of local festivals at that time, while the pensive boatman of Wang's composition conveys the somber and dramatic feelings appropriate to its region- and history-representing message. We see a similar shift in the sung personae involved in the composition of "The East Is Red" discussed below.

What difference do these region- and nation-representing sung personae have when compared with the earlier sung personae of the songs when they were still "small"? If we envision sung personae as "vessels" of meaning, the "small" songs have personae that seem to hold only limited, local meanings; in the case of the bawdy boatman of the festivals of Wang's youth, this would include the risqué humor appropriate to those festivals. However, when taken out of that limited context, the "vessel" of the bawdy boatman would fail to hold other possible meanings—the region as a whole, since there were parts of the region that did not have such characters, nor the nation as a whole, which would not recognize or empathize with such a character. The "bawdy" nature in itself was limiting, closing the door to other meanings; it did not allow for the somber, the dramatic, the nationalistic, or the hopeful. On the other hand, the boatman of Wang's song leaves the door open to many possible interpretations.

The boatman's image is ambiguous, opening a space for multiple meanings. Its fuzziness allows for scalability—the potential to expand the "vessel" created by that persona. He could represent the region, the nation, or even all of humankind. Wang suggested that the boatman "points to many different things." Similar to the banquet singers and spirit mediums of Wang's youth, the boatman's unique identity allows him to connect to two different groups. He is clearly a member of the common people (*laobaixing* 老百姓), but his steering a "boatload of people" also suggests he is a leader—a helmsman—a classic metaphor for leaders such as Mao Zedong. Just as the boatman is responsible for the safe passage of people from one bank to the other, leaders are responsible for the citizens' smooth passage from past to future. The boatman's "steering" thus parallels the decisions of leaders about the direction of the country. "Nowadays," Wang said, "Hu Jintao, he is the one steering the boat." The boatman's dual identity—as a common person and a leader—reminds the listener that people from all walks of life experience difficulties and responsibilities. The fates of commoners and leaders are tied together—they are all in the same boat.

The inherent power of ambiguity, then, is a key factor in constructing these representative songs. M. H. Abrams (1953) suggests that ambiguous literary characters are more relatable to a variety of readers, citing Shakespeare's use of the "generic human type, rather than the individual" as an example (37–38). Similarly, John Fiske, in his study of television culture, suggests that texts with "semiotic excess" offer a range of meanings to viewers with different social backgrounds and thus reach larger audiences (2011, 194, 16). Such a "multiplicity of meanings," says Fiske, is "the textual equivalent of social difference and diversity" (15–16). At the same time, ambiguity calls our attention as we feel compelled to interpret it. "Any verbal nuance...which gives room for alternative reactions to the same piece of language," says William Empson in his classic study on ambiguity, has the effect of focusing our attention as we think over "which of [several possible interpretations] to hold most clearly in mind" (1966, 1, 3). Herein lies the poetic power of ambiguity: not only does it mean more things to more people, but it engages the attention of each person. In this light, the fuzzy image of the boatman persona invites listeners to fill that "vessel" with any number of different types of content, whereas an image too distinct would form an end to the conversation. Multiple possibilities beg the observer to weigh one interpretation against another, then speculate about the existence of a third. Does the boatman's fuzzy image represent all boatmen? Does it symbolize a region? A nation? Does it represent the present or generations from the past—or both? Or all of the above?

This power of ambiguity lies in the ability to connect multiple facets of meaning—a relatability that connects to Bella Dicks' (2003) notion of "visit-ability." A large part of "visitability," Dicks notes, "is dependent on the display of culture," on "how culture comes to be produced in visitable form" (1). She suggests that "cultural display promises…the experience of meaningfulness" (8), and I would add that such "meaningfulness" requires recourse to ambiguity. In terms of visitability, images with specific and/or esoteric meanings become obstacles to coherent visits: "Places whose identity seems inaccessible, confusing or contradictory do not present themselves as destinations. They do not, in other words, seem visitable" (Dicks 2003, 1). To be "visitable," the region had to be recognizable—a balance between specificity and generality that meets in fuzzy images like Wang's boatman.

Together with the transformed persona of the boatman, the image of the boat in Wang's song provides an expandable metaphor—boats come in all sizes and can carry varying numbers of people. In the bawdy festival tune, the boatman is either in the boat with the woman (when they travel down south) or alone (after she abandons him). Together, the two in a boat conjure up the notion of lovers. Alone once again, the boatman becomes a comic character. When Wang described his composition, however, he stressed the boat's inherent ambiguity. The "boatload of people" could include just a few people, several tens of people, or several hundred people—progressively larger and larger groups. Characterizing the boatman as a symbol, Wang outlined a flexible ambiguity extending to larger and larger areas centered around the Yellow River. On one hand, the boatman could represent generations of people who had lived on the banks of the Yellow River or even all the people of the Yellow Earth. At the same time, given the Yellow River basin and Loess Plateau's centrality in narratives of the origins of the Chinese nation, Wang suggested, when we view the boatman "in a bigger way" (*shuo da le* 说大了), he symbolizes the Chinese nation and its people (*Zhonghua minzu* 中华民族). Thus, the boat and boatman metaphors could be variously applied to individual, regional, and national identities. Wang's insight into the development of regional songs helps us look again at one of the most emblematic pieces from northern Shaanxi.

Composing "The East Is Red"

One of the songs that perhaps best epitomizes the transition from local to regional (and on to national) is "The East Is Red." Scholars have described its origins as an "unrefined folk song" (*yuansheng zhuangtai de min'ge* 原生状态的民歌) that, through the process of being continually sung and passed down, became "a powerful, dignified, revolutionary ode" (*yi shou xiongwei zhuangyan de geming songge* 一首雄伟庄严的革命颂歌) (Wei 2004, 65). Referring to the song's final version, one scholar wrote, "This song expressed the extreme love and respect of the People of every ethnic group throughout all of China toward the great leader Mao Zedong and the Chinese Communist Party. It is a heartfelt statement of the feelings of millions upon millions of Chinese people" (Wang Changfa 1998, 85). The use of the music of "The East Is Red" on a radio frequency broadcast from China's first man-made satellite suggests that its music would literally reach beyond the nation to the ends of the Earth and the universe beyond (Wang 1998, 85). What interests us here are the changes involved in the song's transformation into a representation of China's entire population.

The creation and refinement of "The East Is Red" involved changes in tempo, rhythm, and ornamentation along with changes to its lyrics, similar to the process through which Wang Xiangrong transformed a local festival tune into "Pulling Ferries throughout the Year" (Wang Changfa 1998, 84–85). The development of "The East Is Red" also involved, I suggest, the incorporation of a sung persona with a dual identity—both a common person and a representative of common people—as well as expanded imagery to reflect the national and global reach of its content. We can also think about "The East Is Red" as an extension of the "couple going out" paradigm with various mutually constituting couples—the East and the sun, Mao and the People, the Chinese Communist Party (CCP) and the People, and, perhaps, the song's peasant composer and Mao Zedong.

The melody of "The East Is Red" is often traced to earlier love songs where the sung personae are essentially peasant lovers, quite different from the revolutionary-minded sung persona we find in its current incarnations. Although several individuals are said to have had a hand in its composition, "The East Is Red" is associated with a peasant singer said to have spontaneously composed one of the song's early versions. The image of this "peasant composer," Li Youyuan 李有源 (1903–1955), known as "The People's Singer" (*Renmin geshou* 人民歌手), can be seen as a potential "sung persona" for the song (Wei 1994, 35). When the lyrics are heard through his voice, the "peasant composer" image conveniently fuses concepts of the people (*laobaixing*), region, and nation. And yet, given Li Youyuan's place of origin—Jiaxian County in northern Shaanxi—this "peasant composer" persona has ties to a specific locality, similar to Wang's boatman's rootedness in Qileng village, another locality in the region. Both the "boatman" persona in Wang's song and the "peasant composer" persona associated with "The East Is Red" can be seen as imagined voices simultaneously connecting to particular localities and serving as national symbols through their representation of the region of northern Shaanxi (given the region's central role in China's revolutionary history). In this sense, I suggest, the sung personae of these songs serve as bridges connecting the local to the national (cf. Goodman 2002).

The first stanza of "The East Is Red" is frequently attributed to the peasant composer, Li Youyuan, and I would suggest that this image gets attached at some level to the song, providing a potential reading of its sung persona: a musically inclined peasant who praises the country's leaders through song. Although some scholars now question the stanza's attribution to Li, part of the legend surrounding his creative process relates to issues raised earlier concerning the "enlarging" (*fangda*) of lyrics. As related in several accounts, including his own, Li had long desired to write a song reflecting the proletariat masses' feelings that praised Mao and the CCP (Su 2007, 48; Wang Changfa 1998, 83). Previously, he had used the term "Emperor Yao" (*Tang Yao* 唐尧), referring to a legendary Chinese ruler, as a metaphor for Mao, but he sought a better analogy (Su 2007, 48; Zhen et al. 2003, 54). Inspiration came when Li heard the lyrics of another *yangge* leader, Qu Shicai 屈士才, during the Spring Festival of 1942, who sang:

> Chairman Mao is just like a lamp,
> Casting light that makes the whole house bright.
> *Mao Zhuxi haobi yi zhan deng,*
> *Zhaode quanjia ming you ming.*
> 毛主席好比一盏灯，
> 照得全家明又明。(Quoted in Su 2007, 48)

While Li found this metaphor fresh and new, he also found it lacking: a lamp could only illuminate a cave dwelling (*yaodong*, the typical style of home in northern Shaanxi Province), or one household, and thus could not reflect the greatness of Chairman Mao. Su Jian (2007, 48) narrates the story as follows: "At night, Li Youyuan went home and sat beneath the light of an oil lamp. Lost in thought, he took off his hat and covered the lamp. Right away, the interior of his cave dwelling was immersed in darkness. He thought, 'If a lamp can be extinguished this easily, how can it be compared to Chairman Mao?' He made a decision to himself to write a *yangge* song praising Chairman Mao that was better and more fitting."

Like the "Emperor Yao" metaphor before it, the "lamp" metaphor was also found lacking (Zhen et al. 2003, 54). There are several versions of what happened next and how Li came upon the metaphor that would better capture the essence of Chairman Mao's greatness. One reads, "On a winter's night in 1942, as Li Youyuan rested after carrying buckets of excrement [used for fertilizer] on a shoulder pole, his body shivered with cold. Just at that moment, a huge red sun rose from the East, casting a bright-red light over the entire earth, casting its warm rays over Li Youyuan. Inspired by this, he composed, 'The East is red, the sun has risen, China has produced a Mao Zedong'" (Wei 1994, 36). Another version of the story has this: "One morning in the early winter in 1942, Li

Youyuan woke up at dawn and carried a set of buckets into the city. When he had almost arrived at the county town, suddenly, he saw that the East was bright red. A huge, majestic red sun emerged from the clouds, rising slowly. *It shined on the old city of Jiaxian, shined on the northern Shaanxi plateau, shined on the entire Motherland,* causing him to feel warm all over" (Su 2007, 48, emphasis added). A third version goes as follows:

> This morning, as Li Youyuan climbed from the western slope to the summit of a loess ridge, just then, a huge red sun arose from the East. This scene and this feeling sparked an inspiration in a folk singer talented both in composition and singing. Moved by the scenery, what a beautiful and magnificent mood it was! Look—the sun rose slowly from the East, bright red and exceedingly dazzling in its splendor, shining on Li Youyuan and filling him with happiness. He put down the hoe he had been carrying, held his breath, and focused in appreciation at the sight of the sunrise. The golden sunlight shined at an angle on the thousands of mountains and hillsides of the Loess Plateau.... As he looked and looked, a spirit of absolute sincerity surged in his bosom, and he burst forth in song. Using the melody from "Riding a White Horse,"[13] he sang out, "The East is red, the sun has risen; China has produced a Mao Zedong." (Wang Changfa 1998, 84)

The power of the sun imagery gains further nuance when we examine several aspects of these accounts. In each narrative, Li Youyuan is always alone—aside from Chairman Mao, no one else is mentioned. The smallness of this lone figure is contrasted with the grandeur of the surrounding scenery, replete with the numerous mountains and slopes of the Loess Plateau. We are constantly reminded of Li's association with the peasant class. Whether he is carrying night soil (Wei 1994, 36), carrying buckets with unnamed contents (Su 2007, 48), grasping a hoe (Wang Changfa 1998, 84), or on his way to sell vegetables in the county town (Wei 1994, 36), each of these actions connects him with idealized notions of the People, consistent with his honorary title "The People's Singer" (Wei 1994, 35). Regardless of what he is described as doing during the first part of the narrative, the key moment seems to be when Li witnesses the sun's sudden appearance and sings out his improvised melody. Facing the sun as he sings his creation, it is almost as if he is performing a serenade to the warmth that shines down upon him on behalf of the nation's people—an aspect I return to when I discuss Wang's performances of the song.

The sun metaphor proved superior to the "lamp" metaphor for several reasons.[14] Most obviously, the magnitude and reach of its brightness are far superior. Instead of merely illuminating the interior of one cave home, the sun could shine down on "the thousands of mountains and hillsides of the Loess Plateau" (Wang Changfa 1998, 84). This immediately brings to mind a strong connection with the land of northern Shaanxi. The term "loess" (in Chinese, literally "yellow earth" or *huangtu* 黄土) is strongly associated with the geography of this region, as well as its history of droughts and poverty, which would now be washed over by the "redness" of the sun's light. Two of the accounts of the composition of "The East Is Red" mention a coldness that causes Li to shiver—cold being another trope of poverty—and the subsequent warmth and comfort brought on by the sun (Wei 1994, 36; Su 2007, 48). This adds a tactile dimension (and full-body tactility at that) lacking in the lamp metaphor.

However, the sun does not stop there. Bursting beyond the reaches of the region, its rays extend to what might either be translated as "the entire nation" or the entire "earth" (*dadi* 大地) (Wei 1994, 36; Zhen et al. 2003, 54). The account that most closely coincides with Wang Xiangrong's description of "enlargement" progresses from the local to the regional to the national reach of the sun's rays: "It shined on the old city of Jiaxian, shined on the northern Shaanxi plateau, shined on the entire Motherland" (Su 2007, 48). In this way, it reaches the level of providing a "sonic dimension" of nationalism, as described by Sue Tuohy (2001), wherein music functions as "performances of the social imaginary" (108, 124). Thus, through altered imagery, the geographical symbolism of "The East Is Red" was expanded from the extremely local (a small cave home) to the global.[15]

In an a cappella version of "The East Is Red" discussed below that Wang performs in concerts, he draws on this geographical evolution of the lyrics, following the song from the time it began as a local, Jiaxian County love song, "emigrated" from Jiaxian to the revolutionary base at Yan'an, and then became the nationally recognized "final version" around the time that the new nation was established. Wang took the geographical expansion of the song even further during a performance at a Christmas concert held in a five-star Yulin hotel on December 24, 2011, outlining the song's progression from "how the common people of Jiaxian sang it in the past" (*Jiaxian laobaixing guoqu shi zenme chang de* 佳县老百姓过去是怎么唱的) and how it "later became a global song across the whole world" (*houlai zhe biancheng yi ge quanqiu de qiuge* 后来这变成一个全球的球歌). This geographical expansion from a regional folk tune to a "solemn, dignified, stately ode" has been further paralleled with the journey made by Chairman Mao; in detailing the song's transformation, Zhao Shimin (1994) writes, "Mao Zedong also went from being an ordinary person to becoming a giant" (79). As Wang Xiangrong adapted versions of the song over the course of his career, he incorporated stories of Li Youyuan and the song's roots in earlier folk songs into relevant performances set in contemporary contexts.

Performing the Regional Singer

Just as these newer sung personae reframe local roots (Qileng village and Jia-xian County) as representations of the larger region (northern Shaanxi Province), singers must also carefully present their own place-based identities in ways that acknowledge different audiences as they negotiate their status as regional representatives. Every singer is from a particular place, and yet "regional" singers must demonstrate their ability and authority to represent the region in ways that are "visitable." This is less of an issue when performing outside of the region, since outsiders' knowledge of subregional differences is limited, but in different localities within the region a singer's assumption of regional representation can highlight tensions between local and regional identities. Audience members might ask, "What right does this singer—from another part of the region—have to represent us?" If the song they sing is from another locality, the audience may wonder, "Why is this song from a distant village representative of our region, while our local songs are not?" Like singers, songs are associated with particular localities, and when a song from one locality becomes part of the common repertoire of songs representing the region, problems can arise. On the other hand, if the song is a local one but the "regional" singer is from another locality, the audience may ask, "What authority/claim does this singer have to sing our local song authentically?" Does a singer who is not from Jiaxian have the right to sing "The East Is Red" to an audience of Jiaxian people? How should he present the significance of his performance of the song? In essence, what right does a singer have to represent a place any larger than the village in which they grew up? Thus, subregional tensions between locality and region affect both songs and singers and must be dealt with, in part, in conversation with the audience. Performances outside of the region also involve conversations with audiences, often involving questions of how songs are to be understood in different contexts. What happens, for example, when the local connotations associated with a song's imagery and/or sung personae no longer apply? How does the singer establish a sense of connection with the audience while also reinforcing unique place-based identities? These are some of the issues that must be negotiated, often through onstage speech, as "regional" singers perform within and outside of the region.

When Wang Xiangrong performs in northern Shaanxi and elsewhere, he shifts his presentation of self and the songs he sings in response to the way in which he perceives each audience. Often framing his performances as a visit from afar—either arriving from distant northern Shaanxi to cities such as Xi'an or returning to his home region after having been away for a long time—Wang uses his arrival to convey good wishes to the audience from a visiting

Other. The Otherness with which Wang presents himself reflects his vision of the audience as a group and how he chooses to relate to that group. Depending on the context, he may frame himself as an individual (as he sometimes does in his hometown area), a member of the older generation (when younger audience members are present), a Xinmin person (when he wants to affirm his solidarity with a crowd in his home township), a Fugu person (when he wants to do the same with a crowd in his home county), a northern Shaanxi person (to consolidate subregional differences and/or provide a foil for other groups), or a Chinese person (when performing abroad, talking with foreign researchers, or speaking with others about his ability to represent Chinese culture).

Wang's statements of place-based identity—local, regional, provincial, and national—seem to occur in situations where he finds the need to draw a line between bounded groups—including some people while excluding others (cf. Bauman 1972; Barth 1969). In the performances I observed, he would often draw these distinctions during his speeches onstage before and after singing, using the phrase "on behalf of" (*daibiao* 代表) followed by identities ranging from the individual ("myself") to the region ("northern Shaanxi people"). In certain local contexts where he may have felt that it would be too presumptuous to claim to represent the locality or the region (since he was now living in Xi'an), Wang would fall back to presenting himself as an individual. For example, when addressing a local audience in his home county around the time of the Chinese New Year in 2012, he said, "Greetings, relatives and fellow villagers. First of all, *on behalf of (daibiao)* myself, I would like to wish everyone an early Happy Chinese New Year, and to wish everyone an auspicious Year of the Dragon."[16]

However, at another event around the same time, Wang addressed the central Shaanxi audience at a large-scale, televised Chinese New Year's gala performance as a representative of northern Shaanxi: "First of all, *on behalf of (daibiao) our northern Shaanxi elders,* I wish a Happy Chinese New Year to the elders, local people, and villagers of Mei County, the leaders, and the friends out there sitting in front of their televisions!"[17]

In the local event, Wang's visiting Otherness was that of a local who had been away for a long time, achieved fame in the process, and returned home to wish everyone a happy new year. On the other hand, in the central Shaanxi performance he chose to represent the northern part of the province to its central inhabitants—an Other both distinct from and part of their own provincial identity.

Wang's use of the regional "northern Shaanxi" identity in many ways serves as an amorphous bordering Other that pivots between those within the region and those outside—it sits in a usefully ambiguous space between the audience's sense of self and their experience of difference. Revolving around this regional image, Wang's performances, like those of other song kings and queens, bring together disparate subregional groups and provide a sense of rural roots and tradition for outsiders. This promotion of group solidarity works in contrast to the potential threat to that solidarity imposed by individual songs and singers, which often tend to be associated with specific localities and thus point to fractures within the group. In the central Shaanxi example, if Wang had introduced himself as representing "Marugeda people," the audience would have been confused—they had probably never heard of that small mountain village and wouldn't know how to relate to it. If Wang had chosen to represent "Fugu County people," it would have merely framed his conversation with the audience as that of one county visiting the other. By choosing to represent "northern Shaanxi," he honored Mei County with the visit of an entire region, while at the same time promoting a sense of provincial identity that incorporated different localities.

Wang's regional identity not only provided a visiting Other for other regions but frequently proved useful in bridging subregional differences. At a wedding in Xi'an where the bride's and groom's families came from different counties of northern Shaanxi (Qingjian 清涧 and Zizhou 子洲), Wang—a native of a third county, Fugu—could potentially have been seen as an outsider. However, by declaring his "northern Shaanxi" identity, he assumed authority within the context of the event while glossing over differences that might threaten group solidarity: "Dear fellow villagers, friends, and relatives from our Qingjian, from Zizhou, and all of those from Xi'an, good day to you! I [am speaking] both *on behalf of* (*daibiao*) the groom's family and *on behalf of* (*daibiao*) the bride's family. Why? Because I am a real (*didao*) northern Shaanxi person....Seeing everyone, I feel a deep familiarity and affection."[18] Here, Wang's role as a "real" northern Shaanxi person brushes aside the two families' different local ties, while at the same time positioning himself in relation to the Xi'an members of the audience. In a sense, his regional identity served as a bridge between disparate audience segments, providing a "folkier" counterpart to the more urbane central Shaanxi cousins, while at the same time offering an umbrella identity for the two families' localities. By focusing on Wang as an embodiment of northern Shaanxi identity, audience members from Qingjian, Zizhou, and Xi'an could find a way to come together and relate to each other on this happy occasion.

In addition to people, songs also have local identities, even those that have since become known as "regional" songs. Given that the popular repertoire of northern Shaanxi folk songs includes pieces that are said to have originated from particular localities in the region, Wang's performances of those songs could potentially be criticized as inauthentic—after all, if songs are tied to local geography, does someone from another locality have the right to sing them? Once again, Wang's "northern Shaanxi" identity has proved effective in glossing over these subregional differences. This was the case when Wang introduced "The East Is Red" to a group of bankers at a large annual company banquet in an upscale hotel in Yulin city, the capital of Yulin Prefecture. As mentioned earlier, the song is commonly known to have originated in Jiaxian, one of the counties in Yulin. Since there were likely at least some individuals from Jiaxian in the audience and Wang is from another county, his singing of a Jiaxian song could have been critiqued for a lack of local authenticity. Sensing this, Wang preemptively formulated a challenge for himself and the audience—to see how authentically he could sing the song: "Everyone see how authentic (lit. "thick") my Jiaxian flavor is. I am from Fugu, I should make that clear, but I am still... almost the same. When people ask where [I am from], I am a *real*

Figure 3.2 (a) and (b) Yulin City, Shaanxi. 2012. Photographs by author.

(*didao*) *northern Shaanxi person.* In fact, I *am a real* (*didao*) *northern Shaanxi person,* no one can replace me. Thank you all"[19] (emphasis added).

Yet again, Wang's "northern Shaanxi" identity rhetorically trumps any subregional differences. His claims to regional authenticity ("a real northern Shaanxi person") can be understood in part as diverting audience attention from potential criticisms of local inauthenticity, while simultaneously reinforcing his authority as a representative of the region. These claims to an authenticity rooted in physical terrain seem to offset the otherwise amorphous quality of regional identity—they ground it. While localities embody visible plots of land and nations can be "seen" through their flags and maps, regions—as somewhere in between—need to be anchored to images that can pivot between locality and nation. One such image is the singer who connects audiences to a broad patch of land through song.

"The East Is Red" Onstage

Wang performs two different versions of "The East Is Red," depending on the occasion and the people he perceives to be in the audience. The first version, developed in the 1990s, was produced for a televised music video. Wang refers to this as the "MTV East Is Red" ("MTV Dongfang hong" MTV 东方红).[20] Originally staged with a multitude of dancers, the prerecorded MTV version contains orchestral and choral accompaniment, together with a driving rhythm in the middle section. With its upbeat tempo and pulsing cadence, the MTV version appears to be a key example of what Gregory Lee (1995, 102) refers to as "Maoist disco-beat musical eulogies." Wang later developed an a cappella version of "The East Is Red" during the early 2000s. This second version, running between six and eight stanzas, is much longer than the MTV version. In the a cappella version, Wang uses each stanza to evoke a different historical period in the song's development, which he metonymically ties to the history of northern Shaanxi and China itself. Whereas Wang would use the MTV version as a dramatic beginning to his performances, he would usually sing the a cappella version at the end as an artistic finale.

In addition to considerations of the order of songs included in a performance set, the choice of which of these two versions of "The East Is Red" to sing on a particular occasion has a lot to do with Wang's estimation of the composition of the audience and the nature of the event. When I asked how he decides which version to sing in a given context, he said,

> If there are many people [in the audience] who are involved with music, or if it's a gathering with friends, singing the a cappella version is more

suitable. For those who are professionally engaged in music appreciation or musicians, they prefer things to be sung a cappella. Now, as for the MTV–style format, most often when I perform the official "East Is Red," people [e.g., the event organizers] specifically ask for this music. When you say, "The East Is Red," then it must be sung according to that version. That version is most often sung for political occasions...performances of a political nature.

In eleven performances where I observed Wang perform "The East Is Red," he sang the MTV version three times and the a cappella version eight times. Two of the MTV version performances were at formal celebrations commemorating the anniversaries of educational institutions, with references to their revolutionary history. One of these was for the eightieth anniversary of a university located on the outskirts of Xi'an, where Wang's performance was included in a sort of revolutionary medley, culminating at the end with Wang finishing the song while a gigantic portrait of Chairman Mao was projected on the screen at the back of the stage. The other was at the tenth anniversary of an elementary school in Xi'an associated with a prestigious local university. Both of these institutions specifically asked for this version of the song. A third occasion where he sang the MTV version was a wedding held in Xi'an, where a crescent-shaped crowd of guests stood before the stage and recorded Wang's performance with their cell phones, while the MC brought up the bride and groom, best man and maid of honor, and other guests in succession for photo opportunities while Wang was performing the song.

Whereas the MTV version tended to be the first (or only) song performed in certain venues, the a cappella version was always sung either last or second to last. The overall lineup of songs Wang would perform seemed to have a direct impact on the version he chose. In performances that I observed between 2011 and 2012, Wang would usually begin with dramatic, accompanied pieces and then transition to a cappella pieces—often humorous and/or unusual—for his finale. He always began with either the MTV "The East Is Red" or "The Infinite Bends of the Yellow River"—both accompanied, prerecorded songs. Presumably, Wang performed these recorded songs at the beginning to start off strong, meeting audience expectations of what the Folk Song King of Western China ought to sound like (and giving him a chance to warm up his voice if necessary), while the a cappella finales provided an intimate moment at the end to leave the audience with an entertaining twist. The shift from dramatic, accompanied pieces to humorous, a cappella pieces may also reflect another aspect of the expectations of stage performances—the overall order where certain pieces are considered appropriate for the beginning or finale of one's act, and only certain pieces may precede or follow others. A similar tendency to progress from serious to nonserious pieces during a performance has been observed in several cultural contexts, and future research should explore this further (cf. Casey, Rosenberg, and Wareham 1972, 399; Maring and Maring 1997, 37). This shifting during the course of a performance may be tied to another important aspect I look at later on—meeting audiences' expectations before playing with those very expectations.

In addition, audiences with large numbers of people from northern Shaanxi seemed to call for the a cappella version—perhaps performing such an iconic song to people from the region required a unique version to keep them engaged. While all of the three MTV version performances occurred in the vicinity of Xi'an—perhaps seen as a more urban and/or official stage—five of the eight a cappella version performances occurred in northern Shaanxi. There were two weddings (in Shenmu and Fugu), a Christmas performance at the People's Mansion Hotel in Yulin, an annual company party for a bank held at the same venue, and Wang's elementary classmate reunion in Fugu. Of the other three, one could argue that they all contained "music experts" of some kind and/or a larger number of people from northern Shaanxi. At an annual concert of the Northern Shaanxi Xintianyou Promotion Society in Xianyang (near Xi'an), where the audience included other singers, fans of northern Shaanxi folk songs, and many people from northern Shaanxi, Wang sang the a cappella version as his finale. As a special guest performance at the regional finals of a nationally televised singing competition, *Starlight Highway* (*Xingguang dadao* 星光大道), where there were judges and producers for the show, Wang also sang the a cappella version—ostensibly to showcase an artistically talented performance for the competition's contestants and the crowd at large. In addition, at the locally televised Chinese New Year's gala performance in Baoji, where the organizers specifically asked him to sing a cappella (without specifying a particular song), he sang the a cappella version as his finale.

MTV Version of "The East Is Red"

Wang's "MTV 'The East Is Red'" uses orchestral accompaniment and two choirs. The overture begins with a succession of notes struck on bells with the string section of an orchestra beneath.[21] After a high note is struck, the strings take over, horns enter, and the strings and horn section rise in a crescendo, culminating in an even higher note struck on a bell, which reverberates for several seconds as Wang begins to sing the first stanza unaccompanied. He personalizes the classic version of the song ("The East is red, the sun has risen") by calling out to the East and to the sun as two apostrophes. Prefacing each statement with "I say," he sings, "I say East, *you are the one who* is red, I say Sun, *you are the one who* has risen" (emphasis added). While the original lyrics appear as a past-oriented narrative, a story told with no attention paid to the storyteller, Wang's addition of "I say" introduces a new sense of subjectivity, brings the audience into a "lyric event" rather than "a representation of an event," and transforms Wang's song into a performative act (Culler 2015, 131, 137). Wang's sung persona is asserting that these statements are true. As the "I" calls attention to Wang the singer, Wang's calling out to the East as "you" and to the sun as another "you" sets up mutually constructing relationships between the lyric "I" and the two apostrophes. His sung persona constructs the greatness of those two entities, while simultaneously benefiting from their greatness—the persona is worthy of addressing them. In addition, the "I" of Wang's sung persona provides a connecting "and" for what would otherwise be disparate statements (Culler 2015, 54). Whereas "the East," "the Sun," "Mao Zedong," and "the People" might otherwise remain isolated images, the "I" connects them, suggesting that their meanings are intertwined. Wang's "I" provides a focal point around which the other entities Wang constructs in this song world revolve.

People I met during fieldwork pointed to this line as characterizing Wang's unique stylistic stamp on the song. Wang pronounces the "I" in a popularly understood northern Shaanxi dialect pronunciation (*nge* 额).[22] His use of dialect calls attention to the song's sung persona, which we can choose to envision as Wang the "Folk Song King of Northern Shaanxi," as an embodiment of the "peasant composer" of "The East Is Red," or as a peasant singer in general. Again, ambiguity is powerful. This sung persona embodies a dual identity, similar to the boatman in "Pulling Ferries throughout the Year." While clearly the voice of a peasant (Wang's dialect and clothing tell us so), this solo voice commands the authority to represent larger groups, reinforced by the voice's juxtaposition with choirs and orchestral accompaniment.

Wang's "MTV 'The East Is Red'" progresses from his solo, unaccompanied voice to the collective voices of a powerful, conservatory-trained choir of basses, and then an even more expansive four-part, mixed-gender choir alternating lines with Wang before concluding the song. In the first stanza, Wang's solo, peasant voice seems to embody the "subjective in the collective," constructing the greatness of the East, the sun, and Mao Zedong as a symbolic voice of the people (Frith 1996a, 110). When Wang is accompanied by dancers in large-scale performances, the dancers stay relatively still during this first stanza, keeping the focus on Wang and his unaccompanied voice. The second stanza begins with the *rat-a-tat-tat* drums of a marching band, quickening to a regular steady beat that accompanies Wang as he sings a more or less standard version of the song. Whereas Wang uses the first stanza to establish the characters—the East, the sun, Mao, the People—he uses the second stanza to lay out the narrative, animating the audience for what follows. Moving to the beat of the drums, Wang and the dancers spring into action. Wang ends with a high note on "liberator" (*jiuxing* 救星), holding the tail end of the word as the orchestra's string section rises in a crescendo and the bass section of the choir begins to sing the third stanza. The deep, male voices of the bass section seem to embody the determination of the Communist Party as they sing about the CCP bringing liberation to the people. The chorus acts as a "revolutionary bod[y]" (Billings, Budelmann, and Macintosh 2013, 4). The role of progressives in liberating the population as a whole is further expressed in the transition to the fourth stanza, where the entire choir repeats lines about the People being liberated by the CCP—this time in four-part harmony. In the following interplay between Wang's voice and the choir, the voice of a representative peasant echoes the nation-representing choir's statements before the individual and collective merge, the peasant's voice fades, and the choir rises to a sustained high note.

Looking at the arc of the song, the choices in voicing and instrumentation appear to tell a story of the relationship between the individual and the collective. If Wang's sung persona is a representative peasant, the choir's bass section forms a "multiple persona"—what Edward T. Cone describes as "a group in which each member forgoes his individuality to take part in a common enterprise" (Cone 1974, 66). Given the lyrics the bass section sings, the basses seem to embody the CCP—a group of leaders representing the people. The full choir, in turn, represents an even larger "multiple persona" encompassing the nation as a whole (Cone 1974, 66). The repetition of the lines "Wherever there is the Communist Party, the People receive liberation"—first by the basses, then by the entire chorus—suggests the relationship between these two personae: when sung by the basses, the lines emphasize the CCP's power in bringing about liberation; when sung by the full choir, they bring focus to the People who have benefited from that liberation.

Wang's role in relation to the choir is like a lead singer in a group serenade. He calls out to the beloved—in this case the East and the sun—publically projecting the audience's feelings in a way that is beyond what they could do themselves. Wang's addressees remain at a distance, like the beautiful girl in a serenade, and his calling out to them gains meaning through the presence of others (cf. Žižek 2005). The chorus, when joining Wang, offers the popular approval of the vox populi, while the audience members give tacit approval by silently observing—a meaningful silence (Noyes 1995, 91). The audience's presence in a public display of feelings is key to the socialization of emotions.[23] Through the juxtaposition of Wang's sung persona and the chorus, the song emphasizes the interconnectedness of the individual, the People, the nation, and its leaders. The common people (symbolized by Wang's voice) are necessary in constructing the greatness of leaders (Mao Zedong and the Communist Party), who in turn benefit the People. Wang's voice reminds listeners that popular support is crucial for effective leadership—one cannot be considered great until another person "says" one is great and other people follow suit. Whereas in the first half of the song, Wang's solo voice builds up the greatness of the collective voices that follow, after the song reaches a miniclimax when the four-part choir sings about the People's liberation in the fourth stanza, Wang's sung persona now echoes the choir—suggesting that the People continue to express gratitude for the benefits they have received. Both the choir and Wang's sung persona now sing the same message (the East is red and the sun has risen), suggesting that China has arrived, but they do so in distinct voices—the choir in Mandarin, using the standard lyrics, and Wang in his idiomatic, subjective phrasing. The juxtaposition and merging of voices resonates with the "couple going out" paradigm, here with the nation's future acting as a the "other" space into which the couple travels. The choir's voice suggests this to be a collective narrative, and Wang's voice seems to say, "I think so too, based on my own experience." The individual and the collective boost each other, merging into one.

"MTV 'THE EAST IS RED'" ("MTV 'DONGFANG HONG'" MTV 东方红)[24]

Wang:
I [*nge*] say East, you are the one who is red,
I [*nge*] say Sun, you are the one who has risen.
Say China has produced a Mao Zedong,
He is the Great Liberator of the People.
Nge shuo dongfang ni ya jiu yi ge hong,
Nge shuo taiyang ni ya jiu yi ge sheng.
Shuo Zhongguo chu liao ge Mao Zedong,
Ta shi renmin da jiuxing.
额说东方你呀就一个红,
额说太阳你呀就一个升。
说中国出了个毛泽东,
他是人民大救星。

The East is red, the sun has risen,
China has produced a Mao Zedong.
He finds happiness for the People,
Hur hai, hur hai, hur hai, hur hai, hur hai hai hai,
He is the Great Liberator of the People.
Dongfang hong, taiyang sheng,
Zhongguo chu liao ge Mao Zedong,
Ta wei renmin mou xingfu,
Hur hai, hur hai, hur hai, hur hai, hur hai hai hai,
Ta shi renmin da jiuxing.
东方红, 太阳升,
中国出了个毛泽东。

他为人民谋幸福，
呼儿嗨，呼儿嗨，呼儿嗨，呼儿嗨，呼儿嗨嗨嗨，
他是人民大救星。

Bass Section of Choir:
The Communist Party is like the sun,
Bringing brightness wherever it shines.
Wherever there is the Communist Party,
Hur hai ya,
The People receive liberation.
Gongchandang xiang taiyang,
Zhao dao nali nali liang.
Nali you liao Gongchandang,
Hur hai ya,
Nali renmin de jiefang.
共产党像太阳，
照到哪里哪里亮。
哪里有了共产党，
呼儿嗨呀，
哪里人民得解放。

Choir (Four-Part Harmony):
Wherever there is the Communist Party,
Hur hai ya
The People receive liberation.
Nali you liao Gongchandang,
Hur hai ya,
Nali renmin de jiefang.
哪里有了共产党，
呼儿嗨呀，
哪里人民得解放。

Mixed Choir:
The East is red…
Dongfang hong
东方红……

    Wang:
    Say East, you are the one who is red…
    Shuo dongfang ni ya jiu yi ge hong
    说东方你呀就一个红……

Mixed Choir:
The sun has risen…
Taiyang sheng
太阳升……

> **Wang:**
> Say Sun, you are the one who has risen...
> *Shuo taiyang ni ya jiu yi ge sheng*
> 说太阳你呀就一个升......

Mixed Choir:
The East is red...
Dongfang hong
东方红......

> **Wang:**
> Say East, you are the one who is red...
> *Shuo dongfang ni ya jiu yi ge hong*
> 说东方你呀就一个红......

Mixed Choir:
The sun has risen...
Taiyang sheng
太阳升......

> **Wang:**
> Say Sun, you are the one who has risen...
> *Shuo taiyang ni ya jiu yi ge sheng*
> 说太阳你呀就一个升......

After the MTV version was produced, the TV station that put it together gave Wang a complete recording including his recorded voice on a CD. When Wang performs this version, he uses the recorded version, lip-synching, as he does with the recorded MTV version of "The Infinite Bends of the Yellow River." On a few occasions, I asked Wang why he didn't sing this version live. Once, he told me that the TV station had not given him a copy that just included the background orchestra and choir. Another time, he mentioned that it was difficult for certain sound technicians to successfully balance the background choir and his voice if it was live-miked.

A Cappella "The East Is Red"

Unlike the prerecorded MTV version, Wang's a cappella version of "The East Is Red" has a flexible length, with a variable number of stanzas.[25] All of the song's stanzas, with two exceptions, come from versions originating in different historical periods during the development of "The East Is Red." In piecing these stanzas together into a narrative, Wang develops a male sung persona who travels through the various periods of the song's development corresponding to the nation's history before and after the founding of the People's Republic of China. Through contrasting tempos and delivery in each stanza, Wang works to bring the audience into the song world.

Wang acknowledged composing the first stanza of this version, evidently piecing together traditional oral formulae. In the first verse, Wang lays out two of the song's protagonists—the male sung persona (Third Older Brother, the male persona who appears in revolutionary-era verses of the song) and his beloved (referred to as "Little Sister")—and establishes the narrative arc. Third Older Brother is leaving on a long journey and faces an unknown future. The next two stanzas come from traditional folk song verses. According to Wang, in the song's historical narrative, these first three stanzas belong to the time before the revolution and involve "local reflections on love between a man and a woman." He added that the three stanzas' lyrics (including his composed first stanza) "were completely in the *xintianyou* style" and "did not touch at all on politics."

The following stanzas enter into the Revolutionary Period and the Yan'an era, before moving on to the period after the revolution succeeded. The fourth stanza forms a turning point from romantic love to revolutionary fervor (cf. Haiyan Lee 2007). Set during the War of Resistance against Japan and one of the verses most often pointed to as the precursor to "The East Is Red," this verse, in its placement in Wang's narrative, suggests a tension between Third Older Brother's love for his girl and his evolving love for his country. Whereas the second stanza uses images of rustic, home-cooked food as a metaphor for the couple's connection and mutual support, by the fourth stanza, Third Older Brother has journeyed far away without her and must depend on the provisions of the Eighth Route Army. He desires to go back to his beloved but resigns himself to fighting the Japanese with the Eighth Route Army. Now facing a foreign Other, Third Older Brother responds to that Other together with the army, forming a new sense of self. We can think of Third Older Brother and the Eighth Route Army as another couple who form a new shared identity as revolutionary citizens with a national conscience as they head out into the battlefield with Japan.

By the fifth stanza, the male sung persona now embodies the "we" of the region's poor, and the group of poor peasants form a couple with Chairman Mao in the newly created space of the Shaan-Gan-Ning Border Region, heading toward the new territory of a liberated nation. In the sixth stanza, which Wang seems to perform only on more official occasions, soldiers and civilians join together (another couple) as they head toward Yan'an for government-instituted resettlement, building a new life of happy production together.[26]

The seventh stanza follows Wang's MTV version, inserting his innovation— "I say" sung in dialect (*nge shuo*) and direct address of "the East" and "the sun." In the context of Wang's a cappella version, this stanza seems to do several things. First, it inserts Wang's innovative voice—highlighted in the subjectivity of regional dialect—into the arc of the song's development. Second, whereas the earlier stanzas can essentially be interpreted as past-oriented narratives, Wang's "I" once again brings the audience into a "lyric present," which has the added effect of bringing what would otherwise be disparate historical snapshots into the immediate experience of the audience (Culler 2015, 289). As discussed earlier with regard to the MTV version, Wang's solo voice adds an individual subjectivity to what would otherwise be a collective voice. It also positions Wang as someone with the authority to tell this story—drawing on its authority as tradition, while at the same time inserting himself as someone who has a unique viewpoint worthy of the audience's consideration (cf. Bauman 2004, 28). Having emphasized his relevance as a singer, Wang sometimes continues with an upbeat rendition of the eighth stanza (the standard song's first stanza) and ends with a fast, forceful, and loud performance of the ninth stanza.

Before each performance of this song, Wang frequently gave a spoken introduction of variable length outlining the song's historical development. When pressed for time, such as in the following example from a Shenmu wedding on November 10, 2011, where there were many invited performers and Wang had to finish quickly, he gave a bare-bones outline of the development of the song: "I will sing another song, a cappella, for everyone. Since I've come back, I'll take 'The East Is Red,' a Jiaxian folk song, from a *xintianyou* to 'Migration Song' ('Yimin ge' 移民歌) and then on to 'The East Is Red'—this history of [its] development—and sing a stanza for each historical period. Everyone can listen to the flavor of our old home."[27] At a wedding in Fugu on January 6, 2012, where things were a bit more relaxed, he introduced the song at greater length:

"The East Is Red" is a Jiaxian love song. [With that melody] one could sing about love between men and women and *whatever* one wanted to. Whatever you saw, you could sing about it, and whatever you thought, you could sing about it too. When Chairman Mao Zedong brought the Central Red Army to northern Shaanxi, only then did it become a revolutionary folk song. During the War of Resistance against Japan Period, it was called "White Horse Melody" ("Baima diao"). [*Recites lyrics from that version*] During the Great Leap Forward…[*Recites lyrics from that version*] In the period just before the founding of the People's Republic of China, it was finally named "The East Is Red." I will take the history of the development of "The East Is Red" and sing a bit from each historical period. Everyone can hear a little bit of the flavor.[28]

This introduction is almost word for word the same way he introduced it at the regional finals of a national singing competition in Liquan County, central

Shaanxi, on May 15, 2012. However, in the latter, instead of introducing it as a "Jiaxian love song," he introduced it as a "northern Shaanxi love song"—again adjusting his presentation of the song to meet his audience (central Shaanxi people who may not be familiar with the counties in northern Shaanxi).[29]

"A CAPPELLA 'THE EAST IS RED'" ("QINGCHANG 'DONGFANG HONG'" 清唱东方红)[30]

Say, in the bright, blue sky floats a cluster of clouds,
Today, Third Elder Brother is setting off for a journey a long way from home.
But the blowing wind, the pouring rain, the rumbling thunder, *hur hai ya*,
Make my beloved girl feel uneasy.
Shuo lan ge yingying tian piao lai yi ge dada yun,
San gege jin le tian yao chu yuanmen.
Guafeng xiayu xiang leisheng, hur hai ya,
Dao jiao nge meimei bu fangxin a.
说蓝格莹莹天飘来一格垯垯云，
三哥哥今了天要出远门。
刮风下雨响雷声，呼儿嗨呀，
倒叫额妹妹不放心啊。

The sesame oil lamp is clear and bright,
Cabbage hearts braised in sesame oil.
Red string beans with the fibers removed, *hur hai ya*,
Neither of us can disregard our own conscience.
Mayou deng na liang you ming,
Zhimayou hui liao xie baicai xin.
Hongdou jiaor jiaor shuang chou liao jin, hur hai ya,
Shui ye buneng mei liangxin.
麻油灯那亮又明，
芝麻油烩了些白菜心。
红豆角儿角儿双抽了筋，呼儿嗨呀，
谁也不能昧良心。

Snow-white buckwheat flowers,
Third Younger Sister is truly beautiful.
Glistening, beautiful eyes, *hur hai ya*,
Looking at them, I feel my emotions stirred.
Qiaomai hua bai ge shengsheng,
San meimei zhang di shizai shi jun.
Maohua yanyan na shui ge lingr lingr, hur hai ya,
Kan di gege nge dong liao ge qing.
荞麦花白格生生，
三妹妹长得实在是俊。
毛花眼眼那水格灵儿灵儿，呼儿嗨呀，
看得哥哥额动了格情。

Riding a white horse, carrying a foreign gun,
Third Elder Brother has eaten the Eighth Route Army's provisions.
I have it in mind to return home to see my girl, *hur hai ya*,
But fighting the Japanese, I cannot make it back.
Qi baima kua yangqiang,
San gege chi liao Balujun di liang.
Youxin huijia kan guniang, hur hai ya,
Da Riben jiu gubushang.
骑白马挎洋枪，
三哥哥吃了八路军的粮。
有心回家看姑娘，呼儿嗨呀，
打日本就顾不上。

The mountains and rivers are beautiful and Heaven and Earth are at peace,
Chairman Mao has come to our Shaan-Gan-Ning.[31]
Leading us poor people to fight for emancipation, *hur hai ya*,
Our border region, a slice of red.
Shan-chuan xiu tiandi ping,
Mao Zhuxi lai dao zan Shaan-Gan-Ning.
Lingdao zan qiongrenmen nao fanshen, hur hai ya,
Zanmen bianqu yi pian hong.
山川秀天地平，
毛主席来到咱陕甘宁。
领导咱穷人们闹翻身，呼儿嗨呀，
咱们边区一片红。

Emigrating is good, emigrating is good,
The Resettlement Policy has been launched.
Leaving Jiaxian and headed toward Yan'an, *hur hai ya*,
The soldiers and civilians are producing happily.
Yimin hao yimin hao,
Yimin zhengce zhankai liao.
Jiaxian qishen wang Yan'an zou, hur hai ya,
Junmin shengchan letaotao.
移民好移民好，
移民政策展开了。
佳县起身往延安走，呼儿嗨呀，
军民生产乐陶陶。

I [*nge*] say East, you are the one who is red,
I [*nge*] say Sun, you are the one who has risen.
Say China has produced a Mao Zedong,
He is the Great Liberator of the People.
Nge shuo dongfang ni ya jiu yi ge hong,
Nge shuo taiyang ni ya jiu yi ge sheng.
Shuo Zhongguo chu liao ge Mao Zedong,
Ta shi renmin da jiuxing.

额说东方你呀就一个红，
额说太阳你呀就一个升。
说中国出了个毛泽东，
他是人民大救星。

The East is red, the sun has risen,
China has produced a Mao Zedong.
He works for the happiness of the People, *hur hai ya*,
He is the Great Liberator of the People.
Dongfang hong taiyang sheng,
Zhongguo chu liao ge Mao Zedong.
Tai wei renmin mou xingfu, hur hai ya,
Ta shi renmin da jiuxing.
东方红太阳升，
中国出了个毛泽东。
他为人民谋幸福，呼儿嗨呀，
他是人民大救星。

The Communist Party is like the sun,
Bringing brightness wherever it shines.
Wherever our Communist Party is,[32]
Hur hai, hur hai, hur hai, hur hai, hur hai hai hai,[33]
The People will be liberated.
Gongchandang xiang taiyang,
Zhao dao nali jiu nali liang.
Nali you liao zan Gongchandang,
Hur hai, hur hai, hur hai, hur hai, hur hai hai hai,
Nali renmin de jiefang.
共产党像太阳，
照到哪里就哪里亮。
哪里有了咱共产党，
呼儿嗨，呼儿嗨，呼儿嗨，呼儿嗨，呼儿嗨嗨嗨，
哪里人民得解放。

Wang's varying presentations of these two versions of "The East Is Red" reflect considerations of audience, timing, occasion, geography, and other factors. While both versions of "The East Is Red" are Stageworthy—appropriate on large-scale stages—the existence of two versions and the considerations involved in their performance parallel deliberations involved in determining what songs are appropriate for other contexts beyond the large-scale stage. These alternative contexts, which I discuss in chapter 5, often call for additional sorts of songs, as the performer continues to gauge his/her audience.

The examples in this chapter point to complicating factors in representing the region through song. Though songs and singers may adopt broader, more ambiguous personae to gloss over subregional differences, the dangers of "metonymic misrepresentation" linger in local roots, language patterns, and repertoires of individual singers (Fernandez 1988a, 22). Nevertheless, we have seen how "small" songs were "expanded" into "big" songs in the construction of northern Shaanxi's regional identity. A large part of this transformation involved considerations of different performance contexts. Humorous, sometimes bawdy songs performed at rural Chinese New Year's festivities were transformed into dramatic representations of regional history presented on urban stages. Singers and composers altered tempos and lyrics, crafting new sung personae capable of bringing together disparate localities under the umbrella of the region. These nebulous personae—the Yellow River boatman, the peasant singer, the muleteer, and the shepherd—were general enough to be recognized by many, yet unique enough to be associated with the land of northern Shaanxi. Sitting between the self and Other, these personae and the singers who performed them glossed over subregional differences while providing a foil for other regions.

CHAPTER 4

Culture Paves the Way

As we saw in the drinking parties and spirit-medium rituals Wang observed as a youth, songs can bring individuals together while distinguishing the unique abilities of each—a function that continued, albeit on a grander scale, with the rise of song-and-dance troupes (cf. Shepherd 2005).[1] During Wang's professional career, the "gifts" of song performed by banquet attendees to strengthen their interpersonal bonds have been extended to regional governments' "gifts" of performances in cultural exchanges. Both banquets and sponsored performances are sites where gaps between participants (and larger entities with which they are associated) are made narrow through performance, bringing them together and setting them apart as they participate in the emergent flow of events (Shepherd 2005).

The performances of orchestras and song-and-dance troupes are often characterized under umbrella-like terms such as "American" and "Chinese"—powerful and amorphous identities shared by performing bodies as they travel from one place to another. The homes of performing groups and the places they visit ground those amorphous identities, connecting the place from which they originate (locality and nation) and the cities, regions, and nations where they are exhibited. These endpoints set up the parameters of a conversation where various parties participate, hoping to effect a shared meaning and a new perspective as they attempt to define themselves and other participants in the process.

In Wang's work in the Yulin Folk Arts Troupe, the use of performance to bring groups together while highlighting the uniqueness of each was essential. While in the smaller social events of his youth a performance's meanings were created by those present and others who heard about the event, in the large-scale international cultural exchanges of Wang's professional career his performances became relevant to several levels of society, leading multiple voices to engage in the conversation and urge recognition for their desired relationships. When performing abroad, although Wang and the Yulin Folk Arts Troupe had a say in repertoire selection and performance, other entities, including government officials, presidents, and CEOs of multinational corporations chose to comment on the performances in ways that positioned themselves and the groups they represented in relation to the other parties involved in those cultural exchanges. The performance events served as a site for those conversations.

In this chapter, I look at the rhetoric leading up to and surrounding an exchange of performances in the United States and China in which Wang was involved during negotiations for a joint venture between the Shenhua Group,[2] China's largest coal company, and the Dow Chemical Company, an American multinational chemical corporation. In 2008, Yulin—the site of the proposed venture—sent the Yulin Folk Arts Troupe to perform at a "Far East Meets West" event at Dow's global headquarters in Midland, Michigan. Dow later reciprocated by funding the U.S. National Symphony Orchestra's 2009 Asia Tour, with performances in key cities in China. This exchange of performances amidst the development of an economic partnership in many ways paralleled the use of gift exchange in the negotiation of interpersonal relationships. At the same time, the rhetoric surrounding the gift—a *regional* song-and-dance troupe's performance was described as offering an authentic *Chineseness*—ties into recent trends in provincial self-promotion that blur the line between the local and the national. Taken as a whole, the exchange of performances provides an excellent example of culture paving the way for mutually beneficial relationships between larger entities in an era of global capitalism.

Culture as a Bridge

Yulin's desire to use songs to establish and strengthen its relationships with other regions was not unlike the way individuals in Marugeda used songs to strengthen their bonds at drinking parties and communicate with the gods during rituals. Yulin's local government aspired to use northern Shaanxi folk songs as a "window" (*chuangkou* 窗口) through which other places could become familiar with the region. According to Wang,

> First, you would become familiar with northern Shaanxi folk songs. Through a means of culture, [the people promoting Yulin] would first get close to you and set up an exchange. Then, they would get you to learn more about Yulin, and finally about Yulin's economy. The slogan at the time was "culture paves the way, economics comes to sing the opera" (*wenhua pulu, jingji changxi* 文化铺路，经济唱戏). That means that cul-

ture first paves the road nice and good, and then the people who get things done, that is, the economic . . . it means that culture serves as a kind of medium, yes, a weapon for exchange. First, it would be through song and dance. We would go to your Shanghai or your Xi'an, or Yunnan or Beijing. In order to advertise the region of Yulin, first we would bring songs and dances from Yulin. After that . . . things from Yulin would gradually become more familiar and known by people in society, and the initial stages of this market would be set up.[3]

In each context, the goal of the performance was to make a connection with the audience, while at the same time highlighting Yulin's cultural uniqueness and investment potential. Over the years, Yulin has used several international tours and events to advertise the region. The Yulin Folk Arts Troupe has performed in France, Switzerland, Japan, and Brazil, in addition to the 2008 U.S. performance discussed below.[4] While it is difficult to gauge whether and to what degree Yulin's cultural exchanges contributed to its economic growth, the idea that "culture paves the way" appears to have driven much of Yulin's self-promotion in recent years. Several large-scale regional events have highlighted folk songs and folk singers as key cultural attractions. In 2006, Yulin held an international conference and fieldwork project on northern Shaanxi folk music in conjunction with the European Foundation for Chinese Music Research (CHIME), followed by two televised singing contests (2006 and 2010) in search of the "Ten Greatest Northern Shaanxi Folk Singers" (He Feng 2006; Zhang Xijian 2010). The Second Yulin International Folk Song Festival, held in 2007, showcased northern Shaanxi folk songs as one of three major world song traditions, along with Russian and African American folk songs (Chen 2007).[5] More recently, in 2009, northern Shaanxi folk songs were declared a national-level item of intangible cultural heritage, with Wang Xiangrong chosen as one of two national-level representative transmitters for the tradition, as mentioned earlier (cf. Zhao Le 2010, 5).[6] By 2012, Yulin had become known as "China's Kuwait" and was "a major energy and chemical industry base with the exploitation of coal, oil and natural gas" (Xinhua News Agency 2012). On May 24, 2012, the chairman of the Shenhua Group, Dr. Zhang Xiwu, was appointed chairman of the World Coal Association (WCA)—the first time in almost thirty years that the WCA would be led by a Chinese coal producer (World Coal Association 2012). Later that year, the mayor of Yulin presided over a meeting where it was announced that "students in Yulin . . . [would] enjoy totally free education from preschool through high school starting in 2013" (Chinese Business View 2012). Though Yulin's economy slowed soon after, its massive escalation at the time seemed to play into the narrative that cultural exchange brings economic growth.[7]

Yulin's "culture paves the way, economics comes to sing the opera" (*wenhua pulu, jingji changxi*) resonates with similar slogans across China (e.g., "trade [or economy] performing on a stage built by culture" [*wenhua datai, jingmao changxi*]), highlighting the ability of artistic exchange to establish mutually beneficial relationships, and many places in China have established song-and-dance troupes to advertise their localities (Jing Li 2013, 86; Mackerras 1984; Wilcox 2016, 374–375). Certain provinces have similar slogans catered to local industries. For example, Guizhou Province, which relies more heavily on tourism, has used the phrase "trade performing on a stage built by tourism" (*lüyou datai, jingji changxi* 旅游搭台, 经济唱戏) (Oakes 2000, 680). In addition, Wang's use of the term "window" (*chuangkou*) to describe the capacity of folk songs to place his region on the world's mental map is not unique. The use of terms like "window" and "bridge" are found elsewhere in recent discourse: initial joint ventures in areas of interior China have been referred to as "window enterprises," in that they highlight investment possibilities in a local area and may attract additional business ventures in the future (Oakes 1999, 45). A martial arts novel by the famous writer Jin Yong set in Dali 大理, Yunnan Province, has been described as a "bridge" bringing outside interest to that city, eventually leading to the transformation of the place itself. Beth Notar (2006) cites a Chinese scholar who compared the novel "to a *spatial and temporal bridge,* between Dali and the outside, the local and the global, the underdeveloped and the economically developed," saying, "this literary text would allow the place and people of Dali to cross over into prosperity" (4, emphasis added).[8]

Like Yulin, many places in China have established song-and-dance troupes to advertise their localities. Exchanges of performances, such as the Yulin Folk Arts Troupe's Midland performance and the National Symphony Orchestra's Asia Tour, fit into a long history of government- and corporation-sponsored cultural exchanges in China and the United States. A classic example was the famous Peking opera artist Mei Lanfang's 1930 U.S. tour, which was suggested by a departing American minister to China "in the interest of building closer ties between the Chinese and American citizenry" and funded in part by the "president of the Bank of China" (Guy 2005, 50; Joshua Goldstein 2007, 281). "Those who sponsored and cheered Mei's tour," notes Joshua Goldstein, "aimed to . . . wrest control over the representation of China abroad" (266). Mei Lanfang also toured Japan and the Soviet Union, and Peking Opera troupes from the People's Republic of China visited Western Europe in 1955, 1958, and 1964 (Tian 2012, 1; Guy 2005, 50).[9] One of the goals of the 1964 tour was "to promote mutual understanding and friendship" (Ching 1964, 16).

China has hardly been alone in using art to promote cultural understanding. The U.S. National Symphony Orchestra (NSO) that toured China following the Yulin Folk Art Troupe's Midland performance has a history of performances intended to facilitate relations. The NSO's first international tour in 1959 to "19

Latin and South American countries" was "undertaken as part of President Eisenhower's Program for Cultural Presentations, a project of the U.S. State Department, for the purpose of building goodwill throughout the region" (Kennedy Center 2012a). Danielle Fosler-Lussier (2010) has studied U.S. State Department–funded cultural exchanges involving musicians, and she cites a musician-turned-diplomat who suggests that the goals of such exchanges are to "create the conditions for understanding" (62). Meanwhile, in a study of ethnic minority folk song and dance performances sponsored by Yunnan Province at the 2007 Smithsonian Folklife Festival in Washington, D.C., Jing Li (2013) describes the "artifying of politics" (*zhengzhi yishuhua* 政治艺术化), a term used by a Yunnan cultural official that Li says "brings 'art' to the foreground on stage and endows 'art' with a seemingly apolitical position that officials hope will ease the crossing of boundaries and be identified with by all" (88–89). The foregrounding of cultural events as a means of shifting public opinion amidst negotiations resonates with Wang Xiangrong's description of using northern Shaanxi folk songs to help Yulin "gradually become more familiar and known by people in society." Wang, Li, and Fosler-Lussier all point to culture's ability to bridge gaps. They hint at the liminal space opened by cultural exchanges—a liminality offering the potential to realign relations and public opinion—similar to what banquet attendees experience when they are able to strengthen relationships with one another, or what audiences in gala events experience when they engage with a variety of familiar and exotic performances, repositioning themselves in the process (Victor Turner 1969; Shepherd 2005).[10]

The liminalities of banquets and gala performances intersect in an interesting anecdote about Mei Lanfang and his friend and playwright Qi Rushan: "When Qi and Mei entertained foreigners at Mei's home, they welcomed their guests into a carefully constructed 'ultra-Chinese' environment. Guests not only heard Mei sing, but they were also offered tea and snacks and sometimes a full meal. Peking opera was served as one course in a banquet of traditional Chinese culture" (Guy 2005, 49). Just as Peking opera became "one course in a banquet of traditional Chinese culture," in the case of the Midland celebration of Chinese culture and the reciprocal National Symphony Orchestra tour of China, Wang's performance of an *errentai* duet and the NSO's classical music concerts became symbolic gifts of "Chinese" and "American" culture in an exchange meant to bring various parties together while displaying the unique talents of each.

East Meets Midwest

In early 2008, during the process of setting up a joint venture coal-to-chemicals project in Yulin Prefecture between the Dow Chemical Company and China's largest coal company, the Shenhua Group, Dow funded a four-month celebration of China's rich cultural heritage in Midland entitled "A Celebration of China: Far East Meets West."[11] The celebration included an exhibit of two terra-cotta warriors and other ancient relics sent on loan from Shaanxi Province, as well as several performances. The exhibit, entitled "Timeless Warriors & Relics: 1500 Years of Ancient China" in English and "Yellow River Culture" (*Huanghe wenhua* 黄河文化) in Chinese, was put on display at the Alden B. Dow Museum of Science and Art, located at the Midland Center for the Arts, from January 20, 2008 to April 13, 2008 (Dow 2008a).[12] Dow's CEO Andrew Liveris and his wife Paula hosted the opening celebration for the exhibit, with the deputy director of the Shaanxi Provincial Cultural Relics Bureau, Zhang Wen, as their honored guest (Dow 2008c). Northwest Airlines cosponsored the festival with its key corporate client Dow Chemical by funding transportation costs for the forty-member Yulin Folk Arts Troupe, including Wang Xiangrong (Dow 2008c).[13]

The festival's performance series included both Western and Chinese works. The Midland Symphony Orchestra held a concert of Verdi, Mozart, and Dvořák featuring two Chinese pianists, Angela Cheng and Alvin Chow (Dow 2008b). The Yulin Folk Arts Troupe performed at several regional public schools, leading up to "a special ticketed public performance" on March 26, 2008 (MCFTA 2008b). At that concert, Wang Xiangrong performed a love song *errentai* duet, "The Flowers Bloom in May" ("Wuyue sanhua" 五月散花), discussed below. Both the concert of Western classical music and Wang's duet can be seen as metaphors for merging subjectivities—metaphors that then become sites for entities such as Yulin and the Dow Chemical Company to position themselves as valuable players in the evolving web of relationships.

The choice to include Western-trained Chinese pianists performing with the Midland Symphony Orchestra suggests an attempt to honor the hosting community by mirroring them—Chinese pianists showing an appreciation for Western classical music through expert performance in conjunction with the local orchestra. This collaboration forms one of the "couple" metaphors for the merging of subjectivities throughout the celebration, combining Chinese and Midwestern American appreciation of classical music—a celebration of shared aesthetic tastes, albeit from different points of view. In essence, the Chinese pianists' performances attempted to validate Midland, the Midwest, and America by embodying a positive appraisal from the outside, saying I see you, understand you, and appreciate you. This acknowledgment of the hosting community (together with the Yulin Folk Arts Troupe's visits to regional public schools) opened the way for the presentation of "Chineseness" that followed in the celebration's final performance.

Wang's performance of the duet "The Flowers Bloom in May" in the final event brings to mind a similar merging of subjectivities, once more building upon the "couple going out" paradigm. This love song *errentai* duet is a riddle song about flowers that bloom in each month. The song is future oriented, similar to the *errentai* duets celebrating the Chinese New Year discussed in chapter 2. By asking which flowers bloom in which months—metaphors for the "blossoming" relationship of the couple—the song leads listeners to think about relationships and flowers that will blossom in the future. The merging of subjectivities is reinforced by the alternation and union of the male and female voices, similar to what we saw in "Liancheng Pays a New Year's Call" and "Going to the Market." Once again, the couple is entering a new environment—a new relationship evolving amidst future months of blossoming flowers. As they comment individually on what they see, they take part in an exchange of "verbal gift giving," building a relationship instantiated on Mauss' "giv[ing]," "receiv[ing]," and "repaying" (Barbara Herrnstein Smith 1978, 91; Mauss 1966, 10–11). Then, uniting in a shared expression of a merged perspective, they come "to some extent share the same experiential environment" (Barbara Herrnstein Smith 1978, 91). What could be a more fitting metaphor for entities "flirting" with each other in the hopes of a "blossoming" joint venture?

"THE FLOWERS BLOOM IN MAY" ("WUYUE SANHUA" 五月散花)[14]

(M) What flo-flower blooms in the first month?
(F) The "spring-welcoming flower" [i.e., winter jasmine] blooms in the first month.[15]
(M) Which flower?
(F) The spring-welcoming flower.
(M) Which flo-flower?
(F) The spring-welcoming (MF) flo-flo-flo-flowers blossom, *ai le ai hai hai yo yo yo yo yo yo*
(M) Blooming in sevens, (F) Blooming in eights,
(MF) Blooming in sevens and eights, beloved by all.
(M) Seven *bu long dong na* (F) *Ai yo yo*
(M) Eight *ge na ge long dong* (F) in a ga-garden
(MF) One and one and one fresh flo-flowers, flo-flo-flo-flo-flowers blossom, beloved by all.
Zhengyue li lai shenme na hua hua kai yo kai?
Zhengyue li lai yingchun na hua hua hua hua kai yo kai.
Shenme na hua?
Yingchun lei hua.
Shenme na hua hua?
Yingchun hua hua hua hua kai, ai le ai hai hai yo yo yo yo yo yo,
Nai qi kai ba bu ya ge kai,
Na qi kai ba kai hua kai renren ai.
Qi bu long dong na ai yo yo,

Ba ge na ge long dong yi ge yuanr yuan,
Yi duo yi duo yi duo xianhua hua lei hua hua hua hua hua kai kai, hua kai na
  renren ai.
（男）正月里来什么（那）花花开（哟）开？
（女）正月里来迎春（那）花花花花开（哟）开。
（男）什么（那）花？
（女）迎春（嘞）花。
（男）什么（那）花花？
（女）迎春（齐）花花花花开, 哎嘞哎嗨嗨哟哟哟哟哟哟,
（男）乃七开（女）八不呀个开,
（齐）那七开八开花开人人爱。
（男）七不龙冬那（女）哎哟哟,
（男）八个那个龙冬（女）一个圆儿圆,
（齐）一朵一朵一朵鲜花花（嘞）花花花花花开开, 花开那人人爱。

The Western and Chinese performances during the festival modeled the merging of subjectivities, and we see a similar coming together of perspectives in various descriptions of the festival—an advertisement for the final performance, a speech given by a Yulin official during the closing ceremony, and two articles produced by Dow—all pointing to the theme of culture as a bridge that brings people together, while at the same time emphasizing the unique resources Yulin and Dow bring to the table. Each party highlights the value of the performance—its "authentic Chineseness"—while striving to showcase their resourcefulness in sharing that valuable commodity.

The venue's Web site advertised the Midland performance as a bridge to the exotic—one that would take you to "China." The event, entitled "Reflections of the Yellow River" in English and "Winds of the Yellow River—Sentiments of the Yellow Earth" ("Huanghe feng—Huangtu qing" 黄河风—黄土情)[16] in Chinese, was described as follows: "The Yulin Folk Art Troupe from the Chinese Province of Shaanxi will *transport you to a land of beauty and enchantment* through 'Reflections of the Yellow River,' a series of *traditional Chinese performances* featuring dance, acrobatics, and music" (MCFTA 2008a, emphasis added). The performances of this *regional* song-and-dance troupe were billed as both "traditional" and "Chinese," suggesting they represented the nation and its cultural history. Both "Chineseness" and "tradition" are vague, yet familiar-sounding terms perhaps intended to engage Midwesterner audience members who might be unfamiliar with places such as Yulin and Shaanxi. This advertisement, while framing the event's context as one of bringing people together through culture exchange, also suggested Chinese culture was a unique resource that the Yulin Folk Arts Troupe could provide.

The claim to Chineseness is characteristic of recent provincial attempts at self-promotion, where "promoting Chineseness is part of a strategy…to promote a cultural identity attractive to the 'flexible accumulation' of global capitalism" (Oakes 2000, 669).[17] Local claims to Chineseness have been especially common in areas such as northern Shaanxi that are "located in China's interior" and "relatively poor, with economies primarily dependent on agriculture and natural resource extraction," areas with "ancient, unique, and attractive regional cultures that... [could] be called upon to spur a dynamic, innovative entrepreneurialism and sense of self-confidence" (Oakes 2000, 675).[18] This rhetoric of "ancient, unique, and attractive regional cultures" serving as resources for "dynamic, innovative entrepreneurialism" was particularly evident in a speech given during the Yulin Folk Arts Troupe's Midland performance by the party secretary of the Yulin Municipal Party Committee and director of the Yulin Municipal People's Congress Standing Committee, Li Jinzhu 李金柱. In his speech, Li sought to establish common ground by first framing the event within the long history of U.S.–China relations, before focusing attention on Yulin's unique cultural and natural resources and its aspirations to use the relationship with Dow as a springboard to future collaborations with the American business community:

China and the U.S.A. are separated by vast oceans and have completely different historical backgrounds and social systems. However, for a long time, the people of these two countries have held deep feelings of mutual interest and friendship. *Yulin is situated in the northern part of Shaanxi. In addition to having a long history and a deep-seated culture, it also possesses abundant mineral products, energy sources, tourism and human resources, and is a national-level energy and chemical engineering base.* Our collaboration with the Dow Chemical Company has already drawn back the curtain, and we look forward to having more interest and participation from American businesses. At the same time, we also hope to develop a wide-ranging exchange with all walks of life in the U.S....

Culture is a *window* that reflects a nation's historical heritage and inner, spiritual world. It is also the best *bridge* for promoting mutual understanding between different peoples and communicating the heart and soul of the people. Our presentation today for everyone, "Winds of the Yellow River—Sentiments of the Yellow Earth," is an artistic performance with rich, local color. Simple and unadorned, straightforward and uninhibited, bold and powerful—this is the folk song and dance of the plateaus in the northern part of Shaanxi Province, which amply reflects the northern Shaanxi people's attitude of exerting oneself. The graceful, traditional ethnic music reflects the long-term accumulation of northern Shaanxi's long history and culture. This evening's performance will help the American people to gain a deeper understanding of China, and promote exchange and collaboration between the two great nations of China and America. (Wang Xuqin 2008c, emphasis added)[19]

After beginning with a description of the long history of "mutual interest and friendship" between China and the United States, Li immediately focused in on the specific area of Yulin, situating it within China and outlining its history, culture, and natural and human resources. Representing Yulin, Li did not mention the coal company with which Dow was planning to collaborate, but instead framed his speech in terms of Yulin's potential relationships with Dow and other American corporations, placing those relationships within the broader context of Sino–U.S. relations.

While the Yulin party secretary's speech highlighted the unique resources Yulin brought to the cultural exchange, Dow produced articles emphasizing its role as a powerful force in facilitating the exchange, pointing to the positive impact that economics could bring to local culture. Like Yulin, Dow foregrounded the potential for such exchanges to increase understanding between nations, but here, Dow focused on its ability to bring "Chinese" culture to the area surrounding its global headquarters. A public relations article posted on Dow's Web site, subtitled "Dow Contributes to Cultural Exchange Between U.S. and China," portrayed Chinese culture as a scarce, valuable commodity brought to the Midwest by Dow, "a diversified chemical company that combines the power of science and technology with the 'Human Element' to constantly improve what is essential to human progress" (Dow 2008a), as seen in the following excerpt: "Two authentic Chinese terracotta warriors have arrived in Midland, Michigan, the global headquarters of the Dow Chemical Company, as the centerpiece of a four-month celebration of the rich heritage of China. The 2200-year-old warriors will spend their first Chinese New Year in the U.S., and will be cultural ambassadors, sharing stories of the rich history of China" (Dow 2008a).

Framing the terra-cotta warriors as "one of the greatest archaeological discoveries of the twentieth century" and a link to "the ancient culture of China," the article suggests that visitors to the exhibit from all over the Midwest will have a chance "to come and learn about the mysterious Chinese culture first hand" (Dow 2008a). "Ancient" and "mysterious" point to a rare, exotic factor echoing the idea that the Yulin Folk Arts Troupe's performance would "transport you to a land of beauty and enchantment" (MCFTA 2008a). Both the terra-cotta warriors and the Yulin Folk Arts Troupe's performance are characterized by their "authenticity" and "Chineseness." The terra-cotta warriors were referred to as "authentic" and "ancient treasures," while the Yulin Folk Arts Troupe performance was described as "an authentic Chinese art performance" (Dow 2008a, 2008c).

While presenting itself as a broker of cultural exchange, Dow describes the benefits of that exchange differently when speaking to the public and when speaking to its own employees. Perhaps unsurprisingly, the public relations article, "Terracotta Warriors to Spend Chinese New Year in the U.S.: Dow Contributes to Cultural Exchange Between U.S. and China," stresses the benefits for the public at large, quoting Dow's CEO and chairman as saying, "As a global company with growing operations in China, east is meeting west in many exciting ways.... We are pleased to be able to sponsor this cultural exchange as a way to share some of China's important heritage with the people of this region" (Dow 2008a). Around the same time, in Dow's corporate newsletter, *Around Dow*, another article, "Far East Meets West: Dow Celebrates Relationship with China," quotes the CEO as emphasizing the beneficial business relationship that the exchange will foster: "Building a strong relationship with China is a top priority for Dow, and the benefits of this relationship can't be measured.... That relationship is built as we share our strengths with each other. *This kind of cultural exchange, based on trust and goodwill, lays the groundwork for a valuable, long-term relationship*" (Dow 2008c, emphasis added). Taken together, these two articles point to the benefits that cultural exchange can bring to the public and to business, highlighting Dow's role in each case. In the former, Dow serves as a mediator between countries (e.g., "Dow Contributes to Cultural Exchange Between U.S. and China"), while in the latter, it rhetorically places itself in a mutually beneficial relationship with a nation (e.g., "Dow Celebrates Relationship with China").

The Dow newsletter article concluded by discussing the next step in the budding relationship between Dow and Yulin: "The end of the Chinese festival actually marks the beginning of another cultural exchange. Party Secretary Li invited Dow to Shaanxi Province in 2009, to share U.S. culture with our Asian counterparts. It is too soon to say what that effort will be, but employees can be sure it will represent the company and the United States in true Dow fashion" (Dow 2008c). Eventually, Dow decided to share U.S. culture with their Chinese counterparts by sponsoring the 2009 Asia Tour of the National Symphony Orchestra of the John F. Kennedy Center for the Performing Arts, based in Washington, D.C. Although funded by Dow partly in reciprocation for Yulin and Shaanxi's Midland performance and exhibit, the NSO tour, with concerts in Beijing, Xi'an, Shanghai, Macau, and South Korea, was imbued with multiple levels of meaning (Kennedy Center 2012b). While the 2008 Midland event had been *rhetorically* placed within the context of Sino–U.S. relations, the NSO's 2009 Asia Tour was given a clear *official* dimension—it was formally invited by the Ministry of Culture of the People's Republic of China in order to celebrate the thirtieth anniversary of the establishment of diplomatic relations between the PRC and the United States and "to further Sino-U.S. diplomatic relations" (Kennedy Center 2009).

The Asia Tour also marked a ten-year anniversary of the NSO's first tour to China in 1999, when Jiang Zemin had invited it after hearing the NSO perform during his visit to Washington, D.C. in 1997. The National Symphony Orchestra has a history of being associated with U.S. national affairs, including presidential inaugurations and diplomatic goodwill missions, and its Asia Tour was treated as a significant event both by China and the U.S. (Kennedy Center 2009). The presidents of both nations sent congratulatory messages, with Hu Jintao pointing to music's ability to "promote communication between people's hearts of different countries" and "enhance the mutual understanding between the two peoples," and Barack Obama describing music as "a common language of the world that builds up intercultural bridges, pushes forward relations among peoples and nations, strengthens our understanding of history and tradition, and enriches our lives and communities" (China Embassy 2009).

Dow's CEO, in speaking of the tour, pointed to Dow's important role in the relations between the two countries, saying, "This year not only marks the historic anniversary of engaged and positive Sino-U.S. relations, but also the 30th anniversary of Dow's operations in mainland China. As a global company and as a long-standing member of the Chinese business community, Dow is pleased to be a supporter of this tour to showcase the strong cultural ties and increased understanding between China and the United States" (Dow 2009). While Shaanxi, Yulin, Shenhua, and the joint venture were not explicitly mentioned, the tour's destination cities included the capital of Shaanxi Province, Xi'an. An article posted on a Shaanxi news site highlights the business overtones of the NSO's Xi'an performance on June 14, 2009, citing numerous Shaanxi provincial officials who attended the performance and noting that earlier in the day, a member of the Provincial Party Standing Committee had met with a delegation of Dow executives for its Asia Pacific, Middle East, and Africa regions, during which time the Shenhua-Dow Coal-to-Chemicals Project was described as a signature project for Shaanxi's energy and chemical engineering base, with all of the preparatory work moving along at a rapid pace (Zhang Xin 2009).[20]

Though Dow's sponsorship of the NSO's 2009 Asia Tour appears to have been inspired by Li Jinzhu's request for Dow to reciprocate for the Midland performance by sharing U.S. culture with Shaanxi Province, the official rhetoric surrounding the tour focuses attention mainly on the music of the National Symphony Orchestra and its ability to serve as a bridge between nations. Even the article from the Shaanxi news site focuses primarily on the Xi'an concert, while relating the business dealings to the artistic event. Since Dow's sponsorship of the 2009 Asia Tour, it has continued to fund NSO performances amidst negotiations with various countries. Dow sponsored another cultural exchange in 2012—an NSO tour to Mexico, Trinidad and Tobago, Argentina, Uruguay, and Rio de Janeiro. According to Andrew Liveris, "After the re-

CHAPTER 5

Mediating the Rural and Urban

> How does this stranger engage with an audience, reconcil-
> ing the distance not of the stage to the floor but of different
> worldviews rooted in their different, respective social
> identities outside of the performance context?
> —Ian Brodie, 2014

Normally, you do not see performances that are not meant for you. At the CCTV Spring Festival Gala—an annual, nationally televised, four-hour event that has become a viewing tradition during Chinese New Year—audiences see performances chosen for a national viewership. At Wang's 2008 Midland performance, American audiences saw songs and dances chosen for them. At wedding banquets, guests see performances selected to meet their expectations. It is only when we stumble upon alternative versions of songs that we begin to see the complex considerations singers make in meeting each audience. In addition to Wang's performance of "Pulling Ferries throughout the Year" for the TV drama discussed in chapter 3, Wang sang other bawdy versions of the song for friends on various occasions. These additional versions point to different ways that song kings and queens traveling from place to place "read" and respond to audiences, highlighting underlying moral views about what it means to perform in public in China. Wang's discussion below of different interpretations of "erotic" material points to song performance as a site for discussions of public morality—a theme spanning from earlier song god legends to the present.

Moving between audiences, professional folk singers constantly negotiate which types of performance are appropriate for each event. During my conversations with Wang, he would often say that a particular piece could not be performed on a large-scale stage or in a public arena.[1] Two issues of particular concern seemed to be offending public mores—too "bawdy" or "superstitious"—and lacking the aesthetic qualities needed for the stage. However, I also found other contexts, such as gatherings with friends and meetings with folk song collectors, where the same "bawdy" or "superstitious" songs were appropriate. Whereas in chapter 3 I looked at what it means to be worthy of the stage ("Stageworthy"), in this chapter I discuss the ability of "good" singers to adapt performances to a range of contexts, finding material appropriate to each—

what I call (lowercase) *stageworthy*. Choosing songs and performance styles appropriate for an event involves audience-level categorization—performers gauge each audience's expectations and present material that engages without offending. As folk singers mediate rural and urban moral and aesthetic tastes, they address concerns shared by folk song collectors who struggle to represent and anthologize regional groups of the Folk. In what follows, I include discussions with two retired scholars in Xi'an who devoted their lives to folk song collection, research, and teaching—one of whom was involved in Wang's discovery. Both folk singers and folk song collectors mediate between place-based rural and urban moralities in their performances and the documentation of those performances. While singers select songs appropriate for particular audiences, folk song collectors in China and the United States face moral concerns regarding which songs to include in published collections and which to keep in private archives. Particularly "good" singers, as Wang notes below, are able to meet the expectations of their audiences and then take them for a ride.

Gauging Other Stages

While Wang's notion of "Stageworthiness" (see chapter 3) connotes the public presentation of a tradition with an eye towards representation to outsiders—what Catherine Ingram calls "going onstage to sing" (2012, 56) and Sara Davis refers to as "front stage" (2005, 22)—a closer look at the many performance contexts encountered by performers suggests a subtler gradation of song repertoire, with different versions corresponding to specific contexts, rather than a simple dichotomy between "public" and "private" or "insider" and "outsider." This spectrum, which I explore below with reference to "erotic" and "superstitious" songs, reflects the performer's ability to "read" different types of audiences and anticipate their reactions, a sensitivity frequently reflected in discussions about what pieces are "appropriate" for each occasion.

While spirit-medium tunes and bawdy songs like the festival tune mentioned in chapter 3 were not considered suitable for the Yulin stage, they did find other venues for performance in scholarly anthologies and at private parties among friends. Just as Wang playfully imitated spirit-medium tunes as a child, as an adult he also found opportunities to perform them as entertainment for friends. When folk song collectors were amassing material in the late 1970s for the *Big Anthology of Chinese Folksongs,* and again when the music scholar Qiao Jianzhong recorded Wang in Beijing in 1994, Wang found suitable "stages" (i.e., performance contexts) in which to perform spirit-medium tunes. Thus, although these songs were not suitable for performances on large-scale stages, they did find contexts where they were appropriate—what I am calling here (lowercase) *stageworthy*.[2] As I use it, the idea of *stageworthiness* includes pieces that an audience in a particular context expects, accepts, tolerates, and/or enjoys—everything except for pieces they reject, find boring, or those that disgust and/or anger them. As such, Stageworthiness with a capital S can be seen as a subcategory of lowercase *stageworthiness* that is limited to the expectations audiences have for stage performances, while lowercase *stageworthiness* encompasses a broader array of performance contexts, such as public performances, semipublic performances, private performances, performances for scholars, and casual performances for friends.

In addition to the somber and dignified, region-representing "Pulling Ferries throughout the Year" that Wang produced for the TV drama discussed in chapter 3, he would sing another version of the song when asked by folk song scholars and during intimate gatherings with friends. This bawdy version used some of the same lyrics, but presented the sung persona as a bravado playboy intent on having an affair with his wife's sister. Similar to the way Wang found suitable "stages" to perform spirit-medium tunes during visits from folk song–collecting scholars, he also willingly sang a version of this risqué ballad when a group of folk song collectors visited him in 2011 and asked for a bawdy one—locally referred to as a "sour tune" (*suanqu* 酸曲). This risqué version, while building on the bawdy boatman persona from the old festival tune, extends the sung persona in a more explicit direction—mentioning parts of the female anatomy in the third stanza and suggesting an affair between familial relations in the fourth:

"BOAT ROWING MELODY" ("BAN CHUAN DIAO" 扳船调)[3]

When you mention my hometown, it's known throughout the land,
On the banks of the Yellow River—Qileng Village.
For generation after generation, [we] have endured poverty,
Ai, I steer my boat, passing the time.
Tiqi wojia, jia youming,
Huanghe na pan shang Qilengcun.
Zuzu na beibei shou pinqiong,
Ai, banchuan na baidu wo guo shang le guangjing.
提起我家，家有名，
黄河那畔上七楞村。
祖祖那辈辈受贫穷，
哎，扳船那摆渡我过上了光景。

In my boat, there sits a white peony,
I take you, Peony, south to Jiangnan.
In Jiangnan, there's her man,
And she dumps this old boatman.
Ai hai ai hai hai hai yo,
And she dumps this old boatman.

Wo chuanli zuo de ge bai mudan,
Wo ban shang ge mudan ni xia Jiangnan.
Jiangnan na you ta de nanzihan,
Ba wo zhe lao shaogong jiu gechaozhuan.
Ai hei ai hei hei hei yo,
Ba wo zhe lao shaogong jiu gechaozhuan.
我船里坐得个白牡丹，
我扳上个牡丹你下江南。
江南那有她的男子汉，
把我这老艄公就圪超转。
哎嘿哎嘿嘿嘿哟，
把我这老艄公就圪超转。

That white cloth shirt opens at the chest,
Exposing a pair of white breasts.
I have it in mind to give them a squeeze,
But I'm afraid someone outside might see.
Ai hai ai hai hai hai yo,
But I'm afraid someone outside might see.
Baibu shan shan na liekai huai,
Luchu na yi dui dui bai nai nai.
Wo youxin na shangqu ba ta chuai,
You pa na waimian na ren kanjian.
Ai hei ai hei hei hei yo,
You pa na waimian na ren kanjian.
白布衫衫那裂开怀，
露出那一对对白奶奶。
我有心那上去把她揣，
又怕那外面那人看见。
哎嘿哎嘿嘿嘿哟，
又怕那外面那人看见。

Ai, sorghum is growing in the millet field,
In my bosom, the one I'm hugging is my wife's sister,
[I] call to her, "Sister-in-law, don't be shy,
I'm the same as brother-in-law [your husband].
Ai hai ai hai hai hai yo,
I'm the same as brother-in-law."
Ai gaoliang zhang zai na guzi di,
Wo huai libian bao le ge ta yiyi.
Jiao ta yi ni buyao xiu,
Wo he na ta yifu shi yiyang di.
Ai hei ai hei hei hei yo,
Wo he na ta yifu shi yiyang di.
哎，高粱长在那谷子地，
我怀里边抱了个她姨姨。
叫她姨你不要羞，

我和那他姨夫是一样的。
哎嘿哎嘿嘿嘿哟，
我和那他姨夫是一样的。

In a similar, three-stanza version collected earlier by another scholar, Wang sang first and third stanzas similar to the 2011 performance, but with an additional second stanza about climbing up a courtyard wall to see "Second Sister-in-Law" (*er yi* 二姨) and desiring to embrace and kiss her, but relenting due to the presence of annoying people (literally "headless ghosts" [*meitou gui* 没头鬼], pronounced *metou gui* in dialect) in the vicinity (Zhang Ruiting 2009, 59):

Ai, the sun comes out laughing tee-hee,
I'm climbing over a wall to see my wife's sister,
[I] have it in mind to hug her and give her a few kisses,
[But] there are some annoying people standing nearby.
Ai hai hai hai hai ai hai ya,
[But] there are some annoying people standing nearby.
Ai, taiyang chulai me xiaoxixi,
Wo qiangtou shang pazhe wo kan er yi.
Youxin na baozhu ta qin ji kou,
Genqian na zhan liao xie meitou gui.
Ai hai hai hai hai ai hai ya,
Genqian na zhan liao xie meitou gui.
哎，太阳出来么笑嘻嘻，
我墙头上爬着我看二姨。
有心（那）抱住她亲几口，
跟前（那）站了些没头（哦）鬼。
哎嗨嗨嗨嗨哎嗨呀，
跟前（那）站了些没头（哦）鬼。(Zhang Ruiting 2009, 59)

In both versions, the first stanza is similar to the song Wang composed for the TV drama. However, after assessing his audiences, Wang determined that the bawdier verses would entertain—they were *stageworthy*.

Scholars in China often use the term "sour tunes" (*suanqu*) to refer to songs of an erotic, bawdy nature from northern Shaanxi (cf. Zhang Ruiting 2009).[4] Different descriptions of this genre define it either by content or context.[5] In essence, the two are intertwined—for the content of a song to be deemed "erotic," the observer must make a value judgment regarding the public presentation of sexual matters. What is considered obscene or "off-color" is culturally determined, and often there is an interesting contradiction in social contexts where singing about sexual themes is considered wrong, while gossiping about others is not: "It is in the context rather than in the word or the subject. Perhaps the only thing I can say is that pornography, obscenity, lewdity, profanity, and erotica in general are determined by the manner in which they are received by the audience or treated by the informant. Roughly, when they are treated as taboo, they then fall into the above categories" (Beck 1962, 197, 198).

In China, "while the collecting of erotic folk songs has often evoked—and continues to evoke—strong resistance among scholars and government officials," Antoinet Schimmelpenninck's research on folk songs in southern Jiangsu Province found that "villagers largely accept erotic songs as an inherent—rather than shocking or 'immoral'—part of their song culture" (Schimmelpenninck 1997, 142–143). This divergence in views about bawdy songs is evident in certain earlier legends of song gods—such as Zhang Liang singing a flirtatious song to the Goddess of Mercy and being punished and placed under a mountain for it (Schimmelpenninck 1997)—and it is an ever-present issue for individuals who mediate between rural and urban groups in China, including professional folk singers and folk song collectors.

Mediating between Rural and Urban

The concern with how to represent rural populations to urban audiences underlies the work of professional folk singers and folk song collectors in China, bringing to light different frameworks for interpreting the content of songs. In what follows, I discuss some of the experiences of folk song collectors working in Shaanxi Province in the early 1950s, around the time of Wang's birth, to draw parallels between singers' needs to gauge the *stageworthy* and scholar-collectors' needs to produce "representative" folk song anthologies.

One of the people credited with discovering Wang Xiangrong in the late 1970s was the eminent northern Shaanxi folk song collector and scholar Yang Cui, whom I interviewed in 2001 with another retired folk song collector—the southern Shaanxi folk song expert Feng Yalan. During my conversation with Yang and Feng, they spoke at length about their experiences collecting folk songs as college students in the early 1950s and the differing moral and aesthetic views of folk songs they encountered.[6] These disparate points of view led to some of the difficulties the two young women encountered during collection trips in the early 1950s. Both Yang and Feng began collecting in Shaanxi Province in 1952, when they were students at the Xi'an Conservatory of Music. At the beginning of the 1950s, the State Cultural Bureau (*Guojia wenhua zhuguan bumen*) had made a call for "carrying on cultural heritage" (*jicheng yichan*) and "developing traditions" (*fayang chuantong*), and Music Work Groups (*Yinyue gongzuo zu*, abbreviated as *Yingongzu*), responsible for collecting and sorting all types of traditional Chinese music, were set up in every province (Qiao 1998, 327; Wang Yaohua 1999, 10). Based on this work, by the mid-1950s a succession of folk song anthologies, organized geographically, by ethnic group, or by song genre, began to be published (Wang Yaohua 1999, 10).

Yang Cui and Feng Yalan, working in northern and southern Shaanxi Province respectively, used their summer vacations to go to the countryside and later edited published collections and taught courses related to folk songs. While their comments and opinions are not representative of all collectors in all areas during that time period, they do offer insight into individual cases of the practice of folk song collection and related issues of moral judgment. The conversations that the collectors engaged in to gain access to the songs they sought, as well as their considerations of what to do with the material once collected, point to attempts to negotiate along the rural-urban spectrum of the understanding of folk songs. In the process of building trust before the actual collection of songs, the collectors spoke of attempting to "become one with the People" (*he laobaixing dacheng yipian*) by living, working, eating, and singing together with the people in the communities they stayed in. Yang Cui said that this way the people "would feel you didn't draw any lines between them and yourself." However, first they had to convince or "fix the thought problem" (*jiejue sixiang wenti*) of two groups: local officials and the singers themselves. In both cases, the conversations they described appeared to address separate though tangentially related dichotomies: moral vs. immoral and elite vs. low-class culture. According to Yang Cui, local officials tended to consider most folk songs to be about love and/or pornographic in content, and couldn't understand why they wanted to collect them.[7] The collectors, in turn, would talk about how folk songs are intimately connected with the life of the people and reflect the people's heart and spirit.

After having won over the local government workers, the collectors also had to convince the singers themselves, who would often fail to see the value of local songs, which were considered artistically inferior to the large-scale operas that would come to town each year during seasonal festivals. The local singers argued that everyone could sing these songs and that they were *only meant to be sung at home*—a clear echo of the notion of *stageworthiness* discussed earlier. In short, "elite" art was used as a foil with which to criticize crude, worthless, everyday songs. While the singers may or may not have explicitly labeled particular songs as licentious, aspects of their performance suggested that this too was an underlying issue. During the initial period of collection, Feng and Yang frequently ran into the problem that men would be embarrassed to sing certain types of songs in front of female collectors and vice versa with female singers and male collectors. Many of the songs were structured into stanzas corresponding to either the twelve lunar months or the four seasons, with each stanza becoming progressively more risqué. Yang Cui noted that often a male singer would get to a certain point and feel he could not continue. "He felt embarrassed. So, he would say, 'Oh! There's no more! I've forgotten the rest! No more singing for me!'" To avoid this problem, the female collectors eventually began interviewing female singers separately and male collectors would interview the men, allowing the singers to be more forthcoming and relaxed. When I spoke with another retired collector who was involved in a well-known folk song collection project in Hequ, Shanxi Province, in 1953, Zhang Cunliang, he too mentioned separating men and women during collection efforts.[8]

The issue of how to deal with licentious songs once they were collected is one that concerned many folk song collectors. Yang Cui noted that the vast majority of songs collected were love songs, some of which were "healthy" and others that she referred to as "unhealthy." Beyond the issue of how to collect these songs (since the scholars were committed to collecting everything), what remained was how to categorize them. Both Feng and Yang mentioned coming across what they considered to be "bad" songs. This rather broad category included songs that were "bad for the country" (*dui guojia buhao*), "bad towards ethnic groups" (*dui minzu buhao*), "culturally backward," "feudal," "superstitious," "pornographic" (*huangse de*), and those that "talked about love in an unhealthy way." Feng Yalan noted that while these songs could not be published, they should still be collected for teaching purposes, to show the "features of the old society." Furthermore, since they were seen as reflecting "bad" elements that still existed among the folk, they could be examined to determine problems still found in society. In a similar way, another well-known folk song collection project in 1953 categorized and interpreted the songs it collected (some of which described extramarital affairs) in ways promoting the need for land and marriage reform (Gibbs forthcoming 2018b; ZYXZYY 1962).

Although the "bad" songs that Feng mentioned didn't make it into the official anthologies, they were still stored and preserved in "other books" (*lingce* 另册), kept by the collectors to be used for future research. The liminality of these "other books"—the songs were documented without being publicized—is similar to *stageworthy* performances that are performed but not on the big stage. Yang Cui stressed that these songs did have valuable expressive and artistic techniques, but it was simply that their *content* was not good. Certain collectors in Jiangsu Province appear to have made similar considerations—Schimmelpennick (1997) notes that despite "strong resistance among scholars and government officials" regarding the collection of erotic songs, "some scholars in Jiangsu tend to advocate a more objective approach and try to preserve some of the erotic repertoire in archives" (142).

The concept of "other books" bears an interesting similarity with Alan Lomax's (1993) description of how the U.S. Library of Congress would give deposits of erotic lore the Greek symbol delta (Δ) and make them "inaccessible save to specialist scholars and congressmen" in *The Land Where the Blues Began* (378).

A comparison of Confucian and Puritanical attitudes toward erotic folklore is certainly worth exploring in the future. Lomax wrote of his reluctance to publish such material, much of which "display[s] a harshness about sexual matters" that he found "both unpleasant and unreal," the publication of which would foment what he called "the tormenting ambivalence of our social code" (379). These concerns seem to resonate with Yang Cui's and Feng Yalan's worries about the harmful effects of such lore on society and the young in particular— at the same time that they suggest the existence of divergent place-based moral codes.

What weighs heavy on the shoulders of these collectors is the issue of representation, made particularly poignant by their role in serving as a bridge between the rural and urban. In the process of selecting which singers and which songs to represent to a broader public—an audience beyond the scope of the villages in which the singers were born and raised—these collectors have to negotiate what to represent and how to represent it from one social context to another—in short, how to represent the Folk. In considering the concept of "becoming one with the People" within the context of mediating between different worldviews, several aspects of the collection process are highlighted. The resistance that the collectors experienced from local officials and singers can be understood as stemming from concerns that the song collection would present an unflattering view of the locality to outsiders—one of sexual licentiousness and crude aesthetics. The collectors' effort to work, eat, and live with locals was both an attempt to gain trust and potentially an effort to gain an understanding of the local contexts and understandings of the songs they will collect. At the same time, their denotation of certain pieces as "bad" songs exhibited their concerns about how those songs would be viewed in the post-collection context into which they would be presented. Songs perceived as "bad" contradict the collectors' romantic desires to learn from a virtuous rural folk and "become one with the People."

The nature and significance of "other books" takes on a liminal role in this back-and-forth process of mediation. While satisfying the call to collect everything, the songs archived in "other books" were not deemed appropriate for published anthologies, which represented the official portrait of what was being sung and, by extension, the lives of the people. By appropriating "problematic" songs for the analysis of perceived social ills, the "other books" could be seen as functioning as a filter to catch potentially dangerous materials during their flow from rural to urban contexts—one that allowed experts to "analyze" any "impurities" at the source. Such a conceptualization bears resemblance to the designation of delta files in the Library of Congress, whose limitation of access to specialist scholars and congressmen suggests that only two groups were included in the "need to know"—those who analyzed society and those with power to enact social change (Lomax 1993, 378). In both the cases of Yang Cui's "other books" and the Library of Congress' delta files, the selectivity of the audiences to which these songs are presented parallels considerations of *stageworthiness* by professional folk singers in gauging which songs are appropriate for which audiences and performance contexts.

Performance and Place-Based Morality

The similarity between how collectors select songs for anthologies and how singers select songs for particular performance contexts points to divergent views about erotic material separating rural and urban, oral and written social spheres. Several scholars have pointed to the distinct "interpretive frame" that entextualizing folk song lyrics—writing them down—has on how they are contextualized and understood (Bauman 1984; Zhang Ruiting 2009; Legman 1962). What makes transcribing and publishing folk song lyrics especially problematic is that once lyrics are fixed in print, little can be done to control the contexts in which they are read and performed, making them likely to be read in inappropriate ways. In addition, given the Chinese literary tradition that "writing is meant to convey truth" (*wenyizaidao* 文以载道), what is written down is often presumed to promote a sense of moral purpose—an idea similar in some sense to what it means to perform onstage. Both public performances and literary works are implicitly understood as statements of how things should be and how people should act, and many of the controversies that occur revolve around written/performed content clashing with the reader's/audience's ideas of what is proper. The moralizing aspect of literary censorship is not unique to China and has been noted in other cultural contexts as well.[9] When put into writing or placed on a stage, performances essentially enter a new moral paradigm and are seen as a promotion of values. Noting the altered expectations and interpretations brought on by entextualization, Zhang Ruiting (2009) posits that writing down northern Shaanxi "sour tunes" leads to the destruction of their complete meaning, in the sense that it removes them from the performance contexts in which they occur (29). This idea is similar to the opinions expressed by Wang Xiangrong in a conversation we had about the term "sour tunes," where he discussed the distancing effect that classifying songs under that genre can have on songs, removing them from the contexts of local singers:

> *Suanqu* ("sour tunes"), outsiders call them *suanqu*. Local folk artists and local people don't consider them to be *suanqu*. What does "sour" (*suan*) mean anyway? It just means something that's undisguised/explicit/ straightforward.... In the past during the period of the Cultural Revolu-

tion, Chinese people called them "yellow [i.e. pornographic] tunes." In fact, the melodies are nothing special, it mainly has to do with the content, the lyrics. Simply put, the reason that outsiders chose to call certain traditional northern Shaanxi songs *suanqu* was due to the fact that their content touched on issues regarding the relationship between men and women and sex. Directly expressing what is on one's mind in an undisguised manner, without covering up anything, singing with the most simple, plain, and straightforward language possible—these [songs] are called *suanqu*.[10]

Here, Wang argues that such naming practices reflect a worldview different from those of the rural singers who perform these songs (cf. Tuohy 1999, 50; Bourdieu 1984, 479).[11] Specifically, Wang suggests that outsiders' moral objection to the straightforward expression of sexual matters leads them to corral such songs into a separate genre—"sour tunes." Elsewhere, he mentioned that local genre classification is much more fluid—while one might ask a singer to "sing a 'meaty' stanza" (*lai yi duan hun de* 来一段荤的), they would not classify an entire song as "bawdy."[12] Rather, sections of a song may deal with erotic themes, but that does not automatically color the entire song.

By arguing against the classification of songs as "sour tunes," Wang Xiangrong attempts to subvert the moral criticism of outsiders by suggesting instead that such song lyrics are, in fact, moral—simple, plain, straightforward, and undisguised. In doing so, Wang engages with a longstanding conceptualization in China of folk songs serving as a moral barometer for rural populaces (cf. DeWoskin 1982, 22; Cai 2010, 105). Such "brazen" expression of erotic content in rural songs has either been seen as reflecting a lack of education and civilized behavior or a form of purity, untouched by the constraints of Confucian and other moral frameworks.[13] In the context of twentieth-century Marxist criticism, we find scholars of northern Shaanxi folk songs such as Wang Kewen (1986) who refer to "sour tunes" as reflecting "unhealthy" elements in rural society that should be analyzed in terms of their historical contexts (10). This follows a line of social analysis with an urban prejudice that attempts to place particular conditions within a historical-materialist framework, conflating "rural" with "past." Wang Kewen specifically suggests that just because we affirm that a song was proper for a particular historical period does not mean that people should continue to sing it in the present. Similarly, David Hughes notes that a genre of Japanese erotic song (*shunka*) was regarded by most young Japanese "as an embarrassing relic of their country's peasant past, with its frankly bawdy lyrics and raucous behavior to match them" (Hughes 1986, 36, cited in Maring and Maring 1997, 45).

On the other hand, similar to Wang's attempt to counter outsider criticism of rural morality, there have also been other counterarguments to such moral criticisms of rural residents in China. For example, there was Feng Menglong's declaration in the late Ming dynasty that bawdy "mountain songs" (*shan'ge* 山歌) expressed "true feeling" (*zhenqing* 真情) that had been lost in elite culture; and there was the inaugural statement in the Folk Song Movement of 1918 that "there is no such thing as obscenity or vulgarity in the academic field" and all folk song materials could be considered as contributing to the "the voice of the folk" (Hsu 2006, 78–79; Hung 1985, 50). Another rationalization for bucolic moral purity is the idea that any bawdy elements in folk songs have been introduced through the moral contamination of city dwellers. In the "Outline for Chinese Folk Music Research" ("Zhongguo minjian yinyue yanjiu tigang" 中国民间音乐研究提纲), written in 1946 by the influential musicologist, Lü Ji 吕骥, Lü argues against claims that the majority of Chinese folk songs are licentious and asserts that such songs make up an extremely small percentage of the overall repertoire, and moreover that they are not created by the "great masses," but rather edited by "a small number of idle urban scholars, men who visit prostitutes, and morally decrepit young hooligans from rich families" (375). Furthermore, he urges the reader to look at northern Shaanxi folk songs as examples of creations that *really* come from the masses, suggesting that the People's thinking is vast and their feelings are simple hearted, honest, and sincere, completely lacking the slick articulation used by those fallen scholars from the cities.

When songs are moved from various performance contexts to written anthologies and the stage, erotic content takes on new meaning as it is embedded in song categorization, and the resulting "erotic" songs become sites for discussions of public morality that distinguish between rural and urban, past and present, "here" and "there." Amidst the translation of these songs between contexts and media, they mean different things to different people, even in cases where the lyrics remain the same. An excellent example is Wang's performances of a traditional love song that borders on the bawdy, entitled "Yaosanbai" (摇三摆), which evokes a strong sense of intimate familiarity, localness, and nostalgia when Wang sings it back home in Fugu, while providing a humorous finale of risqué rurality when performed in central Shaanxi after songs such as "The Infinite Bends of the Yellow River" and "The East Is Red." "Yaosanbai," titled after the nickname of its female protagonist whose hips sway as she walks down the road, is a song of flirtation sung back-and-forth between a man and woman in alternating stanzas (though the entire song is often performed solo by either a male or female singer). Here are the lyrics from a performance Wang gave on November 12, 2011, with the first, third, and fourth stanzas sung by the male persona and the second stanza in the voice of the female persona, Yaosanbai:

"YAOSANBAI" (摇三摆)

Swinging [her hips] from side to side, *ai der yo, haha,* coming down the road,
Turn your pretty white face around so I can see, *yaosanbai.*
Dayaodabai, ai der yo, haha, dalu shang na ge lai,
Ni ba ni na bai ge lian lian diao guolai, yaosanbai.
大摇大摆，哎得儿哟，哈哈，大路上那个来，
你把你那白格脸脸掉过来，摇三摆。

You want me to turn around, *ai der yo,* Little Sister will turn around for you,[14]
If you tell me what devilish thoughts you have in mind, *yaosanbai.*
Ni shuo na ge diao guo, ai der yo, meimei gei ni diao guolai,
You shenme na hui ge xinshi ni shuo chulai, yaosanbai.
你说那个掉过，哎得儿哟，妹妹给你掉过来，
有什么那灰格心事你说出来，摇三摆。

Arms white as turnips, *ai der yo,* legs like summer radishes,
When Little Sister turns around to see me, I kiss her on the lips, *yaosanbai.*
Bailuobor bor gebo, ai der yo, shuiluobor bor na tui,
Banzhuan meimei na jian liao ba wo qin shang yi ge zui, yaosanbai.
白萝卜儿卜儿胳膊，哎得儿哟，水萝卜儿卜儿那腿，
扳转妹妹那见了把我亲上一个嘴，摇三摆。

Make Older Brother a pair of, *ai der yo,* leather shoes,
And I will wear them and pitter-patter pitter-patter come to see you.
And I will wear them and pitter-patter pitter-patter come to see you![15]
Ni gei gege na zuo shang yi shuang, ai der yo, niu pi pi xie,
Gege wo chuan liao shang ta na deng ger, deng ger deng ger deng ger deng ger, kan le
    meimei lai.
Gege wo chuan liao shang ta deng ger, deng ger deng ger deng ger deng ger, kan le
    meimei lai!
你给哥哥那做上一双，哎得儿哟，牛皮皮鞋，
哥哥我穿了上它那登格儿，登格儿登格儿登格儿登格儿，看了妹妹来。
哥哥我穿了上它登格儿，登格儿登格儿登格儿登格儿，看了妹妹来! [16]

During one intimate banquet with select northern Shaanxi elite, one of
them praised Wang's version of this song as the "most authentic" (*zui didao de*
最地道的) and specifically asked to hear it.[17] On another occasion on an outdoor stage at a business opening in Fugu County Town, Wang clearly framed
his performance of the song as a marker of local authenticity.[18] Referring to the
song as "our Fugu mountain tune" (*zanmen Fugu de shanqur* 咱们府谷的山曲
儿), he told the audience that they could clap if he sang well, but need not ap-
plaud if they felt he had "lost the [local] flavor" after being away too long (see
chapter 6).[19] However, when Wang performed the same song at a large-scale
event in central Shaanxi, he made no reference to local authenticity, but instead
jokingly referred to the song as a "laughter-provoking" (*douqur de* 逗趣儿的)

one about "love between men and women" (*nannü aiqing de* 男女爱情的).[20] The loud, boisterous nature of the song, sung with a rural accent, may have provoked amusement by playing on stereotypes of "country bumpkins," while at the same time the frank dialogue in the song lyrics—the couple kisses at one point, and he later asks her to make shoes for him so he can walk to visit her— may have seemed quaintly nostalgic of simpler times. Here, what is "familiar" to local audiences becomes the "exotic Other" for contemporary urban audiences (cf. Abrahams 1981).

And yet, these two types of audiences—the "rural/local" and the "urban"— only represent two ends of a spectrum defined by shades of difference, a "sliding scale of values" that exists amidst an assortment of place-based identities (Fowler and Helfield 2006, 2–3). During my fieldwork in northern Shaanxi and the surrounding area since 2006, I have observed that instead of a clear dichotomy between "dirty" and "clean" versions of songs, there is a wide spectrum, with nuanced sexual metaphor somewhere in the middle and explicit references to anatomy at one end. Tastes vary and different individuals and audiences prefer certain types.[21] This complicates things when one is trying to determine what is appropriate for an audience—what is *stageworthy*. In deciding what type of song to perform in each context, Wang suggested that there is a question of "degree" (*du* 度). Although the public nature of performances precludes certain content— "Some things can only be done, but cannot be talked about. Especially in public occasions, in front of large, formal audiences, [these things] cannot be talked about"—successful performers develop the ability to determine where to draw the line in each performance context. Wang noted,

> If you want to take [potentially objectionable songs] to a formal stage, *with an audience of many people from both towns and the countryside,* then you should have a measure or "degree" (*du*). This degree must be grasped. If properly grasped, the song becomes a traditional, classic folk song. If you don't grasp it properly—if, for example, the lyrics you sing are too explicit and you use specific language to describe relations between men and women, especially touching on sexual relations—then, you must avoid that. If you just barely touch on it, but go no further, that is okay/good. If you talk about it more deeply, more frankly, then it becomes dregs, it becomes "sour" (*suan* 酸). This is the distinction. (Emphasis added)[22]

Specifically mentioning the range of viewpoints brought into play in rural/ urban mixed audiences, Wang suggests that a sensitivity to the range of expectations implicit in a heterogeneous audience is crucial to a successful performance— to finding a suitable piece. Wang's discussion of "degree" relates more generally to the interaction between artist and audience in emergent performance, discussed by Henry Glassie (1970), Albert Lord (1960), Sandra Stahl (1989), Patrick Mullen (1981), Richard Bauman (2004), and others; it involves the ability to size up one's audience and respond accordingly. Wang viewed this sensitivity to audience needs and reactions as crucial for a singer's rise to professional success—integral to what makes a "good" singer—and he is not alone in this viewpoint. In their discussion of repertoire categorization and performer-audience interaction, Casey, Rosenberg, and Wareham (1972) write, "The 'good' singer is aware of the likes and dislikes of the groups and individuals for whom he performs. He manipulates his repertoire in response to perceived or anticipated performances, giving his constituents what he thinks they would like to hear. He is more or less sensitive to their feedback and thus quick to react in situations in which either his or their expectations are not fulfilled" (397). This ability to adapt repertoires to individual audiences' needs is common to a range of performers. While Wang's comments above focus on bawdy songs, Kyoim Yun's (2006) examination of stage performances of Korean shamanism during the 2002 World Cup paraphrases one shaman (*simbang*) as saying that "being able to adapt a performance to one's audience is a measure of skilled simbang: the greater the simbang, the greater their ability to adapt to different performance venues" (23).

This notion of a "good singer" or "good performer" is further reinforced by examples of "bad" singers who fail to accurately gauge their audiences. Performing a song that offends one's audience will most likely result in not being invited to future performances, at the very least. Casey, Rosenberg, and Wareham (1972) state it clearly: "The singer who is most clearly aware of and responsive to the tastes of different audiences and of certain individuals in these audiences will often be considered 'a good singer,' whereas a singer whose awareness of such distinctions is limited, or who does not respond even when aware of the distinctions may be considered 'not much good'" (400).

Extreme examples of such a lack of awareness include incidents involving the incarceration of singers. The story about Wang Luobin being jailed as a child for singing operatic arias too loudly at night, mentioned earlier, is a good example (Harris 2005, 382). Clearly, Wang Luobin's singing in that context was not *stageworthy*. Similarly, the American folk singer Burl Ives "spent a night in jail in Mona, Utah, in the '30s" for singing a sexually suggestive version of "The Foggy, Foggy Dew," "a song so unsuitable for Mormon ears"—another case of failing to gauge the *stageworthy* (Rockwell 2005, 236). However, since "the version Ives sang by the time he made recordings is less sexually explicit and more elusively poetic," he apparently learned his lesson (Rockwell 2005, 236). Going back to the various struggles encountered by singer-heroes discussed in chapter 1, many of them involved misjudging new contexts and committing faux pas of *stageworthiness*.

The ability to adapt—to "grasp" the degree—seems directly related to itinerant singers' movement between places and audiences. In theory, if singers are better able to respond and adapt to a wider range of performance contexts, they will become more successful. At the same time, the concept of "grasping the degree" involves a bit of pushing the envelope—finding a balance between playing it safe and going overboard. As Wang says, "If you just barely touch on it, but go no further, that is okay/good." Henry Glassie (1970, 29–30) provides an excellent example of adjusting a repertoire to audience tastes, highlighting a different sort of objectionable material—racism. He relates an account of one singer's ongoing composition of a racist song over multiple performances to different audiences:

> After the composition of each new stanza it was presented in a performance of the whole song to his audience. Generally, if it received the correct reaction—laughter—it was retained in the song…if sour or blank looks followed the new stanza, it was eliminated.…His audience…maintained a broad control over its content which acted to prevent it from becoming a totally personal statement and to keep it acceptable; specifically, his audience rejected the most stereotypic and directly offensive of the stanzas…because, on the whole, his audience was less prejudiced, less violent than he.

The singer's negotiation with each new audience attempts to find the appropriate degree on a spectrum of potentially objectionable material. In this case, he does so by overstepping and adjusting: removing new stanzas that receive negative reactions and keeping those that resulted in the desired effect—laughter. As stand-up comedians implicitly understand, the line between humorous and inappropriate is a fine one and bound to vary between individuals, audiences, places, and time periods (cf. Brodie 2014). While singing offers some leeway in the sense that things can be sung that cannot always be spoken, Glassie's example stresses the underlying back-and-forth between performers and audiences concerning taste and opinion.

Wang's sensitivity to context and his ability to "grasp the degree" of the audience allowed him to choose songs and presentations of those songs that were *stageworthy* for each occasion. We have already seen how this sensitivity carried over not only to other locations in Shaanxi and elsewhere in the country but when he traveled abroad as well. In each case, song was a means of connecting places and people, setting up conversations between selves and Others. Wang's success abroad and his border-crossing experiences at home have enabled him to present audiences with a mixture of insider and outsider viewpoints with which to have a conversation and reposition themselves in relation to others.

Between Here and There

Is this not the testimony of the arts and literature? Is not the
first and only purpose of their strange existence the
presentation of this strangeness?
—Jean-Luc Nancy, 2000

WANG Xiangrong strives to meet each audience through performance—but he
does not stop there. After connecting with each audience, he shifts between the
familiar/here and exotic/there, mimicking the border-crossing experiences of
itinerant singers and providing audience members with a miniature journey of
self-realization where they can position their senses of self in relation to others—
all without leaving their seats.[1] Wang's performances blend the familiar and the
exotic in a manner similar to the alternating voices in the "couple going out"
paradigm merging into a new subjectivity—coming together in a new point of
view somewhere between the self and other.

In a world largely defined by "local meets global," relations between places
and identities need to be examined at regular intervals (cf. Liu Kang 2004; Robertson 1992, 1995). Wang's rhetorical shifting between "here" and "there" allows audiences to see the here not only in its own eyes, but through the eyes of
others. In a globalizing world where localities define themselves against ever
more distant places, senses of local authenticity must travel and encounter new
Others in order to maintain their relevance. The stage becomes the meeting
ground where local authenticity is made intelligible to the Other and the world's
praise is brought back to a local self. Onstage, Wang the performer acts as a lens
reflecting back images of the audience's self while letting light through from
elsewhere, blending together images of Others and images of selves bathed in
the light of Others.

Wang's shifting between familiar and exotic was particularly evident in
speeches and performances I observed him give in his home region between
2011 and 2012. Using contrasting imagery and sung personae, Wang "distanced
the local," objectifying it through the lens of an outsider in order to praise it,
presenting familiar themes in ways that "othered" them to local audiences. His
shifting between the local and the global raises the status of the local by com-

paring it to the global and declaring it superior. As a native son who has returned after many years, Wang's dual identity as both insider and outsider allowed him to blend images of self and other—fusing together the components necessary for a sense of identity: a sense of self and a sense of how others view that self (Erikson 1994).

In addition, Wang often explicitly challenged audiences to judge the *local authenticity* (*didao* 地道) of particular songs he sang, compelling them to distinguish between the here/self and the there/other as he presented his performances as objects to be judged (Bauman 2004).[2] Wang's challenge to listen and evaluate the authenticity of his songs not only engages audience attention during longer performances (cf. Bender 1999), but also requires individual audience members to assert their notions of self and other amidst the interplay of familiar and exotic, coordinating the relation between self and performed object(s) through the act of judging.[3] Thus, as with other song kings and queens, Wang's performances compel one to define the "here" in relation to various "theres," drawing connections and differences between them and coming to see each through the eyes of others.

Distancing the Local

Wang's appearances in Fugu County provided him with opportunities to reflect on his choice to leave the area when young and his experiences while away. Though Wang continued to visit the area frequently, his ostensible decades-long absence provided a context for observations of changes in the region. When he was invited back by his home township for a "New Year's" (*Yuandan* 元旦) gathering of local elites in late December 2011, Wang gave a speech that shifted between contrasting images of the local and the distant, the past and the present.[4] Repeatedly alternating between "here" and "there," he was able to construct an image of the local situated in a larger context. Wang's authority to shift rested on his own travels back and forth—he had "been there" and returned—allowing him to praise the local both as an insider (i.e., someone who knows the local firsthand) and as an outsider (i.e., someone who can compare the local with other places).

During his speech, Wang began by addressing the audience in an intimate, familiar manner, before creating a sense of double-awareness with a reference to a foreign holiday: "Dear elders and fellow villagers, dear friends and relatives, and also our beloved 'father-mother officials' (*fumuguanr*),[5] the New Year is almost here, so I wanted to wish you a happy new year. Today is also a foreign holiday for those foreigners, 'Christmas.'" Wang's parallel between the celebration "here" (New Year) and the celebration "there" (Christmas) began his speech by suggesting that this was not an isolated event but rather a local event with an awareness of its relation to the world.[6] Next, Wang painted a picture of local people living elsewhere—himself included—being invited back and returning with great enthusiasm:

> So, already a couple of weeks ago, our town head contacted me and said that every year our Xinmin has a gathering, and all of the Xinmin people who have left and all of the prominent community members in Xinmin—the cream of every profession, outstanding figures—all meet together here, and he asked if I could come back. I said of course. In fact, if you all provide such an opportunity every year I would be even happier. I left over thirty years ago, and this is the first time that our town political commissar, town Communist Party committee, and town government formally invited me to participate in this gathering at Shagoucha.[7]

Similar to the shift from *local* holiday (New Year) to *foreign* holiday (Christmas), here we see a back-and-forth shift from *here* (local people) to *there* (living elsewhere) to *here* (coming home). Valorizing the "there," Wang notes that these esteemed individuals are leading successful lives in other localities, thus meriting invitations from the local government. At the same time, Wang praises the local by emphasizing everyone's eagerness to be invited to return. After this prelude, Wang continued his speech by focusing on the local, stretching back in time to a point where he still lived there and worked as a manual laborer on a local building. This backward shift in time concurrently moves from Wang's current place in the "there" to his past experience in the "here," shifting the audience's attention from Wang's success abroad to the familiarity of home: "Over behind Shagoucha, when they were laying the foundation, I was there using a pickax to prepare the ground. So, frankly speaking, no matter how high you soar or how far you go, nothing is more familiar than your own villagers." Wang then continued his focus on the "here" by praising the local landscape's natural beauty: "The moon is still the roundest here at home, and people are the dearest as well. Mountains—no matter whether they are luxuriant green with flowing water or desolate slopes of yellow earth—to me, the mountains here always look the best." He then shifted back to the "there" of distant lands, before arriving once more at the "here":

> I often say when traveling—I've been to over fifteen…twenty-something countries—after I went to America a couple years ago, which is said to be the biggest, most powerful nation…I have been to many, many countries, and performed on a lot of big stages, but when I dream, I don't dream about anywhere else—I just dream about Xinmin. When I sing

errentai, I think of that old stage (*lao xitai* 老戏台) in Xinmin. When I dream of people, those who are no longer here and those who are still here, I just dream about these people. In the outside, no matter how many talented people there are, I never dream about them. They don't have much to do with me.

After leading the audience abroad on this mental journey, Wang used the image of himself overseas dreaming about home to bring the audience back to Xinmin's "here," declaring it superior. The effect of Wang's shifting back and forth between the local and the global was to praise the "here" not only in and of itself (i.e., through the eyes of a local) but through the eyes of someone who had seen "great and powerful nations" and continued to find the "here" superior. Leaving and returning, Wang now hovered on the border between locals who had lived their entire lives on the land and others who had left and never returned. His ambiguous place-based identity—both insider and outsider—allowed him to simultaneously (1) assert his local identity and (2) use the length of his absence to express "objective" praise for the "here" from a perspective somewhere between the "here" and "there":

I *am* a Xinmin person. I *am* a Fugu person. Back then, I didn't have enough to eat or enough clothes to keep out the cold.[8] Why did I leave? In fact, it's not that Wang Xiangrong has a great skill at making a living, no. At that time, due to my family's poverty... at that time, this place of ours, due to various reasons, hadn't yet begun to develop. This place was poor, you could also say, and I wanted to try my best to "jump out of the Dragon Gate" [i.e., travel to another place to seek professional development],[9] to see how things were in the outside. Well, honestly, after I left and began to "eat from the public rice bowl" (*chi gongjia na yi wan fan*, [i.e., work on the government payroll after he joined the Yulin Folk Arts Troupe]), what do you know, after all these years, Shagoucha and Xinmin have moved heaven and earth. All those former laborers from the past are now trillionaires. I'm jealous, but being jealous does no good, since I can't come back now. I can't come back, but my heart is here. Although I can't come back, now our Xinmin has these many entrepreneurs—old entrepreneurs, new entrepreneurs, small entrepreneurs—and furthermore, I often say, Xinmin is ours and it is also yours, but at the end of the day, it is yours [*audience laughter*].[10]

The final sentence—adapted from a quote attributed to Mao Zedong—juxtaposed the inclusive "ours," grouping together speaker and audience, with "yours," which excludes the speaker from the audience's group. While Wang used "ours" to suggest that he shared in Xinmin's history and helped evoke Xinmin's sense of "here" through song, he used "yours" to refer to those in the audience who had stayed on the land their entire lives. It was to the people of Xinmin that the future belonged, and by rhetorically removing himself from that future Wang could praise Xinmin as a "there." By combining "ours" and "yours," Wang praised Xinmin and its people from the dual perspective of insider and outsider, augmenting how locals see Xinmin with others' praise of it—Xinmin as both "here" and "there."

Shifting Perspectives

In addition to such speeches, Wang enacted a shifting between familiar/here and exotic/there in a range of performances. This shifting was especially evident during an appearance at a business opening in Wang's home area, Fugu County Town, which I attended in late 2011. After an outdoor performance for the local populace, Wang continued his appearance at an indoor banquet that followed. Speaking to the assembled bosses and their friends, Wang discussed how the relationship between their locality (Fugu) and the outside had changed over time (figure 6.1). The emergent flow of songs and speech moved back and forth between the "here" (Fugu) and various "theres" ranging from neighboring counties, other parts of the region, other parts of the province, the nation, and the world as a whole. Through the course of the event, this oscillation be-

Figure 6.1 Speech at a business opening in Fugu. November 12, 2011. Photograph by author.

tween familiar and exotic—local/familiar songs sung in unfamiliar languages and/or by exotic people—offered the audience a chance to reconsider their own sense of identity in a dialogic manner.[11]

Concluding his speech to the assembled banquet crowd, Wang asked me—the young foreign researcher who had been filming the entire event—to come up and sing a couple of Fugu songs. This performance of local songs by a foreigner then served as a springboard for Wang to discuss the uniqueness and value of these songs (and by extension, the locality) in the world, stressing the power of local culture in attracting this foreign scholar. As Wang marveled at the possibility of Fugu songs becoming "global songs" (*qiuge* 球歌), one of the inebriated bosses from the audience walked up to Wang, put an arm around his shoulder, and asked him to have me sing a Fugu song in English. My impromptu, translated version of "Sheep Stomach Towel Rag Three Lines of Blue" ("Yang duzi shoujianr san dao dao lan" 羊肚子手巾儿三道道蓝) provided Wang with a pretext to sing his own "translation" of a Chinese song, saying,

> Since I spent some time in Inner Mongolia in the sixties, I will now sing for everyone—I'm not kidding you—I'll use Mongolian to sing a song that all of the older people here will recognize, "Sailing in the Ocean We Rely on the Great Helmsman / Carrying Out the Revolution We Rely on Mao Zedong Thought." [*applause*] "Fish cannot leave the water / Melons cannot leave the vine / The Revolutionary Masses cannot leave the Communist Party / Mao Zedong Thought is the sun that never sets"—these are the Chinese [lyrics]. I will use Mongolian for everyone....I sing it extremely well—even Mongolian people admire my singing. There are many younger Mongolians who are unable to sing this song. I'm not bragging, everyone have a listen [*sings*].[12]

The overall flow of this emergent performance (including the parts played by Wang and myself) appears to involve repeated juxtapositions of the familiar and the exotic: first, a Fugu song (familiar) sung in local dialect (familiar) by a foreigner (exotic) with some degree of foreign accent (exotic); then, a traditional northern Shaanxi song (familiar) sung again by a foreigner (exotic) in English (exotic); and finally, a popular Chinese revolutionary song (familiar) sung in Mongolian (exotic) by a locally famous singer (familiar).

Since songs, and especially folk songs, are implicitly tied to particular languages and people that sing them, what is "normal" is for a Fugu folk song (familiar song) to be sung by a Fugu person (familiar person) in Fugu dialect (familiar language). Such a performance is what is to be expected and tends to call less reflexive attention to itself. However, when a foreigner sings the same song, the local audience's expectations regarding singer and language are disrupted, and the focus of their attention is shifted to listening for similarities and differences in linguistic and stylistic "flavor." A foreigner (exotic person) singing a local song (familiar song) in a foreign language (exotic language) switches out both person and language from what is expected. In Wang's case, a local/Chinese singer (familiar person) singing a Chinese song (familiar song) in a foreign language (exotic language) switches out the expected language, and one might argue that his singing in Mongolian draws increased attention to the singer himself—after all, why is a Chinese person (and a local one at that) singing Mongolian? Essentially, I argue, both Wang and I were crossing borders of audience expectations in our performances.

The juxtaposition of the familiar and the unfamiliar in each case provided the audience with an experience that played with their sense of self and other, implicitly asking them questions about how they see themselves *and* how others see them. For example, upon hearing a local song sung by a foreigner, an audience member might have asked: Does the experience of a Fugu person hearing a local folk song sung in (unintelligible) English come close to what a non-Chinese–speaking foreigner would hear when the same song is sung in Chinese? Does a familiar song made exotic through altered lyrics (English or Mongolian, instead of Chinese) distance the local, allowing for a moment of more "objective" self-introspection?[13] By distancing the local, the performance encourages the audience to consider how others see them and how they want to define themselves. In a sense, this entire sequence of events epitomized the dialogue that Wang enacts through his speeches and performances—he literally came home from the "there" and brought an "Other" with him. Furthermore, this was not just any Other, but a foreign *scholar* who could engage with the *common people* (*laobaixing*) in the audience and present the praise of an outsider with a certain degree of insider knowledge. One is reminded of the two target demographics for Wang's 2006 CD album: common people and "high-level" intellectuals, including music scholars. This event could be seen as a dialogue between the two. By presenting the audience with this back-and-forth between local identity and foreign perceptions of that identity, Wang established a discursive space where the audience could play with their sense of self and other.

Reflections of Self

As a native son who has returned after many years, Wang has a dual identity as both insider and outsider that allows him to present audiences with images of the self and Other—like a translucent lens moving between the "here" and "there," letting some light through from the Other while simultaneously reflecting the self.[14] In addition to connecting audiences to other places and peoples, song kings such as Wang also provide a window into history—we see Wang reminisce about how things used to be—but that historical vision is fused with geographical movement. Wang did not stay in the mountain village where he was born. When he speaks of his youth, Wang's perspective contains the distance of time as well as the distance of place. The idea of "going away to discover home—is, of course, familiar to any traveller," as Eugene Chen Eoyang (2007, ix) notes, and one of the fundamental functions of storytellers posited by Walter Benjamin (1969) is to provide listeners with windows into other times and places.

To exist in the world is to coexist, argues the French philosopher Jean-Luc Nancy in *Being Singular Plural,* suggesting that "all appearance is co-appearance" and "*the plurality of beings is at the foundation…of Being*" (2000, 12, italics in original). One's "position" can only be defined in relation to others, Nancy posits, either "*from,* in the sense of *with,* other (at least possible) positions" or "*among,* in the sense of *between,* other positions" (ibid., italics in original). This symbiotic nature of identity accounts, in part, for what Nancy calls the "commanding presence" of the strange (10). The elements of otherness in Wang's performances call attention to themselves as they encourage audience members to distinguish their own senses of self against the foil of that otherness. However, that otherness, as we have seen, is a moving target. One moment, Wang is singing a familiar local tune, and the next he is singing in Mongolian. One moment, he is reminiscing about working years ago on a local construction crew and the next he is talking about world tours and international success. Wang's shifting back and forth, combined with the ambiguous nature of each image—the Mongolian song bears a familiar revolutionary tune and the picture of Wang abroad is one of him dreaming of home—encourages audiences to find their positions somewhere between the here and there. This liminality—neither here nor there, now nor then, us nor them—bears the same in-betweenness that characterizes the lives and performances of song kings and queens. It provides the self-defining link-between that facilitates coexistence.

Let us imagine Wang singing a local song to fellow villagers during his youth in Marugeda. Wang's persona, identity, and the song he sang would all be close to the environment in which and the audience to which he performed. Singing a local song for fellow villagers, the performer was one of the crowd. While Wang's performance would objectify the song to a certain extent—another being standing in front of them, performing the song—as he was a fellow villager, Wang's performance might have been seen by the audience as a reflection of themselves. However, once Wang left Marugeda and began to perform for other audiences, the dynamics of his performances shifted along with his physical location. When Wang performed for audiences in Yulin, Xi'an, and

Beijing with the Yulin Folk Arts Troupe, he presented a mediated view of the "here" (be that Marugeda, Fugu, Yulin, or northern Shaanxi) to the audience before him "there." Adapting his performances to the expectations of the stage and presenting repertoires that each "there" would be able to connect to in some way, Wang learned to shift and mediate between audiences. In his performances abroad, such as the 2008 Midland concert described in chapter 4, Wang presented the "local" from Yulin in a manner that sought to connect to the American audience's familiarity with the "common" human emotion of love. Attempting to remind the Midland audience of their own humanity while presenting an "authentic Other," Wang was taking what was locally familiar to the Midland audience (i.e., love), passing it through the lens of another place and culture, and reflecting it back at the audience.

This experience of presenting to other audiences—in Xi'an, Beijing, and abroad—in turn allowed Wang to provide local Fugu audiences with additional perspective on their own identity when he returned. When Wang performed the same local song that he might have performed to local villagers in his youth after returning from his lengthy sojourn elsewhere (as I witnessed several times during my fieldwork in 2011 and 2012), his performance was no longer the same as that of someone who had never left the locality. By now, the image of the local "self" reflected back at the audience had incorporated "other" views of that self amassed during Wang's travels to various "theres." This was a reflection of self, but what seemed to be a translucent reflection of self—one that incorporated other views of that self accumulated through time and space.

In the context of sung personae, each of these performances carries different layers of meaning, even if the performer is singing the same song. To begin with, a local singer performing an *errentai* duet to a local audience (such as the performances of Wang's youth) would effectively provide a local mirror of the "here." Next, the same song presented to people in other places could offer the "here" as an Other to the "there" of the performance venue. Third, the same performance abroad could mirror the humanity of the "there" back to that audience through the lens of the "here," while experienced by those at home as having the "here" seen and appreciated by others. Fourth, upon returning home afterwards, a singer such as Wang would offer a sung persona who had performed for Others and been appreciated by them. The singer's presentation of local songs would now contain an element of how Others see the local self. This fusion of the subjective and the objective played into a fifth sung persona that I saw Wang offer: the sung persona of the foreign researcher-performer played by the author. As a foreign scholar familiar with local songs, my performances were presented as how someone from the "there" who understands the "here" would perform a local song. Wang's choice to include my performances of local songs on several occasions, encouraging audiences to "have a listen" and see for themselves, suggests that observing a foreign scholar sing local songs was an extension of the sort of border-crossing "reflections of self bathed in the light of others" Wang sought to bring about as a song king.

In certain aspects, Wang asking me to sing at his performances was an attempt to present me as one of his sung personae. It followed the same logic of a man who hires a mariachi singer to serenade his beloved—the mariachi singer serves as a mask for the person who hired the singer, allowing the person who ordered the serenade to say things he wants to say (and cannot say himself) in a publically appropriate manner. When Wang had me sing after him to the banquet of Fugu businessmen, I too served as one of his masks. Though I attempted to sing the same songs he sings, I sang them in a way that he could not—a foreign Other's attempt to perform the familiar self, and a *"significant Other"* at that, to use Claire Conceison's term for the role Americans play in China as "privileged marginalized Other[s]" (2004, 3, italics in original). If Wang had attempted to sing the same song *as if he were a foreigner,* the result would be parody at best—a chance to laugh at the goofy Otherness of the stranger. If his caricature of the Other accentuated the differences to the point where the familiar song became unrecognizable, the overall effect would be to laugh at the foreign Other. If, on the other hand, his caricatured persona sang *too authentically*—too *didao*—audiences would question his ability to impersonate a foreigner. After all, one might ask, how could a foreigner sing the local so well and what would be the point of that anyway? However, with my performance authorized by Wang, Wang could maintain a distance from the sung persona while providing "evidence" of the local's attractiveness to the global. Just as Wang's anecdotes about dreaming of home while abroad and his performance of familiar revolutionary songs in foreign languages valorized the local, his "foreign scholar" persona showed an appreciation for the local culture through the eyes of Others.

Performance as a Conversation between Familiar and Exotic

While the performance sequence described above might seem a bit unusual—after all, it is not every day that Wang has a foreign scholar contribute to his performances—even when Wang sings "traditional" songs in Chinese, he often highlights issues of local identity by challenging audiences to distinguish authentic local flavor. When he performs a "local" song in Fugu after a long absence, he invites the audience to judge if he has maintained his local flavor, using applause as a means of expressing their opinion. Likewise, when he performs local songs from other areas of northern Shaanxi, he poses similar challenges to audiences in those localities: Is he, as an authentic (*didao*) northern Shaanxi folk singer (albeit from a different part of the region), able to sing their locality's local song in an authentic (*didao*) way? In each of these cases, Wang's challenge to the audience focuses their attention on the "flavor" of the song and whether it conforms to their own understanding of local identity. At the same time, Wang seems to be suggesting the value of a "traveled" local authenticity.

"Flavor" is an intangible concept that permeates an entire performance and must be continually gauged at each moment by the observer. This sustained act of observation requires the audience to constantly refer back to what the "local" sounds like and what it means to be "local," thus reinforcing the audience members' own sense of local identity, self, and other. At the same time, the focus on distinguishing local authenticity places an implicit value on local identity—it is something to be applauded, something to be sought out. "Authentic" local culture is conceptualized as a "pure" product, as Wang suggests through his frequently used phrase "original pure flavor" (*yuanzhiyuan-wei* 原汁原味). The value of "local authenticity" is also put forward in Wang's presentation of foreign adaptations of the local—the revolutionary song sung in Mongolian, the local song sung by a foreigner—suggesting that local and Chinese values are attractive to the world at large. Just as Mao Zedong Thought–inspired songs were purportedly sung in over one hundred foreign countries, Wang presents Fugu culture, as embodied by its folk songs, as similarly attractive on a global level.[15]

When Wang asks Fugu audiences to clap if he has maintained the local flavor of a song, he is not merely asking them to judge if he is presenting a song that is locally authentic. What seems to be key here is Wang's ability to maintain a sense of local authenticity (*didao*) *after having been away*. Rather than the authenticity of an elderly performer who has remained in the same village his entire life, Wang's "local authenticity" has traveled, encountered other peoples and places, and endured the passage of time. It is a self that has been elsewhere and back—a self that has met with other selves and become stronger for it. While some might argue that the local authenticity Wang maintains stems from earlier traditions that he observed before leaving his village, thus "preserving" what has since disappeared or changed, his performances today are not the same as Marugeda performances in the 1950s. If the "authentic" of that time and place were magically transplanted to the present here and now, it would not, I suggest, have the same *didao* quality as Wang's performances today. Instead, Wang's present "authenticity" is equivalent to what would have happened if that earlier authenticity grew legs, traveled around the world, and returned.[16]

This idea of a "traveled" local authenticity does not necessarily contradict Philip Bohlman's assertion that "authentic" folk music involves "consistent representation of the origins of a piece (or a style or a genre) in subsequent versions or at later moments in the tradition's chronology," adding, "with regard to those aspects that are salient, the piece remains the piece" (1988, 10). Indeed, Bohlman suggests a range of cultural interpretations of authenticity among which Wang's *didao* would fit nicely. What both Bohlman and Wang implicitly suggest is that authenticity is relational. On the one hand, "authenticity only emerges when it is counter to forces that are trying to screw it up" (Keil and Feld 1994, 296). On the other hand, as James Clifford suggests, "entertainers" positioned along the margins of societies offer us chances to "[look] at culture (along with tradition and identity) in terms of travel relations" (1992, 101).[17] Faced with difference, authenticity reacts, and songs, similar to stories, can thus accrue authenticity as they travel based in part on the claims to authority that the singer makes with them (cf. Shuman 2005, 120).

In the pursuit of authenticity, the stage represents the meeting ground between self and other, where the local *didao* is adapted to become intelligible to the other. On the one hand, without such "stageification" (Qiao 2011), the local would be too unfamiliar and could not be appreciated. At the same time, Wang's conversations with local audiences point to another concern—whether the local changed too much in the process and has become something else. Locals might worry that an iconic performer who has traveled and enjoyed success elsewhere may have changed so much engaging with others that he or she is no longer locally authentic. They might worry that in adapting to the stage, the singer has changed the flavor of the songs to such a degree that it is no longer *didao*. The fear is that the performed material that allowed the singer to become iconic and that is so appreciated by various audiences no longer belongs to what the local folk judge to have the same place-based essence.

Part of Wang's claim to authenticity rests on his expressions of "emotional sincerity" and "solidarity with an audience"—his onstage banter about having just returned, wishing to have more time to sit and chat with the audience, and his repeated declarations that he is a "real" (*dididaodao*) northern Shaanxi person and/or Fugu person (P. David Marshall 2006, 205, 206; cf. Von Hallberg 2008). As Bourdieu would have it, Wang frames himself as "a legitimate speaker...in a legitimate situation...address[ing]...legitimate receivers" (1977, 650). These moves to connect with the audience constitute a crucial step in establishing Wang's authenticity. While Charles Lindholm notes "two overlapping modes" for claiming authenticity, including "genealogical or historical (*origin*) and identity or correspondence (*content*)," he also suggests that focusing audiences' attention on "the character of the artist" provides an alternative path to authenticity that can sidestep sticky notions of content (2008, 2, 33). "If *real* country musicians perform the music," Lindholm posits, "then it *is* country music, whatever the instrumentation, orchestration, or venue" (33). Wang's onstage assertions that he is a "real" northern Shaanxi person and a "real" Fugu person suggest to audiences that they should listen to his performances to see what the flavor of an authentic regional representative sounds like.

Determining whether something is *didao* is both consensus based and subjective. *Didao* is defined in one's emotional reaction to something. In Yulin's traditional architecture, what "looks '*didao*'" is what "looks good" (Jiang Lu 2007, 196). What "sounds *didao*" in traditional songs seems to be what "sounds good."[18] Part of a song's familiarity and much of its authority lies in the music. "Musicality authenticates poetry," notes Robert Von Hallberg in *Lyric Powers* (2008, 10), and the nexus of melody, pronunciation, and delivery in Wang's songs comes together in a *didao*-ness that "feels right" to the ears of individual locals. Wang's challenges for the audience to judge his authenticity position him as a fellow observer—it is as if he is listening together with them to see whether his song is authentic. One of song's unique effects is that singers often seem to be "joining in on" the words they sing—relating rather than creating— and that act of identification is then replicated by the audience (Booth 1981, 177).[19] David Pattie notes a similar tendency for rock musicians and audiences to position themselves as fellow observers, writing, "both the audience and the performer look to the music to provide the ultimate validation, the ultimate proof of authenticity" (2007, 12).

Performed authenticity is integral to Simon Frith's conception of identity as "an experiential process which is most vividly grasped *as music*" (1996a, 110). Frith notes that "music seems to be a key to identity because it offers, so intensely, a sense of both self and others, of the subjective in the collective" (ibid.). When Wang's audiences decide that what they are hearing "sounds *right*," that determination of *didao* is an act through which "we both express ourselves, our own sense of rightness, and suborn ourselves, lose ourselves, in an act of participation," losing and then finding ourselves again (ibid., italics in original). Not everyone will agree on whether a particular song or turn of phrase is *didao*, but through "cultural activity" and "aesthetic judgement," social groups "get to know themselves *as groups* (as a particular organization of individual and social interests, of sameness and difference)" (111). When we appreciate music, we are to a certain degree identifying with it, and therefore our "aesthetic response is, implicitly, an ethical agreement" (114).

A sense of identity, as "something we put or try on, not something we reveal or discover," seems particularly suited to the play of sung personae Wang provides (Frith 1996a, 122). If personal identity "arises from play-acting and the adoption of artificial voices," Wang's juxtaposition and fusion of familiar and exotic elements in the sequences of his performances offer the perfect means for audiences to "try on" different perspectives (Rée 1990, 1054; Frith 1996a, 122). Indeed, Stuart Hall suggests that identities are "points of temporary attachment to the subject positions which discursive practices construct for us"

(1996, 6; cf. Hall 1995). Similar to Frith's observation of music and identity, Deborah Kapchan suggests, "Performance genres are intertextual fields where the politics of identity are negotiated" (1995, 482). Wang's performances provide a litmus test for audiences to feel their identity.

By asking audiences to focus on the flavor of the performance while at the same time playing with their horizon of expectations, Wang's performances force audience members to question their own sense of identity and reposition themselves in relation to others. Only through interacting with others do we define and position ourselves in relation to others, and allowing for that interaction to happen is one of the important reasons for mediating between groups and views (Cantwell 1993). When Wang challenges audiences to determine the presence/absence of authentic local flavor in his songs, he asks them to look anew at the relations between "here" and "there," "self" and "Other." The repeated nature of Wang's questioning and performances suggests that these issues of identity must be reevaluated at frequent intervals—there are changes over time in relationships between places and ways of thinking about things, due, for example, to recent urban migration and the interaction of the global and the local. "Boundary-making" is an implicit part of establishing a sense of self (cf. Barth 1969). As such, the questions of who one is and who one is not *need to be asked at regular intervals*—the world is in flux and so are we.

Audiences can compare their senses of self with multiple aspects of Wang's performances (cf. Fiske 2011). He is folk. He is rural. He is tradition. He is of the land. He is of the Yellow River. He is of the Yellow Earth. He is steeped in the past, yet thriving in the present. He is famous. In shorter cameo appearances, Wang's singing often appears to shift the overall flow of performance toward a reflection on history and the rural folk. At an elementary school anniversary in Xi'an, Wang's performance of "The East Is Red" and a pastoral love song provided a focus on the revolutionary history of the region and the nation, as well as evocations of nearby folk culture. Pop songs and ethnic minority-style dance arrangements preceded his performance, and two elementary school student emcees dressed in tuxedo and ballroom gown introduced each act. Likewise, at the ninetieth anniversary of a nearby university, adult emcees in tuxedos and ballroom gowns introduced a range of pop singers, dance acts, and rock stars, with Wang appearing in a sequence reminiscing about the school's connection to revolutionary history—singing "The East Is Red" as a massive image of Mao Zedong was projected on the screen at the back of the stage.

When juxtaposed with magicians, acrobats, drummers, dancers, and pop singers, Wang's performances present audiences with a mixture of things they can relate to and others against which they can define themselves. His face and voice, his persona as a singer and the sung personae of his songs, all merge into a translucent lens that shifts between the here and there, allowing audiences to simultaneously see Others and themselves. This combination of similarities and differences brings audiences on a journey where they encounter others and redefine themselves—an important exercise in the continual redefinition of self in a world that is increasingly interconnected. A range of performed others and selves, such as those presented in large-scale Chinese gala performances including the opening ceremony of the 2008 Beijing Olympics and annual CCTV Spring Festival Galas, mirror the interplay between various social forces, popular trends, historical periods, and ethnic groups involved in individual constructions of Chinese identity. Among those multifaceted stages and performances, we find song kings such as Wang.

CHAPTER 7

Connecting Past, Present, and Future

We require a visible past, a visible continuum, a visible
myth of origin, which reassures us about our end.
—Jean Baudrillard, 1994

As families gathered around China to watch the 2014 CCTV Spring Festival
Gala, toward the end of the four-hour marathon event, Wang appeared singing
"The Infinite Bends of the Yellow River" in between a patriotic song by a Hong
Kong pop singer and a jazzy duet by two Mongolian singers.[1] There were stark
differences between Wang and the audience that sat before him. Singing with a
northern Shaanxi accent, head wrapped in a knotted, white towel—traditional
for northern Shaanxi men—Wang faced an audience dressed in suits and ties
(figure 7.1). And yet, despite appearing as if from another time and place, Wang
was undoubtedly Chinese. And, as that modern, urban audience viewed his
performance evoking rural history fused with aspirations for the future, they
were offered a chance to negotiate their sense of self in time and space with a
trajectory aimed at things to come.

The patriotic song performed before him, "Chinese Dream," was sung by a
Hong Kong singer dressed in a black suit with a flowing white scarf draped
around his neck, surrounded by female dancers in pink flamingo tutus (figure
7.2). As the Hong Kong singer sang "The country's prosperity is my glory,"[2] images of the modern city, beautiful natural landscapes, and the Beijing Olympics
were projected in the background, and he too fused personal and national narratives in song. The individual singer, connected to both region and nation,
became a symbol for the integrity of both. China's territory was celebrated (natural landscapes) together with its modernity (the city), and the narrative of
progress culminated in global recognition (the Olympics). Presented with this
"Chinese Dream," the audience could reflect on their own connections to region and nation, and how they too experienced a sense of self that bridged the
individual and the collective.

"The country's prosperity is my glory"—as these words rang out and the
song ended, a computer-generated image of the Great Wall appeared, followed

Figure 7.1
Contrasting
clothing at
Wang's 2014
CCTV Gala
performance.

Figure 7.2 Hong Kong singer performs "Chinese Dream" at 2014 CCTV Gala.

by a shot of the audience, and then Wang began to sing, "Do you know how many bends the Yellow River has? And how many boatmen are on those bends?" with images of the river above and behind him. This succession of images—Great Wall, people, singer, Yellow River—points to the song as a vocal expression of China's long and winding history. Following images of China's modernity and progress, the line of questioning sung by Wang points the audience back in time—although there are no longer boatmen on the Yellow River, they have become a symbol for China's strength and tenacity. Wang's song urges listeners to reflect on the past, before answering the questions it raises—there are an infinite number of bends in the Yellow River and an infinite number of boatmen on those bends. Questioning of the past ends in confirmation of the present and confidence in the future.

Now considered one of Wang's "must-sing" songs, "The Infinite Bends of the Yellow River" is prominently placed at the beginning of several folk song anthologies in the section of work songs (*haozi*), symbolically framing it as an epic, primordial song, and it is taught in music conservatories across the country (cf. Lü 1994; Qiao 2002; Cao 2004; Huo 2006).[3] The song is also the title track on his 2006 CD (Wang Xiangrong 2006). During my research, Wang performed this song in a range of large-scale events where it seemed to offer audiences a dialogue between the context of the event and a broad sense of history. Each of the events where Wang performed the song, including New Year's galas, weddings, and business openings, appears to represent changes from one state to another: the transition of old year to new, the joining together of two individuals in marriage, the birth of a new business. People involved in such moments of social change tend to question aspects of their identity, asking themselves where they have come from and where they are going—similar, as we will see, to the questions laid out in this song. Perhaps due to the song's questioning nature, it has a history of being tied to transitional events.

First composed and performed by a Yellow River boatman and amateur performer at rural Chinese New Year's festivities in 1920, the song's melody was adapted from a popular festival tune (Huo 2006, 4; Yang Cui 2007). The song's composer, Li Simin 李思敏 (1891–1963), wrote a stanza of probing questions that became known as "The Boatman's Song" ("Chuanfu diao" 船夫调) (Huo 2006; Yang Cui 2007):[4]

Do you know—in the whole world, how many bends does the Yellow River have? *Ai!*
And how many boats are on those bends? *Ai,*
And how many poles are on those boats? *Ai,*
And how many boatmen, *yo ho,* move those boats?
Ni xiaode, tianxia Huanghe jishiji dao wan ai!
Jishiji dao wan shang jishiji zhi chuan ai,

Jishiji zhi chuan shang jishiji gen gan ai,
Jishiji ge na shaogong ya ha lai ba chuan lai ban.
你晓得，天下黄河几十几道湾哎！
几十几道湾上几十几只船哎，
几十几只船上几十几根杆哎，
几十几个那艄公呀哈来把船来搬。[5]

Li's song appeared at a time when May Fourth intellectuals were questioning the fate of the nation. Following the devastation caused by the Opium Wars and the collapse of the Qing dynasty in 1911, China's intellectuals were asking how China had come to its present state and where the country was heading. Li sang each question to the simulated rhythm of rowing a boat, leaving each query unanswered to linger in the minds of his listeners. The imagery he used invites symbolic interpretation—the bends of the Yellow River could represent the breadth of China's territory and the anonymous boatmen its vast population.

Though the song's questions are asked in the present tense, they lead the listener to think about the past: How long have there been boatmen on the Yellow River? How many boatmen were there before? How far back does Chinese history go?[6] Chinese folk song scholar Qiao Jianzhong characterizes the song's steady, driving rhythm as "appear[ing] like a cry out, a question posed, and a deep sigh to oneself all rolled into one, as if pouring out all at once the five thousand years of changes our nation and people have been through" (2002, 1:2). At the same time, listeners' thoughts about China's history and present state would lead them to think about the future—in keeping with the intellectual concerns of the May Fourth period. The relation of the song to past, present, and future, I would suggest, continued during later periods.

While the song's questions interrogate China's past and future, their lack of answers can also be seen as focusing the listener's attention on the unknowable. One is reminded of another poetic collection of inquiries—the *Heavenly Questions* (*Tianwen* 天问), a series of questions about the creation of the world and various mythical and/or historical personages attributed to Qu Yuan and included in the anthology of *Chuci* 楚辞. While various theories exist regarding the nature of that text, David Hawkes suggests that the poem's questions are riddles, in that a riddle "does not ask for information but playfully challenges it" (1985, 46). Repeated questions about the unknowable can evoke a sense of wonder, as well as helplessness. Writing on the *Heavenly Questions*, Mark Edward Lewis notes,

> This decision to deny any answers must be taken seriously. The repeated posing of questions that have no answer, the refusal to answer questions that do, and the questioning of Heaven's morality are all formal equiva-

lents of the substantive focus on marvels and the miraculous, which are by definition that which defies explanation or answer. In its relentless questioning the poem presents the cosmos as a set of impenetrable riddles, the earth as an array of uncanny regions, and human history as a field of inexplicable occurrences. The ultimate theme of the poem is the manner in which the world escapes all man's feeble attempts to give account of it. (1999, 183)

In a similar manner, Li Simin's stanza of questions can be seen as evoking a lack of control over China's history and future, while at the same time raising up that uncertainty to mythic stature.

The gravitas and import of the song's questions depend largely on the perceived identity of the singer. The eminent northern Shaanxi folk song scholar Yang Cui suggests that Li Simin's dual identity as a boatman in real life *and* a lead performer in Chinese New Year *yangge* performances of "boat on dry land" (*pao hanchuan* 跑旱船) skits infused his song with an aesthetic element transcending the mere description of one person's life experience (2007, 14). The two components of Li's dual identity, in a sense—his work/life experience and his talent as a performer—were combined into a feeling of performed authenticity in his song. The two narratives—life story and performed story—fused together in his performances while at the same time suggesting the possibility of supplementing additional narrative layers from other sources in the future.

Beginning in the 1980s, this song was used in films and performances involving questions of social and cultural identity in the midst of transition. The 1984 film *Life* (*Rensheng* 人生), based on a novel by the northern Shaanxi writer Lu Yao 路遥 (1949–1992), uses the song to bookend a story about the struggles of negotiating the rural-urban divide. The song is played once at the beginning of the film, paired with images of a farmer hoeing the earth on a rugged mountain, and again near the end of the film when the male protagonist returns to his village, standing before a bridge, after a sojourn in the city. The single stanza of questions—unanswered—seems to evoke the long, winding path of tradition. Li Zhiwen, the singer from whom Wang learned the song, performed a version arranged by the Xi'an Film Studio composer Xu Youfu 许友夫 in the film (Yang Cui 1995, 32).[7]

Sometime during the 1980s, a second stanza of answers was added to the song's lyrics. The new two-stanza version continued to allow audiences to ponder the string of ambiguous questions in the first stanza, but now it answered each question in the second stanza with the number "ninety-nine," which in Chinese signifies an infinite number. Here is how Wang Xiangrong performs the second stanza nowadays:

I know—in the whole world, there are ninety-nine bends in the Yellow River, *ai,*
Ninety-nine boats on those bends, *ai,*
Ninety-nine poles on those boats, *ai,*
And ninety-nine boatmen, *yo ho,* moving those boats, *ai hai! Ai hai! Ai hai!*
Nge xiaode, tianxia Huanghe jiushijiu dao wan ai,
Jiushijiu dao wan shang, jiushijiu zhi chuan ai,
Jiushijiu zhi chuan shang, jiushijiu gen gan ai,
Jiushijiu ge na shaogong yo he lai ba chuan lai ban, ai hai! Ai hai! Ai hai!
额晓得，天下黄河九十九道湾哎，[8]
九十九道湾上，九十九只船哎，
九十九只船上，九十九根竿哎，
九十九个那艄公哟嗬来把船来扳，哎嘿！哎嘿！哎嘿！

Whereas the earlier one-stanza version appeared to critically question tradition and the past, this new version declares a triumphant answer—"*I know.*" Though these two stanzas were written over sixty years apart, they are now leveled into one "lyric present" that we as listeners experience in the moment (Culler 2015, 289).[9] As a literary form, the lyric has the potential to conjure up a "discursive time" where different time periods, subjectivities, and viewpoints converse (ibid., 226–228).[10] Even if we watch a performance of this song at some point during the new millennium, it is as if we are witnessing a conversation between questions posed in 1920 about the nation's past and answers provided in the 1980s by someone who benefited from the economic progress following China's opening up and reform—a narrative of progress that we will see reinforced below.

This conversation between past and future is especially evident in the song's appearances at the beginning and end of each episode of the controversial 1988 TV documentary series *River Elegy* (*Heshang* 河殇), which questions the cultural utility of China and the West, once again echoing concerns from the May Fourth era (Su and Wang 1991, 101).[11] Each episode of the series opens with an unidentified male singer singing the first stanza, emphasizing the series' critical theme of questioning Chinese tradition, and ends with a male-female duet singing the second stanza, suggesting that a future of "infinite" possibilities lies in the ideological strategy promoted by the series—opening China to Western ideas—symbolized by the final images of the Yellow River (Chinese tradition) meeting the ocean (Western modernity). The progression from a single male voice questioning Chinese tradition to a couple singing in unison, "I know—the Yellow River has ninety-nine bends," appears to be yet another extension of the "couple going out" paradigm examined earlier. Just as the Yellow River merges with the ocean and China with the West, the two voices of the couple come together in a combined subjectivity—a new sense of "I" that brings together self and Other into a new sense of self. Once again, we find the song used in a moment of conversation between continuity and change, similar, albeit on a smaller scale, to the role of the song in many of Wang's performances in recent years. Wang's performances, in turn, build on the song's symbolic power by incorporating several narrative layers.

The Fusion of Parallel Narratives

For both Li Simin and Wang Xiangrong, the singer's authority to present the song's narrative draws on a combination of lived authenticity and performing talent. This dual identity fuses a sense of "realness" with the "as if" nature of performance and invites others to do the same. A boatman without performing experience would not carry the same weight, and neither would a trained performer with no other authenticating life experience to draw upon. As Wang never worked as a boatman and readily admits to never having set foot on a boat until well into adulthood, he instead validates his performances of this song by drawing on his rise from rural poverty to folk song king.[12]

When Wang was younger, northern Shaanxi as a whole was largely unknown and often looked down upon for its poverty. Speaking to a local crowd at one performance, Wang noted how outsiders used to conflate "northern Shaanxi" with the revolutionary base in Yan'an 延安 (the southern part of northern Shaanxi), unaware of the existence of the northern half of the region, Yulin 榆林, where Wang is from. In several speeches intended to place value on the local, Wang drew parallels between Yulin's remoteness and the invisibility of his home village Marugeda, which does not appear on any map. During an elementary school reunion in 2012, he spoke about Marugeda village, Fugu County, and northern Shaanxi Province:

> What is greatness? What is uniqueness? The more local something is, the closer it is to the people (*minjian*), the more it belongs to the entire world. I often say that with Fugu, maybe you can [find it on a map]. Marugeda, you will never ever find it on any map, but Marugeda, this place, *does exist*. You can't say that just because you can't find it on a map that this place doesn't exist.…I am a Fugu person. I only want to take our Fugu things and use them so that outsiders can get to know Fugu, to see our northern Shaanxi, to see our Marugeda.[13]

While local isolation leads to invisibility, Wang suggests such isolation also nurtures the unique value of a place—its cultural capital. His assertion that "the more local something is…the more it belongs to the entire world" echoes Arif Dirlik's (1999) observation of how "the local…is rendered into a commodity available for global circulation" (160). Elsewhere, Wang draws parallels between the cultural attention his performances have brought to the region and the economic interests attracted by the region's natural resource industry—conveniently summed up by the local slogan "culture paves the way, economics comes to sing the opera" (*wenhua pulu, jingji changxi*) (see chapter 4; cf. Gibbs 2017). Just as Wang became famous by bringing songs rooted in local mountains and rivers to the outside, Fugu also became nationally recognized for the natural resources hidden in its landscape.[14]

Speaking at a banquet for a local business opening in 2011, Wang drew parallels between his own experiences overcoming obstacles and his home region's dramatic transition from invisibility to economic success:

> In the past, people had never heard of Fugu....Nowadays, Shenmu and Fugu...no matter where you go, as soon as you mention them, even if they have never been here, they say right away, "Yes! I have heard of them. They were in the news." Fugu and Shenmu are now number one in Shaanxi Province. So, I am proud. Wherever I go, I stick my queue up like a peacock, and hold my head up high....Although I am not the boss of a [local] company, I belong to this land. When this region does well, I bask in its glory. That is also the glory of Fugu people, and the glory of the Yellow River Basin. So, just now outside down there, I sang "The Infinite Bends of the Yellow River."[15]

Wang's statement that "when this region does well, I bask in its glory" echoes the fusion of personal and national fate evoked in the line, "the country's prosperity is my glory," from the Hong Kong singer's "Chinese Dream." In this speech and elsewhere, Wang lays out several mutually reinforcing narratives: he presents his own struggle and success as intertwined with the fate of the region, and together these narratives reinforce a third—that of the song, which has become a symbol for the nation's history. The personal, regional, national, and lyrical are thus joined together.

One of the ways these narrative layers come together is through the song's sung persona. Having observed Wang perform the song on large stages with LCD projections of the rushing waters of the Yellow River in the background, it often seemed that he was meant to appear as an elderly boatman standing on the river's edge. When I asked Wang about the song's boatman persona, he noted its scalability:

> Some people see it as an old boatman on the Yellow River—standing on the bow, ferrying the boat—this kind of feeling. Now then, as for myself, I see it more as the boatman and the world of the Yellow River represent-

ing the hardships and the difficulties in the lives of all the people who have lived in the Yellow River Basin. Generation after generation, they have traveled down countless winding paths, not smooth at all, just like the numerous, tortuous paths that the Chinese people have traveled during modern times. One could say that this is embodied through an expression of deep distress—my understanding of this song is mainly from this point of view. This is because Chinese people call the Yellow River "Mother River," and the Yellow River Basin and the Yellow Earth comprise the birthplace of the Chinese nation. That is to say, Chinese people believe that they originated from the Yellow River Basin area, and when humankind first appeared in China, they lived on the banks of the Yellow River. Therefore, I see the "Song of the Yellow River Boatmen" as the history of China—the history of the Yellow River, China's history, and the human affairs that took place on the Yellow River, the relationship between nature and mankind—this is my understanding of it.[16]

The persona's flexible ambiguity allows for various scales to be fused together, including the area of the Yellow River Basin and the nation as a whole.

Wang adds additional nuance to the persona's significance by using a regional dialect word for "I" in the second stanza—connecting the persona both to the region and to the nation's rural population. Like Li Zhiwen, Wang answers the question "Do you know?" with "I know," and he answers each of the following questions with the number ninety-nine. Unlike Li Zhiwen, Wang does not use the standard Mandarin word for "I" (*wo* 我), but rather the northern Shaanxi dialect pronunciation *nge* (额). Similar to Wang's use of *nge* in "The East Is Red" (see chapter 3), different audiences could read Wang's use of this widely recognized dialect word in "The Infinite Bends of the Yellow River" in different ways. To those from northern Shaanxi, there is no doubt a sense of familiarity upon hearing this word, as well as a linking together of regional identity to the whole of Chinese history and Chineseness at large. For those from other parts of China, the dialect word might evoke broader notions of the "Folk"—after all, folk material from northern Shaanxi was some of the first to be used by the CCP during the revolutionary period in Yan'an. In this latter sense, one could see this as an emphasis that *everyone* in China, *including the peasants,* has arrived, and China's present and future are bright.

Wang's performances of "The Infinite Bends of the Yellow River" build on these mutually reinforcing personal, regional, and national narratives to present audiences with a narrative of progress connecting the struggles of history to China's recent rise. Although Wang's vocals and the accompanying music for the song are prerecorded and his gestures remain largely similar in each event, the diverse occasions where these performances take place—weddings, business openings, Chinese New Year celebrations, and Christmas concerts—offer different "frames" through which to read Wang's performances (Bauman 1984, 9; cf. Goffman 1974). At a business opening, the backdrop might be a sign with the company's logo and four large characters in an arc reading "Great Fortune in Starting a Business" (*Kaiye daji* 开业大吉) (figure 7.3), or two giant red balloon arches announcing the opening of the business and the appearance of "The Northern Shaanxi Song King, Wang Xiangrong," with a dozen cannons lined up in front of the stage to offer a thunderous salute to the new enterprise (figure 7.4). At a wedding, the backdrop might be a small sign with the word "wedding" in English (figure 7.5) or a large picture of the happy couple projected on a screen (figure 7.6). At one New Year's event in the local government building of his home township in late December of 2011, there was a sign that read "Artistic Gathering to Welcome the New Year" (*Ying xinnian wenyi lianhuanhui* 迎新年文艺联欢会) (figure 7.7), while at a Christmas gala held the evening before at a five-star hotel in the regional capital, there was a large sign that said "Merry Christmas" (figure 7.8). In each of these cases, the song connected the event at hand to a sense of the past and hopes for the future.

During the song's lengthy overture, Wang would stand off to the side, leaving the audience to focus on the backdrop of the stage. The tinkle of wind chimes would bring to mind mist rising from the Yellow River after the spring thaw. Four notes would sound on ancient Chinese *bianzhong* 编钟 bells (a symbol of tradition), foreshadowing the four questions to be asked. Then, as an orchestra's powerful string section began to play, Wang would walk out in measured pace

Figure 7.3 "Great Fortune in Starting a Business." Dingbian, Shaanxi. December 23, 2011. Photograph by author.

Figure 7.4 "The Northern Shaanxi Song King, Wang Xiangrong." Fugu, Shaanxi. November 12, 2011. Photograph by author.

Figure 7.5 "Wedding." Xi'an. March 8, 2012. Photograph by author.

Figure 7.6
Wedding with
projected image
of happy couple.
Shenmu, Shaanxi.
November 10,
2011. Photo-
graphs by author.

Figure 7.7 "Artistic Gathering to Welcome the New Year." Xinmin, Shaanxi. December 25, 2011. Photograph by author.

Figure 7.8 "Merry Christmas." Yulin, Shaanxi. December 24, 2011. Photograph by author.

towards the center, gazing wistfully back at whatever backdrop was there—the business announcement, the photo of the bride and groom, or the New Year's wishes. He would pause for a moment as piano arpeggios rose in a crescendo and the house and stage lights brightened, and then turn his head around to face the audience as he sang, "Do you know how many bends the Yellow River has?" (figure 7.9). This turn from backward- to forward-looking and from the anonymous back of his head to his highly recognizable face in many ways parallels Wang's narratives of struggle and success that highlight the invisibility of the past and the hypervisibility of the present.

During the first stanza of the song, the musical accompaniment was slow and simple—following the rhythm of rowing a boat. As Wang stood in one place, he would sing each question, echoed by a choir of children.[17] The alternation between Wang's advanced age and the youth of the children suggested a backward- and forward-looking trajectory as the audience would mull over the meaning of these questions. Wang's age and rustic outfit gave him the appearance of a bearer of tradition who might very well have seen boatmen on the river in the past and could tell us about them. The children's voices, on the other hand, evoked a sense of youthful wonder about what was yet to come—what would the Yellow River and the region and the nation look like when they were Wang's age? This backward-and-forward sensation paralleled the song's rhythm—oars being pulled backward and forward.

As the second stanza began, the tempo quickened into a driving rhythm evoking an upbeat mood. At that point, Wang would lift his head up high and

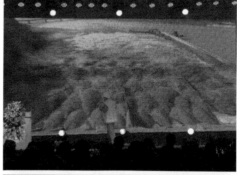

sing, "I know—there are ninety-nine bends on the Yellow River." If anyone from the audience was going to present him with a bouquet of flowers, this was when they usually did so. In venues with runwaylike walkways protruding from the front of the stage, Wang would walk forward into the middle of the audience. In general, his gestures during this second stanza were more forward oriented than during the first, where he had largely stood in one place. Rather than being echoed by a children's choir, Wang would sing the second stanza in unison with a choir of adult male baritones, the answers to the riddles punctuated by powerful blasts from the horn section. As Wang walked forward and smiled at the audience, he would confidently point with his finger at each mention of "ninety-nine." In one televised performance, audience members are seen singing along at this point, waving glow sticks and beaming with smiles.[18] When I listen to this section, I hear a sense of authority, pride, and conviction. At the end of the song, Wang would gaze forward or upward into the distance and wave his right hand (with or without flowers), his final three high-noted cries of *"ai hai!"* seeming to say, "We made it! We made it! We maaaaaaaade it!"[19]

The alternation between Wang's voice and the two choruses is similar to the interplay of solo and choral voices in his "MTV 'The East Is Red'" performances described in chapter 3. The shifting between solo voice and chorus juxtaposes the personal and collective, individual and nation in mutually reinforcing ways. A similar arrangement of individual and collective voices can be seen in the renowned Chinese operatic soprano Guo Lanying's (b. 1929) iconic rendition of "My Motherland" ("Wo de zuguo" 我的祖国) in the 1956 film *Battle on Shangganling Mountain*.[20] Playing the role of a young female soldier named Wang Lan, Guo Lanying sings "My Motherland" to a unit of soldiers sitting in a cave bunker, her solo voice alternating stanzas with a four-part choir. Similar to Wang's "MTV 'The East Is Red,'" there is a progression from a largely male choir in the second stanza to a fuller, brighter mixed choir with more prominent female voices in the final stanza. Again, this progression seems to represent larger and larger collective entities.

In *Battle on Shangganling Mountain*, Guo Lanying's song begins with a close-up of Guo singing the first stanza about growing up on the banks of a wide river, hearing the songs of boatmen and watching the white sails of their boats.[21] As she sings, the other soldiers, some bandaged and others smoking cigarettes, gaze on nostalgically. The beginning of the second stanza switches to a shot of two male soldiers seated in the foreground singing, "This is the beautiful motherland, the place where I was born and raised," in unison with a soft, largely male choir. As they sing the second stanza's final two lines—"In this vast land, there are bright and beautiful sights everywhere"—the camera pans from the cave's interior to its opening, revealing a bright, expansive landscape outside. As the camera moves out of the cave, the image dissolves into a sequential montage of billowing white clouds, the majestic Great Wall, gushing rivers, and vast mountains. Guo Lanying sings the third stanza solo. As she sings the third stanza's two final lines, "To build a new frontier and awaken the slumbering mountains, / Let us transform the river's appearance," the images shift from a serene river flanked by karst mountains and a rushing waterfall to images of progress—panning shots of immense dams and factories billowing with smoke. As these images of industrial progress fill the screen, a fuller choir with more prominent female voices sings the fourth stanza about the "heroic" motherland, adding, "In this ancient land, the spirit of youth is everywhere." Following the montage of factory images, we see another shot of bright, white clouds—seeming to suggest a bright future—and the camera reenters the cave, panning across a row of seated soldiers, back to a close-up of Guo Lanying. The fifth and sixth stanzas alternate once again between her solo voice and an even fuller, more resonant choral voice filled with female high notes.

In both "My Motherland" and "The Infinite Bends of the Yellow River," we see references to the river's expansiveness. Guo Lanying sings about the "wide" river, while Wang Xiangrong sings about its numerous bends. In addition to lyrics about rivers, boats, and boatmen, we see other similar choices in imagery. During "My Motherland," the "powerful images…projected on screen: the Great Wall, gorgeous mountains, beautiful rivers, and modern industrial factories that billow smoke" resemble the images preceding and accompanying Wang's 2014 CCTV Spring Gala performance—the Yellow River, Great Wall, natural landscapes, and modern buildings (Pickowicz 2010, 359). In both cases, the voice of the individual singer is paired with symbolic images of the nation, alternating between individual and collective experiences and perhaps using the individual and the collective to authenticate each other.

What distinguishes Wang's performances of "The Infinite Bends of the Yellow River" from Guo Lanying's performance of "My Motherland" and Wang's performances of his "MTV 'The East Is Red'" is the combination in "The Infinite Bends" of Wang's voice first with a children's choir and then with an adult choir. In an analysis of televised musical events celebrating Macau's return to the People's Republic of China in 1999, Lauren Gorkfinkel (2014, 100) describes a solo performance during the 1999 *CCTV Spring Festival Gala* by a Macau girl with a local accent echoed by adults singing Mandarin. Both Wang Xiangrong and the girl present a sense of local authenticity and individual subjectivity, with the echoing choirs offering "supportive emulation" (Gorfinkel 2014; cf. Van Leeuwen 1999). However, the two singers' contrasting ages create different effects. Whereas the young girl presents Macau as "a young child [who] needs his or her mother…a small but treasured part of a powerful Chinese nation" and the adult choir that echoes her represents the "mainland 'mother'" (Gorfinkel 2014, 100), Wang's pairing with the children's choir directs the questions of "The Infinite Bends" in two directions, toward the past and toward the future. Like the adult choir in the Macau example, the children's choir in Wang's song echoes the solo voice's dialect-inflected words with standard Mandarin, suggesting the merging "of the local entity with the bigger collective nation" (ibid.). When Wang is later joined by the adult choir in the second stanza of "The Infinite Bends," the local individual has found his place in the collective.

In China's search for the voice of the nation, Sue Tuohy (2001, 115) notes the complexity involved in choosing from the nation's diverse options:

> When musical activists searched for the people's voice, they found vocal diversity; no one voice represented the nation as a whole, let alone met their goals for a national future. Because defining the voice of the people is tantamount to defining the nation, the activists had different opinions as to what such a voice should sound like. Should the nation's voice be an urban sound from the metropolitan coast or a rural sound from the inland provinces? Were the people to sound traditional, or modern, or "futuristic"—an ideal sound of a Chinese people united in the future? Some advocated maintaining a Chinese "essence" from the past, only to be countered by those arguing China needed a new, stronger voice to meet both nationalist and popular demand.

Wang's juxtaposition with the two choirs offers a combination of desired representations. His questions, echoed by the children's choir, are both rooted in tradition and the past and forward looking. His dialect pronunciation evokes China's inland rurality, fused with the "new, stronger voice" of the baritone choir (Tuohy 2001, 115). In both "MTV 'The East Is Red'" and "The Infinite Bends of the Yellow River," the Mandarin-singing choir serves an integral part in Wang's regional-cum-national singer persona.

Wang's performances usually occurred near the end of an event, offering a sense of history and tradition to the context at hand. When I watched Wang sing "The Infinite Bends of the Yellow River" at a wedding in northern Shaanxi Province in late 2011, he first gazed back at a projected portrait of the wedding couple and then turned around to sing to the assembled guests. Singing a song that ties local imagery to China's larger history after gazing back at the couple to be married, Wang seemed to be saying, "This is where you come from, and this is where you are going." The images that Wang gazes back at in each performance appear to symbolize changes—the couple will be married and start a new family, the new year will replace the old, before it too is replaced by another new year. Wang's gazes at the backdrops draw audiences' attention to these transformations. His turns to face each audience then acknowledge those present in the moment of the event. By following Wang's turning gaze as he sings "you" first to the backdrop and then to the audience, we can visualize him connecting the background image's transition from past to future to the live audience in front of him, fusing the two into one subjectivity that he constructs as he calls out to it (Althusser 2001). This connecting gaze places the audience and event in the center of an arc from past to future, in a "now" firmly situated between what has been and what will come—bringing them into "an iterable *now*" that connects the audience to all other audiences of past and future performances, placing them in a stream of history (Culler 2015, 294–295, italics in original).

By situating each event in this way, Wang's performances suggest to those present that they will be able to transition smoothly from one state to another—a message Wang reinforces with multiple "crossing over" narratives of struggle and success: his life story, the questions and answers of "The Infinite Bends of the Yellow River," and the history of the region and nation he connects to the song. Wang's merging of narratives resonates with Jeff Todd Titon's characterization of folk artists as individuals "whose enacted or performed stories—or 'little narratives,'…instantiate and in turn are validated by one of their community's metanarratives" (Titon 2012, 230; Lyotard 1984). Here, the dyadic structure of "The Infinite Bends of the Yellow River" can be seen as a performed metaphor for Wang's personal and regional identity. Just as Wang moves from the anonymous back of his head to his famous face and the song's lyrics move from the anonymity of the past (we do not know how many boatmen have been on the Yellow River) to the confident "I" of the present (e.g., "I know"), so have Wang and the region crossed over from invisibility to hypervisibility.[22] The narratives of the song, region, and nation thus reinforce the significance of Wang's life, bolstering his authority to serve as a link between past, present, and future, and his story reinforces the narratives of the song, region, and nation.

The song's message of a great past and a greater future can apply to a range of situations.[23] In several events I observed, Wang's role seemed to be that of an "intermediary" offering a sense of continuity amidst social change. In Arnold van Gennep's classic study of rites of passage, he suggests that such individuals "serve as…bridges, chains, or links," and "facilitate the changing of condition without violent social disruptions" (1960, 48). Such a smooth transition in a changing world is something any enterprise, couple, or local government might desire, especially when that transition is anchored between a rich history of tradition and a future filled with prosperity.

For audience members, Wang's performances of a "traditional" song merging personal, regional and national narratives show how the experience of an individual can embody collective experiences, enacting what Titon (1988, 461) calls the "passing [of] tradition through individual experience to forge communal truth." When Wang fuses his own narrative to the narratives around him, he encourages listeners to consider how their lives might also connect to larger metanarratives of struggle and success. When Wang challenges each audience to respond to the string of riddles at the beginning of the song, he takes them on a mental journey to the Yellow River of the past, destabilizing their senses of self. Then, when he sings the answers together with the bass choir—suggesting that the audience might join in, too, even if subvocally—Wang brings the audience back to a renewed sense of the here and now. This chance to join in offers audience members a site to assert their personal and group identity by saying "I know" with undertones of "we know"—as seen in the televised crowd singing along while waving glow sticks. When audiences do join in, they engage in a collective experience of the individual, a "feeling together" of the "subjective in the collective" (Fernandez 1988b, cited in Noyes 2003, 30; Frith 1996a, 110). Though the "you" in "do you know" ambiguously refers to each audience member, the audience responds as a group with "I," individually and collectively reaffirming their senses of place in the broader historical and geographical contexts of the event's "here and now."

Once again, we see the power of a song's ambiguity. Though the song provides an answer—ninety-nine—at the same time, it refuses to provide a real number. Ninety-nine is a metaphor for an infinite number, a generality with the illusion of specificity—as if the word "many" could at the same time be a countable number. In a sense, "there are ninety-nine bends in the Yellow River" continues to marvel at the unknowability raised by the question, "answering" without really answering. One is reminded of the iconic "How many roads must a man walk down / Before you call him a man?" from the American singer Bob Dylan's "Blowin' in the Wind," to which Dylan responds, "The answer is blowin' in the wind" (Dylan 2016, 53). The specific yet vague nature of "ninety-nine" in "The Infinite Bends of the Yellow River" is similar to the fuzzy firmness of Dylan's answer. Mike Marqusee suggests that Dylan's "ambiguous refrain...gropes for the unnameable" while "the 'answer'...remains elusive" (2005, 60). Dylan himself described the answer as floating "just like a restless piece of paper" (cited in Marqusee 2005, 61).

Symbolic answers to questions about the unknowable have, I suggest, an important social function. "Riddles," writes Ian Hamnett, "are often 'objectively' susceptible of more than one reasonable and appropriate solution, but in fact only one solution 'counts' as correct" (1967, 384). While a host of alternatives could potentially respond to "how many bends does the Yellow River have," the agreed-upon answer "ninety-nine" has a unifying effect. Lee Haring notes, "the connection between question and answer is fixed by tradition and popular acceptance" (Haring 1974, 197). Savely Senderovich sees the answer as a shared "social property": "The folk riddle as it functions in the folk ritual of riddling is not intended to be solved by the individual's wit—the riddle's answer is a social property; both sides in the riddling ritual are supposed to be in possession of it, or one teaching and the other learning it" (2005, 20).

This idea that the *answer is not supposed to be guessed* is key. While the competitive nature of many riddling situations appears to value "individual wits" who can "outsmart" others, the "shared social property" of the answers often reinforces group identity. For audiences around China, "ninety-nine bends" connects them to the stream of Chinese history, complete with all of its zigs and zags. For American audiences, the answer "blowin' in the wind" links them to a similar sense of stability amidst contemporary American history's various twists and turns.

By connecting individuals to broader narratives that surround them, Wang's performances of "The Infinite Bends of the Yellow River" offer audiences a means to incorporate social change into a dynamic sense of self. If not addressed, social change can be disorienting, and it is precisely the ability to connect our stories to those around us that helps us maintain a "stable" sense of self. This feeling of stability is not unlike what someone sitting on a boat feels as they float down a river—though their position is constantly shifting in relation to others, when they sit still it feels as though they are hardly moving at all. If all goes smoothly, they move from one point to the next, observing the changes in the scenery on the banks while not being disturbed by them. However, when the water becomes turbulent, the same movement from one point to the next becomes a dramatic affair.

"The Infinite Bends of the Yellow River" serves as a site for a perpetual public conversation, linking the social choices at hand to choices made in the past and those to be made in the future. The dialogic nature of song allows these singers to converse with past (upstream) and future (downstream) and other places and peoples (along the banks). This conversation is ongoing—incorporating new voices as it both builds on old voices and allows them to fade away. Whereas "myths seem to reinforce the established order," Elli Köngäs Maranda suggests that riddles "question at least certain kinds of established order…mak[ing] a point of playing with conceptual borderlines and crossing them for the pleasure of showing that things are not quite as stable as they appear" (1971, 53). The destabilizing effect of such questioning is precisely the sort of push into liminality that we need to help us adapt to social change. At the same time, the "mythic" quality of the ninety-nine boatmen on the ninety-nine bends of the Yellow River could be seen as bolstering a sense of tenacity amidst such changes. Perhaps "The Infinite Bends of the Yellow River" fuses elements of myth and riddle to alternately question and reaffirm the current social state within the larger stream of history.

The repeated performances of "The Infinite Bends of the Yellow River," furthermore, form a site for negotiations of public memory. Benjamin Filene argues that public memory is largely formed through repetition and involves "revisiting and reevaluating the culture of the past in the light of the present" (2000, 8). By hearing songs such as "The Infinite Bends of the Yellow River" and "The East Is Red" again and again, year in and year out, the songs are able to "read" the audiences at intervals as the audience members continue to grow and change with life experience and the passage of time. Each of Wang's performances of "The Infinite Bends" exhibits a "double grounding" situated in relation to previous performances as well as the context of the immediate event, similar to Paul Connerton's notion of the double identity of each day of the year—the individual day and the echoes it carries of the same date in previous years (Bauman 2004, 149; Connerton 1989, 65). Each performance draws on a sense of repetition stemming from earlier performances, both by Wang and his predecessors.

In this manner, multiple iterations of "one" song can provide personal and social meanings for individuals and groups of various scales, connecting them across time and space while highlighting their relevance in the present. Wang's performances of "The Infinite Bends of the Yellow River" serve as sites where singers and audiences negotiate personal and collective meanings, "articulat[ing] private but common desires" in "a shared public language" (Grossberg 1992, 207). The song acts as a tapestry of meanings that weaves in new narratives and contexts with each performance. Part of the reason "The Infinite Bends of the Yellow River" and "Blowin' in the Wind" have become iconic seems to be their ability to serve as such tapestries, amassing power with each performance. One is reminded of John Miles Foley's notion of "word-power," where a phrase—or in this case a song—gains power over time as it gathers accumulated meanings (1995, xiv).[24] Though "Blowin' in the Wind" was composed in the 1960s, a 2003 *Boston Globe* article noted that Dylan's song was still one of the protest songs of choice in peace rallies against the Iraq War (Kennedy 2003). Perhaps the repeated performances of "Blowin' in the Wind" reminded protesters of the powerful social movements of the 1960s in the United States, suggesting that song's ability to link the issue at hand to a larger history of social struggle—a means to connect audiences to a sense of stability without getting pinned down.

A similarly poignant example of one song tying together social conversations from different periods can be seen in a performance of "The Infinite Bends of the Yellow River" Wang gave during a Christmas Concert at a five-star Yulin hotel on December 24, 2011. In that concert, Wang's backward gaze at the beginning of the song was met by an image of revolutionary martyrs that morphed into the words "Merry Christmas" after Wang turned around. Though the two images might seem unconnected, Wang's turning gaze as he sang "you" fused together the nostalgia for a revolutionary past with the "romance" of the Christmas Eve luxury event (Christmas Eve's "romance" was a theme that the event's emcees highlighted several times). Once again, Wang's backward- and forward-looking performance connected the arc of history to the moment of the event, presenting nostalgia for the past in the present with an eye toward the future.

As song kings and queens move us from place to place, it is as if they are boatmen guiding our boats. They navigate us away from dangerous rocks while helping us to interact with various Others along the banks, enriching our senses of self. Each iconic singer assumes a unique position as if riding the crest of a wave—lifted up by previous singers who push the singer from behind, while pushing along other singers into the future.

Rivers, like desires, flow toward ever-receding destinations. Songs, too, call out to ever-receding addressees (cf. Žižek 2005). While a singer might imagine his or her words are heard by an Other, the singer's desire to call out is really a desire to move forward in a particular direction, pulling the audience along. Song kings and queens sing out to elusive targets "up ahead," propelling singer, tradition, and audience toward those targets. As we the audience sit along the river's banks or in the singer's boat, we observe it all, sometimes identifying with the singer, sometimes with the Other they are singing to, and sometimes reflecting on the desire that drives the singer to call out. When Wang sings "East, you are that red, Sun, you have risen," he moves rhetorically toward the points of view embodied by the East and the Sun, allowing audiences to follow along. In a similar fashion, when guest performers sing "oh say can you see" at American baseball games, the "you" in the lyrics addresses a symbolic entity who feels pride in "the land of the free and the home of the brave"—and audience members decide how to relate to that entity.[25] When Bob Dylan sings "the answer is blowin' in the wind," he summons a fluttering "piece of paper" audiences can choose to relate to, connecting themselves to a never-ending conversation about social change (cited in Marqusee 2005, 61). Similarly, when Wang Xiangrong sings about "ninety-nine bends" in the Yellow River, he offers audiences a tangible yet amorphous entity simultaneously connected to the moment and to a stream of conversations about stability and change that have occurred as society moves between tradition and modernity.

In Wang's performances of "The Infinite Bends," he stands with his audiences on the banks of the river, conjuring up images of boats and boatmen while observing them together with the audience. The song sets up a public conversation that audiences join in on, and Wang provides the conversation's voices at the same time that he joins the crowd.[26] Through lyrics and gestures, he merges subjective and objective points of view. Walking into the crowd during the second stanza, Wang brings a sense of continuity with tradition into the audience's present. Wang's steps forward suggest that the future is rooted in a past integrated with the present. As Wang walks into the crowd, he pulls the Other of tradition and the past into the audience's present self, "kneading" the Other into the self to produce a stronger subjectivity (figure 7.10). Just as a bread maker pulls the dough's outer edges into its heart, building an internal structure and a redefined sense of self and other, Wang pulls the edges of the exotic—those which border on the familiar—into the audience's focus, shifting back and forth between self and Other, here and there, past and present, just as a baker rocks back and forth as he kneads dough to make bread.

Returning once again to the 2014 CCTV Spring Festival Gala, as the Hong Kong singer finished singing "the country's prosperity is my glory"—fusing personal and national fate in a manner similar to Wang's juxtaposed narratives—there was an image projected of the Great Wall, another symbol of China's long and winding history. After a shot of the audience, Wang Xiangrong began to sing, "Do you know?" This time, however, his questions were answered by a younger singer (figure 7.11). As the younger singer sang out "I know," the

Figure 7.10 Wang "kneading" the audience. Shenmu, Shaanxi. November 10, 2011. Photograph by author.

Figure 7.11 Younger singer answers "I know" at 2014 CCTV Gala.

Figure 7.12 River of dancers at 2014 CCTV Gala.

accompanying male dancers—spread out like a river between the two singers—gazed upward into the distance (figure 7.12). Just as Wang Xiangrong's life, songs, and performances were influenced by earlier individuals who placed their own stamps on the traditions in which they engaged, Wang also provides a model for younger generations as they search for meaning in their own encounters between self and Other. The river flows on.

Epilogue

GLOBAL SONG KINGS AND QUEENS

There is no self-knowledge without other, and no knowledge of other without metaphor.
—Robert Cantwell, 1993

ALTHOUGH the terms "song king" (*gewang*) and "song queen" (*gehou*) may be uniquely Chinese, there are singers around the world who move from rural to urban landscapes, transforming themselves and the local traditions they carry with them into symbols of larger regions, nations, peoples, and epochs. These singers physically embody mediation between groups through their movement, lives, and performances. The songs they sing, as well as events from their life stories that spark public interest, become discursive sites for social tensions as people strive to redefine themselves as the world changes. Many of these singers live during transitional times, their lives coinciding with the rise of new nations and historical periods. Umm Kulthūm (1904–1975), the "Voice of Egypt," brought a rural art form to urban Cairo and connected a national Egyptian identity to the surrounding Arab world through her performances (Danielson 1997). The "Queen of Enka" Misora Hibari (1937–1989) became a national icon in the years of postwar Japan (Tansman 1996). The Scottish folk singer Jeannie Robertson (1908–1975) represented Traveller culture and the past to large audiences through her songs and performances of Child Ballads (Porter and Gower 1995). Leadbelly (1889–1949) brought rural African American folk music to affluent, mostly Caucasian audiences in the New York area (Wolfe and Lornell 1999). Each involved a movement in time and space between the context in which the performer first encountered songs and the places and people to whom he/she later performed them. Through such performances, the singers were able to mediate between ethnic groups, socioeconomic classes, localities, regions, nations, and eras.

Each of these singers rose to fame in large part due to their perceived authenticity—not only in the intense emotions of performances that fused talented artistic expression with "real" lives, but in "local authenticity" tied to the past and particular places and peoples evoked through their songs. This

Table 2. Global singers, titles, and areas of representation

Singers	Titles	Areas of Representation
Joe Heaney	"Bright Star of the West"; "Irish Song-Man"	Irish
Michael Jackson	"King of Pop"	Global Pop/American
Robert Johnson	"King of the Delta"	Delta Blues
Umm Kulthūm	"Voice of Egypt"	Egypt/Arab World
Leadbelly	"King of the Twelve-String"	American Folk and Blues
Hibari Misora	"Queen of Enka"; "The People's Singer"; "The People's Voice"; "The Singing Queen"; "Japan's Greatest Postwar Singer"	Post-World War II Japan
Frank Mitchell	"Navajo Blessingway Singer"	Navajo
Luciano Pavarotti	"King of High Cs"	Italy/Bel Canto Opera
Jesse Ponce	"Conjunto Master"	Tejano (Texas-Mexican)
Elvis Presley	"Cat King"; "King of Rock 'n' Roll"	American Rock 'n' Roll
Esma Redžepova and Stevo Teodosievski	"King and Queen of Romani Music"	Romani/Macedonian
Pete Seeger	"America's Tuning Fork"	American Folk Music
Mercedes Sosa	"The Voice of Latin America"; "The Voice of the Voiceless"; "The Nation's Most Beloved Voice"	Chile/Latin America
Muddy Waters	"Father of Modern Chicago Blues"	Downhome Folk Blues/ Old-Time Roots Music

Note: Select references include Sean Williams 2011; Williams and Ó Laoire 2011; Tansman 1996; Bourdaghs 2012; Wald 2004; Danielson 1997; Wolfe and Lornell 1999; Frisbie and McAllester 1978; Harnish 2009; Marcus 1991; Silverman 2014; Filene 2000; Dunaway 1990; and Sloan 2011.

sense of authenticity often offset the technological aspects involved in their rise to fame—distribution networks such as high-powered radio, record companies, and regional satellite TV stations—providing a counterargument to critics who might accuse them of commercialization. And yet, while authenticity constitutes a major part of these singers' claim to fame, a singer's categorization as "song king" or "song queen" is contestable and always in flux; as individuals who are simultaneously insiders and outsiders, these singers straddle amorphous borders, shifting their presentations of powerful yet fuzzy identities in different ways to different audiences, constantly drawing and redrawing lines between "here" and "there" and self and other in the process. Audienes who identify with the singers' placement of those lines declare them kings and queens. Those who do not call them imposters.

Although the archetypical song kings and queens move from countryside to city (in modern times at least), it is their mediating function that defines them, not their birthplace. Some singers come from urban spaces and bring rural traditions back to the cities—think of Pete Seeger (1919–2014) and an early Bob Dylan (b. 1941) in the days when Dylan impersonated Woody Guthrie (1912–1967). Such singers may be criticized as "interlopers" or "imitators," or, if seen as authentic representatives, they may be praised as "folk stylists" (Titon 2012; Filene 2000).[1] Likewise, singers moving from the countryside to the city may become "song kings" or "song queens" if they maintain their authenticity in the process, but they may also be seen as having "lost their flavor," "walked onto the stage," or otherwise severed their connections with the rural contexts from which their songs emerged, becoming "Countrypolitans" (Titon 2012, 239). While song kings and queens are celebrated for their "traveled" authenticity, adapting too completely to their new audiences means losing their roots and title.

The obstacles song kings and queens encounter—the moments of tension and conflict in their stories—reflect choices that people in society are making at the time about who they are and who they are not. The stage represents a meeting ground between self and Other, and audiences' reactions to what they see onstage contribute to a sense of identity. When Bob Dylan played an electric guitar at the 1965 Newport Folk Festival, one of the resulting controversies revolved around what constituted folk music, and by extension, who was folk and who was not.[2] If Dylan had performed in an electric band for fans of that style of music or with an acoustic guitar for an audience who liked acoustic, none of the audience members' beliefs, tastes, or senses of self would have been questioned. When a performer offends the audience, controversies over what it means to relate between self and Other in an appropriate way emerge. Communication breaks down and distinct choices come into view. "Untrained" singing style or "scientific" vocal training? Acceptance of singing in public or respect for urban noise ordinances? Arranged marriage or free love? Country or city? Tradition or modernity? Local or regional? Or national? Or global?

These choices surface after we encounter different ways of doing things and thinking about how we live. By recognizing different options available to us, we are compelled to respond by either sticking with what we have, opting for something else, or forging a blend in between. No matter how we react, the choice engages us, drawing us out of our comfort zones, before we return to a renewed sense of self with a decision. What a singer like Wang Xiangrong offers to audiences is an opportunity to encounter similarity and difference. He brings these experiences through his travels and expresses them aesthetically through his songs and speeches. Through the performances of Wang and other song kings and queens, audiences are able to redefine themselves amidst a range of what is familiar and what is not. Singers are not the only ones who mediate between people, periods, and places—we might think of any number of writers, artists, dancers, and other performers who adapt and present some artistic expression from one "place" or "state" to another, highlighting commonalities and differences in the process. Like Wang's life and songs, their lives and expressions too become sites for discussions of choices as the world evolves.

NOTES

Introduction

1. This performance occurred during the Eleventh CHIME Conference/Fieldwork Project in northern Shaanxi Province in the summer of 2006. I am indebted to the organizers, especially Antoinet Schimmelpenninck and Frank Kouwenhoven, for all of the arrangements.

2. For the complete translated lyrics and original Chinese, see chapter 2. In many of the love songs examined in this book, "little sister" (*meimei* 妹妹) is the term used to refer to the female lover and "older brother" (*gege* 哥哥) refers to the male lover. Unless otherwise noted, all translations of song lyrics and excerpts from Chinese interviews are my own.

3. For other recent works looking at the relationship between individual musicians and larger traditions, see Stock (2001), Rees (2009), Kouwenhoven and Schimmelpenninck (2009), Danielson (1997), and Tansman (1996). For examinations of aspects of this dynamic among a range of traditions, see Cashman et al. (2011).

4. For more on the history of intangible cultural heritage preservation in China, see Rees (2012). For a study of other musical traditions in northern Shaanxi, including storytelling bards (*shuoshu* 说书) and shawm bands, see Jones (2009).

5. For other studies of the lives of individual Chinese folk singers, see Kouwenhoven and Schimmelpenninck (2009) and Zhang Junren (2004).

6. Sarah Allan (1997) notes that for the Chinese philosopher Confucius and the pre-Socratic Greek philosopher Heraclitus, "the imagery of the river suggests time passing" (11), and suggests that "water, in the form of the stream with a natural spring as its source, provides a model for ideas of both transience and continuity" (13).

7. Another metaphor brought to mind by rivers is the expression of emotion through song and poetry. When Wang spoke of singing as a means of emotional release, he used a verb (*xuanxie*) meaning "to unbosom oneself" or literally "to drain off (liquids)" (interview, July 19, 2006). The metaphor "to drain off liquids" is reminiscent of Wordsworth's characterization of poetry as "the spontaneous overflow of powerful feelings" in his "Preface" to *Lyrical Ballads* (1800, xiv). Abrams (1989) points to the word "overflow" as an instance of the "water-language" often used to discuss feelings (13).

8. John Fiske (2011) has suggested that multiple potential meanings of a sign contribute

to the sign's popularity among diverse audiences. In his study of television culture, Fiske writes, "the polysemy of the text is necessary if it is to be popular amongst viewers who occupy a variety of situations within the social structure" (16). A similar dynamic seems to be at play with the ambiguous regional personae of song kings and queens, as well as the sung personae of their songs.

9. Wang Xiangrong interview, July 14, 2010.

10. Similar to the "song gods" who "created" local genres that helped people and places to position themselves in relation to others, Chinese kings are traditionally credited with creating culture and civilization (*wen*) (Xu 2006, 9; D. Howard Smith 1957, 183).

11. Wang used this term "half a peasant" in a speech to his former classmates at an elementary school reunion in Fugu County Town on March 27, 2012.

12. Amy Shuman (2005) calls this aspect of stories "transvaluing the personal to the more than personal" (4).

13. Other terms for what I am calling "sung personae" include "lyric speaker" (DuBois 2006, 212) and "fictional speaker/character" (Culler 2015, 350).

14. See Wang's (2006) CD.

15. In Jonathan Culler's (2015) study of lyric poetry, he defines "triangulated address" as "addressing the audience of readers by addressing or pretending to address someone or something else, a lover, a god, natural forces, or personified abstractions" (8). Gregory Nagy (1996) notes, "The concept of lyrical dialogues...lies at the heart of the medieval *troubadour* traditions, where one side of a dialogue, the side of the lover, is highlighted as if it were a monologue. As a performance, such a monologue is of course implicitly a dialogue with the audience who is being addressed, as also with the beloved, real or imaginary" (38).

16. Jia Pingwa was born in the same year as Wang Xiangrong in rural southern Shaanxi. Like Wang, Jia moved to Xi'an during the course of his professional career and has been described as having a "double identity"—simultaneously inhabiting a rural identity and an urban residency, which required a constant shifting between the two (Lai Daren 2000, cited in Wang 2006, 32). Both Jia and Wang, similar to many other regional writers and singers in China, have been elected committee members in the Chinese People's Political Consultative Conference (CPPCC), positions that are intended to offer popular representation in dialogue with the government. Another writer, Lu Yao 路遥 (1949–1992) from rural northern Shaanxi, coined the term "urban-rural intersection" (*chengxiang jiaocha didai* 城乡交叉地带) to describe the work that he and similar writers were engaged in (Yasumoto 1999). Another term, "urban residence with rural association" (*nongyi chengji* 农裔城籍), has been used to describe writers from rural areas who have later become urban residents, although they still attach themselves to their original hometowns (Li Xing 1989). This dual nature applies to Wang Xiangrong as well, living as he does in urban Xi'an while continuing to identify himself with his (now almost deserted) rural mountain village hometown.

17. Cited in Yang Yinliu (1980, 1:47).

18. For a translation of the story, see Cai (2002, 41–42). See also Sue Tuohy's discussion (2001, 112) of Confucius discerning the character of a state by hearing its music.

19. The periphery is brought onto stage for the center in a manner through which the urban audience's "psychic tourism" allows them to construct their own modernity and centrality, "for time passes and 'provincial' and 'anachronistic' tend to coincide. Out from the center means backwards in time" (Levenson 1967, 280, 274).

20. Both "rich" and "poor" attribute value to money, while "modern" and "not modern" imply that how we associate with time affects the way we think.

21. Shuman (2005) suggests that "storytelling acknowledges and invents patterns as part

of a dynamic relationship between chaos and pattern," similar to the life stories and performances of song kings and queens (13).

22. Wang Xiangrong interview, July 14, 2010.

Chapter 1: The Meanings of a Life

1. Schimmelpenninck 1997, 125.

2. The actual distance traveled varies between song kings. Wang Luobin 王洛宾 (1913–1996) traveled all over the Northwest, adapting songs from various minority ethnic groups, while Qian Afu 钱阿福 (1909–1993) went to work in a bakery in the city of Wuxi, where he learned a great deal of folk songs from a coworker, before returning to his village (Harris 2005; Schimmelpenninck 1997, 59). Campbell (2004) discusses such variability in the "separation from the world" part of the story, and, referring to the future "boon" that the hero will bring back, suggests, "The deed of the hero in the second part of his personal cycle will be proportionate to the depth of his descent during the first" (296). While it is questionable whether Campbell's theory applies here, it is certainly true that Wang Luobin is far more nationally and even internationally recognized than Qian Afu. Such correspondences are by no means conclusive but deserve to be examined further in the future.

3. Myron L. Cohen (1991) notes how "examination system lore deeply penetrated popular thinking" (124). The connection between individual ability, geography, and social mobility implied in such lore is evident in Henrietta Harrison's (2002) study of a Qing dynasty scholar from Shanxi Province's sense of rural/urban place as evoked in his diary: "Liu define[d] the political hierarchy of settlements in terms of a hierarchy of ability" (92).

4. Wang Xiangrong interview, Fugu, Shaanxi, July 19, 2006.

5. Helen Rees (2012) translates the term *yuanshengtai min'ge* as "original ecology folksongs" (34). For more on the recent rise in interest surrounding *yuanshengtai* folksongs and how it connects to discourse on environmental and cultural preservation in China, see Rees (2016).

6. For more on the drive toward "being scientific (*kexuehua*)" in the development of a "homogenized pan-Chinese music style," see Lau (2008, 27).

7. In China, and perhaps elsewhere, there seem to be certain similarities between the implications of performing something onstage and writing something down. The latter involves the Chinese literary tradition of "writing is meant to convey truth" (*wenyizaidao* 文以载道), where what is written down—similar to what is performed onstage—is often presumed to promote a sense of moral purpose.

8. It should be noted that although Wang Luobin was called a "folk song king," he was known more as a composer rather than a professional singer.

9. The imprisonment of folk singers for political reasons is hardly unique to China. One year after Wang Luobin received fifteen years at a labor camp, the American folk singer Pete Seeger received ten years (which could be served concurrently) after being made to testify before the House Un-American Activities Committee (HUAC) and was sentenced to "a year and a day in federal prison," although he was later acquitted (Dunaway 1990, 200–210). Nevertheless, he was blacklisted and effectively barred from television appearances for several years, again for singing songs inappropriate to the political context of the medium at the time (Dunaway 1990).

10. Among the older generations of singers in northern Shaanxi, there are several examples. Ding Xicai, who was from the same county as Wang and later went on to teach at the Shanghai Conservatory, participated in one such contest in 1953; Yang Jinshan 杨进山

(1912–1987) attended several such events both at the county and prefectural level; and Chen Weiye, who was from the same county as Wang but of an older generation, was invited to perform in a large-scale performance conference in 1975 (Huo 2006, 2:949–950). At that time, Wang was still not well known outside of his home area and did not participate (Li Shibin interview, Xi'an, July 14, 2010). Li Zhiwen, like Wang, attended multiple levels of song contests beginning in 1977 and won awards in each, although their careers diverged in the 1980s, with Li playing older characters in films and working as a consultant for the Yulin Folk Arts Troupe and Wang working as a member of the troupe (Huo 2006, 2:950–951).

11. There is a photo of the all-female a cappella folk song troupe, of which Ma Ziqing was a member and lead singer, meeting Zhou Enlai in the collection of pictures at the beginning of the first volume of Huo 2006.

12. Examples might include Elvis meeting U.S. president Richard Nixon, Michael Jackson meeting U.S. president Ronald Reagan, Misora Hibari's connection with Emperor Hirohito, Umm Kulthūm's friendship with Egyptian president 'Abd al-Nāsir, and countless others (Tansman 1996; Danielson 1997).

13. Wang Xiangrong has served as a spokesman for various northern Shaanxi products, including *baijiu* liquor, regional cell phone services, clothing, and dried bean curd. In a similar fashion, the hugely popular ethnic Miao singer A You Duo 阿幼朵 has helped to advertise regional products and tourism in Guizhou Province (Schein 2010). Regarding A You Duo's product promotion, Louisa Schein (2010) writes, "A You Duo's ethnic image has saturated popular culture in Guizhou. An advertisement for a telephone information service featured six photos of A You Duo in costume and appeared on billboards all over the province. She has become a celebrity worthy of doing product endorsements. In Guiyang, her smiling face appeared on a three-story-high billboard on the side of a building" (159).

14. For discussion of Wang Xiangrong's lectures on northern Shaanxi folksongs and their social history at various universities and music conservatories, see Luo (2006) and Chu and Jiang (2005, 16).

15. See http://cn.chinagate.cn/culture/2013-01/10/content_27643519.htm (accessed April 29, 2017).

16. This two-character Chinese term combines *chuan* 传, meaning to pass on, hand down, impart, teach, transmit, and so on, and *cheng* 承, meaning to bear, hold, carry, continue, or carry on. As this process is institutionally understood and constructed, unique cultural traditions are to be transmitted from "representative transmitters" to "receivers of tradition" known as *jichengren* 继承人. The goal is make sure there is "no lack of successors" (*houjiyouren* 后继有人) for the items of intangible cultural heritage; promotion among youth is especially encouraged (GBM 2005, 12; cf. UNESCO 2003).

17. See http://www.sxwht.gov.cn/20160126/100018156.html and http://cn.chinagate.cn /culture/2013-01/10/content_27643519.htm (accessed April 29, 2017).

18. Wang spoke fondly of eating the "fruits" of this plant as a child, which could be picked, boiled, and made into a sort of porridge. There is also a local song about a couple going out to pick these fruits, which I discuss in chapter 2. The plant is variably referred to as *maru* 马茹 or *maruru* 马茹茹. For a description and photos of the yellow *maru* flower and its red fruit, see http://bbs.tianya.cn/post-96-709323-1.shtml (accessed February 23, 2016).

19. *Geda* 疙瘩 in northern Shaanxi dialect literally means "clump," but it also refers to the round-topped, steep-sided hills commonly found in this area.

20. A general from the Three Kingdoms period (220–265 CE) who later became deified as the God of War.

21. A typical style of home in northern Shaanxi province.

22. The song "Picking *Maru* Fruits" discussed in chapter 2 mentions the blooming of *maru* flowers in the sixth lunar month.

23. His older brother notes that Wang was the youngest of his entire generation in the Wang clan (Wang Shangrong 2011, 44).

24. Wang concluded that the degree of environmental destruction was extremely serious. Wang Xiangrong interview, January 2, 2012.

25. Wang Xiangrong interview, June 20, 2012.

26. Different articles about Wang appear to offer different dates for when he started teaching. Chu and Jiang (2005) write that it was in 1970 (9). The term *minban jiaoshi* refers to "teachers in rural citizen-managed or state-managed schools who do not receive the normal remuneration from the government" (http://www.iciba.com/民办教师, accessed April 10, 2013).

27. This date was given in a 2006 interview, although Wang used the word "probably" (*keneng* 可能), suggesting he wasn't sure.

28. Miao Meng (2008) refers to it as a "commune pioneering brigade" (*gongshe chuangye dui* 公社创业队) (73).

29. The information about the Gang of Four song comes from an interview with Wang.

30. Miao Meng (2008) refers to it as a "national peasant art selection" (*quanguo nongmin yishu diaoyan* 全国农民艺术调演) (73).

31. According to Wang, he adapted the melody with Li Shibin, while Dang Yong'an wrote the lyrics. Wang added that younger singers nowadays follow his adapted melody when they sing "Liancheng Pays a New Year's Call," also known as "Paying a New Year's Visit" (interview, May 30, 2012).

32. Wang's performance at this National Rural Amateur Performance Selection could also be seen as representing a sort of grassroots praise for the newly established "open markets" and the abundance of goods for sale, symbolizing peripheral support for the political center and providing an excellent example of the meeting of cultural and political capital in encounters between song kings and national leaders.

33. Wang Xiangrong interview, May 21, 2012.

34. Certain parallels can be observed with rags-to-riches tales in Western narratives. Dorothy Noyes writes, "The story of the young person who leaves home, encounters tests and obstacles, accomplishes a task, and is recognized, rewarded, and installed in a new home, remains a prominent cultural script" (2016, 300–301).

35. "Renwu: shaanbei gewang—Wang Xiangrong" 人物: 陕北歌王——王向荣 ("People: The King of Northern Shaanxi Folksongs—Wang Xiangrong"). http://space.tv.cctv.com/act/article .jsp?articleId=ARTI1225776921003914&nowpage=0 (accessed April 12, 2013).

36. Wang Xiangrong interview, July 24, 2006; cf. Rosenberg 1986; Harkness 2014.

37. The story is also reminiscent of Mao Zedong's articles criticizing the tragic position of women brought on by traditional arranged marriage (Schram 1969, 337; Witke 1967, 128).

38. In a preface to the book, Zhao Xirong 赵喜荣 notes that only about 40 percent of the book is actually about Wang and that "the author's writing of each chapter was motivated from the point of view of educating people" (*zuozhe xie mei pian wenzhang dou shi cong jiaoyu ren de jiaodu chufa de* 作者写每篇文章都是从教育人的角度出发的) (2011, 3, 9). In the introduction, Wang's brother Wang Shangrong 王尚荣 writes that he includes stories about a great-grandfather who worked as a traveling doctor in Inner Mongolia to "provide later generations something with which to learn from his spirit and moral character as an upright

person" (*gong houbeimen xuexi ta de jingshen he zuoren de pinde* 供后辈们学习他的精神和做人的品德) (2011, 4–5).

39. The chapter ends with a photograph of Wang Xiangrong, his now estranged wife, and Wang's mother (Wang Shangrong 2011, 71).

40. Wang Xiangrong interview, May 21, 2012.

41. Wang Xiangrong interview, Xi'an, October 4, 2011. I was fortunate enough to meet and interview several of Wang's disciples during my fieldwork, including Feng Xiaohong 冯小红 (b. 1975), Li Chunru 李春如 (b. 1977), Zhou Jinping 周金平 (b. 1961), Zhang Liaojun 张辽军 (b. 1982), and Li Zhengfei 李政飞 (b. 1980).

42. Wang Xiangrong interview, Beijing, August 8, 2016.

43. For more on the recent *yuanshengtai* trend in China, see Rees (2016).

44. In many such contests, the most honored judges tend to be placed in the center section of the panel of judges.

45. Wang Xiangrong interview, Beijing, August 8, 2016.

46. At this point, I refrain from suggesting to what degree Wang's interpretations of the tradition and its history have influenced the views of others, although Gramsci's notion (1992, 3) of the "organic intellectual," in which "intellectuals are distinguished less by their professions...than by their function in directing the ideas and aspirations of the class to which they organically belong" is intriguing.

47. Wang Xiangrong interview, May 30, 2012.

48. See "Dianying 'Yi duidui yuanyang shuishang piao' zai Yulin juxing kaiji yishi" 电影一对对鸳鸯水上漂在榆林举行开机仪式 ("The Film *Pairs of Mandarin Ducks Float on the Water* Holds Ceremony to Commemorate the Start of Filming"). http://yulin.sanqin.com/2014/0527/7021.shtml (accessed October 12, 2015).

49. See "Dianying 'Yi duidui yuanyang shuishang piao' zai Yulin juxing kaiji yishi."

Chapter 2: An Education through Song

1. As elsewhere, different genres often provide channels for different types of information (cf. Bauman 2004, 7; Briggs and Bauman 1992, 140; Cashman 2011, 367).

2. For more on the history of *yangge* in northern Shaanxi and its use in revolutionary propaganda, see Holm (1991, 155 ff.).

3. More recently, Frank Kouwenhoven and Antoinet Schimmelpenninck (2013) have argued that mountain songs (*shan'ge*) form a widespread, pan-Chinese genre with local variations.

4. Antoinet Schimmelpenninck (1997, 17–18) described *xiaodiao* as "lyrical, mellifluous songs in a regular rhythm, often sung indoors in a soft voice and to instrumental accompaniment."

5. For a more detailed discussion of the general categories of mountain songs (*shan'ge*) and little ditties (*xiaodiao*), see Schimmelpenninck (1997, 16–22).

6. In writing about the history of this genre, Chinese scholars frequently frame it as evidence of "ethnic unity and cooperation" (E'erdunchaolu et al. 1992, 20; YDW 1983), and there is often a narrative about how ethnic Mongols and Han, living in close proximity over a long period of time, began sharing their musical cultures and created this new genre together. One article writes, "*Manhandiao*'s coming-into-being is the crystallization of ethnic unity. It is an 'exotic flower' of art born through the continuous process of the blending of ethnic Mongol and ethnic Han folk culture" (Guo 2005, 75). The actual timeline of the history of this genre is unclear. Many scholars suggest the genre was formed sometime between

the mid-nineteenth and the early twentieth centuries (Zhang Fa 2005, 69), while at least one scholar believes it took shape much later, during the Cultural Revolution (1966–1976), when Han suspicion of lyrics they couldn't understand forced Mongolian singers to sing in Chinese. For more on the genre, see Du (2005).

7. For more on temple fairs in northern Shaanxi, see Chau (2006b).

8. For a description of a contemporary festival where *errentai* were performed in a small village in Shanxi Province, across the Yellow River from Wang's home county in Shaanxi, see Yang Hong (2006, 200–201). For a description of temple fairs in southeastern Shanxi Province and their staging of Shanxi village opera, see Johnson (2009).

9. In fact, Wang's choice of the *kang* as stage may have been rooted in common performance practices at the time. Yang Hong 杨红, a scholar at the China Conservatory of Music who has done extensive research on *errentai,* recorded the recollection of an old resident of Fugu 府谷 County (where Wang's home village is located) who remembered how *errentai* was performed when he was young during the Chinese lunar new year. According to this old resident, the performers would sit cross-legged on the *kang* and sing, with the audience sitting on the floor. In this way, the *kang* would serve as a makeshift "stage" (Yang Hong 2006, 51).

10. One of Wang's disciples, Li Chunru, also described joining an operatic troupe in order to leave her home village (Li Chunru interview, November 22, 2011). Nowadays, with the influx of rural migrant workers to the cities and the resulting dearth of young people in the countryside, perhaps traveling troupes no longer offer the same attraction.

11. The following description of Sun Bin is based on Chu and Jiang 2005, 15–16.

12. These lines come from "You Are Older Brother's Pretty-Eyed Gal" ("Ni shi gege de maoyanyan" 你是哥哥的毛眼眼).

13. Wang Xiangrong interview, June 6, 2012.

14. Wang noted that some rooms would have one large *kang,* while others would have two smaller *kang.* He estimated anywhere from ten to fifteen people could sleep together on a large *kang.*

15. On larger occasions, one might even have one's neighbors and nearby relatives help out, offering their homes for additional seating.

16. In recent years, a regional liquor company has tapped into this cultural market by hiring professional folk singers to promote its products in restaurants (Qiao et al. 2011).

17. For a description of youth participation in finger-guessing drinking games in northern Shaanxi, see Chau (2006a, 169–170).

18. Wang believes that seeking spirit mediums for cures was more or less pervasive throughout the countryside of northern Shaanxi when he was young, and, except for medical facilities in larger cities, they were one of the main means used at the time. Bonnie B. O'Connor and David J. Hufford (2001, 20) note that "a significant number of folk medical systems recognize magical and supernatural elements in disease etiology."

19. For additional descriptions of spirit mediums in this area as they relate to "fox cults," see Kang (2006). Stephen Jones (2009, 24) mentions the presence of spirit mediums throughout northern Shaanxi. For descriptions of spirit mediums and their rituals in the Yan'an region of northern Shaanxi, see Ka-ming Wu (2015).

20. For more information on fox spirits and the spread of the fox cult, including ethnographic information from Wang's home area of Yulin prefecture in northern Shaanxi, see Kang (2006).

21. These ancestral gods were called *zu wei shen* 祖为神 or *zong wei shen* 宗为神 (see "Treating an Illness" later in this chapter).

22. The *bricoleur* image manages to bridge together two otherwise seemingly contradictory notions—namely, "tradition as process and tradition as resource" (Cashman, Mould, and Shukla 2011, 3).

23. Here and in later references to Wang's songs, the songs recorded on Wang's CD are listed by track number. See Wang Xiangrong (2006).

24. Wang Xiangrong interview, March 5, 2012.

25. The close spacing of the second crop of Chinese leeks is compared to the difficulty of assembling together the guests, and the connection between toasting, drinking, and talking freely is made explicit in the third and fourth lines of the first stanza.

26. Wang Xiangrong interview, March 5, 2012.

27. Wang Xiangrong interview, March 5, 2012.

28. Wang Xiangrong interview, March 5, 2012.

29. Wang Xiangrong interview, March 5, 2012.

30. Wang pronounces the *shi* as *si* and the *yo* as *yue*. He also uses the northern Shaanxi dialect pronunciation for "I" (*nge*). I have put Wang's dialect pronunciations in the English translations throughout and kept the standard Mandarin pronunciations in the song lyric transliterations.

31. Here and elsewhere, Wang often pronounces *de* as *di*, a common pronunciation found in sung Chinese.

32. For additional spirit medium tunes from northern Shaanxi, several recorded from Wang, see Huo (2006, 2:897–907); Lü (1994, 1:596–606); and Li and Li (2003, 249–330).

33. Cf. Wang Xiangrong interview, May 18, 2012.

34. Wang Xiangrong interview, May 18, 2012.

35. Wang Xiangrong interview, May 18, 2012.

36. Hu Jintao served as president of the People's Republic of China from 2003 to 2013. Wang Xiangrong interview, May 18, 2012.

37. Wang Xiangrong interview, May 18, 2012.

38. Wang Xiangrong interview, May 18, 2012. Xiaofei Kang (2006, 101) notes master-disciple relationships established both between spirits and mediums and between older and newer mediums.

39. Wang Xiangrong interview, May 18, 2012. For a fuller discussion of Wang's disciples mentioned here, see chapter 1. Later on, when discussing various *shenguan* of the past, Wang mentioned that they also had different grades/classes (*dangci* 档次), just like modern-day singers. He said,

> In the past, *shenguan* were also divided into various ranks, just like singers. As for singers, some are vocalists (*gechangjia*), while others are mere singers (*geshou*). Some are first-class performers (*yiji yanyuan*, referring to the nationally allocated ranking system), while others are unranked. The latter are just artistic aficionados, amateur singers. There is a difference. There were also some *shenguan*, the old *shenguan* in the past, who had books (*shuben*) from old masters, who would teach them word-by-word. Furthermore, what they did was all traditional, scrupulous and methodical—they understood everything very clearly. Now then, these younger/lesser *shenguan*, after so many generations, the number of things they have learned is much less. Furthermore, though they may have received some of the same songs, when an old master-singer sings it and a beginner sings it—they both "know how to" sing it, but though you can sing it and he can also sing it, the level (*chengdu*) at which you can sing it is different. This is how it works. (Interview, May 18, 2012)

40. Wang Xiangrong interview, May 18, 2012.

41. Wang Xiangrong interview, May 18, 2012.

42. When defining the term "welcoming guests" (*yingjie*), Wang said, "When people or gods come, you should go to the entrance to meet them. This shows your respect for them. Now then, when the gods come, how could you not go out to meet them? They were invited by you! Your invited guests" (interview, May 18, 2012). When he said this, it reminded me of his behavior during my mother's visit to Xi'an. During my frequent visits to Wang's home to conduct interviews, he had become increasingly relaxed with my arrivals, and I would often arrive to find his apartment door wide open and Wang playing online Chinese card games in an undershirt or pajamas. However, when I told him that I was going to bring my mother to visit while she was in town, we arrived to find the door closed. After we knocked, Wang came to the door dressed in a traditional silk Chinese-style shirt of the type that he tends to wear on public occasions. He smiled and greeted my mother warmly, while I translated. This varying behavior in relation to the identity of a guest seems to be consistent with Wang's description of how to "host" the gods.

43. Wang Xiangrong interview, May 18, 2012.

44. Wang Xiangrong interview, May 18, 2012.

45. For a similar line in the context of a drinking song, see "I Beg the Magnanimity of Our Host," discussed earlier.

46. According to Wang, the "golden lamps" refer to candles with metal bases (interview, May 18, 2012).

47. A poetic term for a steel helmet, which Wang compared to the helmets worn by American soldiers (interview, May 18, 2012).

48. Wang likened this to a bulletproof vest, which would protect one against arrows and bullets (interview, May 18, 2012).

49. With regard to this line, Wang noted that you couldn't very well continue to wear the clothes you had worn on the train on the way to get here when visiting a host, but instead you should change into something suitable for a visit (interview, May 18, 2012).

50. The "host" refers to the ritual host (*shizhu* 事主) who has invited the deities on this occasion. In the case of a sick child, the father would usually host the gods, while if the father had already passed, the mother could also do it (Wang Xiangrong interview, May 18, 2012).

51. The wine is "clear" (*qingjiu* 清酒) because most deities are vegetarian. Therefore, they are never offered dishes with meat in them, and even the oil in the lamps mentioned in the following line is vegetable oil ("clear oil" *qingyou* 清油). The "cold tea" does not necessarily refer to the temperature of the tea itself but rather its property of "reducing internal heat" (*qinghuo* 清火) in accordance with the principles of Chinese medicine. Wang notes that teas with cooling properties all have a bitter taste (interview, May 18, 2012).

52. The Supreme Being here refers to the deity that is being invited on this occasion (Wang Xiangrong interview, May 18, 2012).

53. Wang noted that given the oral nature of these songs, the word *shu* 数 could be any one of four characters, depending on personal interpretations (interview, May 18, 2012).

54. Wang compared this to himself, since due to a stomach ulcer he can no longer drink wine or tea but only plain boiled water (interview, May 18, 2012).

55. Since the gods have already transcended the mortal world (*tuofan* 脱凡), Wang says that they no longer have the same desires to eat certain foods that humans do. Instead, they search for a different flavor (*weidao* 味道), which they find in incense smoke. With regard to the name of the Altar, Wang said that each of the Five Directions has an Immortal (*Daoren* 道人). For example, for the East it's "Black Five Directions" (*Hei wudao* 黑

五道), while for the South it's "Red Five Directions" (*Hong wudao* 红五道) (interview, May 18, 2012).

56. The Eight Immortal Cave refers to the place where the gods reside. (Immortals tend to live in the mountains.) The Eight Cave Immortals (*Badong Shenxian*), also known as the Eight Immortals (*Baxian* 八仙), refer to Zhongli Quan 钟离权, Zhang Guolao 张果老, Lü Dongbin 吕洞宾, Tieguai Li 铁拐李, Han Xiangzi 韩湘子, Cao Guojiu 曹国舅, Lan Caihe 蓝采和, and He Xiangu 何仙姑 (cf. Ho and O'Brien 1990). Wang used the term "cave abode" (*dongfu*, literally "cave city") to describe the abode of each god, noting that there was a city in each cave, one suitable for the gods. Each major god had his own cave. There were not just eight caves. Some people said there were sixteen (i.e., eight plus eight) or even sixty-four (i.e., eight times eight), as there were many lesser gods in addition to the main leaders (interview, May 18, 2012).

57. The Ninth Heaven is the highest heavenly realm.

58. This deity has two eyes to observe the heavens and two to observe the mortal realm. He sees everything that occurs and is considered a Heavenly General (*Shenjiang* 神将) in the Heavenly Palace (*Tiangong* 天宫) (Wang Xiangrong interview, May 18, 2012).

59. According to Wang, this refers to a constellation of twenty-eight stars, where each star is a deity with unique abilities. They appear in the novel *Journey to the West* (*Xiyou ji* 西游记) and save the Monkey King hero Sun Wukong when he is trapped. Although at least one dictionary translated the name of this set of gods as the "Twenty-Eight Lunar Mansions," when I asked if they were located on the moon, he insisted they were stars, not located on the moon (interview, May 18, 2012).

60. Wang noted that some *shenguan* referred to this deity as *Jiutian Xuannü* 九天玄女 and others as *Jiutian Xiannü* 九天仙女. He related this variation to the fact that some *shenguan* were illiterate and might not distinguish between the two characters (*xuan* 玄 and *xian* 仙) (interview, May 18, 2012).

61. Wang said that the phrase could also be sung as "I ask the gods to ascend [*sheng*] to their seats," but here it had the meaning of "to find" their seats. He listed different possible verbs that might be used here, emphasizing once again the flexibility of the lyrics (interview, May 18, 2012).

62. The flags (*biaogan* 标杆) are the symbols/signs for each god and their assistants. Wang described the spirit tablets as "ID cards" (*shenfenzheng* 身份证) for the spirits, representing them (interview, May 18, 2012).

63. The "wall with carved murals" (*yingbiqiang* 影壁墙) refers to a decorated wall immediately inside of the main door, which shields the rest of the house from outside view. It is also referred to as a screen wall (*zhaobi* 照壁). Wang noted that the "wall with carved murals" might also refer to the wall at the back end of the home, immediately behind the *kang* (brick bed), which could also be used to set up the spirit tablets. When I commented that his childhood home did not have such a wall near the entrance, he said that Marugeda was too small a village to pay attention to such rules of etiquette, but the nearby town center had courtyard houses with such walls, as did the regional capital of Yulin (interview, May 18, 2012).

64. This is a ritual saying of a host to a guest, asking the latter to forgive the "inattentiveness" of the former. Wang said this was meant to ask the gods' forgiveness if the host had been ignorant of their relative rank (*guanwei daxiao* 官位大小) and unintentionally seated them in an incorrect order (interview, May 18, 2012).

65. Barack Obama, American president from 2009 to 2017.

66. Wang Xiangrong interview, May 18, 2012.

67. Wang Xiangrong interview, May 18, 2012.

68. Wang Xiangrong interview, May 18, 2012.

69. Wang Xiangrong interview, May 18, 2012.

70. Beyond providing instructions for an herbal prescription, one could argue that the spirit medium is also providing a conceptual framework through which to deal with the uncertainty caused by illness. Lévi-Strauss (1966) has emphasized how providing people with ways to talk about a difficult situation and how it might be resolved can alleviate anxiety and affect the functioning of the body. In his key example, he describes a case where the chants of a Native American shaman from the Cuna of Panama brought relief to a woman caught in the midst of a difficult labor, by "provid[ing] the sick woman with a *language*" (Lévi-Strauss 1996, 374). Here too, the spirit medium could be seen as providing a similar function for the ill individual and those attending to him or her.

71. Wang Xiangrong interview, May 18, 2012.

72. The *zong* 宗 can be read as self-referential, as in "I," where the "I" refers to a god that represents the ancestors (*daibiao zuxian de yi ge shen* 代表祖先的一个神) (Wang Xiangrong interview, May 18, 2012).

73. Wang said this was an immortal (*xianjia* 仙家) from Marugeda, where all of the villagers had the surname Wang (hence the phrase "of your Wang family"). There was a special hall (*tang* 堂) dedicated to this deity, who was said to be entirely black, to ride black clouds, wear black clothes, ride a black horse, and carry black flags. Other deities might have similar monochromatic accoutrements in red, white, and so on. In the case of fox spirits, their color would correspond to that of their fur—such as white, red, or yellow (Wang Xiangrong interview, May 18, 2012).

74. Wang said that the phrase *youyouwanwan* 游游玩玩 translated here referred to "turning" and "moving from side to side" (*zhuanyou* 转游). In a video of a *shenguan* that I discussed with Wang, the *shenguan* did in fact turn to face various directions (interview, May 18, 2012).

75. The gate here refers to the gate in the city wall, used in entering the city. The color used here is difficult to translate, as the Chinese word "*qing* 青" can refer to blue, green, and black, depending on context. When I asked Wang whether this meant black, he answered in the affirmative, but it is unclear how this differs from the "black" (*hei* 黑) used in the fourth stanza, which can only refer to black and is therefore unambiguous (interview, May 18, 2012).

76. Cf. Wang Xiangrong interview, Yulin, July 24, 2006.

77. In the following version of "Picking *Maru* Fruits," I have combined two of Wang's performances of this song. During an interview on July 24, 2006, he performed the first two stanzas and talked about his mother and some memories of his home village. In 2010, when I interviewed him again at his home in Xi'an, I sang those two stanzas that I had learned from my recording of the 2006 interview and asked him to sing "the rest of the song," thinking that there was a set number of stanzas in a specific order. At that time, he sang the following four stanzas, saying that there were many more, but he couldn't remember them all (Wang Xiangrong interview, July 15, 2010). As he would later repeat over and over to me during my fieldwork from 2011 to 2012, nothing is set in stone, and different stanzas, lines, and lyrics can be mixed and matched according to the whims and abilities of the performer and the influence of the performance context. For another version of this song collected in 1962 from the Baota 宝塔 area of Yan'an, which contains some similar lyrics, see Huo (2006, 2:663).

78. Wang Xiangrong interview, July 15, 2010.

79. The "red" here refers to the fruit of the yellow flowers. For photos of the flowers and fruits, see http://bbs.tianya.cn/post-96-709323-1.shtml (accessed February 23, 2016).

80. The line is a bit ambiguous here and could also refer to the male protagonist following her on her way to pick the fruit.

81. With regard to the imagery of the final stanza, one might note that two millstones coming together are used in certain regions of China as a metaphor for harmonious marital relations (cf. Mair and Bender 2011, 56–57).

82. For different versions of the story, see Idema (2010).

83. Wang Xiangrong interview, June 6, 2012.

84. This "your dear" (qinqin 亲亲) is self-referential to the singer and could also be translated as "I" or "me."

85. During the Spring Festival of 2012, I observed smoked, dried mutton legs in vacuum-packed plastic being sold in a large supermarket in Xi'an.

86. The "der" here and below ends in a rolled "r" sound.

87. In this version from Wang's 2006 CD, the couple doesn't make it past the first marker.

88. The lyrics for this song come from Wang's solo version on his CD. I have added the indications for male, female, and duet voices based on an undated performance Wang gave with Wang Erni 王二妮 (b. 1985). See http://m.kuaigeng.com/video/6210868885235698688 (accessed April 28, 2017). In that performance, an additional second stanza was included in between these two stanzas, where she invites him to eat a New Year's meal.

89. The singers in the video cited above sing shi as si. In the track on Wang's CD, he alternates between shi and si and I have adjusted the translation accordingly. I have kept the pinyin version in the middle column in standard Mandarin.

90. The "drrrrrrr" in the final line includes a trilled "r" sound (similar to the rolled "r" in Spanish), which approximates the noise of festive firecrackers.

91. Wang Xiangrong interview, May 30, 2012.

92. Wang Xiangrong interview, May 30, 2012.

93. The Chinese lyrics are from Wang Shangrong (2011, 220–221), although the book mistakenly labels the song "Brother and Sister Go to the Market," conflating Wang's 1980 national competition performance piece and this piece, which Wang recalled performing later in a Shaanxi Province Professional Festival of Literature and the Arts (Shaanxi sheng zhuanye wenyi huiyan) in 1982 or 1983, followed by the shooting of his first music video with the singer Zhao Qing 赵青 singing the female role. Wang wrote the lyrics to this piece and adapted the melody from the errentai tune "Soft Cakes" ("Ruan gaomian" 软糕面), also known as "Kneading Cakes" ("Nie gaomian" 捏糕面) (Wang Xiangrong interview, May 30, 2012). I have added "M" for male and "F" for female to indicate who sings what, according to an MTV version of the song that Wang Xiangrong showed me.

94. The shifting between narration and playing the role of a character (in this case, the male migrant farmworker who must leave his wife to go find work beyond the Western Pass) shares similar dynamics with certain Yuefu 乐府 ballads from the Han dynasty (206 BCE–220 CE). Hans Frankel (1985, 107) refers to the two modes of singing as "objective narration" and "impersonation."

95. The fifth year of the Qing dynasty's Xianfeng reign was 1855.

96. Most versions have "Shanxi" rather than "Shaanxi." I have included "Shaanxi" here because those are the lyrics printed on Wang's (2006) CD insert.

97. In the stanza, the muleteer refers to himself as "older brother" (gege 哥哥).

98. Embroidered red shoes were often a key part of marriage dowries, and they appear in several northern Shaanxi folk songs, often with romantic or sexual connotations.

99. During our interview, perhaps in part due to my identity as a foreigner, Wang also connected the song lyrics with the history of foreign aggression and opium sales in China

during the nineteenth century, culminating in the Opium Wars (1839–1842 and 1856–1860). The Chinese term for opium is literally "foreign smoke" (*yangyan* 洋烟), highlighting the song's connection to foreign influence.

100. Cashman (2011, 376) writes, "Springboard for social commentary and moral proclamation, index of his predispositions or orientations to the world, Packy Jim's versions of this story do much more than explain the origin of the fairies or offer us another instantiation of tradition that can be dated, located, and archived."

101. For the "dangerous" qualities attributed to permanent bachelors, see Chabrowski (2015, 219) and Sommer (2002).

Chapter 3: Representing the Region

1. Wang Xiangrong interview, November 1, 2011. The Yulin Folk Arts Troupe was already functioning in an "amateur" capacity by 1982 and was officially established on July 1, 1984. For more on the work conducted leading up to the founding of the troupe and descriptions of its early history, see Shang (1996a, 1996b, and 1996c).

2. Wang talked at length about the onstage/offstage dichotomy in an interview on June 20, 2012.

3. There are several works that touch on the adjustment of length in consideration of different performance contexts. Patrick Mullen (1981, 273, 277) describes how the Texas storyteller Ed Bell began to tell shorter and funnier stories after he started performing more frequently for national festival audiences in order to attract passing festivalgoers. James Porter (1976, 13) relates how Jeannie Robertson, the Scottish traveler singer, cut down the length of a ballad for a television performance. While both Ed Bell and Jeannie Robertson shortened their pieces, Albert B. Lord (1976, 13) notes that the groups of men listening to epics all night long at coffee houses during Ramadan helped foster long songs.

4. Meeker (2013) and Hughes (2008) have pointed to similar phenomena in North Vietnam and Japan respectively.

5. Kyoim Yun describes a similar transformation as enacted by Korean shamans (*simbang*), who "by reframing and drawing upon customary ritual activities...adroitly transformed their activities into a recontextualized presentation or enactment for a festival audience" (2006, 23).

6. Feng Xiaohong interview, October 18, 2011.

7. Feng Xiaohong interview, October 18, 2011.

8. Feng Xiaohong interview, October 18, 2011.

9. Li Chunru interview, November 22, 2011.

10. For another case study where a melody from a shaman song of the Sibe nationality in Xinjiang was transformed into a revolutionary song praising Chairman Mao, see Harris (2004, 179–187).

11. Wang Xiangrong interview, November 1, 2011. Wang pronounced the word "peony" as *maodan*.

12. Wang Xiangrong interview, November 1, 2011.

13. One verse of "Riding a White Horse" (also known as "White Horse Melody") appeared in the 1953 anthology mentioned earlier (ZMWY 1953, 304).

14. Isabel K. F. Wong notes a similar use of sun imagery much earlier, in a Taiping song text, where Hong Xiuquan is referred to as "The Sun King, illuminating all corners of the world" (1984, 114).

15. This transformation is largely in keeping with Frederick Lau's observation that "re-

gional cultures…are sometimes appropriated into national culture for political purposes" (Lau 2008, 60). One might also think of it as "the localization of national essence in the poetic language of the folk" (Haiyan Lee 2008, 25).

16. Wang Xiangrong performance, Fugu, Shaanxi, January 6, 2012.

17. Wang Xiangrong performance, Baoji, Shaanxi, January 5, 2012.

18. Wang Xiangrong performance, Xi'an, March 8, 2012.

19. Wang Xiangrong performance, Yulin, Shaanxi, January 10, 2012.

20. Wang Xiangrong interview, November 1, 2011. In at least one television presentation of this version of the song, the famous composer Li Huanzhi 李焕之 is listed in the credits for arranging the version. See http://xiyou.cntv.cn/v-eee71f66-bc1e-11e0-b474-a4badb4689bc.html (accessed February 23, 2013).

21. The bells sound like a combination of clock tower bells and ancient Chinese *bianzhong*, both calling to mind tradition, authority, and the passage of time.

22. In song lyrics, this is sometimes written as 俺.

23. Barbara Herrnstein Smith (1978) talks of the function of audience as an occasion to process feelings, noting "the occasion they offer us to verbalize and thus integrate, discriminate, appreciate, and indeed experience our own otherwise elusive perceptions" (109).

24. Wang performed this recorded version of the song on several occasions during my fieldwork from 2011 to 2012.

25. Wang always began with the first stanza, but he would sometimes switch the two traditional love song verses that followed or skip them entirely if the occasion called for it. At a more official performance in a televised Chinese New Year gala in Baoji, Shaanxi, on January 5, 2012, he went straight from the first stanza to the fourth stanza about fighting the Japanese during the War of Resistance, followed by the fifth, seventh, eighth, and ninth stanzas—essentially shifting the weight of the song toward its political history. At a Christmas concert in a Yulin hotel on December 24, 2011, Wang played to the event's apparent theme of romantic nostalgia (the "romance" of Western Christmas combined with nostalgia for China's revolutionary history) by adding in the sixth stanza on the revolutionary-era policy encouraging resettlement in Yan'an.

26. Wang noted that this stanza comes from the Army and People's Large-Scale Production Period (*Junmin da shengchan shiqi* 军民大生产时期).

27. Wang Xiangrong performance, Shenmu, Shaanxi, November 10, 2011.

28. Wang Xiangrong performance, Fugu, Shaanxi, January 6, 2012.

29. Wang Xiangrong performance, Liquan, Shaanxi, May 15, 2012.

30. I have compiled these nine stanzas based on multiple performances I observed Wang give between 2011 and 2012. The title given is how Wang referred to this version. To give an idea of the variability of Wang's emergent performances, here are the stanzas he performed on three occasions: At the Christmas concert at a Yulin Hotel on December 24, 2011, he sang stanzas 1, 2, 3, 4, 5, 6, 7, and 9. At a corporate performance for Yulin bankers on January 10, 2012, he performed stanzas 1, 3, 2, 4, 5, 7, and 9. At a televised Chinese New Year's performance in Meixian County, Baoji, Shaanxi, on January 5, 2012, Wang sang stanzas 1, 4, 5, 7, 8, and 9. Wang's older brother includes a seven-stanza version of this song titled "Riding a White Horse, Carrying a Foreign Gun (Folk Song)" in his book on Wang Xiangrong and their family, including the following stanzas in this order: 1, 2, 3, 5, 4, 8, 9 (Wang Shangrong 2011, 304).

31. Shaan-Gan-Ning: An abbreviation of the Shaan-Gan-Ning Border Region, which was comprised of parts of modern-day Shaanxi, Gansu, and Ningxia, with its capital in Yan'an.

32. In a performance Wang gave of the a cappella version at a Christmas concert in a

Yulin hotel on December 24, 2011, he added "our" (*zan* 咱) before "Communist Party." This variation seemed to fit in with the revolutionary nostalgia evoked during the evening's performances.

33. At a televised Chinese New Year's performance in Baoji, Shaanxi, on January 5, 2012, the audience was clapping during this and the previous stanzas, and Wang first completed this stanza with the standard "hur hai ya" to maintain the pace, before repeating the last three lines with the extended "hur hai" sequence to slow the melody down to his regular finale on a high note.

Chapter 4: Culture Paves the Way

1. For descriptions of the growth of professional troupes in China, see Mackerras (1984, 212–217) and Wilcox (2016, 374–375). For a relatively recent study of tourism and musical performing arts in China, see Mackerras (2011).

2. More specifically, its subsidiary, China Shenhua Coal Liquefaction Corporation Limited, also referred to as China Shenhua Coal to Liquid and Chemical Company Limited.

3. Wang Xiangrong interview, May 21, 2012.

4. Wang Xiangrong interview, May 21, 2012.

5. The "African American folk songs" section was represented by the American blues and R&B singer Bobby Rush.

6. The other "representative transmitter" for northern Shaanxi folk songs was He Yutang 贺玉堂 (1949–2013), who appeared in Chen Kaige's 1984 film *Yellow Earth* (*Huang tudi* 黄土地) (cf. He Yutang 2007; Yin 2007; Jones 2009, 11). For an excellent description of China's efforts to preserve intangible cultural heritage, see Rees (2012).

7. Reports suggest that a slowing down of the coal industry beginning in late 2012 contributed to a decline in Yulin's overall economy in recent years (Coco Liu 2015; Sue-Lin Wong 2016). Dow reportedly withdrew from the joint venture in 2013, although Shenhua and the local government decided to proceed with the coal-to-chemicals project (ICIS News 2014; Xinhua Finance Agency 2015). The Yulin plant began producing "coal-based low-density polyethylene" in December 2015, churning out an estimated 220,000 metric tons in 2016 (CCFGroup 2016; Nina Ying Sun 2016).

8. In addition to a bridge, the Chinese scholar also compared Jin Yong's novel "to a traditional matchmaker who arranges a marriage between locals and tourists" (Notar 2006, 4).

9. Mei Lanfang "made his international debut in 1919 at the Imperial Theatre in Tokyo, Japan," performed in the Soviet Union in 1935, and again in Japan in 1956 "in an effort to help reestablish [a] friendly relationship between China and Japan" (Tian 2012, 1, 11).

10. While Turner (1969) is discussing the liminal aspects of rites of passage and how the liminality of those rites allows individuals to move from one social category to another (thus realigning their relationships with other people), I am suggesting that the liminal space of cultural performances allows audiences to realign their impressions of and perceived relationships with the cultures represented onstage.

11. Andrew Watson, Yang Xueyi, and Jiao Xingguo (1999) note, "Shaanxi forms part of the Shanxi-Shaanxi-Inner Mongolia coal field, which holds over 50 per cent of China's total coal reserves. The emphasis on the energy sector adopted as part of the revision of national industrial strategy in 1994 was seen as a significant gain for the province, and especially as an avenue of development for the poor north" (80). For background on the history of China's coal industry, see Wright (2012).

12. The exhibition of Chinese relics was sponsored by the Shaanxi Provincial Cultural

Relics Bureau, the Museum of Emperor Qin Shihuang's Terracotta Warriors and Horses, the Shaanxi Provincial Institute of Archaeology, the Shaanxi Cultural Heritage Promotion Center, the Dow Chemical Company, Northwest Airlines, Dow Corning Corporation, McKay Press, and local television and media (MCFTA 2008b).

13. According to Northwest Airline's corporate newsletter, "Northwest co-sponsored the festival with key corporate customer Dow Chemical, investing in the communities we jointly serve." The newsletter also noted, "Demonstrating Northwest's support of this cultural exhibit, Steve Sear, vice president sales and customer care, attended 'Reflections of the Yellow River,' a program of traditional Chinese performances" (NWA 2008).

14. This is a version of the song sung by Wang Xiangrong and Guo Yunqin 郭云琴 transcribed and published in Huo (2005, 32–33). I have added "M" for male, "F" for female, and "MF" for both, to indicate the singers of each line. There is a rhythmic play throughout the song with repetitions of *hua* 花 ("flower"), which I have attempted to recreate with "flo-flo-flower" and the like.

15. Huo (2005, 33) notes that performances of this song may have up to three verses, adding on the third lunar month, when peach and apricot blossoms (*taoxinghua* 桃杏花) appear, and the fifth lunar month, when five-petaled plum blossoms (*wumeihua* 五梅花) arrive. Though Huo writes the character for "five," another possibility with a similar pronunciation would be "dark plum" (*wumei* 乌梅).

16. In Chinese, the characters *feng* 风 ("wind") and *qing* 情 ("feelings/sentiments"), when combined into the word *fengqing* 风情, can mean both "local conditions and customs" and "fine taste" or "refined feelings."

17. Colin Mackerras (2011), in an article on tourism and musical performing arts in China, noted that "Some…performances for tourists take on a nationalist edge by glorifying some aspect of Chinese history and/or culture" (160).

18. Oakes (2000) provides examples from Shanxi, Anhui, and Guizhou.

19. This article was entitled "The Yulin Folk Arts Troupe Attends the 'Chinese Music and Culture Festival' in the U.S.: Li Jinzhu Gives a Speech at the Closing Ceremony." Another article with similar content, attributed to the same editor and also in *Yulin Daily* (*Yulin ribao*), was entitled "Northern Shaanxi Culture in America" (Wang Xuqin 2008b).

20. Early estimates suggested that the coal-to-chemicals complex in Yulin could be operational by 2016, and it eventually achieved this goal, beginning production in December 2015 (ICIS News 2009; Nina Ying Sun 2016).

Chapter 5: Mediating the Rural and Urban

Epigraph. Brodie 2014, 63.

1. Cf. Wang Xiangrong interview, June 20, 2012.

2. This also relates to the idea that certain contexts can move particular pieces in and out of a performer's active and inactive repertoires (cf. Kenneth S. Goldstein 1971).

3. This version was recorded by Professor Huang Hu 黄虎 in Xi'an on July 20, 2011. I would like to thank Professor Huang for sharing his recording and lyric transcription with me. I added the *pinyin* and English translation.

4. The term "sour tunes" (*suanqu*) is sometimes used to refer to love songs in general but more often those that are considered licentious and/or pornographic.

5. Qiao Jianzhong has suggested twelve categories through which Chinese folk song genres may be classified, including subject matter, style, function, ethnic group, region, singing technique, and so on, and has grouped *suanqu* along with other genres that are "situationally" (*huanjing fenleifa* 环境分类法) defined (Qiao, cited in Zhang Ruiting 2009, 21).

Whereas other genres Qiao relegates to this group are clearly associated with certain types of performance spaces (e.g., those always sung indoors or always sung in the wilds outside of town), Zhang Ruiting argues that the concept of *suanqu* does not contain such spatial limitations. There are no such set environments where *suanqu* are always sung. Zhang points to another definition of *suanqu* that Qiao gives elsewhere, namely, that "*suanqu* are love songs with sexual content," to argue that the genre should be classified instead according to its "content," thus placing it in Qiao's category of genres defined by "subject matter" (*ticai huafenfa* 题材划分法) (Zhang Ruiting 2009, 21).

6. Interview with Yang Cui and Feng Yalan, Xi'an, August 6, 2001.

7. The terms Yang used were *suangezi* and *suanqu* (both referring to "love" songs, especially those with "unhealthy" [i.e., pornographic] content). Similarly, the collectors in the 1953 collection project discovered that local officials had banned a local folk opera genre *errentai* for being immoral (ZYXZYY 1962, 205–206; Holm 1991, 331; Jones 1995, 45).

8. Zhang Cunliang interview, Hequ, Shanxi Province, July 24, 2010.

9. Legman (1962, 201) has suggested that the categorization of "sexual folklore" is a by-product of literary censorship, perpetrated predominantly by collectors who feel the need to separate erotic elements from the rest. This "need to separate" is evident in the U.S. Library of Congress's delta file system, discussed earlier.

10. Wang Xiangrong interview, May 3, 2012.

11. Perhaps the distinction in conflicting naming practices and categories is most succinctly displayed in a scene in Chen Kaige's 1984 film *The Yellow Earth,* where a PLA soldier who has come to collect "northern Shaanxi folk songs" (*Shaanbei de min'ge* 陕北的民歌) is rebuffed by an old peasant. "The old man laughs, 'What folk songs?! [*Sha min'ge*]. Sour tunes [*suanqu'r*]'" (Tuohy 1999, 45).

12. Wang Xiangrong interview, May 3, 2012.

13. For this latter portrayal, see articles in the May Fourth-era journal *Folksong Weekly* (*Geyao zhoukan*) as well as the Ming dynasty Feng Menglong's "Preface to *Mountain Songs,*" both discussed later in this chapter.

14. "Little Sister" (*meimei* 妹妹) is the term for the generic female persona in love songs, and, depending on context, can be self-referential (meaning "I"), as it is here, or an invocation in the second person (meaning "you"), as it is in the third and fourth stanzas.

15. The Chinese onomatopoeia for the sound of walking in the leather shoes is *deng ger deng ger deng ger.*

16. Wang Xiangrong performance, Fugu, Shaanxi, November 12, 2011.

17. Wang Xiangrong, banquet, Dingbian, Shaanxi, December 22, 2011.

18. Wang Xiangrong performance, Fugu, Shaanxi, November 12, 2011.

19. Wang Xiangrong performance, Fugu, Shaanxi, November 12, 2011.

20. Wang Xiangrong performance, Liquan, Shaanxi, May 15, 2012.

21. This note regarding variable tastes coincides with Zhang Ruiting's (2009) observation that the classification of "sour tunes" varies on an individual basis, depending upon whether the content of a song as performed in a particular context makes an individual audience member feel embarrassed (27).

22. Wang Xiangrong interview, May 3, 2012.

Chapter 6: Between Here and There

Epigraph. Nancy 2000, 10.

1. My notions of "shifting" here and below attempt to build on ideas put forward in Mark Bender's (1999) "Shifting and Performance in Suzhou Chantefable."

2. Cf. Wang Xiangrong performance, Fugu, Shaanxi, November 12, 2011.

3. The positioning of "local authenticity" as a focal point for sustained audience attention is similar in some respects to focuses on the "feeling" (*qing* 情 or *ganqing* 感情) of performances (cf. Bender 2003, 147–149). Both require judging an essential quality of a performance from moment to moment. David Pattie suggests that rock enthusiasts' search for authenticity involves a similar judgment of "a series of tropes: gestures, poses, characteristic tones and images, which, in the eyes of an engaged audience, metaphorically suggest the presence of the authentic performer" (2007, 13).

4. Wang Xiangrong performance, Xinmin Township, Shaanxi, December 25, 2011.

5. A popular term for a county magistrate, here used by Wang to address the local officials who were present at the event.

6. Although New Year (January 1) is celebrated internationally, in the context of this event it was seen as a local/Chinese holiday.

7. The town where Xinmin's government offices are located.

8. Once again, there seem to be certain parallels here with Western rags-to-riches narratives: "The tales of peasant protagonists are set in motion by material lack. You leave home because you are hungry" (Noyes 2016, 305).

9. The phrase "jump through the Dragon Gate" (*tiao longmen* 跳龙门) traditionally meant to pass the civil-service examinations, but Wang uses it here more colloquially to refer to trying his luck at a career away from home.

10. Wang Xiangrong speech at New Year's event held by Xinmin Township government on December 25, 2011. The part about "Xinmin is ours and it is also yours, but at the end of the day, it is yours" is a reference to a speech Mao Zedong gave in 1957 (cf. http://www.people.com.cn/GB/shizheng/252/7955/7958/20020422/714354.html [accessed April 14, 2013]).

11. M. M. Bakhtin (1981, 62) writes, "After all, it is possible to objectivize one's own particular language, its internal form, the peculiarities of its world view, its specific linguistic habitus, only in light of another language belonging to someone else, which is almost as much 'one's own' as one's native language."

12. Wang Xiangrong performance, Fugu, Shaanxi, November 12, 2011.

13. One might think of Freud's famous example of his grandson's self-devised game where he throws a toy out of sight, shouting "gone!" and then goes to retrieve it, shouting, "here!" In the alternation between distancing and bringing closer a valued object to oneself, the child could both learn to deal with separation and, perhaps, gain a new sense of self (Freud 1955, 15–16).

14. This "translucent lens" metaphor has both reflective and transmissive properties. Needless to say, lens and mirror metaphors abound in literary, cultural, and philosophical studies. Pamela Crossley has used the term "translucent mirror" in her work on Qing history to describe an approach to historical documents that juxtaposes their "back layers" (i.e., "the past of the event") with their "reflections" (i.e., future portrayals of those events), making "the images…translucent as a result" (1999, 23, 31). The Otherness of "historical narratives" is seen as having "a didactic, morally informative, or partisan import" when viewed through the mirror's glass together the reflections of those narratives through history (ibid., 23). Michel Foucault (1986) describes mirrors as a combination of the real and the unreal—a type of site he refers to as a "heterotopia." Looking at oneself in a mirror allows one to see what appears to be an objective view of oneself, and though what one sees is not the physical object it appears to be, the viewing of that object provides a reference point for the observer. "In the mirror," Foucault writes, "I see myself there where I am not, in an unreal, virtual space that opens up behind the surface; I am over there, there where I am not, a sort of shadow that gives

my own visibility to myself, that enables me to see myself there.... It exerts a sort of counter-action on the position that I occupy" (24). This notion is similar to Eugene Chen Eoyang's idea of the "two-way mirror" in his cross-cultural study of Chinese and Western literature and culture, describing "the kind of study that, in focussing on the other, reveals as much about the self and where object becomes self and self becomes object" (2007, ix).

15. "Li Yuwen yu 'dahai hangxing kao duoshou'" 李郁文与《大海航行靠舵手》("Li Yuwen and 'Sailing in the Ocean We Rely on the Great Helmsman'"). www.sina.com.cn, May 11, 2007. http://news.sina.com.cn/o/2007-05-11/033811795794s.shtml (accessed on January 28, 2013).

16. In addition, Wang's "traveled" authenticity suggests that he has brought the benefit of local authenticity to larger social power structures. Dorothy Noyes (2016, 314) suggests, "An infusion of authenticity from below is required to revitalize and justify an otherwise preda-tory elite."

17. Clifford points to "traveling 'indigenous' culture-makers" in particular and cites the example of "a musician and non-academic historian of music, who for some years now has been bringing traditional Hawaiian music into the Continental United States" (1992, 101). This musician's family had traveled and performed for over five decades, hardly ever return-ing to the home they represented, which led Clifford to ask, "How, for fifty-six years in tran-sient, hybrid environments, did they preserve and invent a sense of Hawaiian 'home?'" (102). Such "travel" of performers and performances is now a significant component of displays of culture in China and elsewhere and can be seen as implying a certain degree of disconnect between performances and their (traditional) meanings. In a recent book on the cultural politics of folk traditions in northern Shaanxi Province, Ka-ming Wu uses the term "hyper-folk" to refer to "the late socialist cultural condition in which the practice and representation of folk culture is no longer associated with any ritual reality, rural environment, or cultural origin" (2015, 20). While we may find instances of such disconnects, this book attempts to look at ways that meanings carry over from earlier contexts to later contexts, building on earlier dynamics and layering narratives through the power of performance.

18. Using *hua'er* from China's northwest as a case study, Sue Tuohy has noted how local scholars found local songs sung in Mandarin to have a non-*didao* flavor (*wei'er bu didao*), a phrase that she translated as "flavor not typical" (2003, 180).

19. Booth suggests that audiences take songs as "familiar poetry... the poetry of common experience" (1981, 201).

Chapter 7: Connecting Past, Present, and Future

Epigraph. Baudrillard 1994, 10.

1. See (3:41:25) of https://www.youtube.com/watch?v=Co_Qhzynkr8 (accessed Decem-ber 15, 2015).

2. 国家的兴旺是我的光荣.

3. The song's earliest publication (discussed below) did not place it first but rather mixed it in with other "work songs" (*haozi*) in the anthology's first section entitled "Livelihoods" (*Shenghuo lei*), only including the stanza of questions composed by Li Simin (ZMWY 1953). In the monumental *jicheng* series compiled in the late 1970s and 1980s, the two-part Shaanxi volume places the song at the beginning of the first volume in the "work song" (*haozi*) sec-tion, still recording the one-stanza version of the song (Lü 1994, 1:47). Later volumes con-tinue to place the song first in opening sections on "work songs," though anthologies began to include the second stanza of answers discussed below (cf. Qiao 2002, 1:1–2; Cao 2004, 3;

Huo 2006, 4). For a description of the *haozi* genre in general and various subtypes, see Han (1989, 113–116).

4. Li Simin's name is sometimes written as Li Siming 李思命.

5. This earlier version of the song containing one stanza of questions without answers was collected from Li Simin in 1942 and published in the 1953 collection, *An Anthology of Folksongs from the Shaanxi, Gansu, and Ningxia Old Revolutionary Base Area* (ZMWY 1953, 11). The song is labeled as being popular all along the Yellow River, and a footnote refers to Li Simin as an "old boatman from the Yellow River" who was already sixty years old and had composed many songs (ibid.). The character *ba* 把 in the final line is sometimes also written as 吧.

6. This past-oriented interpretation of the questions is even more pronounced nowadays, since there are no longer boatmen of the type described in the song working on the Yellow River.

7. For a description of Li Zhiwen's version of the piece, see Yang Cui (1995, 32–33).

8. While 额 is commonly used to write *nge* (the dialect word for "I"), some televised recordings of Wang's performances use the character 俺.

9. Culler suggests that lyrics "create the impression of something happening now, in the present time of discourse" (2015, 37).

10. According to Culler, while third-person pronouns tend to imply the narration of past events with "temporal movement from A to B," the second-person calling out to another entity as "you" in lyrics brings the listener into "a time of discourse" where we experience the "reversible alternation" of "discursive time"—"a play of presence and absence governed not by time but by poetic ingenuity or power" (2015, 226–227).

11. While not the focus of my discussion here, one could consider the effect, if any, of the numerous performances of this song on television, film, and in live events on later performances of the same song. What "baggage might it carry over from its prior incarnations? In this sense, we could consider the song a "heritage palimpsest," to use a term coined by Barbara Kirshenblatt-Gimblett that describes "when one site is landmarked repeatedly, each time for a different reason, and used for different purposes, even at one point in time" (1998, 156). I thank David Rolston for urging me to consider the "baggage" of this song.

12. Wang's age undoubtedly forms a component of his "performed authenticity." In CedarBough Tam Saeji's (2013) research on traditional Korean dance performers, she suggested the idea of "age as a marker of authenticity," whereby a performer's old age may link him or her to the past in the audience's imagination.

13. Wang Xiangrong speech at Elementary School Reunion, Fugu, Shaanxi, March 27, 2012.

14. Wang's speeches during my fieldwork in 2011 and 2012 coincided with a booming local economy. Later reports suggest a decline in the following years (Coco Liu 2015; Sue-Lin Wong 2016).

15. Wang Xiangrong speech at Business Opening, Fugu, Shaanxi, November 12, 2011.

16. Wang Xiangrong interview, June 20, 2012.

17. In places where Wang's pronunciation varies from standard Mandarin, the lines that the children repeat are phrased in standard Mandarin. For example, in the line asking how many boats are on the bends of the Yellow River, Wang sings the measure word for boats (只) as *zi*, while the children echo the line using the standard Mandarin pronunciation of *zhi*.

18. This was a broadcast of a large-scale concert in Yulin in 2009. http://my.tv.sohu.com /u/vw/2615283 (accessed February 23, 2013).

19. Part of my impression of this section stems from observing broad smiles on guests' faces at a wedding as the guests stood and kneeled in a semicircle in front of the stage, recording Wang's performance on their iPhones.

20. *Battle on Shangganling Mountain* (*Shangganling*), 1956, directed by Sha Meng and Lin Shan, Changchun Film Studio.

21. The description that follows and the select lyrics I have translated come from the film. See previous note.

22. Louisa Schein describes a similar phenomenon with the ethnic Miao singer mentioned earlier, A You Duo, noting that she "gives Guizhou good press; *her success makes the province, and her home region, hypervisible in a Chinese cultural economy* where regions are vying to be 'on the map' for ethnic tourism, joint venture investment and national prestige" (2010, 160, emphasis added).

23. The song's lyrics are not unlike the positive yet general message of a greeting card, which is given particular meaning through its signing and delivery on a specific occasion (Barbara Herrnstein Smith 1978).

24. The mutual reinforcement of narratives brought about in Wang's performance relates to Foley's discussion of metonymy, where the "word-power" of certain oral formulae accumulates meaning from repeated occurrences in a range of performances over time (1995, xiv). Just as Foley notes how the phrase "grey-eyed Athena" in the Homeric tradition "would serve as an approved traditional channel or pathway for summoning the Athena not just of this or that particular moment, but rather of all moments in the experience of audience and poet," Wang's performances of this song bring to mind the continual public conversation about stability and change discussed earlier (5).

25. The quoted lyrics come from "The Star-Spangled Banner," the American national anthem traditionally sung at the beginning of sports events in the United States.

26. This aspect of Wang's "observing" in "The Infinite Bends of the Yellow River" is different from his embodiment of the boatman persona in "Pulling Ferries throughout the Year" (see chapter 3).

Epilogue

Epigraph. Cantwell 1993, 184.

1. Pete Seeger, who grew up in New York state, brought a largely Southern, rural repertoire to mostly northern audiences, educating them in the process. Another example raised by Filene (2000) was Bob Dylan.

2. For different readings of how Dylan's performance that night "split" audiences, see Wald (2015, 1–8) and Lee Marshall (2007, 88–92).

REFERENCES

Abrahams, Roger D. 1981. "Shouting Match at the Border: The Folklore of Display Events." In *"And Other Neighborly Names": Social Process and Cultural Image in Texas Folklore,* edited by Richard Bauman and Roger D. Abrahams, 303–322 (Austin: University of Texas Press).

Abrams, M. H. 1953. *The Mirror and the Lamp: Romantic Theory and the Critical Tradition.* New York: Oxford University Press.

———. 1989. *Doing Things with Texts: Essays in Criticism and Critical Theory.* New York and London: W. W. Norton & Company.

Allan, Sarah. 1997. *The Way of Water and Sprouts of Virtue.* Albany: State University of New York Press.

Althusser, Louis. 2001. "Ideology and Ideological State Apparatus." In *Lenin and Philosophy, and Other Essays,* 85–126. Ben Brewster, trans. (New York: Monthly Review Press).

Anderson, Benedict. 1991. *Imagined Communities: Reflections on the Origin and Spread of Nationalism.* Revised ed. London and New York: Verso.

Attinasi, John, and Paul Friedrich. 1995. "Dialogic Breakthrough: Catalysis and Synthesis in Life-Changing Dialogue." In *The Dialogic Emergence of Culture,* edited by Dennis Tedlock and Bruce Mannheim, 33–53 (Urbana: University of Illinois Press).

"Bainian hunlian Wang Xiangrong" 百年婚恋王向荣 ["A Hundred Years of Love and Marriage: Wang Xiangrong"]. 2003. http://v.youku.com/v_show/id_XMTMwOTQ0Mzk2.html (accessed July 21, 2017).

Bakhtin, M. M. 1981. *The Dialogic Imagination: Four Essays by M. M. Bakhtin.* Edited by Michael Holquist. Translated by Caryl Emerson and Michael Holquist. Austin: University of Texas Press.

Bantly, Francisca Cho. 1996. "Archetypes of Selves: A Study of the Chinese Mytho-Historical Consciousness." In *Myth and Method,* edited by Laurie L. Patton and Wendy Doniger, 177–207 (Charlottesville and London: University Press of Virginia).

Barth, Fredrik, ed. 1969. *Ethnic Groups and Boundaries: The Social Organization of Culture Difference.* Boston: Little, Brown.

Baudrillard, Jean. 1994. *Simulacra and Simulation.* Sheila Faria Glaser, trans. Ann Arbor: University of Michigan Press.

Bauman, Richard. 1972. "Differential Identity and the Social Base of Folklore." In *Toward New Perspectives in Folklore,* edited by Américo Paredes and Richard Bauman, 31–41 (Austin: University of Texas Press).

———. 1984. *Verbal Art as Performance.* Second ed. Prospect Heights, IL: Waveland Press.

———. 2004. *A World of Others' Words: Cross-Cultural Perspectives on Intertextuality.* Malden, MA: Blackwell Publishing.

Beck, Horace P. 1962. "Say Something Dirty!" *Journal of American Folklore* 75 (297): 195–199.

Bender, Mark. 1999. "Shifting and Performance in Suzhou Chantefable." In *The Eternal Storyteller: Oral Literature in Modern China,* edited by Vibeke Børdahl, 181–196 (London: Curzon Press).

———. 2003. *Plum and Bamboo: China's Suzhou Chantefable Tradition.* Urbana and Chicago: University of Illinois Press.

———. 2010. Review of Jiang Jing's *Women Playing Men: Yue Opera and Social Change in Twentieth-Century Shanghai. Chinese Historical Review* 17 (1): 120–122.

Benjamin, Walter. 1969. "The Storyteller: Reflections on the Work of Nikolai Leskov." In *Illuminations,* 83–110. Harry Zohn, trans. (New York: Shocken).

Billings, Joshua, Felix Budelmann, and Fiona Macintosh. 2013. "Introduction." In *Choruses, Ancient and Modern,* edited by Joshua Billings, Felix Budelmann, and Fiona Macintosh, 1–11 (Oxford and New York: Oxford University Press).

Blader, Susan. 1983. "'Yan Chasan Thrice Tested': Printed Novel to Oral Tale." *CHINOPERL Papers* 12:84–111.

———. 1999. "Oral Narrative and Its Transformation into Print: The Case of *Bai Yutang.*" In *The Eternal Storyteller: Oral Literature in Modern China,* edited by Vibeke Børdahl, 161–180 (Surrey, UK: Curzon Press).

Bohlman, Philip V. 1988. *The Study of Folk Music in the Modern World.* Bloomington: Indiana University Press.

Booth, Mark W. 1981. *The Experience of Songs.* New Haven and London: Yale University Press.

Borland, Katherine. 1998. "'That's Not What I Said': Interpretive Conflict in Oral Narrative Research." In *The Oral History Reader,* edited by Robert Perks and Alistair Thomson, 320–332 (London and New York: Routledge).

Bourdaghs, Michael K. 2012. "Mapping Misora Hibari: Where Have All the Asians Gone?" In Michael K. Bourdaghs, *Sayonara Amerika, Sayonara Nippon: A Geopolitical Prehistory of J-Pop,* 49–84 (New York: Columbia University Press).

Bourdieu, Pierre. 1977. "The Economics of Linguistic Exchanges." *Social Science Information* 116 (6): 645–668.

———. 1984. *Distinction: A Social Critique of the Judgement of Taste.* Richard Nice, trans. Cambridge, MA: Harvard University Press.

———. 1990. *The Logic of Practice.* Richard Nice, trans. Stanford, CA: Stanford University Press.

Brenneis, Don. 1986. "Shared Territory: Audience, Indirection and Meaning." *Text: An Interdisciplinary Journal for the Study of Discourse* 6 (3): 339–347.

Briggs, Charles L., and Richard Bauman. 1992. "Genre, Intertextuality, and Social Power." *Journal of Linguistic Anthropology* 2 (2): 131–172.

Brodie, Ian. 2014. *A Vulgar Art: A New Approach to Stand-Up Comedy.* Jackson: University Press of Mississippi.

Bronner, Simon. 1998. *Following Tradition: Folklore in the Discourse of American Culture.* Logan: Utah State University Press.

Brown, Marshall. 2004. "Negative Poetics: On Skepticism and the Lyric Voice." *Representations* 86 (1): 120–140.

Cai, Zong-qi. 2002. *Configurations of Comparative Poetics: Three Perspectives on Western and Chinese Literary Criticism.* Honolulu: University of Hawai'i Press.

———. 2010. "Evolving Practices of *Guan* and Liu Xie's Theory of Literary Interpretation." In *Interpretation and Literature in Early Medieval China,* edited by Alan K. L. Chan and Yuet-Keung Lo, 103–132 (Albany: State University of New York Press).

Campbell, Joseph. 2004 [1949]. *The Hero with a Thousand Faces.* Princeton and Oxford: Princeton University Press.

Cantwell, Robert. 1993. *Ethnomimesis: Folklife and the Representation of Culture.* Chapel Hill & London: University of North Carolina Press.

Cao Shiyu, ed. 2004. *Suide wenku—min'ge juan* 绥德文库民歌卷 [*Suide Library: Folksong Volume*]. Three vols. Beijing: Zhongguo wenshi chubanshe.

Carriaga, Daniel. 1969. "Ballet Folklorico de Mexico: Controlled Creativity, Styled Authenticity." *Los Angeles Times,* February 1, 1969.

Casey, George J., Neil V. Rosenberg, and Wilfred W. Wareham. 1972. "Repertoire Categorization and Performer-Audience Relationships: Some Newfoundland Folksong Examples." *Ethnomusicology* 16 (3): 397–403.

Cashman, Ray. 2011. "The Role of Tradition in the Individual: At Work in Donegal with Packy Jim McGrath." In *The Individual and Tradition: Folkloristic Perspectives,* edited by Ray Cashman, Tom Mould, and Pravina Shukla, 303–322 (Bloomington: Indiana University Press).

———. 2016. *Packy Jim: Folklore and Worldview on the Irish Border.* Madison: University of Wisconsin Press.

Cashman, Ray, Tom Mould, and Pravina Shukla, eds. 2011. *The Individual and Tradition: Folkloristic Perspectives.* Bloomington: Indiana University Press.

CCFGroup. 2016. "Shenhua Yulin, First Coal-to LDPE Maker, Gains Its Talk in PE Market." www.ccfgroup.com, January 19, 2016. http://www.ccfgroup.com/newscenter/newsview.php?Class_ID=D00000&Info_ID=20160119099 (accessed January 3, 2017).

Chabrowski, Igor Iwo. 2015. *Singing on the River: Sichuan Boatmen and Their Work Songs, 1880–1930s.* Leiden and Boston: Brill.

Chau, Adam Yuet. 2006a. "Drinking Games, Karaoke Songs, and *Yangge* Dances: Youth Cultural Production in Rural China." *Ethnology* 45 (2): 161–172.

———. 2006b. *Miraculous Response: Doing Popular Religion in Contemporary China.* Stanford, CA: Stanford University Press.

Chen, Lin. 2007. "East and West to Sing in Shaanxi." www.china.org.cn, August 15, 2007. http://www.china.org.cn/english/culture/221020.htm# (accessed August 9, 2014).

China Embassy (Embassy of the People's Republic of China in the United States). 2009. "President Hu Jintao and President Barack Obama Send Congratulatory Messages to the United States National Symphony Orchestra (NSO) (06/12/09)." June 16, 2009. http://www.china-embassy.org/eng/zmgx/t567959.htm (accessed January 6, 2013).

Chinese Business View. 2012. "Local Governments Offer Free Education." *Global*

Times, December 23, 2012. http://www.globaltimes.cn/content/751746.shtml (accessed January 4, 2013).

Ching, Chung-hwa. 1964. "The Chinese Theatre in Western Europe." *China Reconstructs* 13 (12): 16–18.

Chu Kebao 初克堡 and Jiang Yanmei 姜艳梅. 2005. "Huangtu lian'ge: xibei min'gewang Wang Xiangrong de gushi" 黄土恋歌—西北民歌王王向荣的故事 ["Love Song of the Yellow Earth: The Story of Wang Xiangrong, the King of Northwestern Folksongs"]. *Minsu wenxue* 2:4–17.

Clifford, James. 1992. "Traveling Cultures." In *Cultural Studies,* edited by Lawrence Grossberg, Cary Nelson, and Paula A. Treichler, 96–116 (New York: Routledge).

Cohen, Myron L. 1991. "Being Chinese: The Peripheralization of Traditional Identity." *Daedalus* 120 (2): 113–134.

Conceison, Claire. 2004. *Significant Other: Staging the American in China.* Honolulu: University of Hawai'i Press.

Cone, Edward T. 1974. *The Composer's Voice.* Berkeley: University of California Press.

Connerton, Paul. 1989. *How Societies Remember.* New York: Cambridge University Press.

Creed, Gerald W., and Barbara Ching. 1997. "Recognizing Rusticity: Identity and the Power of Place." In *Knowing Your Place: Rural Identity and Cultural Hierarchy,* edited by Barbara Ching and Gerald W. Creed, 1–38 (New York and London: Routledge).

Crossley, Pamela Kyle. 1999. *A Translucent Mirror: History and Identity in Qing Imperial Ideology.* Berkeley: University of California Press.

Culler, Jonathan. 2015. *Theory of the Lyric.* Cambridge, MA, and London: Harvard University Press.

Danielson, Virginia. 1997. *"The Voice of Egypt": Umm Kulthūm, Arabic Song, and Egyptian Society in the Twentieth Century.* Chicago: University of Chicago Press.

Davis, Sara. 2001. "The Hawaiification of Sipsongbanna: Orality, Power, and Cultural Survival in Southwest China." *Drama Review* 45 (4): 25–41.

———. 2005. *Songs and Silence: Ethnic Revival on China's Southwest Borders.* New York: Columbia University Press.

DeWoskin, Kenneth J. 1982. *A Song for One or Two: Music and the Concept of Art in Early China.* Ann Arbor: Center for Chinese Studies, University of Michigan.

Di Ma 狄马. 2010. "Ting Wang Xiangrong changge xiang dao de" 听王向荣唱歌想到的 ["Thoughts After Hearing Wang Xiangrong Sing"]. *Dangdai Shaanxi* 10:15.

Dicks, Bella. 2003. *Culture on Display: The Production of Contemporary Visitability.* Maidenhead, Berkshire, UK: Open University Press.

Dirlik, Arif. 1999. "Place-Based Imagination: Globalism and the Politics of Place." *Review (Fernand Braudel Center)* 22 (2): 151–187.

Dow (The Dow Chemical Company). 2008a. "Terracotta Warriors to Spend Chinese New Year in the U.S.: Dow Contributes to Cultural Exchange Between U.S. and China." January 30, 2008. http://www.dow.com/news/corporate/2008/20080130a.htm (accessed September 14, 2012).

———. 2008b. "Event Calendar." http://www.dow.com/greaterchina/en/events/calendar .htm (accessed December 18, 2012).

———. 2008c. "Far East Meets West: Dow Celebrates Relationship with China." *Around Dow* (June 2008): 6–7. http://msdssearch.dow.com/PublishedLiteratureDOWCOM/dh

_0132/0901b80380132224.pdf?filepath=news/pdfs/noreg/162–02418.pdf&fromPage =GetDoc. (accessed December 18, 2012).

———. 2009. "National Symphony Orchestra Tour to Celebrate 30th Anniversary of U.S.-China Friendship." June 10, 2009. http://www.dow.com/greaterchina/en/news /2009/20090610a.htm (accessed January 4, 2013).

Du Rongfang, ed. 2005. *Manhandiao yishu yanjiu* 漫瀚调艺术研究 [*Research on the Art of Manhandiao*]. Hohhot: Neimenggu renmin chubanshe.

DuBois, Thomas A. 2006. *Lyric, Meaning, and Audience in the Oral Tradition of Northern Europe*. Notre Dame, IN: University of Notre Dame Press.

Dunaway, David King. 1990. *How Can I Keep from Singing: Pete Seeger*. New York: Da Capo Press.

Dylan, Bob. 2016. *The Lyrics: 1961–2012*. New York: Simon & Schuster.

E'erdunchaolu 额尔敦朝鲁, Wang Shiyi 王世一, Da Sangbao 达·桑宝, Zhang Shan 张善, and Bao Yulin 包玉林, eds. 1992. *Zhongguo minjian gequ jicheng: Neimenggu juan* 中国民间 歌曲集成内蒙古卷 [*Grand Compendium of Chinese Folksongs: Inner Mongolia Volume*]. Two vols. Beijing: Renmin yinyue chubanshe.

Empson, William. 1966. *Seven Types of Ambiguity*. Fourteenth ed. New York: New Directions.

Eoyang, Eugene Chen. 2007. *Two-Way Mirrors: Cross-Cultural Studies in Glocalization*. Lanham, MD: Lexington Books.

Erikson, Erik H. 1994. *Identity and the Life Cycle*. New York: W. W. Norton & Company.

Faure, David, and Tao Tao Liu, eds. 2002. *Town and Country in China: Identity and Perception*. Hampshire, UK, and New York: Palgrave.

Fernandez, James W. 1988a. "Andalusia on Our Minds: Two Contrasting Places in Spain as Seen in a Vernacular Poetic Duel of the Late 19th Century." *Cultural Anthropology* 3 (1): 21–35.

———. 1988b. "Isn't There Anything Out There That We Can All Believe In?: The Quest for Cultural Consensus in Anthropology and History." Paper read at the Institute for Advanced Study School of Social Science, Princeton, NJ.

Feuchtwang, Stephan. 2001. *Popular Religion in China: The Imperial Metaphor*. Richmond: Curzon Press.

Filene, Benjamin. 2000. *Romancing the Folk: Public Memory & American Roots Music*. Chapel Hill: University of North Carolina Press.

Fiske, John. 2011. *Television Culture*. Second ed. London and New York: Routledge.

Foley, John Miles. 1995. *The Singer of Tales in Performance*. Bloomington: Indiana University Press.

Fong, Grace S. 1990. "Persona and Mask in the Song Lyric (*Ci*)." *Harvard Journal of Asiatic Studies* 50 (2): 459–484.

Fosler-Lussier, Danielle. 2010. "Cultural Diplomacy as Cultural Globalization: The University of Michigan Jazz Band in Latin America." *Journal of the Society for American Music* 4 (1): 59–93.

Foucault, Michel. 1986 [1967]. "Of Other Spaces." Jay Miskowiec, trans. *Diacritics* 16 (1): 22–27.

Fowler, Catherine, and Gillian Helfield, eds. 2006. *Representing the Rural: Space, Place, and Identity in Films about the Land*. Detroit: Wayne State University Press.

Frankel, Hans H. 1974. "The Chinese Ballad: 'Southeast Fly the Peacocks.'" *Harvard Journal of Asiatic Studies* 34:248–271.

———. 1985. "The Relations between Narrator and Characters in Yuefu Ballads." *CHINOPERL Papers* 13:107–127.

Freud, Sigmund. 1955. *The Standard Edition of the Complete Psychological Works of Sigmund Freud, Translated from the German under the General Editorship of James Strachey in Collaboration with Anna Freud.* Vol. 18 (1920–1922): *Beyond the Pleasure Principle, Group Psychology, and Other Works.* London: Hogarth Press.

Frisbie, Charlotte J., and David P. McAllester. 1978. *Navajo Blessingway Singer: The Autobiography of Frank Mitchell, 1881–1967.* Tucson: University of Arizona Press.

Frith, Simon. 1996a. "Music and Identity." In *Questions of Cultural Identity,* edited by Stuart Hall and Paul du Gay, 108–127 (London: SAGE Publications).

———. 1996b. *Performing Rites: On the Value of Popular Music.* Cambridge, MA: Harvard University Press.

GBM (Guowuyuan bangongting mishuju) 国务院办公厅秘书局. 2005. "Guowuyuan bangongting guanyu jiaqiang woguo feiwuzhi wenhua yichan baohu gongzuo de yijian" 国务院办公厅关于加强我国非物质文化遗产保护工作的意见 ["Suggestions from the Secretariat of the State Council on Strengthening China's Intangible Cultural Heritage Preservation Work"]. Document No. 18.

Gibbs, Levi S. 2011. "Min'ge zhi wang: wenhua renwu chuanqi yingxiang shenghuo lishi de chubu tansuo" 民歌之王:文化人物传奇影响生活历史的初步探索 ["Folksong Kings: A Preliminary Exploration of the Influence of Culture Hero Legends on Life Histories"]. *Wenzhou daxue xuebao* 24 (1): 19–25.

———. 2017. "Culture Paves the Way, Economics Comes to Sing the Opera: Chinese Folk Duets and Global Joint Ventures." *Asian Ethnology* 76 (1): 43–63.

———. Forthcoming (2018a). "Chinese Singing Contests as Sites of Negotiation among Individuals and Traditions." *Journal of Folklore Research.*

———. Forthcoming (2018b). "Forming Partnerships: Extramarital Songs and the Promotion of China's 1950 Marriage Law." *The China Quarterly.*

Gilman, Stephen. 1968. "The *Romancero* as a Literary Genre." Public Lecture at Yale University, October 9, 1968.

Glassie, Henry. 1970. "'Take That Night Train to Selma': An Excursion to the Outskirts of Scholarship." In *Folksongs and Their Makers,* edited by Henry Glassie, Edward D. Ives, and John F. Szwed, 1–68 (Bowling Green, OH: Bowling Green University Popular Press).

Goffman, Erving. 1959. *The Presentation of Self in Everyday Life.* Garden City, NY: Doubleday.

———. 1967. "On Face-Work: An Analysis of Ritual Elements in Social Interaction." In Erving Goffman, *Interaction Ritual,* 5–45 (New York: Pantheon).

———. 1974. *Frame Analysis: An Essay on the Organization of Experience.* New York: Harper & Row.

Goldstein, Joshua. 2007. *Drama Kings: Players and Publics in the Re-creation of Peking Opera, 1870–1937.* Berkeley: University of California Press.

Goldstein, Kenneth S. 1971. "On the Application of the Concepts of Active and Inactive Traditions to the Study of Repertory." *Journal of American Folklore* 84 (331): 62–67.

Goodman, David S. G. 1994. "The Politics of Regionalism: Economic Development, Conflict and Negotiation." In *China Deconstructs: Politics, Trade and Regionalism,* edited by David S. G. Goodman and Gerald Segal, 1–20 (London and New York: Routledge).

———. 2002. "Structuring Local Identity: Nation, Province and County in Shanxi during the 1990s." *The China Quarterly* 172:837–862.

Gorfinkel, Lauren. 2012. "From Transformation to Preservation: Music and Multi-Ethnic Unity on Television in China." In *Music as Intangible Cultural Heritage: Policy, Ideology, and Practice in the Preservation of East Asian Traditions,* edited by Keith Howard, 99–112 (Surrey, UK, and Burlington, VT: Ashgate).

———. 2014. "Multimodal Constructions of the Nation: How China's Music-Entertainment Television Has Incorporated Macau into the National Fold." In *Critical Multimodal Studies of Popular Discourse,* edited by Emilia Djonov and Sumin Zhao, 93–108 (New York and London: Routledge).

Gramsci, Antonio. 1992 (1971). *Selections from the Prison Notebooks of Antonio Gramsci.* Quintin Hoare and Geoffrey Nowell Smith, trans. New York: International Publishers.

Grossberg, Lawrence. 1992. *We Gotta Get Out of This Place: Popular Conservatism and Postmodern Culture.* New York and London: Routledge.

Guo Limin 郭立民. 2005. "You wo de congyi jingli kan manhandiao de xingcheng yu fazhan" 由我的从艺经历看漫瀚调的形成与发展 ["A View of *Manhandiao*'s Formation and Development Based on My Artistic Experience"]. In *Manhandiao yishu yanjiu* 漫瀚调艺术研究 [*Research on the Art of* Manhandiao], edited by Du Rongfang, 75–79 (Hohhot, China: Neimenggu renmin chubanshe).

Guy, Nancy. 2005. *Peking Opera and Politics in Taiwan.* Urbana and Chicago: University of Illinois Press.

Hall, Stuart. 1995. "Fantasy, Identity, Politics." In *Cultural Remix: Theories of Politics and the Popular,* edited by Stuart Hall, D. Held, and T. McGrew, 63–69 (London: Lawrence and Wishart).

———. 1996. "Introduction: Who Needs 'Identity'?" In *Questions of Cultural Identity,* edited by Stuart Hall and Paul du Gay, 1–17 (London: SAGE Publications).

Hamnett, Ian. 1967. "Ambiguity, Classification and Change: The Function of Riddles." *Man* 2 (1): 379–392.

Han, Kuo-Huang. 1989. "Folk Songs of the Han Chinese: Characteristics and Classifications." *Asian Music* 20 (2): 107–128.

Haring, Lee. 1974. "On Knowing the Answer." *Journal of American Folklore* 87 (345): 197–207.

Harker, Dave. 1985. *Fakesong: The Manufacture of British 'Folksong' 1700 to the Present Day.* Milton Keynes, UK, and Philadelphia: Open University Press.

Harkness, Nicholas. 2014. *Songs of Seoul: An Ethnography of Voice and Voicing in Christian South Korea.* Berkeley: University of California Press.

Harnish, David. 2009. "Tejano Music in the Urbanizing Midwest: The Musical Story of Conjunto Master Jesse Ponce." *Journal of the Society for American Music* 3 (2): 195–219.

Harris, Rachel. 2004. *Singing the Village: Music, Memory and Ritual among the Sibe of Xinjiang.* Oxford and New York: Oxford University Press.

———. 2005. "Wang Luobin: Folk Song King of the Northwest or Song Thief?: Copyright, Representation, and Chinese Folk Songs." *Modern China* 31 (3): 381–408.

Harrison, Henrietta. 2002. "Village Identity in Rural North China: A Sense of Place in the Diary of Liu Dapeng." In *Town and Country in China: Identity and Perception*, edited by David Faure and Tao Tao Liu, 85–106 (Hampshire, UK, and New York: Palgrave).

Hawkes, David, trans. 1985. *Ch'u tz'ŭ, The Songs of the South: An Ancient Chinese Anthology*. New York: Penguin Books.

He Feng 何凤. 2006. "Shaanbei min'ge dasai zongjuesai jiang tuichu 'shi da Shaanbei mingeshou'" 陕北民歌大赛总决赛将推出十大陕北民歌手 ["Northern Shaanxi Folksong Contest Finals Will Present the Public with the 'Ten Greatest Northern Shaanxi Folksingers'"]. www.cnr.cn, April 17, 2006. http://www.cnr.cn/2004news/whyl/200604/t20060417_504195235.html (accessed August 9, 2014).

He Yutang 贺玉堂, ed. 2007. *He Yutang yanchang min'ge xuan* 贺玉堂演唱民歌选 [*Anthology of Folksongs Performed by He Yutang*]. Guangdong: Zhongguo changpian Guangzhou gongsi.

Holm, David. 1991. *Art and Ideology in Revolutionary China*. Oxford: Clarendon Press.

Howard, Keith, ed. 2012. *Music as Intangible Cultural Heritage: Policy, Ideology and Practice in the Preservation of East Asian Traditions*. Farnham, UK, and Burlington, VT: Ashgate Publications.

Hsu, Pi-Ching. 2006. *Beyond Eroticism: A Historian's Reading of Humor in Feng Menglong's* Child's Folly. Lanham, MD: University Press of America.

Hughes, David W. 2008. *Traditional Folk Song in Modern Japan: Sources, Sentiment and Society*. Folkestone, UK: Global Oriental.

Hung, Chang-tai. 1985. *Going to the People: Chinese Intellectuals and Folk Literature*. Cambridge, MA, and London: Harvard University Press.

Huo Xianggui 霍向贵. 1996. "Nongmin de zhongshi erzi—ji zhuming mingeshou Wang Xiangrong" 农民的忠实儿子–记著名民歌手王向荣 ["A True Peasant Son: Some Notes on the Celebrated Folksinger Wang Xiangrong"]. *Yinyue tiandi* 5: 27.

———, ed. 2005. *Shaanbei min'ge jingxuan* 陕北民歌精选 [*A Choice Selection of Northern Shaanxi Folksongs*]. Xi'an: Shaanxi lüyou chubanshe.

———, ed. 2006. *Shaanbei min'ge daquan* 陕北民歌大全 [*A Complete Collection of Folk Songs from Northern Shaanxi*]. Two vols. Xi'an: Shaanxi renmin chubanshe.

Hymes, Robert P. 2002. *Way and Byway: Taoism, Local Religion, and Models of Divinity in Sung and Modern China*. Berkeley: University of California Press.

ICIS News. 2009. "Shenhua and Dow to Invest $10bn in Yulin Chemicals Complex." November 6, 2009. http://www.icis.com/Articles/2009/11/06/9261371/shenhua-and-dow-to-invest-10bn-in-yulin-chemicals-complex.html (accessed January 7, 2013).

———. 2014. "China Shenhua, Dow Chemical Scrap Yulin Coal-Chemical Project." May 14, 2014. http://www.icis.com/resources/news/2014/05/14/9780947/china-shenhua-dow-chemical-scrap-yulin-coal-chemical-project/ (accessed January 3, 2017).

Idema, Wilt L., ed. and trans. 2010. *The Butterfly Lovers: The Legend of Liang Shanbo and Zhu Yingtai: Four Versions, with Related Texts*. Indianapolis: Hackett Publishing Company.

Ingram, Catherine. 2012. "*Ee, mang gay dor ga ey* (Hey, Why Don't You Sing)? Imagining the Future for Kam Big Song." In *Music as Intangible Cultural Heritage: Policy, Ideology, and Practice in the Preservation of East Asian Traditions,* edited by Keith Howard, 55–75 (Surrey, UK, and Burlington, VT: Ashgate).

Isaku, Patia R. 1981. *Mountain Storm, Pine Breeze: Folk Song in Japan.* Tucson: University of Arizona Press.

Jacobs, Andrew. 2012. "A Star in China Both Rises and Sets." *New York Times,* November 16, 2012.

Jeffreys, Elaine, and Louise Edwards. 2010. "Celebrity/China." In *Celebrity in China,* edited by Louise Edwards and Elaine Jeffreys, 1–20 (Hong Kong: Hong Kong University Press).

Johnson, David. 2009. *Spectacle and Sacrifice: The Ritual Foundations of Village Life in North China.* Cambridge, MA, and London: Harvard University Press.

Jones, Stephen. 1995. *Folk Music of China: Living Instrumental Traditions.* Oxford: Clarendon Press.

———. 2009. *Ritual and Music of North China.* Vol. 2: *Shaanbei.* Farnham, Surrey, UK, and Burlington, VT: Ashgate.

Kang, Xiaofei. 2006. *The Cult of the Fox: Power, Gender, and Popular Religion in Late Imperial and Modern China.* New York: Columbia University Press.

Kapchan, Deborah A. 1995. "Performance." *Journal of American Folklore* 108 (430): 479–508.

Keil, Charles, and Steven Feld. 1994. *Music Grooves: Essays and Dialogues.* Chicago: University of Chicago Press.

Kennedy, Louise. 2003. "Activists Ask, Where Have All the Peace Songs Gone?" *Boston Globe,* March 17, 2003. http://www.sfgate.com/entertainment/article/Activists-ask -where-have-all-the-peace-songs-2662316.php (accessed March 14, 2017).

Kennedy Center (The John F. Kennedy Center for the Performing Arts). 2009. "National Symphony Orchestra, Iván Fischer, Principal Conductor, to Tour China and Republic of Korea, June 2009." Press Release, March 11, 2009. http://www.kennedy -center.org/nso/pdf/090311_nso_china_pressrelease.pdf (accessed January 4, 2013).

———. 2012a. "Americas Tour—National Symphony Orchestra—The John F. Kennedy Center for the Performing Arts." http://www.kennedy-center.org/nso/americastour/ (accessed January 4, 2013).

———. 2012b. "Donors Make a Difference: The Support of Donors Like the Dow Chemical Company and Whirlpool Corporation Has Enabled the NSO to Continue Its Proud Tradition of International Touring." http://www.kennedy-center.org/support /corporate/spotlight.pdf (accessed January 4, 2013).

Kirshenblatt-Gimblett, Barbara. 1989. "Authoring Lives." *Journal of Folklore Research* 26 (2): 123–149.

———. 1998. *Destination Culture: Tourism, Museums, and Heritage.* Berkeley: University of California Press.

Klusen, Ernst. 1986 [1967]. "The Group Song as Group Object." In *German Volkskunde: A Decade of Theoretical Confrontation, Debate, and Reorientation, 1967–1977,* edited by James R. Dow and Hannjost Lixfeld, 184–202 (Bloomington: Indiana University Press).

Kouwenhoven, Frank. 2014. "Love Songs and Temple Festivals in Northwest China: Musical Laughter in the Face of Adversity." In *Music, Dance and the Art of Seduction,* edited by Frank Kouwenhoven and James Kippen, 115–165 (Delft, The Netherlands: Eburon).

Kouwenhoven, Frank, and Antoinet Schimmelpenninck. 2009. "Zhao Yongming: Portrait of a Mountain Song Cicada." In *Lives in Chinese Music,* edited by Helen Rees, 23–44 (Urbana and Chicago: University of Illinois Press).

———. 2013. "'I Prefer a Man Who Is Fresh Like a Jumping Fish': Gender Issues in *Shan'ge,* Chinese Popular Rural Song." In *Gender in Chinese Music,* edited by Rachel Harris, Rowan Pease, and Shzr Ee Tan, 156–176 (Rochester, NY: University of Rochester Press).

Lai Daren 赖大仁. 2000. *Hun gui hechu: Jia Pingwa lun* 魂归何处: 贾平凹论 [*Where Can the Soul Settle: On Jia Pingwa*]. Beijing: Huaxia chubanshe.

Lau, Frederick. 2008. *Music in China: Experiencing Music, Expressing Culture.* New York and Oxford: Oxford University Press.

Lawless, Elaine J. 1991. "Rescripting Their Lives and Narratives: Spiritual Life Stories of Pentecostal Women Preachers." *Journal of Feminist Studies in Religion* 7 (1): 53–71.

Lee, Gregory. 1995. "The 'East Is Red' Goes Pop: Commodification, Hybridity and Nationalism in Chinese Popular Song and Its Televisual Performance." *Popular Music* 14 (1): 95–110.

Lee, Haiyan. 2007. *Revolution of the Heart: A Genealogy of Love in China, 1900–1950.* Stanford, CA: Stanford University Press.

———. 2008. "Meng Jiangnü and the May Fourth Folklore Movement." In *Meng Jiangnü Brings Down the Great Wall: Ten Versions of a Chinese Legend,* edited and translated by Wilt L. Idema, 24–41 (Seattle and London: University of Washington Press).

Lee, Leo Ou-fan. 1990. "In Search of Modernity: Some Reflections on a New Mode of Consciousness in Twentieth Century History and Literature." In *Ideas Across Cultures: Essays on Chinese Thought in Honor of Benjamin I. Schwartz,* edited by Paul A. Cohen and Merle Goldman, 109–135 (Cambridge, MA, and London: Harvard University Press).

Lee, Tong Soon. 2009. *Chinese Street Opera in Singapore.* Urbana and Chicago: University of Illinois Press.

Legman, G. 1962. "Misconceptions in Erotic Folklore." *Journal of American Folklore* 75 (297): 200–208.

Levenson, Joseph. 1967. "The Province, the Nation and the World: The Problem of Chinese Identity." In *Approaches to Modern Chinese History,* edited by Albert Feuerwerker, Rhoads Murphey, and Mary C. Wright, 268–288 (Berkeley: University of California Press).

Lévi-Strauss, Claude. 1966. *The Savage Mind.* Chicago: University of Chicago Press.

———. 1996 [1963]. "The Effectiveness of Symbols." Claire Jacobson and Brooke Grundfest Schoepf, trans. In *Readings in Ritual Studies,* edited by Ronald L. Grimes, 368–378 (Upper Saddle River, NJ: Prentice Hall).

Lewis, Mark Edward. 1999. *Writing and Authority in Early China.* Albany, NY: State University of New York Press.

Li, Jing. 2013. "The Making of Ethnic Yunnan on the National Mall: Minority Folksong and Dance Performances, Provincial Identity, and 'The Artifying of Politics' (*Zhengzhi yishuhua*)." *Modern China* 39 (1): 69–100.

Li, Kwok-sing, comp. 1995. *A Glossary of Political Terms of the People's Republic of China.* Mary Lok, trans. Hong Kong: Chinese University Press.

Li Xing 李星. 1989. "Lun 'nongyi chengji' zuojia de xinli shijie" 论农裔城籍作家的心理世界

["On the Psychological World of Writers of 'Urban Residence with Rural Origin'"]. *Dangdai zuojia pinglun* 2:114–122.

Liang, Zhao. 2009. "'Liu Sanjie' and the Changes and Shapings of Ethnic Culture in Lingnan of China." *Journal of Cambridge Studies* 4 (2): 37–54.

Linde, Charlotte. 1993. *Life Stories: The Creation of Coherence.* New York: Oxford University Press.

Lindholm, Charles. 2008. *Culture and Authenticity.* Oxford: Blackwell Publishing.

Liu, Coco. 2015. "What Happens in a Coal Boomtown as China Heads toward 'Peak Coal'?" www.eenews.net, March 18, 2015. http://www.eenews.net/stories/1060015235 (accessed January 3, 2017).

Liu, Kang. 2004. *Globalization and Cultural Trends in China.* Honolulu: University of Hawai'i Press.

Liu, Tao Tao. 1996. "Local Identity in Modern Chinese Fiction and Fiction of the Native Soil (*Xiangtu Wenxue*)." In *Unity and Diversity: Local Cultures and Identities in China,* edited by Tao Tao Liu and David Faure, 139–160 (Hong Kong: Hong Kong University Press).

Liu, Xin. 2000. *In One's Own Shadow: An Ethnographic Account of the Condition of Post-Reform Rural China.* Berkeley: University of California Press.

Liu Yulin 刘育林 et al. 2010. *Shaanbei min'ge tonglun* 陕北民歌通论 [*General Survey of Northern Shaanxi Folksongs*]. Xi'an: Shaanxi renmin chubanshe.

Loh, Wai-fong. 1984. "From Romantic Love to Class Struggle: Reflections on the Film *Liu Sanjie*." In *Popular Chinese Literature and Performing Arts in the People's Republic of China, 1949–1979,* edited by Bonnie S. McDougall, 165–176 (Berkeley and Los Angeles: University of California Press).

Lomax, Alan. 1993. *The Land Where the Blues Began.* New York: New Press.

Lord, Albert B. 1960. *The Singer of Tales.* Cambridge, MA, and London: Harvard University Press.

Lu, Guang, and Xiaoyu Xiao. 2000. "Beijing Opera during the Cultural Revolution: The Rhetoric of Ideological Conflicts." In *Chinese Perspectives in Rhetoric and Communication,* edited by D. Ray Heisey, 223–248 (Stamford, CT: Ablex Publishing Corporation).

Lu, Hanchao. 2002. "Urban Superiority, Modernity and Local Identity—A Think Piece on the Case of Shanghai." In *Town and Country in China: Identity and Perception,* edited by David Faure and Tao Tao Liu, 126–144 (Hampshire, UK, and New York: Palgrave).

Lu, Jiang. 2007. "The Art of Traditional Architectural Ornaments in Northern China." PhD diss., Indiana University.

Lü Ji 吕骥. 1962. "Zhongguo minjian yinyue yanjiu tigang" 中国民间音乐研究提纲 ["An Outline for Chinese Folk Music Research"]. Manuscript completed on September 15, 1946. Reprinted in *Zhongguo xiandai yinyuejia lun minzu yinyue* 中国现代音乐家论民族音乐 [*Modern Chinese Musicians Discuss Chinese Traditional Music*], edited by Zhongyang yinyue xueyuan Zhongguo yinyue yanjiusuo minzu yinyue yanjiu ban 中央音乐学院中国音乐研究所民族音乐研究班. Beijing: Zhongyang yinyue xueyuan Zhongguo yinyue yanjiusuo minzu yinyue yanjiu ban.

———, ed. 1994. *Zhongguo minjian gequ jicheng: Shaanxi juan* 中国民间歌曲集成: 陕西卷

[*Grand Compendium of Chinese Folksongs: Shaanxi Volume*]. Two vols. Beijing: Zhongguo ISBN zhongxin.

Luo Xi 罗希. 2006. "Wang Xiangrong lai woyuan juban jiangchanghui" 王向荣来我院举办讲唱会 ["Wang Xiangrong Visits Our School to Hold a Singing-Speaking Lecture"]. *Jiaoxiang—Xi'an yinyue xueyuan xuebao* 1:20.

Lyotard, Jean-François. 1984. *The Postmodern Condition: A Report on Knowledge.* Geoff Bennington and Brian Massumi, trans. Minneapolis: University of Minnesota Press.

Ma Yumei 马玉梅 and Zhang Jingyan 张敬艳. 2007. "Nadada dou buru an shangougou hao—ji xibei ge'wang Wang Xiangrong" 哪垯垯都不如俺山沟沟好—记西北歌王王向荣 ["No Place Is as Good as Our Gully: Notes on the Folksong King of the Northwest, Wang Xiangrong"]. *Jinqiu* 4:11–14.

Mackerras, Colin. 1984. "Folksongs and Dances of China's Minority Nationalities: Policy, Tradition, and Professionalization." *Modern China* 10 (2): 187–226.

———. 2011. "Tourism and Musical Performing Arts in China in the First Decade of the Twenty-First Century: A Personal View." *CHINOPERL Papers* 30:153–180.

Mair, Victor H., and Mark Bender, eds. 2011. *The Columbia Anthology of Chinese Folk and Popular Literature.* New York: Columbia University Press.

Malone, Bill. 2011. *Music from the True Vine: Mike Seeger's Life and Musical Journey.* Chapel Hill: University of North Carolina.

Maranda, Elli Köngäs. 1971. "Theory and Practice of Riddle Analysis." *Journal of American Folklore* 84 (331): 51–61.

Marcus, Greil. 1991. *Dead Elvis: A Chronicle of a Cultural Obsession.* New York: Doubleday.

Maring, Joel M., and Lillian E. Maring. 1997. "Japanese Erotic Folksong: From Shunka to Karaoke." *Asian Music* 28 (2): 27–49.

Marqusee, Mike. 2005. *Wicked Messenger: Bob Dylan and the 1960s, Chimes of Freedom, Revised and Expanded.* New York: Seven Stories Press.

Marshall, Lee. 2007. *Bob Dylan: The Never Ending Star.* Cambridge and Malden, MA: Polity.

Marshall, P. David. 2006. "The Meanings of the Popular Music Celebrity: The Construction of Distinctive Authenticity." In *The Celebrity Culture Reader,* edited by P. David Marshall, 196–222 (New York and London: Routledge).

Mauss, Marcel. 1966. *The Gift: Forms and Functions of Exchange in Archaic Societies.* Ian Cunnison, trans. London: Cohen & West Ltd.

McDougall, Bonnie S., ed. 1980. *Mao Zedong's "Talks at the Yan'an Conference on Literature and Arts."* Ann Arbor: University of Michigan Press.

———, ed. 1984. *Popular Chinese Literature and the Performing Arts in the People's Republic of China, 1949–1979.* Berkeley: University of California Press.

MCFTA (Midland Center for the Arts). 2008a. "Celebrate China: Reflections of the Yellow River." http://www.mcfta.org/A_ABDow/ChinaSpecialEvents.htm#Dancers (accessed December 18, 2012).

———. 2008b. "Timeless Warriors & Relics: 1500 Years of Ancient China." http://www.mcfta.org/A_ABDow/ChinaHome.html (accessed December 15, 2012).

McLaren, Anne E. 2008. *Performing Grief: Bridal Laments in Rural China.* Honolulu: University of Hawai'i Press.

Meeker, Lauren. 2013. *Sounding Out Heritage: Cultural Politics and the Social Practice of Quan ho Folk Song in Northern Vietnam.* Honolulu: University of Hawai'i Press.

Miao Jing 苗晶 and Qiao Jianzhong 乔建中. 1987. *Lun Hanzu min'ge jinsi secaiqu de huafen* 论汉族民歌近似色彩区的划分 [*The Division of Han Folksongs into Approximate Color Regions*]. Beijing: Wenhua yishu chubanshe.

Miao Meng 苗萌. 2008. "Huangtu lian'ge—Shaanbei gewang Wang Xiangrong sumiao" 黄土恋歌—陕北歌王王向荣素描 ["Love Song of the Yellow Earth: A Sketch of the Northern Shaanxi Folksong King Wang Xiangrong"]. *Renmin yinyue* 11:71–73.

Moore, Allan F. 2012. *Song Means: Analysing and Interpreting Recorded Popular Song.* Surrey, UK, and Burlington, VT: Ashgate.

Mote, Frederick W. 1973. "A Millennium of Chinese Urban History: Form, Time and Space Concepts in Soochow." *Rice University Studies* 59:35–65.

Mullen, Patrick B. 1981. "A Traditional Storyteller in Changing Contexts." In *"And Other Neighborly Names": Social Process and Cultural Image in Texas Folklore,* edited by Richard Bauman and Roger D. Abrahams, 266–279 (Austin and London: University of Texas Press).

Nagy, Gregory. 1996. *Poetry as Performance: Homer and Beyond.* Cambridge: Cambridge University Press.

Nan Xiangyu 南翔宇. 2003. "'Shaanbei gewang' Wang Xiangrong" 陕北歌王王向荣 ["'The King of Northern Shaanxi Folksongs': Wang Xiangrong"]. *Qianjin luntan* 5:23–24.

Nancy, Jean-Luc. 2000. *Being Singular Plural.* Robert D. Richardson and Anne E. O'Byrne, trans. Stanford, CA: Stanford University Press.

Nora, Pierre. 1989. "Between Memory and History: Les Lieux de Mémoire." *Representations* 26:7–24.

Notar, Beth E. 2006. *Displacing Desire: Travel and Popular Culture in China.* Honolulu: University of Hawai'i Press.

Noyes, Dorothy. 1995. "Façade Performances: Public Face, Private Mask." *Southern Folklore* 52 (2): 91–95.

———. 2003. "Group." In *Eight Words for the Study of Expressive Culture,* edited by Burt Feintuch, 7–41 (Urbana and Chicago: University of Illinois Press).

———. 2016. "Fairy-Tale Economics: Scarcity, Risk, Choice." In *Humble Theory: Folklore's Grasp on Social Life,* 297–322 (Bloomington and Indianapolis: Indiana University Press).

NWA (Northwest Airlines Corp.). 2008. "Northwest Sponsors 'A Celebration of China' Cultural Festival. April 2008. http://www.nwa.com/asia/en/newsletter/apr08_2.html (accessed December 18, 2012).

Oakes, Tim. 1995. "Shen Congwen's Literary Regionalism and the Gendered Landscape of Chinese Modernity." *Geografiska Annaler* 77 B (2): 93–107.

———. 1999. "Selling Guizhou: Cultural Development in an Era of Marketisation." In *The Political Economy of China's Provinces,* edited by Hans Hendrischke and Feng Chongyi, 31–67 (London and New York: Routledge).

———. 2000. "China's Provincial Identities: Reviving Regionalism and Reinventing 'Chineseness.'" *Journal of Asian Studies* 59 (3): 667–692.

Pattie, David. 2007. *Rock Music in Performance.* Basingstoke, UK: Palgrave Macmillan.

Pearson, Barry Lee. 1984. *"Sounds So Good to Me": The Bluesman's Story.* Philadelphia: University of Pennsylvania Press.

Pickowicz, Paul G. 2010. "Revisiting Cold War Propaganda: Close Readings of Chinese and American Film Representations of the Korean War." *Journal of American-East Relations* 17 (4): 352–371.

Plummer, Ken. 2001. "The Call of Life Stories in Ethnographic Research." In *Handbook of Ethnography,* edited by Paul Atkinson, Sara Delamont, Amanda Coffey, John Lofland, and Lyn H. Lofland, 395–406 (London and Thousand Oaks, CA: SAGE Publications).

Porter, James. 1976. "Jeannie Robertson's My Son David: A Conceptual Performance Model." *Journal of American Folklore* 89 (351): 7–26.

Porter, James, and Herschel Gower. 1995. *Jeannie Robertson: Emergent Singer, Transformative Voice.* Knoxville: University of Tennessee Press.

Qiao Jianzhong 乔建中. 1998. "Hanzu chuantong yinyue yanjiu sishi nian" 汉族传统音乐研究四十年 ["Forty Years of Research on Traditional Han Chinese Music"]. In *Tudi yu ge* 土地与歌 [*Songs of the Land in China*], 322–348 (Jinan: Shandong wenyi chubanshe).

——, ed. 2002. *Zhongguo jingdian min'ge: jianshang zhinan* 中国经典民歌鉴赏指南 [*Classic Chinese Folksongs: A Guide for Appreciation*]. Two vols. Shanghai: Shanghai yinyue chubanshe.

——. 2011. "Yuanshengtai min'ge de wutaihua yu 'feiyi' baohu: Zhongguo yuanshengtai min'ge shengdian xueshu yanjiuhui fayan tigang" 原生态民歌的舞台化与非遗保护—中国原生态民歌盛典学术研讨会发言提纲 ["The Stageification of *Yuanshengtai* Folksongs and the Preservation of 'Intangible Cultural Heritage': Outline for a Speech Given at the Academic Symposium on Chinese *Yuanshengtai* Folksongs"]. *Renmin yinyue* 8:47–49.

—— et al. 2011. "Shaanbei min'ge diaocha baogao" 陕北民歌调查报告 ["Investigation Report on Northern Shaanxi Folksongs"]. Unpublished manuscript.

Raglan, FitzRoy Richard Somerset, Baron. 2003 [1936]. *The Hero: A Study in Tradition, Myth and Drama.* Mineola, New York: Dover Publications, Inc.

Rée, Jonathan. 1990. "Funny Voices: Stories, Punctuation, and Personal Identity." *New Literary History* 21 (4): 1039–1058.

Rees, Helen, ed. 2009. *Lives in Chinese Music.* Urbana and Chicago: University of Illinois Press.

——. 2012. "Intangible Cultural Heritage in China Today: Policy and Practice in the Early Twenty-First Century." In *Music as Intangible Cultural Heritage: Policy, Ideology, and Practice in Preservation of East Asian Traditions,* edited by Keith Howard, 23–54 (Surrey, UK, and Burlington, VT: Ashgate).

——. 2016. "Environmental Crisis, Culture Loss, and a New Musical Aesthetic: China's 'Original Ecology Folksongs' in Theory and Practice." *Ethnomusicology* 60 (1): 53–88.

Robertson, Roland. 1992. *Globalization: Social Theory and Global Culture.* London: Sage Publications.

——. 1995. "Glocalization: Time-Space and Homogeneity-Heterogeneity." In *Global Modernities,* edited by Mike Featherstone, Scott Lash, and Roland Robertson, 25–44 (London: Sage Publications).

Rockwell, John. 2005. "The Foggy, Foggy Dew." In *The Rose and the Briar: Death, Love and Liberty in the American Ballad,* edited by Sean Wilentz and Greil Marcus, 231–240 (New York and London: W. W. Norton & Company).

Rosenberg, Neil V. 1986. "Big Fish, Small Pond: Country Musicians and Their Markets." In *Media Sense: The Folklore Popular Culture Continuum,* edited by Peter Narváez and Martin Laba, 149–166 (Bowling Green, OH: Bowling Green State University Popular Press).

Rubin, David C. 1995. *Memory in Oral Traditions: The Cognitive Psychology of Epic, Ballads, and Counting-Out Rhymes.* Oxford: Oxford University Press.

Ruskin, Jesse D., and Timothy Rice. 2012. "The Individual in Musical Ethnography." *Ethnomusicology* 56 (2): 299–327.

Saeji, CedarBough Tam. 2013. "Learning Is Never Done: Age and Performance in the Korean Context." Paper Presented at the Association for Asian Studies Annual Conference on March 22, 2013.

Said, Edward W. 1996 [1994]. *Representations of the Intellectual: The 1993 Reith Lectures.* New York: Vintage Books.

Samei, Maija Bell. 2004. *Gendered Persona and Poetic Voice: The Abandoned Woman in Early Chinese Song Lyrics.* Lanham, MD: Lexington Books.

Sawin, Patricia. 2004. *Listening for a Life: A Dialogic Ethnography of Bessie Eldreth through Her Songs and Stories.* Logan: Utah State University Press.

Schechner, Richard. 1988. *Performance Theory.* Revised and expanded ed. New York and London: Routledge.

Schein, Louisa. 2010. "Flexible Celebrity: A Half-Century of Miao Pop." In *Celebrity in China,* edited by Louise Edwards and Elaine Jeffreys, 145–168 (Hong Kong: Hong Kong University Press).

Schimmelpenninck, Antoinet. 1997. *Chinese Folk Songs and Folk Singers: Shan'ge Traditions in Southern Jiangsu.* CHIME Studies in East Asian Music, vol. 1. Leiden: CHIME Foundation.

Schram, Stuart, ed. 1969. *The Political Thought of Mao Tse-tung.* New York: Praeger.

Scott, Clive. 1998. *The Poetics of French Verse: Studies in Reading.* Oxford: Clarendon Press.

Senderovich, Savely. 2005. *The Riddle of the Riddle: A Study of the Folk Riddle's Figurative Nature.* London: Kegan Paul.

Shang Airen 尚爱仁. 1996a. "Shang Airen nianbiao" 尚爱仁年表 ["A Chronology of Shang Airen's Life"]. In *Shang Airen zuopin xuan* 尚爱仁作品选 [*Selection of Shang Airen's Works*] (Xi'an: Xi'an yinyue xueyuan yinshuachang).

———. 1996b. "Yulin diqu wengongtuan de shi nian" 榆林地区文工团的十年 ["A Decade of the Yulin Prefecture Song and Dance Troupe"]. In *Shang Airen zuopin xuan* 尚爱仁作品选 [*Selection of Shang Airen's Works*], 249–253 (Xi'an: Xi'an yinyue xueyuan yinshuachang).

———. 1996c. "Yulin minjian yishutuan de dansheng—cong gai tuan fu Ou yanchu qude jida chenggong tanqi" 榆林民间艺术团的诞生—从该团赴欧演出取得极大成功谈起 ["The Birth of the Yulin Folk Arts Troupe: A Discussion Beginning with Its Immensely Successful European Tour"]. In *Shang Airen zuopin xuan* 尚爱仁作品选 [*Selection of Shang Airen's Works*], 244–248 (Xi'an: Xi'an yinyue xueyuan yinshuachang).

Shay, Anthony. 2002. *Choreographic Politics: State Folk Dance Companies, Representation and Power.* Middletown, CT: Wesleyan University Press.

Shepherd, Eric T. 2005. *Eat Shandong: From Personal Experience to a Pedagogy of a Second Culture.* Columbus, OH: Foreign Language Publications.

Shuman, Amy. 1986. *Storytelling Rights: The Uses of Oral and Written Texts by Urban Adolescents*. Cambridge: Cambridge University Press.

———. 2005. *Other People's Stories: Entitlement Claims and the Critique of Empathy*. Urbana and Chicago: University of Illinois Press.

Silverman, Carol. 2014. "Esma Redžepova: 'Queen of Gypsy Music.'" In *Romani Routes: Cultural Politics and Balkan Music in Diaspora*, 201–219 (Oxford: Oxford University Press).

Siu, Helen F., ed. 1990. *Furrows: Peasants, Intellectuals, and the State: Stories and Histories from Modern China*. Stanford, CA: Stanford University Press.

Skinner, G. William, ed. 1997. *The City in Late Imperial China*. Stanford, CA: Stanford University Press.

Sloan, Kathryn A. 2011. *Women's Roles in Latin America and the Caribbean*. Santa Barbara, CA: ABC Clio/Greenwood.

Smith, Barbara Herrnstein. 1978. *On the Margins of Discourse: The Relation of Literature to Language*. Chicago and London: University of Chicago Press.

Smith, D. Howard. 1957. "Divine Kingship in Ancient China." *Numen* 4 (3): 171–203.

Snow, Edgar. 1938. *Red Star Over China*. New York: Random House.

Sommer, Matthew H. 2002. "Dangerous Males, Vulnerable Males, and Polluted Males: The Regulation on Masculinity in Qing Dynastic Law." In *Chinese Femininities/Chinese Masculinities: A Reader,* edited by Susan E. Brownell and Jeffrey N. Wasserstrom, 67–88 (Berkeley: University of California Press).

Stahl (Dolby), Sandra. 1989. *Literary Folkloristics and the Personal Narrative*. Bloomington: Indiana University Press.

Stock, Jonathan P. J. 2001. "Toward an Ethnomusicology of the Individual, or Biographical Writing in Ethnomusicology." *World of Music* 43 (1): 5–19.

Stokes, Martin. 1994. "Place, Exchange and Meaning: Black Sea Musicians in the West of Ireland." In *Ethnicity, Identity and Music: The Musical Construction of Place*, edited by Martin Stokes, 97–115 (Oxford and Providence, RI: Berg).

Su Jian 苏简. 2007. "'Dongfang hong' shi zenyang dansheng de" 东方红是怎样诞生的 ["How Did 'The East Is Red' Come into Being?"]. *Lantai neiwai* 2:48–49.

Su Xiaokang and Wang Luxiang. 1991. *Deathsong of the River: A Reader's Guide to the Chinese TV Series* Heshang, edited and translated by Richard W. Bodman and Pin P. Wan. Ithaca, NY: Cornell University Press.

Sun, Cecile Chu-chin. 2011. *The Poetics of Repetition in English and Chinese Lyric Poetry*. Chicago and London: University of Chicago Press.

Sun, Nina Ying. 2016. "China to Add 1.3 Million Metric Tons of PE Capacity in 2017." www.plasticsnews.com, December 13, 2016. http://www.plasticsnews.com/article/20161213/NEWS/161219958/china-to-add-1-3-million-metric-tons-of-pe-capacity-in-2017 (accessed January 3, 2017).

Sun, Wanning. 2014. *Subaltern China: Rural Migrants, Media, and Cultural Practices*. Lanham, MD: Rowman & Littlefield.

SWB (Shaanxi sheng wenhuating bangongshi) 陕西省文化厅办公室. 2007. "Guanyu yinfa 'Shaanxi sheng feiwuzhi wenhua yichan xiangmu daibiaoxing chuanchengren rending yu guanli zanxing banfa' de tongzhi" 关于印发陕西省非物质文化遗产项目代表性传承人认定与管理暂行办法的通知 ["Notice Concerning the Printing and Distribution of 'Provisional Measures for the Selection and Administration of Representative Transmitters for Shaanxi Province Intangible Cultural Heritage Items'"]. Document Number 6.

Tansman, Alan M. 1996. "Mournful Tears and *Sake*: The Postwar Myth of Misora Hibari." In *Contemporary Japan and Popular Culture,* edited by John Whittier Treat, 103–133 (Richmond, UK: Curzon Press).

Thurston, Timothy. 2013. "'Careful Village's Grassland Dispute': An A mdo Dialect Tibetan Crosstalk Performance by Sman bla skyabs." *CHINOPERL: Journal of Chinese Oral and Performing Literature* 32 (2): 156–181.

Tian, Min. 2012. *Mei Lanfang and the Twentieth-Century International Stage.* New York: Palgrave Macmillan.

Titon, Jeff Todd. 1980. "The Life Story." *Journal of American Folklore* 93 (369): 276–292.

———. 1988. *Powerhouse for God: Speech, Chant, and Song in an Appalachian Baptist Church.* Austin: University of Texas Press.

———. 2012. "Authenticity and Authentication: Mike Seeger, the New Lost City Ramblers, and the Old-Time Music Revival." *Journal of Folklore Research* 49 (2): 227–245.

Tonkin, Elizabeth. 1992. *Narrating Our Pasts: The Social Construction of Oral History.* Cambridge: Cambridge University Press.

Tuohy, Sue. 1999. "The Social Life of Genre: The Dynamics of Folksong in China." *Asian Music* 30 (2): 39–86.

———. 2001. "The Sonic Dimensions of Nationalism in Modern China: Musical Representation and Transformation." *Ethnomusicology* 45 (1): 107–131.

———. 2003. "The Choices and Challenges of Local Distinction: Regional Attachments and Dialect in Chinese Music." In *Global Pop, Local Language,* edited by Harris M. Berger and Michael Thomas Carroll, 153–185 (Jackson: University Press of Mississippi).

Turner, Graeme. 2004. *Understanding Celebrity.* London: Sage.

Turner, Victor. 1969. *The Ritual Process: Structure and Anti-Structure.* Chicago: Aldine Publishing Company.

UNESCO. 2003. *Convention for the Safeguarding of the Intangible Cultural Heritage.* Paris: UNESCO.

Van Gennep, Arnold. 1960. *The Rites of Passage.* Monika B. Vizedom and Gabrielle L. Caffee, trans. Chicago: University of Chicago Press.

Van Leeuwen, Theo. 1999. *Speech, Music, Sound.* London: Macmillan.

Van Zile, Judy. 2001. "Ch'oe Sŭng-hŭi: A Korean Dancer in the United States." In *Perspectives on Korean Dance,* 185–219 (Middletown, CT: Wesleyan University Press).

Von Hallberg, Robert. 2008. *Lyric Powers.* Chicago and London: University of Chicago Press.

Wald, Elijah. 2004. *Escaping the Delta: Robert Johnson and the Invention of the Blues.* New York: HarperCollins Publishers Inc.

———. 2015. *Dylan Goes Electric! Newport, Seeger, Dylan, and the Night That Split the Sixties.* New York: Dey St.

Wang Changfa 王长发. 1998. "'Dongfang hong' gequ de dansheng jiqi zuozhe kaozheng" 东方红歌曲的诞生及其作者考证 ["The Emergence of 'The East Is Red' and a Verification of Its Composer"]. *Zhangjiakou shizhuan xuebao (shehui kexue ban)* 1:83–85.

Wang Kewen 王克文. 1986. *Shaanbei min'ge yishu chutan* 陕北民歌艺术初探 [*A Prelimi-*

nary Exploration of the Art of Northern Shaanxi Folksongs]. Beijing: Zhongguo minjian wenyi chubanshe.

Wang Shangrong 王尚荣. 2011. *Wang Xiangrong jiazu jishi* 王向荣家族纪事 [*Wang Xiangrong Family Chronicle*]. Taiyuan: Sanjin chubanshe.

Wang Xiangrong 王向荣. 2006. *Shaanbei gewang Wang Xiangrong* 陕北歌王王向荣 [*Wang
Xiangrong, The King of Northern Shaanxi Folksongs*]. Compact Disc. Chinese Original Ecosystem Folk Series 中国原生态民歌演唱家系列. Beijing: China Record Corporation.

Wang Xuqin 王旭芹. 2008a. "Li Jinzhu shuai woshi youhao daibiaotuan yingyao fang-
wen Meiguo—Woshi yu Meiguo Beidun shi jiewei youhao chengshi" 李金柱率我市友好
代表团应邀访问美国—我市与美国贝敦市结为友好城市 ["Li Jinzhu Leads Yulin Goodwill
Mission to Accept Invitation and Visit America: Yulin and America's Baytown Become Sister Cities"]. *Yulin ribao*, March 28, 2008. http://news.xyl.gov.cn/content/ylrb
-wz/2008-3/28/20080328063819743.html (accessed January 6, 2013).

———. 2008b. "Shaanbei wenhua zai Meiguo" 陕北文化在美国 ["Northern Shaanxi Culture
in America"]. *Yulin ribao*, April 10, 2008. http://news.xyl.gov.cn/content/photonews
/2008-4/10/20080410094020306.html (accessed January 6, 2013).

———. 2008c. "Yulin minjian yishutuan zai Mei canjia 'Zhongguo yinyue wenhua jie'—
Li Jinzhu zai bimushi shang zhici" 榆林民间艺术团在美参加中国音乐文化节李金柱在闭幕式
上致辞 ["The Yulin Folk Arts Troupe Attends the 'Chinese Music and Culture Festival'
in the U.S.: Li Jinzhu Gives a Speech at the Closing Ceremony"]. *Yulin ribao*, April 1,
2008. http://news.xyl.gov.cn/content/ylrb-wz/2008-4/1/2008040105480870.html (accessed December 14, 2012).

Wang Yaohua. 1999. "Zhongguo chuantong yinyue yanjiu wushi nian zhi huigu yu si-
kao" 中国传统音乐研究50年之回顾与思考 ["Review and Thoughts on the Research on
China's Traditional Music in the Past 50 Years"]. *Yinyue yanjiu* 3:10–16.

Wang, Yiyan. 2006. *Narrating China: Jia Pingwa and His Fictional World*. London and
New York: Routledge.

Watson, Andrew, Yang Xueyi, and Jiao Xingguo. 1999. "Shaanxi: The Search for Comparative Advantage." In *The Political Economy of China's Provinces*, edited by Hans
Hendrischke and Feng Chongyi, 73–107 (London and New York: Routledge).

Wei Shicheng 卫世诚. 1994. "Li Youyuan shi 'Dongfang hong' de cizuozhe ma?" 李有源是
东方红的词作者吗? ["Did Li Youyuan Write the Lyrics to 'The East Is Red'?"] *Renmin
yinyue* 5:34–36.

Wilcox, Emily E. 2013. "Representative Works: Authoring Tradition in Chinese Dance."
Paper Presented at the American Folklore Society Annual Meeting.

———. 2016. "Beyond Internal Orientalism: Dance and Nationality Discourse in the
Early People's Republic of China, 1949–1954." *Journal of Asian Studies* 75 (2): 363–386.

Williams, Raymond. 1973. *The Country and the City*. New York: Oxford University
Press.

Williams, Sean. 2011. "The Visiting Artist as Culture Broker: Joe Heaney and the Negotiation of Identity." In *Ethnomusicological Encounters with Music and Musicians: Essays in Honor of Robert Garfias*, edited by Timothy Rice, 49–63 (Surrey, UK, and
Burlington, VT: Ashgate).

Williams, Sean, and Lillis Ó Laoire. 2011. *Bright Star of the West: Joe Heaney, Irish Song-
Man*. New York: Oxford University Press.

Witke, Roxane. 1967. "Mao Tse-tung, Women and Suicide in the May Fourth Era." *The China Quarterly* 31:128–147.

Woetzel, Jonathan, Lenny Mendonca, Janamitra Devan, Stefano Negri, Yangmel Hu, Luke Jordan, Xiujun Li, Alexander Maasry, Geoff Tsen, Flora Yu, et al. 2009. *Preparing for China's Urban Billion.* N.p.: McKinsey Global Institute.

Wolfe, Charles K., and Kip Lornell. 1999. *The Life and Legend of Leadbelly.* New York: Da Capo Press.

Wong, Isabel K. F. 1984. "*Geming Gequ*: Songs for the Education of the Masses." In *Popular Chinese Literature and Performing Arts: The People's Republic of China, 1949–1979,* edited by Bonnie S. McDougall, 112–143 (Berkeley, Los Angeles, and London: University of California Press).

Wong, Sue-Lin. 2016. "Former China Boom Town Learns Hard Lessons about Service Economy." www.reuters.com, August 22, 2016. http://www.reuters.com/article/us -china-economy-yulin-idUSKCN10W0ZZ (accessed January 3, 2017).

Wordsworth, William. 1800. *Lyrical Ballads, with Other Poems.* Two vols. Second ed. London: T. N. Longman and O. Rees.

World Coal Association. 2012. "World Coal Association Elects New Chairman." May 25, 2012. http://www.worldcoal.org/extract/world-coal-association-elects-new-chairman -920/ (accessed August 1, 2014).

Wright, Tim. 2012. *The Political Economy of the Chinese Coal Industry: Black Gold and Blood-Stained Coal.* London and New York: Routledge.

Wu, Ka-ming. 2015. *Reinventing Chinese Tradition: The Cultural Politics of Late Socialism.* Urbana: University of Illinois Press.

Wu Yue 吴越. 2005. "Shandandan kaihua hong yanyan: xintianyou gewang Abao de gushi" 山丹丹开花红艳艳—信天游歌王阿宝的故事 ["Wild Lilies Blossom a Brilliant Red: The Story of the King of Xintianyou Songs, Abao"]. *Minsu wenxue* 1:4–10.

Xinhua Finance Agency. 2015. "Shenhua Yulin Coal-Chemical Project Moves Forward." en.xfafinance.com, March 4, 2015. http://en.xfafinance.com/html/Industries /Energy/2015/60696.shtml (accessed January 3, 2017).

Xinhua News Agency. 2012. "'Kuwait' on Northwest China's Loess Plateau." *Global Times,* November 4, 2012. http://www.globaltimes.cn/content/742140.shtml (accessed April 25, 2015).

Xu Shen 许慎. 2006. *Shuowen jiezi zhuyin ban* 说文解字注音版 [*Phonetic Notation Edition of the* Shuowen Jiezi]. Changsha: Yuelu shushe.

Xue Ming 雪明. 2005. "Gesheng fei 'yang': yangguan gewang Shi Zhanming de gushi" 歌 声飞"羊"—羊倌歌王石占明的故事 ["A Voice that Flies 'Like Sheep': The Story of the Shepherd Song King, Shi Zhanming"]. *Minsu wenxue* 1: 11–14.

Yang Cui 杨璀, ed. 1995. *Lushui dili chuan hongxie—xintianyou quji* 露水地里穿红鞋—信天游曲集 [*Wearing Red Shoes on the Dew-Covered Ground: A Collection of* Xintianyou *Pieces*]. Beijing: Renmin yinyue chubanshe.

———. 2007. "Cong 'chuanfuqu' de chansheng mantan min'ge de yanbian" 从船夫曲的产 生漫谈民歌的衍变 ["An Informal Discussion on the Development of Folksongs Starting from the Emergence of the 'Boatman's Song'"]. *Yishu jie* 98:12–15, 70.

Yang Hong 杨红. 2006. *Dangdai shehui bianqian zhong de errentai yanjiu: Hequ minjian xiban yu diyu wenhua zhi hudong guanxi* 当代社会变迁中的二人台研究: 河曲民间戏班与地 域文化之互动关系 [*Research on* Errentai *in the Midst of Contemporary Social Change:*

The Mutual Relationship between Hequ Folk Theatrical Troupes and Regional Culture]. Beijing: Zhongyang yinyue xueyuan chubanshe.

Yang, Mayfair Mei-hui. 1994. *Gifts, Favors, and Banquets: The Art of Social Relationships in China*. Ithaca, NY: Cornell University Press.

Yang Yinliu. 1980. *Zhongguo gudai yinyue shigao* 中国古代音乐史稿 [*A Draft of the History of Ancient Chinese Music*]. Two vols. Beijing: Renmin yinyue chubanshe.

Yao Lang 姚浪. 2015. "Yulin shi guojiaji feiwuzhi wenhua yichan xiangmu" 榆林市国家级非物质文化遗产项目 ["Yulin Municipality National-Level Items of Intangible Cultural Heritage"]. *Yulin ribao,* April 14, 2015. http://www.ylrb.com/2015/0414/281825.shtml (accessed April 29, 2017).

Yasumoto, Minoru. 1999. "Lu Yao wenxue zhong de guanjian ci: jiaocha didai" 路遥文学中的关键词:交叉地带 ["Key Term in Lu Yao's Writings: Intersection"]. *Xiaoshuo pinglun* 1:91–96.

YDW (Yulin diqu wenhuaju) 榆林地区文化局, ed. 1983. *Errentai yinyue* 二人台音乐 [*Errentai Music*], collected and arranged by Li Shibin 李世斌 et al. Xi'an: Shaanxi renmin chubanshe.

Yin Sheng 银笙. 2007. "Shanliang shang piaolai xintianyou—ji 'Zhongguo min'ge dawang' He Yutang" 山梁上飘来信天游—记中国民歌大王贺玉堂 ["*Xintianyou* Come Floating Across the Mountain Ridge: A Record of the Great King of Chinese Folksongs, He Yutang"]. In *He Yutang yanchang min'ge xuan* 贺玉堂演唱民歌选 [*Anthology of Folksongs Performed by He Yutang*], edited by He Yutang 贺玉堂, 1–4 (Guangdong: Zhongguo changpian Guangzhou gongsi).

Yun, Kyoim. 2006. "The 2002 World Cup and a Local Festival in Cheju: Global Dreams and the Commodification of Shamanism." *Journal of Korean Studies* 11 (1): 7–40.

Zhang Fa 张发. 2005. "Manhandiao gailun" 漫瀚调概论 ["An Introduction to *Manhandiao*"]. In *Manhandiao yishu yanjiu* 漫瀚调艺术研究 [*Research on the Art of Manhandiao*], edited by Du Rongfang, 68–72 (Hohhot: Neimenggu renmin chubanshe).

Zhang Junren 张君仁. 2004. *Hua'er wang Zhu Zhonglu—renleixue qingjing zhong de minjian geshou* 花儿王朱仲禄—人类学情境中的民间歌手 [*Zhu Zhonglu, King of Hua'er: The Anthropology of a Folksinger*]. Lanzhou: Dunhuang wenyi chubanshe.

Zhang Ruiting 张睿婷. 2009. "Shaanbei suanqu de kaocha yanjiu jiqi jiazhi chongsu" 陕北酸曲的考察研究及其价值重塑 ["An Investigation and Re-Evaluation of Northern Shaanxi Sour Tunes"]. In *Gezhe yuan xing—minzu yinyuexue yanjiu wenji* 歌者远行—民族音乐学研究文集 [*Singers on a Long Journey: A Collection of Ethnomusicological Research*], edited by Chen Huiwen 陈慧雯, 17–73 (Beijing: Wenhua yishu chubanshe).

Zhang Xijian 张曦健. 2010. "Di'er jie Shaanbei min'ge dasai choubei gongzuo yi kaishi" 第二届陕北民歌大赛筹备工作已开始 ["Preparations for the Second Northern Shaanxi Folksong Contest Have Begun"]. shaanxi.cctv.com, May 5, 2010. http://shaanxi.cctv .com/20100505/102773.shtml (accessed August 9, 2014).

Zhang Xin 张鑫. 2009. "Meiguo guojia jiaoxiangyuetuan zai Xi'an renmin dasha jinxing fang Hua yanchu" 美国国家交响乐团在西安人民大厦进行访华演出 ["American National Symphony Orchestra Performs at the People's Mansion in Xi'an during Its Visit to China"]. www.cnwest.com, June 15, 2009. http://news.cnwest.com/content/2009-06 /15/content_2142320.htm (accessed January 6, 2013).

Zhao Le 赵乐. 2010. "'Huangtuqi' shi Shaanbei min'ge de 'hun'" 黄土气是陕北民歌的魂

["'Emanations from the Yellow Earth' Are the 'Soul' of Northern Shaanxi Folksongs"]. *Guangbo gexuan* 334:4–6.

Zhao Xirong 赵喜荣. 2011. "Du Wang Xiangrong jiazu jishi yougan" 读王向荣家族纪事有感 ["Thoughts After Reading *Wang Xiangrong Family Chronicle*"]. In Wang Shangrong, *Wang Xiangrong jiazu jishi* 王向荣家族纪事 [*Wang Xiangrong Family Chronicle*], 1–9 (Taiyuan: Sanjin chubanshe).

Zhen Shengzhi 甄生枝 et al. 2003. "'Dongfang hong' gequ ci zuozhe daodi shi shei" 东方红歌曲词作者到底是谁 ["Who Wrote 'The East Is Red'?"]. *Zhongguo dang'an* 9:54–55.

Žižek, Slavoj. 2005. *The Metastases of Enjoyment: Six Essays on Women and Causality*. London and New York: Verso.

ZMWX (Zhongguo minjian wenyijia xiehui) 中国民间文艺家协会. 2005. "Guanyu shishi Zhongguo minjian wenhua jiechu chuanchengren diaocha rending he mingming xiangmu de tongzhi" 关于实施中国民间文化杰出传承人调查认定和命名项目的通知 ["Notice Concerning Implementing the Project to Survey, Select, and Name Outstanding Transmitters of Chinese Folk Culture"]. Document Number 17.

ZMWY (Zhongguo minjian wenyi yanjiuhui), ed. 1953. *Shaanganning lao genjudi min'ge xuan* 陕甘宁老根据地民歌选 [*An Anthology of Folksongs from the Shaanxi, Gansu, and Ningxia Old Revolutionary Base Area*]. Shanghai: Xin yinyue chubanshe.

ZSSX (Zhonggong Shaanxi shengwei xuanchuanbu) 中共陕西省委宣传部 [Propaganda Department of the Chinese Communist Party Shaanxi Provincial Party Committee], ed. 2009. *Shoujie Shaanbei min'ge yijie quanguo xueshu yantaohui* 首届陕北民歌译介全国学术研讨会 [*Inaugural National Academic Symposium on the Translation and Introduction of Northern Shaanxi Folksongs*]. Xi'an: Xi'an Conservatory of Music.

ZYXZYY (Zhongyang yinyue xueyuan Zhongguo yinyue yanjiusuo) 中央音乐学院中国音乐研究所, ed. 1962. *Hequ minjian gequ: diaocha yanjiu zhuanji* 河曲民间歌曲:调查研究专辑 [*Hequ Folk Songs: A Collection of Investigations and Research*]. Beijing: Yinyue chubanshe.

INDEX

Page numbers in **boldface** type refer to figures, tables, and maps.

Benjamin, Walter, 18, 180
biography. *See* life stories
Blader, Susan, 59
"Blowin' in the Wind," 206–209. *See also* singers, mentioned: Dylan, Bob
boatmen, 11, 52; bawdy, 104, 114–115, 159–161 (*see also* sour tunes); dual identities, 133, 192, 194; elderly, 195, 236n.5; heroic helmsmen, 96, 115–116, 120; scalability of, 195–196; song kings and queens as, 208–209; symbols of Chinese history, 190–191, 207, 236n.6; transformation of bawdy to heroic, 110, 118–121; Yellow River, 70, 143, 190, 236n.6. *See also* "Infinite Bends of the Yellow River"; songs, mentioned: "My Motherland"
boats. *See under* imagery
Bohlman, Philip, 183–184
border-crossing, 17, 51–52, 54, 86–87, 172–173, 182
Bourdieu, Pierre, 59, 167, 184
bricolage, 59–60, 227n.77
Brodie, Ian, 13, 157, 172, 232

calling out: to an Other, 12, 70, 104, 132–134, 236n.10. *See also* addressees; "East Is Red": East and sun as addressees; imagery: sun
Campbell, Joseph, 25, 219n.2
Cantwell, Robert, 186, 212
Cashman, Ray, 60, 103–104, 217n.3, 222n.1, 224n.22, 229n.100
cave homes (*yaodong*), 37, **38**, **39**, 52, 54, 63, 123, 124, 125
CCTV Spring Festival Gala, 157, 187, 188–190, **189**, 203, 209–211, **210**, **211**; "I Want to Be on the CCTV Gala," 45
celebrities, 19, 27; selling out, 9; and singing competitions, 30; vs. public figures, 44–45
centers and peripheries, 4, 15–16, 30–31, 218n.19, 221n.32
Chairman Mao. *See* Mao Zedong
changes, social: continuity amidst, 7, 18, 21, 194, 205–209, 217n.6, 237n.24
Chau, Adam Yuet, 223n.7, 223n.17
CHIME (European Foundation for Chinese Music Research), viii, 146, 217n.1

China: as exotic, 151, 153; Gansu Province, 27, 34, 230n.31, 236n.5; Guangxi Province, 34; Guizhou Province, 108, 147, 220n.13, 232n.18, 237n.22; Jiangsu Province, 26, 28, 65, 162, 164; Macau, 154, 203–204; Qinghai Province, 27, **33**, 34; Shanghai, 15, 35, 146, 154, 219n.10; Yunnan Province, 108, 109, 146, 147, 148. *See also* Beijing; Inner Mongolia; Shaanxi Province; Shanxi Province; Xi'an
Chineseness, 6, 13, 106, 145, 149, 153, 196; fusion with localness; 156, fuzzy notions of, 16, 20, 110, 151; provincial claims to, 151–152; as a rare commodity, 156. *See also* ambiguity: of sung personae
Chinese People's Political Consultative Conference, 31, **33**, 37, 45, 218n.16
choruses, 110, 136–137; children, 200, 202, 203; children vs. adult, 203–204; interplay with solo voice, 14, 133–134, 200, 202; progression of larger and larger, 133, 202–203; representing the People, 134–135; as revolutionary bodies, 134; similarities to group serenades, 134; singing in Mandarin Chinese, 135, 204; stand-ins for the audience, 206
Christmas, 174, 175. *See also* events: Christmas concerts
cities. *See* migrants, rural: urban migration; rural-urban divide
class, 6, 8–9, 37, 57, 124, 222n.46. *See also* folk and elite: social mobility
Clifford, James, 184, 235n.17
coal, 52, 76, 77, 145, 148–149, 153, 155, 231n.2, 231n.7, 231n.11, 232n.20; World Coal Association, 146. *See also* Shenhua Group
Cohen, Myron L., 219n.3
comedians, 13, 157, 172
common people (*laobaixing*), 6, 43, 120, 122, 125, 163, 179; becoming one with, 163, 165
communities: *communitas*, 68; connecting individuals to, 22, 205 (*see also* narratives: parallel); delineation of, 6, 34, 76–77, 138; heterogeneity of, 9–10, 16, 106, 113–114, 170; imagined, 106, 110. *See also* nationalism

175, 197, **199**, 200, 234n.6, 234n.10; official, 4, 42, 131, 138; private gatherings, 21, 158, 159; school anniversaries, 4, 131, 186; weddings, 4, 5, 18, 128, 139, 157, 190, 196, 197, **198**, **199**, 204, **210**, 236n.19

exotic Others. *See* Others; shifting: between familiar and exotic

Faure, David, 15

Feng Menglong, 168, 233n.13

Feng Yalan, 162–165, 233n.6

festivals. *See* events; temple fairs

Feuchtwang, Stephan, 67

Filene, Benjamin, 3, 207, **213**, 214, 237n.1

finger-guessing games, 55, 60, 61–65, 223n.17. *See also* events: banquets

Fiske, John, 12, 100, 120, 186, 217–218n.8

Foley, John Miles, 208, 237n.24

folk and elite, 17, 31, 235n.16; conversations between, 2, 163; dual identities of song kings, 7, 9; singers as bridges between, 6, 37, 57; as target demographics, 6; tensions between, 8, 24, 26–28, 163, 168

folk songs: *Big Anthology* (*jicheng*), 34–35, 158, 235n.3; collectors, 21, 35, 157–159, 162–166, 233n.7, 233n.9; entextualization, 166; *Folksong Weekly* (*Geyao zhoukan*), 233n.13; history of collection (*caifeng*), 14–15, 167–168

foreigners, 6–7, 138, 148, 174, 182–183, 228–229n.99; scholars, 1, 6, 21, 178–179, 181–182. *See also* Others: foreign

Fosler-Lussier, Danielle, 148

Foucault, Michel, 234–235n.14

fox spirits, 56, 223nn.19–20, 227n.73

frames, interpretive, 4, 70, 162, 166–167, 196–197

Frankel, Hans, 12, 228n.94

Frith, Simon, 12, 18, 19, 99, 133, 185–186, 206

Gang of Four, 41

gaps, social: bridging of, 13, 62, 68, 144, 148

genres, song: continuum of, 51; *errentai* (folk opera), 41–42, 51–53, 57–59, 90–100, 106, 113, 148–151, 176, 181, 223nn.8–9, 228n.93, 233n.7; expressing different types of information, 222n.1; founding of, 15, 34, 218n.10; hybrid, 53; *manhandiao* (*see* Mongol-Han tunes); mountain songs, 27, 34, 38, 51, 168, 222n.3, 233n.13; organization of anthologies by, 163; representing places, 30; *shanqu*, 38, 51, 100, 169; and social relations, 69, 186; *xintianyou*, 30, **32–33**, 51, 132, 138, 139; *yangge*, 51, 123, 192, 222n.2. *See also* drinking songs; sour tunes; spirit-medium tunes

gentlemen (*junzi*), 65–66

gestures: evoking rural-urban divide, 8, 28; merging event to sense of tradition, 196–202, 209; stage performances, 107, 108, 110–111 (*see also* Stageworthy)

ghosts, 56, 82, 99, 104, 161

gift exchange. *See* songs: as gifts

Glassie, Henry, 14, 171, 172

globalization, 17, 21, 145–148, 151–152, 156, 173–174

Goddess of Mercy. *See* Guanyin

gods. *See* spirit-medium tunes

"Going beyond the Western Pass" (*zou xikou*): as discursive site, 59; historical migration, 51–52; song, 1, 13, 19, 43, 52, 97–100; TV dramas and novels about, 99, 100. *See also* songs: "couple going out" paradigm; songs, mentioned: "The One Who Walked beyond the Western Pass Has Returned"

Goldstein, Joshua, 147

Goldstein, Kenneth S., 232n.2

Gramsci, Antonio, 222n.46

Great Leap Forward, 139

Great Wall, 2, 5, 52, 188, 190, 202, 203, 210

groups. *See* communities

Guanyin, 24, 26, 162

guest-host relationships, 50, 54–55, 60–66, 69, 71, 85, 225n.42, 225n.49, 226n.64

habitus, 59, 234n.11

hailing. *See* calling out

Hall, Stuart, 185–186

Han ethnic group, depiction in song, 53, 58, 88, 222–223n.6

Haring, Lee, 206

Harris, Rachel, 29, **33**, 171, 219n.2, 229n.10

parallel); as models for incorporating personal into social, 8; as overlapping arcs, 47–48; as sites for social discourse, 42–48, 212

liminality. *See* cultural exchanges: as liminal spaces to realign relations; singer-heroes: dual identities

Lindholm, Charles, 184

lip-synching. *See* songs: prerecorded

Liu, Kang, 173

Liu Sanjie, 24, 26, 27, 29, 34

Liu, Tao Tao, 15, 16

Liu, Xin, 71

local authenticity (*didao*), 21, 169, 173–174, 182–185, 235n.18. *See also* authenticity

Loess Plateau, **32**, 106, 121, 124, 125

Lomax, Alan, 164–166

Lomax, John, 29

Lord, Albert B., 171, 229n.3

Lu Yao, 192, 218n.16

lyric "I", 11, 133, 139, 193, 205, 228n.84, 233n.14; of an ancestral god, 227n.72; of a spirit medium, 71; use of regional dialect word, 196, 224n.30, 230n.22, 236n.8

lyric songs: being of two minds, 13; inherent desire for dialogue, 10, 19, 193; iterability of, 10, 19, 205; lyric present, 12, 18–19, 193, 205, 236n.9

Mackerras, Colin, 147, 231n.1, 232n.17

Mandarin Chinese. *See* choruses: singing in Mandarin Chinese; dialects: contrasted with Mandarin

Mao Zedong, 5, 6, 15, 30, 42, 46, 70, 120–125, 133–135, 141–142, 176, 178, 183, 186, 221n. 37, 234n.10

Marqusee, Mike, 206, 209

marriages: arranged, 12, 27, 43–44, 103–104, 214, 221n.37; reform, 164; views on love and, 8, 19, 26, 37, 43–44, 214. *See also* events: weddings

Marugeda (Wang Xiangrong's home village), 7, 23, 42, 106, 128, 145, 180–183 *passim*, 226n.63; ancestral gods, 56, 77, 78, 227n.73; ancient local culture, 59; geography, **3**, 5, 37–38; invisibility, 194; local spirit medium, 57, 69; natural environment, 40; performancescape,

51–57, 113; photographs, **38, 39, 54**; temples, 37–38, **39**; topography mentioned in song, 54–55, **54**, 67, 76–77, 85–88, 106; Wang's recollections, 38–40

masks. *See* sung personae

master-disciple relationships. *See* Wang Xiangrong: disciples

Mauss, Marcel, 55, 61, 150, 156

McDowell, John, 103

McLaren, Anne E., 43

mediums. *See* singers: as mediums

memory, public, 10, 207–208

metaphors: expanded, 107–108, 117–121, 123–125; for relationships, 60–63, 67–69, 86–96, 99, 149–150, 212, 228n.81 (*see also* songs: "couple going out" paradigm)

Midland, Michigan (U.S.), 21, 145, 147–156, 157, 181

migrants, rural, 2–3, 11, 15–16, 43, 100–101, 223n.10 (*see also* "Going beyond the Western Pass"); urban migration, 17, 42, 186

modernity: and cities, 15–16, 188; vs. tradition, 2, 7, 17, 23, 43, 188, 209, 214

Mongol-Han tunes (*Meng-Han diao*), 52–54, 57–58, 88–90, 222–223n.6

moralities: place-based, 13, 27, 29, 118, 158, 165–172; tensions between Confucian and folkways, 8, 26–27, 164–168

Mullen, Patrick, 171, 229n.3

multinational corporations, 21, 49, 145, 147, 153, 156. *See also* Dow Chemical Company

music videos, 46–47, 95, 113, 130, 228n.93

Nagy, Gregory, 218n.15

Nancy, Jean-Luc, 173, 180, 233

narratives: little, 205; meta-, 205; overcoming obstacles, 8, 23, 25–26, 36–37, 195, 214, 221n.34; parallel, 194–202, 205, 207–211; rags-to-riches, 43, 221n.34, 234n.8; song, 190–194. *See also* life stories; singers: as storytellers

nationalism: and music, 125, 156, 204, 232n.17

national leaders: Deng Xiaoping, 2, 29, 30, 42; Hirohito, Emperor (Japan), 220n.12; Hu Jintao, 68, 75, 120, 155, 224n.36; Jiang

Zemin, 155; Nāsir, 'Abd al- (Egypt), 220n.12; Nixon, Richard (U.S.), 220n.12; Obama, Barack (U.S.), 75, 155, 226n.65; Reagan, Ronald (U.S.), 220n.12; Zhou Enlai, 30, 220n.11. *See also* Mao Zedong

Newport Folk Festival (1965), 214, 237n.2. *See also* singers, mentioned: Dylan, Bob

northern Shaanxi (*Shaanbei*), 42, 46, 47; performancescape, 51, 53, 55; revolutionary history, 46. *See also* regional identities

nostalgia, 40, 168, 208, 230n.25, 231–232n.32

Notar, Beth E., 147, 231n.8

Noyes, Dorothy, 34, 134, 206, 221n.34, 234n.8, 235n.16

obstacles. *See* narratives: overcoming obstacles

Olympics. *See* Beijing: Olympics; Wang Xiangrong: Olympic torchbearer

operas, regional. *See* genres, song: *errentai*

oral formulae, 138, 227n.77, 237n.24

Others: exotic, 5, 170; foreign, 13, 138, 182; geographical and temporal, 18; significant, 182. *See also* shifting: between familiar and exotic

peasant singers. *See* sung personae: revolutionary peasant

People. *See* common people

"People's Singer." *See* singers, mentioned: Li Youyuan

performances: aesthetics (see *stageworthy*; Stageworthy); contexts (*see* events); liminality (*see* cultural exchanges: as liminal spaces to realign relations); prerecorded (*see* songs: prerecorded)

performer-audience interactions, 170–171. See also *stageworthy*

peripheries. *See* centers and peripheries

personal experiences: gleaned from descriptions of the traditional, 103–104; socialization of, 104

places, promotion of. *See* cultural exchanges: to attract investment; Yulin: promotion of

Porter, James, 10, 104, 212, 229n.3

poverty, 1, 17, 23, 43, 101, 104, 115, 125, 138, 152, 176, 194. *See also* narratives: rags-to-riches

prerecorded songs. *See under* songs

public: figures, 44–45; memory, 10, 207–208

Qiao Jianzhong, vii, 108, 158, 162, 184, 190, 191, 223n.16, 232–233n.5, 235n.3

recordings, 34, 137, 171; China Record Corporation, 110. *See also* songs: prerecorded

Red Song Contest, **32**, 45, **46**

Red Star Over China, 46

Rees, Helen, 16, 28, 30, 35, 36, 217nn.3–4, 219n.5, 222n.43, 231n.6

regional identities, 130; appropriation in national politics, 229–230n.15; glossing over subregional differences, 142–143; subregional heterogeneity, 113–114; visitability, 121. *See also* singers: regional personae

repertoires: active and inactive, 158, 232n.2; constructing regional, 16, 107–108, 111–121

revolutionary history. *See* northern Shaanxi, revolutionary history

riddles, 150, 191; answer as shared social property, 206–207

rites of passage, 25, 205, 231n.10

rituals. *See* spirit mediums; spirit-medium tunes

rivers. *See* imagery: rivers

"Root-Seeking" movement, 15, 16

Rosenberg, Neil V., 132, 171, 221n.36

rural-urban divide, 4, 7, 8, 14–17, 42–43, 44, 110, 163, 192, 214. *See also* hierarchies, social: between country and city; migrants, rural

Said, Edward, 45

Schechner, Richard, 70

Schein, Louisa, 30, 220n.13, 237n.22

Schimmelpenninck, Antoinet, viii, 7, 15, 23–29 *passim*, **33**, 37, 65, 69, 162, 217n.1, 217n.3, 217n.5, 219nn.1–2, 222nn.3–5

self and Other. *See* shifting: between

familiar and exotic; subjectivities: merging of
separation. *See under* songs
serenades, 124, 134, 182
Shaanbei. See northern Shaanxi
Shaan-Gan-Ning Border Region, 138, 141, 230n.31
Shaanxi Province, 2, **3**, 13, 21, **32**, 34, 36, 42, 75, 97, 149, 151–155 *passim,* 162–163, 172, 195, 228n.93, 228n.96, 230n.31, 231n.11, 231–232n.12, 235n.3, 236n.5; Dingbian County, **3**, **197**, 233n.17; Fugu County, **3**, 37, 41, 127–129, 132, 139, 168, 174, 194; Fugu County Town, 112, 169, **177**, 218n.11; Jiaxian County, **3**, 96, 122, 124–126, 129, 139–141; Jingbian County, **3**, 96; Mizhi County, **3**, 35, 96, 111–112; Qiangtou village, **3**, 112; Shenmu County, **3**, 42, 52, 132, 139, 195, **199**, **210**, 230n.27; Suide County, **3**, **32**, 35, 111–112. *See also* Marugeda; northern Shaanxi (*Shaanbei*); Xinmin Township; Yulin
Shanxi Province, 2, **3**, 37, 51–52, 99, 112–113, 164, 219n.3, 223n.8, 228n.96, 231n.11, 232n.18, 233n.8; Baode County, **3**, 112; Hequ County, **3**, 52, 112, 164, 233n.8
Shay, Anthony, 109
Shenhua Group, 145, 146, 149, 155, 231n.2, 231n.7
shifting: between familiar and exotic, 6, 9, 11, 21, 148, 173–179, 180, 182–187, 209; between local and global, 173–174, 176; Mark Bender's notion of, 233n.1; between place-based identities, 2, 107, 213–214, 218n.16; between serious and nonserious pieces, 131–132; between solo voice and chorus (*see* choruses, interplay with solo voice); between voices in a duet (*see* songs: "couple going out" paradigm)
Shuman, Amy, 8, 24, 184, 218n.12, 218–219n.21
singer-heroes, 5, 8, 14, 19; as demigods (*banxian*), 7, 57, 69; dual identities, 7, 8–9, 57; journeys, 9, 18, 25–26, 30, 36, 47; legends, 20, 23–35, 162; semiofficial nature, 7, 37; Shen Qige, 29; teaching people to sing, 31, 34–36; Zhang Liang, 26, 162

singers: authority, 20, 50, 81, 105, 184, 194; "bad," 171; banquet, 57, 65, 69, 106–107, 120; facilitating dialogues, 7–8, 55, 56, 68–69, 77, 92; genealogy, 36; "good," 157–158, 171–172; iconic, 2–10, 16–17, 31, 34, 208; incarceration, 29, 171, 219n.9; as intermediaries, 7–8, 205 (*see also* changes, social); itinerant, 2, 5, 7, 13–14, 17, 19–22, 23–27, 173; as mediums, 3, 7–10; professional, 14, 27–28, 42, 49, 50, 60, 68, 105, 109, 157, 162, 171, 223n.16 (*see also* Wang Xiangrong: professional career); regional personae, 108, 126–130; regulating social events, 55, 60, 65–66, 75; as spokespeople, **31**, 220n.13; as storytellers, 17–19, 180; teaching others, 31, 34–36
singers, mentioned: A You Duo, 220n.13, 237n.22; Abao, 24, 28, 30, **32**; Cui Miao, **32**; Ding Xicai, 35, 219n.10; Dylan, Bob, 206, 208, 209, 214, 237nn.1–2; Feng Xiaohong, 68, 113–114, 222n.41; Guo Lanying, 202–203; Guthrie, Woody, 214; He Yutang, **32**, 231n.6; Heaney, Joe, **213**; Hong Kong singer, 188, **189**, 195, 209–210; Ives, Burl, 171; Jackson, Michael, **213**, 220n.12; Johnson, Robert, **213**; Kulthūm, Umm, 212, **213**, 220n.12; Leadbelly, 29, 212, **213**; Li Chunru, 113–114, 222n.41, 223n.10; Li Simin, 190–191, 192, 194, 235n.3, 236nn.4–5; Li Youyuan, **32**, 122–125; Li Zhengfei, **32**, 68, 222n.41; Li Zhiwen, 30, **32**, 35, 111, 192, 196, 219–220n.10, 236n.7; Ma Ziqing, 30, 102, 220n.11; Mei Lanfang, 147, 148, 231n.9; Misora Hibari, 212, **213**, 220n.12; Mitchell, Frank, **213**; Pavarotti, Luciano, **213**; Peng Liyuan, 30; Ponce, Jesse, **213**; Presley, Elvis, **213**, 220n.12; Qian Afu, **32**, 219n.2; Redžepova, Esma, **213**; Robertson, Jeannie, 104, 212, 229n.3; Rush, Bobby (R&B singer), 231n.5; Seeger, Pete, **213**, 214, 219n.9, 237n.1; Shi Zhanming, **33**, 110, 111; Sosa, Mercedes, **213**; Sun Bin, 53, 57, 59, 223n.11; Sun Zhikuan, **33**; Teodosievski, Stevo, **213**; Wang Erni, **33**, 228n.88; Wang Luobin, 29, **33**, 171, 219n.2, 219nn.8–9; Waters,

Muddy, **213**; Yang Zhongqing, 112, 113; Zhang Tian'en, 35; Zhu Zhonglu, 29, **33**. *See also* Wang Xiangrong

Smith, Barbara Herrnstein, 92–93, 150, 230n.23

Smithsonian Folklife Festival, 109, 148

Snow, Edgar, 46

social mobility, 15–16, 19, 27, 43, 44, 219n.3

song: -and-dance troupes (*gewutuan*), 2, 16, 26, 27, 30, 35, 106, 109, 144–145, 147, 151, 231n.1 (*see also* Yulin: Folk Arts Troupe); gods and goddesses (*geshen*), 7, 15, 21–24 *passim*, 25–37, 57, 69, 157, 218n.10 (*see also* singer-heroes); immortals (*gexian*), 15, 27; kings (*gewang*) and queens (*gehou*), 3–11, 18–21, 23–37, 47–48, 57–58, 128, 157, 174, 180, 208–209, 212–215, 217–218n.8, 218–219n.21; worlds, 9–11, 69–71, 133, 138

songs: adaptation of local into regional, 113–121, 121–125; "bad," 164–165; battles, 26–27; competitions, 30, **32**, 45, 132, 139; as conversations between different desires, 2, 6, 10, 19–20, 49–50, 87, 96, 98–99, 208; "couple going out" paradigm, 85–96, 102, 107–108, 118, 122, 135, 149–150, 173, 193; and courtship, 8, 14, 20, 26; familiar, 168, 170, 173–185; as gifts, 34, 52, 55, 60–61, 92–93, 144–145, 148, 150, 156; grounded in particular places, 16, 20, 50, 54–55, 76–77, 85–90, 106; karaoke, 28, 99; love, 14, 50, 85–92, 111–112, 122, 156, 164, 217n.2, 232n.4, 232–233n.5, 233n.7, 233n.14; nation-representing, 6 (*see also* nationalism: and music); nonsense syllables, 51, 90; prerecorded, 130, 131, 137, 196; as public conversations, 5, 10–14, 17, 19, 23–25, 48–49, 104, 207, 209, 237n.24; region-representing, 6, 11, 16, 20, 70, 106–108, 111, 114–121; rhyme, 60–61; of separation, 14, 52, 59, 97–100; as tapestries of meanings, 10, 208; transmission, 31, 34–36; triangulated address, 12, 218n.15; "unhealthy," 164, 167, 233n.7. *See also* a cappella; addressees; choruses; lyric songs; serenades; *yuanshengtai* singing styles

songs, mentioned: "Boatman's Song," 190; "Chinese Dream," 188, **189**, 195; "Drinking Opium," 102–104; "Flowers Bloom in May," 53, 149–151, 232nn.14–15; "Going to the Market," 46, 53, 95–96, 150; "Herding Livestock," 111–112; "Liang Shanbo and Zhu Yingtai," 43, 54, 88; "My Motherland," 202–203; "The One Who Walked beyond the Western Pass Has Returned," 100–101; "Pulling Ferries throughout the Year," 11, 109, 114–121, 122, 133, 157, 159, 237n.26; "Riding a White Horse," 124, 139, 141, 229n.13; "Song of the Muleteer," 11, 111–112, 143; "Two Wives" (bawdy festival tune), 117–118; "Who Is That?" 112–113; "Yaosanbai," 168–170. *See also* "Blowin' in the Wind"; drinking songs; "East Is Red"; genres, song; "Going beyond the Western Pass"; "Infinite Bends of the Yellow River"; Mongol-Han tunes; sour tunes; spirit-medium tunes

sour tunes (*suanqu*), 159–162, 166–167, 232n.4, 232–233n.5, 233n.7, 233n.11

spirit mediums (*shenhan*, *shenguan*), 11, 55–56; authority bestowed by gods, 58; dual identities, 69; "three rings" and sheepskin drum, 81–82; trances, 78; voices that command authority, 69, 71, 81

spirit-medium tunes (*shenhandiao*), 55–57, 67, 69–70; "Curing an Illness," 77–81; hyperbole, 70; "Inviting the Gods," 70–76; "Preparing the Sacrificial Altar," 76–77; "Scattering Grains and Fodder," 81–84; "Sending Off the Gods," 84–85; social hierarchy in, 67–69, 85

stages: as meeting ground between self and other, 173, 184, 214. See also *kang*, used as stage; Stageworthy

stageworthy, 158–166; and Wang's notion of degree (*du*), 170–172

Stageworthy, 20, 108–111, 142, 157–159; order of songs, 131–132; stageification (*wutaihua*), 108, 184

Stahl, Sandra, 24, 47, 171

Starlight Highway (Xingguang dadao), 30, **32–33**, 132. *See also* songs: competitions

"Star-Spangled Banner" (U.S. national anthem), 209, 237n.25
status, social. *See* hierarchies, social
storytellers. *See under* singers
strange, commanding presence of, 173, 180. *See also* Others; shifting: between familiar and exotic
subjectivities: meeting of, 50; merging of, 9–10, 14, 205, 209 (*see also* songs: "couple going out" paradigm)
suicide, 12, 103
sung personae, 20, 58; adaptation from local to national, 11, 58, 114–121, 121–125; ambiguous regional, 16 (*see also* ambiguity: of sung personae; singers: regional personae); audience identification with, 12–13, 99–100; bridges connecting local to national, 122; expressing desires, 49; expressing different types of sentiments, 11; muleteer, 11, 102, 111–112, 143, 228n.97; revolutionary peasant, 6, 11, 12, 110, 122, 143 (*see also* choruses: as revolutionary bodies); shepherd, **33**, 43, 110, 143; vessels of meaning, 6, 14, 119–121. *See also* boatmen

"Talks at the Yan'an Conference on Literature and Art," 15, 42
temple fairs, 50, 52, 57, 58, 85, 97, 99, 106, 223nn.7–8
tempo, 20, 92, 113, 117, 122, 130, 200, 231n.33
tensions, social. *See* folk and elite: tensions between
Third Sister Liu. *See* Liu Sanjie
Titon, Jeff Todd, 9, 24, 44, 205, 214
toasting, 55, 60–61, 66, 224n.25. *See also* drinking songs; events: banquets
tourism, 147, 152; and performing arts, 231n.1, 232n.17; psychic, 218n.19; singers and, 31, 220n.13, 237n.22
tradition, 59; transmission of (*chuancheng*), 36, 47, 220n.16
Tuohy, Sue, 30, **33**, 111, 125, 167, 204, 218n.18, 233n.11, 235n.18
Turner, Graeme, 9, 44–45
Turner, Victor, 63, 68, 148, 231n.10

UNESCO, **33**, 35–36, 45, 220n.16
United States, 90–96 *passim,* 145–149, 153–158, 175, 181–182, 208, 209, 235n.17, 237n.25; "American," 144, 148, 156; Midwest, 17, 148–149, 153; Sino-U.S. relations, 153–155
U.S. National Symphony Orchestra: Asia Tour (2009), 145, 147, 154–156; history of, 147–148

Van Gennep, Arnold, 7, 25, 205
visitability, 107, 116, 121
voices, alternation and merging. *See* songs: "couple going out" paradigm; sung personae
Von Hallberg, Robert, 184, 185

Wang Xiangrong: advertisements featuring, **31**, 220n.13; CD album (2006), 6, 67, 78, 110, 179, 190, 224n.23; childhood, 2, 14, 37–40; clothing, 133, **189**, 225n.42; disciples, viii, 36, 45, 68, 113; 222n.41; elementary school reunion, 194, 218n.11; father, 38, 40; film and TV roles, 45, 46–47, 222n.48; hometown (*see* Marugeda; Shaanxi Province: Fugu County; Xinmin Township); judge in singing competitions, 45, **46**; marriage, 40–41, 43–44; mother, 27–28, 38, 40, 44, 86, 88, 103, 222n.39, 227n.77; national-level representative transmitter designation, 2, **33**, 35–36, 37, 45, 47, 113, 146, 231n.6; older brother, 40, 43–44, 221n.23, 230n.30; Olympic torchbearer, 47; professional career, 20, 52, 144; shifting place-based identities, 2, 108, 126–130; similarities to cultural anthropologists, 56, 59; singing competitions, **33**, 41–42, 53, 90, 132, 228n.93; sisters, 38; speeches, 2, 5, 8, 17–18, 43, 100–101, 127–130, 173–176, **177**, 178–179, 194–196, 215; titles, 2, **33**; work as community-supported teacher, 40–41, 221n.26
Wang, Yiyan, 13, 218n.16
War of Resistance against Japan, 138, 139, 230n.25
wenyizaidao ("writing is meant to convey truth"), 166, 219n.7

ABOUT THE AUTHOR

Levi S. Gibbs is assistant professor of Chinese in the Department of Asian and Middle Eastern Languages and Literatures at Dartmouth College.